TO HEAVEN'S HEIGHTS

TO HEAVEN'S HEIGHTS
AN ANTHOLOGY OF SKIING IN LITERATURE

COMPILED BY INGRID CHRISTOPHERSEN, MBE

Forewords by:
LORD MOYNIHAN (4th Baron Moynihan)
SIR JOHN HENRY RITBLAT (FRICS)

UNICORN

This edition first published in the UK by Unicorn
an imprint of the Unicorn Publishing Group LLP, 2021
5 Newburgh Street
London W1F 7RG

www.unicornpublishing.org

10 9 8 7 6 5 4 3 2 1

ISBN 978-1-913491-76-5

Design by Vivian@Bookscribe

Printed in the Czech Republic by Latitude Press

——·——

This anthology is dedicated to Sir John Ritblat, a very inadequate
thank-you for what he has done for British skiing over the last 42 years.

The profits from this anthology will go to supporting Snow-Camp,
UK's National Snowsports charity, giving young inner-city children the
opportunity to experience the mountains and in many cases turn their
lives around. Please see www.snow-camp.org.uk

——·——

FOREWORD
BY LORD MOYNIHAN

A book to fill a much-needed gap in the market for ski-lovers everywhere. This anthology spans a thousand years, from the most memorable to lesser-known authors – from Hemingway and Greene, to Balzac and Agatha Christie, the Icelandic Sagas and 'James Bond'. All hold a passion for the world of skiing. There are chapters for children, there is mystery and skulduggery, romance and humour and every one of the Norwegian vignettes takes the reader back to a childhood on skis, when the world was new and unpretentious and the annual journey to the mountains full of Christmas excitement.

Ingie grew up with a father who trained the Heroes of Telemark so no surprise to find detailed encounters of the importance of skiing in warfare; the challenges of Arctic and Antarctic exploration, including the longest ski-competition in history and the remarkable duel between Scott and Amundsen to the South Pole one hundred years ago. This labour of love captures the magic of skiing which Ingie has imbued in the generations of children she has guided through their first experiences of racing on the ski slopes of the world. Here she has given every one of them a gift.

This anthology will surely grace the sitting rooms of ski enthusiasts around the world and give life-long pleasure to all, beginners and experts alike with all proceeds going to www.snow-camp.org.uk – a very worthy cause.

—•—

Lord Moynihan
Lifetime skier
Minister for Sport 1987–1990; Olympic and World Silver Medallist (rowing); Chairman of the British Olympic Association for the London 2012 Olympic Games. (Former) Chairman and Founder of the British Ski Federation and President of the British Biathlon Union. Enthusiastic Alpine skier.

FOREWORD

BY SIR JOHN HENRY RITBLAT (FRICS)

This is not so much a Skiing anthology, as a reflection on the author's dedication and charm. Nobody has attracted more love and respect than Ingrid Christophersen, whose life and adventures in the mountains are unrivalled.

Born and bred in the snowy winters of Norway, she is the epitome of resolution, determination and indefatigable enthusiasm for snow sports and all who engage in them.

Imagine more than 70 years on skis and an icon to whom we can all genuflect and bow very low!

Ingie's selection of authorship, is so much the embodiment of her sensitivity and personality, and in themselves, an endorsement of her lifemanship and offer something for everyone who loves competition, a generous selflessness and single-minded commitment.

As with all the best anthologies, I encourage you to dip and delve as the mood takes you and be stirred by these sagas of courage and love, fortitude and survival. Remembering always the glamour and joyfulness of the author behind the selections illuminating Ingie's spirit ever present as the all-pervading influence.

Such a lovely book which I am sure you will enjoy and relate to these magical reminiscences that are so redolent of my author friend and her distinguished lifetime.

Truly the éminence grise of skiing competition in the mountains.

—————•—————

Sir John Ritblat has been the principal sponsor of The British National Alpine Ski Championships for the last 42 years and is the longest serving sponsor in British sport. He is the President of British Ski & Snowboard National Foundation and President of GB Snow Sport Federation.

CONTENTS

INTRODUCTION

BY INGRID CHRISTOPHERSEN

I was brought up and educated in Norway – land of the Midnight Sun (and midnight Fun) and very much The Cradle of Skiing.

Norway in the 50s and 60s was a safe and innocent country. Little children with labels round their necks were sent off to kindergarten, up the mountain on the tric, electric, as was I, clothed like little Michelin men, to bask in the abundant snow. Skiing was not something you learnt; skis were just an addition to your feet. You would never dream of crossing them – as adult beginners do when they first put skis on. Norway had emerged from five years of occupation and there was nothing to buy in the shops, certainly no toys or such frivolous things – I never had a doll – so skis it was. Laminated wood, screw on metal edges and Kandahar bindings which could be adjusted for walking. Plus-fours, red woolly stockings and leather boots, homespun sweaters and knitted woolly mitts.

We were reared on trolls and whale meat – and tales of Nansen and Amundsen – Scott never got a look in. The Heroes of Telemark featured prominently, my father had trained them in Scotland before they jumped into Norway to sabotage the Heavy Water Plant at Rjukan, and I knew them all. They should have asked him before producing that stupid film The Heroes of Telemark with Kurt Douglas, because it was as wrong as it could be.

So, when it came to collecting stories for the anthology, I very much wanted both winter warfare and arctic exploration to be part of it.

My mother was an Australian, a concert pianist, that is how she came to England – to study at the Royal Academy. Daddy gave her small baby skis and we all died laughing every time she tumbled. So, she gave up. My father skied reasonably well, and once broke both his shoulders in one go ski jumping. There were ski jumps all around Oslo. My brother was brilliant and jumped 49 metres when he was only 9 years old. I suppose if the jump is big enough you cannot avoid jumping a certain length. It taught me about the speed of sound. Standing far off and seeing him land, the sound of the skis hitting the down-run reached us at least a second later.

Oslo's backyard, the vast area of hill, forest and lakes that backs onto the capital, was just the ideal playground and did we make use of it – every day after school, and every weekend.

My brother was sent to my father's old school in England – Cheltenham College – but I was already showing promising signs at ski competitions, and my name at a girls' school in Esher was quickly withdrawn – glory be. Not for me the rather sweet, demure, well-behaved sort. A very lucky escape. A gentle and organised landscape – gentle and disciplined children: a rough and tumble country – rough and tumble children. And I certainly would have missed the company of boys. For me the most important thing was to beat them at skiing. They were not good for much else!

I was Oslo champion at 14 and then competed in British Junior Championships and was surprised to realise that there were some very good young British girls – Gina Hathorn and Davina Galica to mention two. But one thing led to another and in 1963 I was asked to join the British Team at a training session in Val d'Isere. The rest is really history and it has been a truly charmed life. And all because the girl loved skiing......

Bentley Farm during lockdown July 2020

ACKNOWLEDGEMENTS

With thanks to the following for granting permission to reproduce and translate the wonderful stories contained in this collection.

Kjell Aukrust 2 short stories for children. Permission from Aukrust Senter and Cappelen Damm Publishers. Translation by Ingrid Christophersen.

Alf Prøysen Three short stories published in agreement with Tiden Norsk Forlag and Elin Prøysen. Copyright Tiden Norsk Forlag. Translation by Ingrid Christophersen.

Odd Børretzen *Heroes*. Kind permission from Odd Børretzen's son. Translation by Ingrid Christophersen.

Swain Wolfe from *I Invented Skiing* by kind permission of the author.

Karsten Alnæs *The Fifty Kilometre* by kind permission of the author. Translation by Ingrid Christophersen.

Oakley Hall from *The Downhill Racers* by kind permission of InkWell Management.

Peter Kray from *The God of Skiing* by kind permission of the author.

Garrison Keillor *Winter from Lake Wobegone Days* by kind permission of Faber & Faber.

Bill Bryson part of chapter *Fun in the Snow* from *Notes from a Big Country* by kind permission of PenguinRandomHouse.

Fergus Fleming *Fridtjof Nansen* from *Tales of Endurance* by kind permission of Aitken Alexander Associates.

Roland Huntford from *Scott and Amundsen* by kind permission of the author.

Jan Ove Ekeberg *Birkebeinerferden* by kind permission of the author. Translation by Ingrid Christophersen.

Mikkjel Fønhus *The Skier* by kind permission of Even Råkil @osloliteraryagency. Translation by Ingrid Christophersen.

Dag Helleve *The Flight* by kind permission of the author. Translation by Ingrid Christophersen.

Johan Borgen *The Youth of Today* by kind permission of Nina Pedersen @Gyldendal. Translation by ingrid Christophersen.

Ian Fleming from *On Her Majesty's Secret Service* by kind permission of the Fleming Estate and Ciara Finan @ Curtis Brown.

Christopher Matthew from *The Amber Room* by kind permission of the author.

The Finnish Winter War Additional material by Mitch Swenson by kind permission of the author.

Jan Kjærstad from *The Seducer* by kind permission of the author.

Lars Saabye Christensen *Ideal Time* by kind permission of the author.

Sylvia Plath from *The Bell Jar* by kind permission of Faber and Faber.

Graham Green from *Dr Fischer of Geneva* by kind permission of PenguinRandomHouse.

John Cheever from Collected Stories *The Hartleys* by kind permission of The Random House Group.

John Updike from the Early Stories *The Rescue* and *Man and Daughter in the Cold* by kind permission of The Random House Group.

Marc Paul Kaplan from *Over the Edge* by kind permission of the author.

Unni Lindell *The Race* by kind permission of the author. Translation by Ingrid Christophersen.

Clare Francis from *Wolf Winter* by kind permission of the author.

Brad Thor from *The Lions of Lucerne* by kind permission of Simon & Schuster.

Hammond Innes from *The Lonely Skier* by kind permission of The Random House Group.

Arnold Lunn from *In Praise of Skiing* by kind permission of his grandson Bernard Lunn.

Leni Riefenstahl *Escape to the Mountains* from *Memories* by kind permission of Holger Roost.

Karl Ove Knausgård from *Boyhood Island* by kind permission of PenguinRandomHouse

Laila Stien *Birkebeineren* by kind permission of the author. Translation by Ingrid Christophersen.

Dick Dorworth *The Perfect Turn* by kind permission of the author.

Ragnar Hovland *Ole Hagen* by kind permission of the author. Translation by Ingrid Christophersen.

Odd Selmer *The World was Reborn* by kind permission of the author's son Aksel. Translation by Ingrid Christophersen.

Ernest Hemingway *Christmas on the Roof of the World* by kind permission of Simon & Schuster. From *The Snows of Kilimanjaro* and *Cross Country Snow* by kind permission of PenguinRandomHouse.

Ron Watters *Snowshoe Thomson* by kind permission of the author.

Erica Jong *For an Earth Landing* by kind permission of the author.

Irwin Shaw *Top of the Hill* by kind permission of the Orion Publishing Group.

John Marsden *Checkers* by kind permission of the author.

Italo Calvino *The Adventures of a Skier* by kind permission of The Wylie Agency (UK) LTD.

CHAPTER 1
STORIES FOR CHILDREN

This anthology has been 6 years in the making. I have scoured my own bookshelf and the internet, asked friends and borrowed a few ideas from a Norwegian anthology. I have greedily pounced on everything and anything and must by now be Amazon's very best customer.

I've translated the Norwegian short stories and considered how they resonate with my upbringing in Norway. Always an abundance of snow, always skis on my feet, and always wallowing in deep, deep powder.

Norway was awarded the 1952 Winter Olympics just as the country was emerging from five years of occupation. There was little money to spare and my father was given the job of general announcer in English, French and German. We had front row seats for everything. I was torn between wanting to be a figure skater, wearing frilly tutus and whiling around on the ice, or a downhill skier. We had a chalet in the mountains at Norefjell (site of the downhill and giant slalom competitions) and skiing won out. It also helped that Stein Eriksen was my hero and his brother Marius, equally good looking, owned the shop where we bought all our skis.

Here is an article I wrote for the *DHO Journal*.

A CHILDHOOD ON SKIS
Ingrid Christophersen

'Norwegian children are born with skis on and the midwife is there with a saw.' That's my story and I'm sticking to it.

We arrived in Norway in the winter of 1947. Norway had been occupied for five years and there wasn't a spare house in sight. In fact, there was nothing spare at all. The country had been robbed and cleaned out of anything useful. My father's workplace at Oslo University had been ravaged and was unusable. The British Institute was moved to a hotel in the country outside Oslo and that is where I took my first faltering ski steps, aged just 18 months. I hated it. Red, runny nose, wet bottom, my mother never getting me to the loo in time, having to peel off seven layers of clothing first, and always being cold. My nickname was 'Piddly Pants Penelope'. It was so cold that year that the fjord froze over. You could walk on the ice from Norway to Denmark and the fish died in the water. My Australian mother thought she had come to hell; nothing to buy in the shops, rationing, and two runny-nosed children.

But things started to look up. Our church received masses of warm clothes from a branch church in America, (I always thought it was the Marshall Aid) and we were lent a summer house by the fjord. There was no electricity or running water. We had to break the ice in the well and haul water out in buckets, but at least it was our own. The house was next to Amundsen's house. He was the Polar explorer who beat Scott to the South Pole. No wonder he got there first. Anyone brought up in those conditions would find the walk to the Pole a doddle. My poor mother.

Things looked up even further. More houses were built, and we moved up the hill overlooking Oslo, close to the famous Holmenkollen ski jump, with a thousand square miles of wilderness as our backyard. This wilderness would often encroach on our life, with elk and deer appearing in the garden in winter and ptarmigan and capercaillie courting in the summer. What a life. And so much snow! If it had gone by May 17th. I would be allowed to exchange my thick, brown woollen stockings, which were kept up by an old-fashioned suspender belt, for short socks, to march in procession. 17th of May is Norway's National Day. Constitution Day. Every Norwegian marches; in the capital Oslo to the King's palace and afterwards gets sick; the children by eating too many ice creams (the first of the summer) and the grownups by drinking too much.

I skied to school every day and took the 'tric – electric' home in the afternoon. The 'tric' in winter is furnished with leather straps on the outside to which you fasten your skis. Sometimes the number of skis fastened to the outside would completely obscure the view. Oslo hosted the Winter Olympics in 1952 and we lived close to the venue of the slalom. The slope was floodlit – a necessity, as it was pitch black by 3 o'clock in the afternoon – and there was a T-bar. If my current heartthrob was skiing too, I would maneuver in the lift queue or dawdle on the slope to make sure we went up together, holding hands, thick gloves on of course. We'd then ski home through the woods, down the floodlit trails with the lights of Oslo twinkling and blinking far below us. Bliss!! Romance par excellence!

I had long, very long, wooden skis. The edges were screwed on in sections. I had leather boots and wore plus fours and red stockings. The bindings could be loosened for walking. Wax was usually rubbed on. My brother and I started an enterprise, a ski wax production company. We melted my mother's candles and tried to pour the wax into empty toothpaste tubes. My brother was an excellent ski jumper. He jumped 49 metres when he was only nine years old. He always wore 'the fat man', a beautifully warm fur coat that had been in one of the 'Marshall Aid' crates from America. That is how we recognised him at the top of the jump. My father ski jumped too but he once broke both shoulders and had to have them re-broken when it was found that they had been badly set.

If I wasn't ski racing during the weekend, I was rushing round on my cross-country skis in Nordmarka (the vast wilderness that surrounds Oslo), collecting points. Every child is issued with a card which you stamp at your starting point and then stamp again at the furthest away point in one of the many small restaurants, huts, chalets or shelters that are scattered around this enormous area that backs on to the capital. 32 kilometres was considered a good day's ski. At the end of the winter, the card went to the Norwegian Ski Federation who would jot up your mileage and award gold for 500 kilometres, silver for 250 and bronze for 100. I never got beyond silver but some of my classmates got double gold! At Easter, my father and I would pack two rucksacks and ski into the heart of Norway (the home of the Trolls) and spend nights in mountain chalets. We'd cover huge distances in the day, over glacier and plateau, moorland and mountain. Peer Gynt country, two tiny dots in the vast forever.

It was extraordinary visiting England and not seeing snow and children in short pants and no central heating. What did they do in the winter? Cricket? My father imported a cricket team once and held an exhibition game. It never caught on. Norwegians thought it was too boring.

My childhood paradise was a whirl of powder snow and empty white spaces, floodlit trails in the forest, snow crunching under boots and horses breathing clouds into the frozen air. And always an abundance of snow.

FIVE SHORT STORIES FOR CHILDREN translated from Norwegian by Ingrid Christophersen

THREE VIGNETTES BY ALF PRØYSEN:

Alf Prøysen (1914–1970) was a Norwegian author, poet, playwright, songwriter and musician. Prøysen was one of the most important Norwegian cultural figures in the second half of the 20th century. He worked in various media, including books, newspapers and records. He also made significant contributions to music as well as to television and radio. He wrote in dialect and his stories for children are warm, engaging and full of humour.

THE SCHOOL SKI RACE

I would have loved to have written a book about my memories from the nursery slopes. They are something else.

It all started with our school ski race. Miss said we all needed to enter the ski jumping competition. Fourteen hands flew in the air as if on command. The fifteenth right hand remained glued to the desk. That hand was mine.

"Don't you want to take part Alf," said Miss.

"No," I said.

"You need to start taking part in the ski jumping competitions, and not be such a wimp."

I never answered. But twenty-eight eyes were searching for mine. I looked down.

"Well, you mustn't think you can skip school. Everyone must at least show up and spectate. Now we'll sing: 'Courage, valour, wit and humour, arms and legs and minds of steel. Such are boys Old Mother Norway wants.' The volume increased when they got to that part.

Especially Olaf Mobakka.

On the road home, everyone who had entered nagged and hassled me. Olaf Mobakka was the worst. But then he knew he was in line for first place. The day dawned, a big day for all the others. I just stood around, frozen and shivering in the cold. I hadn't eaten anything that morning, so to add to my misery I was hungry too. The others were practising. They waved their arms around and were candidates for the Norwegian Ski Team. Especially Olaf Mobakka.

They whistled through the air like wounded crows whilst I stood by the side of the jump, watching. Then came Olaf Mobakka. And just as he was about to take off and launch himself into thin air I fainted. Olaf rolled, head over heels, all the way down the slope, I heard them say afterwards. They took me home on a sledge, I remember.

Olaf was given a second go, but by then he had the shakes and got nowhere. He went home alone, crying all the way. Well, those are my memories from the ski jumping competition. Everyone has forgotten the race, but I remember. And so does Olav Mobakka.

VICTORY

In the whirlwind of Olympic fervour, a small breeze escaped from my village. It was about a cousin who was about to take part in a race. Not an ordinary club race, you understand. No, all villages in the area were to nominate someone they thought was good enough to compete in Holmenkollen. On every track and trail, from all the rural areas, skiers on Huitfeldt bindings and hickory skis, ventured forth.

My cousin came from Lismarken. He was a man of few words, quiet and discreet. We had never seen him before, but the start list had been published and he was number 83. So, we knew who he was when he spotted him in the air and heard the crack of the landing. Then he swung round on the flat and kicked up a lot of snow. He jumped twice and stood upright twice.

At the end, mother walked over to him and invited him back to supper. We had meat balls and stewed prunes. He ate little and said even less. When his mouth was full anyhow. The prune stones he deposited on the side of the plate and they kept on sliding into the milk.

He was leaving on the 7 o'clock train. We did not accompany him to the station. It had started to snow and he skied a lot faster on his own. But we rushed out and watched the train as it meandered by like a glow worm. He had been chosen to take part in Holmenkollen.

"He'll win," we children said.

"Well, there are a lot of good ones taking part,' said mother. "All the best take part in Holmenkollen. From abroad too, so we must not expect too much."

Two veteran ski club members travelled south to watch.

"I wonder if you'll see him," said mother.

"Oh, we'll see him," they said, "but no doubt we won't get near enough to greet him."

"Oh, there are so many people on that hill," said mother. The next day the result list was in the newspaper. We never had a newspaper, but our neighbour lent us hers. He was sixteenth.

"Gosh, there were people who were better than him," we children said.

"But some who were not so good," said mother, "and he is related to us." Then she cut out the result list and hid it in the hymn book.

CROSS COUNTRY IN MY HOME VILLAGE

There was to be a cross-country race in my village. Not a big race, where the likes of Grønningen and Martinsen would take part. Oh no, this was a tiny race for anyone who was a member of the village ski club. The course crossed a field, continued through a shaw, then over a railway bridge and on over the Skyberg straights. Little snow had fallen that winter and the bridge was snow-free. So, what to do? Not a problem when there were eager competitive boys around. Jarle, Magne and Gunnar took it upon themselves to carry snow onto the bridge to make a track, and for this they would receive one pound.

The race was set for Sunday and early in the morning the boys set out furnished with shovels and a toboggan with which to ferry the snow.

"I'm wondering how our Oscar fares," said Jarle. "He's on form to take first place today."

"Braggart," said Magne. "When Oscar and my brother Johan skied a training run Thursday evening, Johan finished four minutes in front of your Oscar."

"Rubbish," Gunnar shouted. "Show me anyone who is going to beat the twins today."

"Ha, we'll see," Jarle sniggered. "Your twins were pretty tanked up in the pub last night."

One word followed the other. They blasted each other with snowballs and never came to their senses until they saw the first competitor approach the bridge. The bridge!... the bridge which was snow-free! The boys ran. They heard the skiers swear as they clambered over the wooden bridge. More arrived. How would this end? Well, it ended like most races do, the best won. Some had used the wrong wax, some just never got going and those who never got a prize blamed the boys who had dawdled instead of shovelled. They never claimed the one-pound note.

TWO VIGNETTES BY KJELL AUKRUST:

Kjell Aukrust (1920–2002) was a Norwegian author, poet and artist. He is most famous for his memoirs of his childhood in Alvdal in the books Simen, Bonden and Bror Min as well as his creation of the fictional Norwegian village of Flåklypa and its cast of idiosyncratic characters. This setting was the basis of the 1975 animated film "Flåklypa Grand Prix". The film was the first full-length animated feature film made in Norway. It became an international success and has been translated into more than seventy languages. In Britain, it is known as "Pinchcliffe Grand Prix" and was translated by my father. Go to Google and type in 'The Pinchcliffe Grand Prix'.

It is impossible to capture the humour of these vignettes. They are written in dialect and are incredibly colourful. Norwegian has a lot of words pertaining to snow, skiing and ski jumping, and even ski wax, for which there is no equivalent in English. Even the feel of the cold, the frosty morning, the frost smoke issuing forth out of mouths… one has to have experienced Norway on a cold winter's day to really know what it is all about.

THE 17 KILOMETRE RACE

My Brother raced round the barn, 17 times, gloveless, the day Grøttumsbråten won the 17 kilometre in Lahti. In the evening his ears were plugged up, he caught a fever and was fed Trondheim soup with raisins.

On Monday, The Nationen announced that the Norwegians had messed up the wax in soggy conditions in Sollefteå. Utterstrøm won on klister it said. Over in his bed my Brother became very agitated. Following a business-like attack aimed at the leadership of the Norwegian Ski Federation he succumbed to a coughing fit.

When the fever subsided, he boiled klister. The mess smelt curiously like rubber; an obstinate struggle ensued. Forks and spoons were twisted into spirals when the stuff came out of the pan. Berthe, the maid threw her arms in the air. The stuff was poured into empty mustard tins. However, it was a bit trickier to stuff the concoction into used toothpaste tubes. My Brother was the paragon of patience.

Afterwards invitations to take part in the Holmenkollen Ski Race were sent out. The interest was immense. Competition-hungry villagers in home-knitted cross-country deerstalkers turned up in droves.

My Brother installed himself in the kitchen window with an alarm clock. From this vantage point he handed out oilcloth bibs with a safety pin in return for the entry fee. The rubber klister was a great hit. Outside, in the sunshine, hot-tempered skiers fought the wonder concoction. They rubbed and polished. Homespun shag and tufts of hair stuck to their fingers. A soldering iron made the rounds. Now the klister became manageable. The rubber bubbled and ran down the skis in great globs and the wax held on the uphill. Simen rushed up and down the barn footbridge. Snowballs and large lumps of earth stuck to the skis.

Agonising scenes followed. The klister manufacturer behind the window was taken to task. Tempers were boiling. Under threat of compensation old knives and broken scythe-blades were doled out with which to scrape the skis.

At midday, my Brother set the first competitor off, knocking his knuckle on the glass. The echo of famous names fought and struggled about seconds. Lauritz Bergendahl got tangled up in some fencing. Utterstrøm blew his top behind the garden shed and Lappalainen and Gjermund Muråsen struggled in the underbrush down by the river. Ernest Johan, who came from Tynset, refused to play ball. He went home to the vicarage and stayed there.

The combined ski jumping competition followed straight afterwards. My Brother was the judge. We pulled him, wrapped in warm woolly blankets, on the milk sledge over to the ski jump. After the competition, we went home to modest festivities on the kitchen steps. The purchase of prizes had been made with view to a margin of pecuniary safety. My Brother tore the notebook in two and carefully coaxed the rubber off the top of the pencil. That turned into a nice little prize. Later he cut the pencils in two on the meat cleaver for consolation prizes.

The combined calculation process was complicated. My Brother had his own method. The extraordinary results were much guided by one's relationship to the Organising Committee.

Before the prize-giving he gave a speech. "Sportsmen: as we now stand in front of the prize-giving table it will of course cause happiness and sorrow. I want to remind you of Kristian Mikkelsen's words: *it is not important to win but to take part.*"

My Brother spoke without notes. Following the ceremony, he closed the kitchen window and opened his mouth wide – Berthe was there with the cod-liver oil.

HALF A METRE SHORT

Us 8- and 9-year-old boys went dizzy all over when we got our hands on a box of 'Record'. This most precious of ski wax, this mystical, fabulous tar re-hash smelling of 3 times 19 and a phenomenal hill record.

This was before Thorleif Scheldrup, Hyvarainen and Andreas Däscher suspended themselves in Swiss wind tunnels with their hands on their back pockets. It was during these historic times that I jumped 29½ metres on the Sandegg Hill. New skis, with three grooves, were promised if I could manage 30 metres.

I immediately started dry training on the sofa at home. Double take-offs made the sofa springs sing. My rock-solid landings rattled the sideboard.

One Sunday in January the record-beating jump was to become a reality. Time was carefully spent preparing the skis… in the kitchen. The women folk were given serious lectures on the deep mysteries of ski jumping wax. Iron, hot plate and all other conceivable aids and remedies were put to use. And in between the layers of wax I returned to the double take-offs on the sofa.

Saturday night was restless. Every now and again I got up to have a peek at the thermometer outside the office window. The corridor was freezing. The soles of my bare feet stung and I slid down the banisters. The window was glazed over with frost and I had to scrape the glass to read the thermometer. Minus 30! The moon hung yellow and frosty pale. A black, troll-like cat hurried into the barn. On the other side of the river Sandegg Hill lay in the shadow of the looming and brooding Baugs Mountain.

I got dressed the next day, hugging the radiator. Everyone lent a hand. First long johns, then a few editions of Nationen, front and back, followed by more long johns to keep it all in place. Two pairs of stockings, two pairs of thick woolly socks. And two sweaters. The Nationen, Christmas edition in front, the Østerdalen Post at the back. Two pairs of gloves, a beany, a fur-lined hat, and a long scarf to top it all.

It was fiendishly difficult to move. When I breathed, the wrapping rattled. I needed to pee. It was heavy going and my tummy was in turmoil. The third time my dad exploded. A biting wind blew over Glåmma and frost smoke hovered like fine spray when we breathed. Dad's glasses misted up. Beards were white with hoarfrost. The snow crunched and barked for every pole plant that brought us closer to the Sandegg Hill. It lay ahead of us frozen, blue and scary. Walking up took an eternity. On top of the scaffolding I glimpsed Dad raking the jump. He looked like a North Pole explorer. Frost smoke escaped out of him with every shovel. It looked intimidating. Round about in the snow were yellow ice cream cornets deposited by nervous ski jumpers. I showed off by peeing into the largest one. I was sure this one was made by Per Samuelshaug. Gosh, that felt better.

To climb up ice-encrusted scaffolding encased in lots of newspaper is hairy enough. But when I got to the top I recognised what a hazardous undertaking it was. The village lay below me, white and beautiful and a thought rushed around my head. Will I see my childhood valley again after the jump? I lent forwards in the newspapers and buckled my skis on. My heart was pounding behind the Nationen. Surely, this could be heard for miles.

Dad was on the judges' stand in his sheepskin coat, waiting, expectant.

"Is it clear?" I screamed, alarmed at the hollowness of my voice ringing out over the void.

"Yes," came the answer out of the sheepskin coat.

"On my way," I screamed, and remained standing. Oh my God, how horrible, I had to pee.

An irritated voice from the judges' stand: "come on boy."

"But is it clear Dad?"

"Yes, it is clear."

"The landing is not too hard, Dad?"

"No!"

"There's not too much lip on the jump?"

"Not at all."

"It's blowing up here."

"Not down here, come on boy."

"I'm on my way."

I pray to God and let go. I rush down the in-run, the lip of the jump rushes towards me, tears running down my cheeks like frozen peas. "Oh dear, oh dear… why on earth did I think of this?" I launch myself into the abyss. The ski tips brush the bump. I waive my arms around. The body is stiff in its encasement. The packaging crackles and rustles underneath the sweaters. With one big gasp, I give up the ghost, close my eyes and the newspapers disintegrate as I hit the ground. Dad comes sliding down on his bum.

"That looked bad Kjell."

"How far Dad, I moaned."

"As far as the top marker."

"How far's that? "

"29½ metres," said Dad.

CRISS-CROSSED SKIS by Harold M. Sherman

Harold Morrow Sherman (1898–1987) was an American author, lecturer and psychical researcher who wrote several popular boys' sports and adventure books (notably the Tahara series). He also produced two plays on Broadway. 'Criss-Crossed Skis' is featured in Sherman's collection, 'Down the Ice: And Other Winter Sport Stories', published in 1932.

Skiing is loads of fun. If you don't believe it, ask Mr. Sylvester B. Turner who owns the only hill in town worth skiing on. He'll tell you what fun it is and if you're not hit over the head with the nearest thing at hand, you'll be lucky. But maybe Mr. Turner's cooled down some since last winter. Honest, he was hot enough that time to have melted snow!

How'd it all happen? Well, you see, we fellows used to slide and ski on Randolph Hill before Mr. Turner bought it. After that, he puts up 'Don't Trespass' signs all over the place but even then we don't think he means us. The first time we put our feet on his ground though, he raises an awful holler. And the worst of it is, Mr. Turner's one and only son, Ronald, tattles on us.

Ronnie, we call him, is a mamma's boy if there ever was one. He's thin and scared looking, if you get what I mean – the sort who wears rubbers if there's a cloud in the sky. You can't point your finger at him without his running home and telling about it. Talk about sensitive! Mack Sleder asked him "how come his hair wasn't combed?" one morning and Ronnie almost busts out crying. Perhaps he can't help it. But you know how fellows are, if a guy acts that way, they poke a lot of fun at him. Ronnie steers pretty clear of us, though. He knows what's good for him. Besides, Ronnie doesn't go in for sports. He hates to get bumped or dirtied up and then, too, there's always the chance of getting hurt.

"What's the sense in it?" he asks us one time. "I'd much rather sit in a hammock and read a good book."

"Aren't you afraid the hammock might turn over with you?" kids Tommy Fox.

"I'd never thought of that," says Ronnie, soberly. "That's worth considering, isn't it?"

And he sits on the porch steps after that.

Ronnie's dad is as big and blustering as Ronnie is timid and quiet. And talk about dignified! Mr. Sylvester B. Turner expects everyone to bow and scrape before him since he's the richest man in town and owns the biggest factory besides the biggest hill. Everything has to be big with Mr. Turner. That's his style. The biggest house, the biggest car, the biggest noise... and the biggest boob for a son. That's how we feel, anyhow, after Mr. Turner's high and mighty manner and Ronnie's yelling: "Dad, look what the fellahs are doing!"

Are we downhearted? You can just imagine! Being chased off old Randolph Hill is like having our sleds and skis taken away from us on account of there being no other decent place. We could understand this high hat business if Mr. Turner was using the hill for anything else but it slopes off for over a mile behind his big house, going down on one side to Mitchell Creek and down the other to a meadow that's fenced in with an old rail fence. We've been sliding and skiing straight down the hill, though, the long way, which carries us across the old Strawtown Pike and up against a bank that finally stops us. It's one grand ride, whether you take it by sled or by skis ... only, of course, it's lots more exciting on skis. We figured this year that we'd grade the bank, too, and use it for a jumping off place. Whether you know it or not, ski jumping is the real sport. You may land on your head or back or some other part of your anatomy but that's half the sport! And here Mr. Turner is so stingy that he closes his estate to the whole neighborhood!

"You must remember, James," my father says to me, "Mr. Turner has a perfect right to do this. It's his property. Old Mr. Randolph was very nice to let you boys use the hill but you shouldn't feel too hard against Mr. Turner because he refuses. After all, it can't be so enjoyable to have a mob of kids tracking all over. Maybe Mrs. Turner is very high strung. Maybe their boy is nervous and can't stand strenuous exercise or excitement. Maybe that's why Mr. Turner bought the place, so he could be off by himself with his family. You must take this all into consideration."

"I still think he's just doing it to be mean," says I. "He likes to put on airs. As for his son, if Ronnie's mother would let him be himself, we'd make a man out of him in no time!"

My Dad throws back his head and lets loose a laugh.

"You fellows had better leave well enough alone," he warns. "You ought to know by this time that Ronald has a 'Don't Trespass' sign hanging on him, too. And since Mr. Turner has phoned me and complained about your being on his property, I don't care to have any further trouble with our new neighbor. You mustn't forget, either, that my company does considerable business with Mr. Turner's factory. We can't afford to have Mr. Turner down on us."

"You're right, Dad," I agrees. "I guess I'm still peeved, that's all. Made me feel like I wanted to get even. The other guys feel that way, too. Some of 'em were going to take it out on Ronnie – but I'll have a talk with 'em and fix it up. I wouldn't want to do anything that would interfere with your business."

"I know you wouldn't," Dad replies, then puts a hand on my arm. "I'm sorry about that hill. If I owned it I'd turn it over to the town for a public playground."

"Picture Mr. Turner doing a thing like that!" I explodes. "He's not interested in this community. He's just interested in what he can take out of it."

Dad nods. "The answer probably is," he says; thoughtfully, "that Mr. Turner's never learned how to play."

And, do you know – Dad's explanation all of a sudden soaks in! The more I think it over, the sorrier I commence to feel for Mr. Turner for what he's been missing all his life. And the tough part is that his son's starting out the same way.

"Maybe we could return good for evil," it occurs to me. "I'll have to get the gang together and see what they think about it."

Talk about a conference! There's just six of us fellows and each of us has more ideas than we know what to do with ... which means that there's usually six leaders and no followers. Some don't want to have anything more to do with the Turners; others claim, if we did try to be nice, it wouldn't be appreciated; and Tommy Fox asks me what I expect to gain for my trouble.

"Probably nothing," I rejoins, "except the satisfaction of playing missionary to the heathen on the hill!" This brings a laugh.

"Okay!" seconds Mack Sleder. "It's going to be torture for us, but mamma's boy Ronnie gets invited to join our gang the next time we see him."

"And he'll turn us down flatter than a fallen cake," Eddie Hale predicts.

"Well, it's Jim's idea," says Mack. "I'm for trying anything once."

Getting ahold of Ronnie isn't so easy. Every time he sees us coming he runs around the block or cuts across lots. We're just so much poison to him and he figures, since his father's laid down the law about our using the hill, that we'll pretty near scalp him if we get the chance.

But one snowy day we get Ronnie from in front and behind. His arms are full of groceries which he wouldn't have been getting himself only the delivery truck is stuck in a drift and his mother has to have the food for dinner.

"Let me go, you guys!" he begs. "If you dare touch me, my Dad'll...!"

"Listen, you!" says Mack, with his hand on Ronnie's shoulder. "Don't cry before you're hurt. We've been trying to catch you for some time."

"Y-yes, I – I know," says Ronnie, trembling from head to foot. "D-don't make me d-drop these eggs, or you'll b-be sorry."

"Oh, he's got eggs!" says Mack, and winks at the bunch. For a minute I think he's going to change his mind and pull something.

"You don't like us, do you?" Tommy demands.

"Why – why – I certainly do."

"Then why do you try to beat it every time you see us?"

Ronnie swallows and looks the next thing to miserable.

"I – I've got to be getting home with these groceries," he says. "My mother's waiting...."

"Answer my question!" demands Tommy, looking vicious.

"I – I've forgotten it," stammers Ronnie. "It's storming harder, isn't it?"

"Yes – it'll be great weather for skiing after this snow packs down," says Eddie, pointedly.

Ronnie blinks and glances around like he's going to yell for help.

"Cut it," says I, pushing the fellows back and taking matters in my own hands. "Ronnie, old boy, this must be a pretty lonely life you're living," I begins.

"These groceries are getting heavy," Ronnie answers, shifting his packages around. "And I'm getting snow down the back of my neck."

"You shouldn't be alone so much," I keeps on. "It's bad for a guy to play by himself all the time. It makes him self-centered and mean. Besides, there's no fun in it. What you need is to get out with the gang – to be one of us!"

"What?" Ronnie's mouth comes wide open.

"There goes the eggs!" shouts Mack, making a grab at the sack. He picks it out of a snowbank and looks inside. "Okay – only a couple cracked – none of 'em broken."

"Yes, Ronnie," I repeats, as I help hold him up. "One of us! We'd be proud to count you as a member of our Rough and Ready Club."

"You – you would?" Ronnie stares at us suspiciously.

"You bet we would!" assures Mack. "We'd be tickled to initiate you!"

"Initiate?" gulps Ronnie and tries to get away. "No, sir! I don't want to join your club. I want to go home!"

"Listen," says I, kicking Mack in the shins, "we're willing to make an extra special exception in your case – and let you join without any initiation."

"Well...," considers Ronnie, "I – I'd have to ask my Dad first. He doesn't believe much in joining things. He says a man should be able to stand alone."

"He's wrong," speaks up Tommy. "Doesn't your Dad know that 'united we stand, divided we fall'?"

Ronnie stares. "I don't believe he ever heard of that," he says. "But I'll tell him."

"Don't you tell him a thing!" I orders. "Can't you decide anything for yourself. Do you have to run home and ask papa or mamma every time you want to blow your nose?"

Ronnie's face gets red. "Not exactly," he says, faint-like. "These groceries...!"

"We'll help you carry 'em home," I volunteers, "as far as the bottom of the hill, anyway."

"Sure!" says Mack and grabs the sack of eggs. "Oh, oh! There's another one cracked! Man, – these eggs are tough – you can crack 'em but you can't break 'em."

"Mother will throw a fit," Ronnie observes, ruefully. He stares about him, badly worried, because his groceries are divided up between six fellows, and he's probably wondering if he's ever going to get 'em back.

"We're not a bad bunch – honest!" I tells him, as we walk along, keeping our heads down against the wind and the snow. "Trouble is – you and us haven't ever gotten acquainted. We think you're a real guy underneath."

Say – you ought to see Ronnie warm up! I guess he's been starved for talk like this ... someone to take an interest in him. He's still afraid we're going to take a backhanded slap at him, though.

"I – I don't get out much," he confesses. "There's lots of things I'd like to do if...!"

"Fine!" busts in Mack. "You come with us and you can do 'em!"

"Could I learn to ski?" Ronnie asks.

"Ski?" we cry, and now it's our turn to gasp for breath. "Ski?... Would you really like to learn to ski?"

We can't believe our ears. Can you imagine this? It just goes to show that you can't judge any fellow until you get right on the inside of him. If Ronnie was asking us to teach him how to play checkers or blindman's buff ... but – skiing! Maybe he's spoofing us.

"Skiing looks like fun," says Ronnie. "Mother thinks it's too dangerous, but you fellows don't seem to get hurt."

"Naw, of course we don't," I replies. "I tell you what you do, Ronnie! You come out with us and we'll show you how to ski and then, after you know just how to do it, you can surprise your mother! Just imagine the look on her face when she sees you skiing up the hill to the house!"

"Y-yes, I – I can imagine!" falters Ronnie. Then his face takes on a hopeful expression. "I guess she'd feel all right about it when she saw how perfectly safe it was, wouldn't she?"

"Sure!" declares Mack, slapping Ronnie on the back and almost dropping the egg sack. "Every mother's that way! Too bad, though, that your old man – I mean – your father – kicked us off the hill." Mack nudges me and I try to stop him, but he's got what he thinks is a great idea and he goes on. "I guess you weren't so crazy to have us on the hill, either. Just the same – it's the best place around here to learn to ski."

We're just at the foot of the hill as Mack says this. It's the street side of the hill and we're looking up the steps to the big house on top. Somehow it reminds us of a fort that's almost lost in the snow. We're half expecting to hear some words fired out at us from Mr. Turner's booming voice, but we evidently can't be seen from up above. Ronnie hasn't said anything yet in answer to Mack's bold crack about the hill for skiing and I'm thinking to myself that he's spoiled everything.

"I had the wrong idea about you fellows," Ronnie suddenly blurts out as we return his groceries. "That's why I told Dad. He seldom goes out on the back hill. I don't see how the tracks you'd make in the snow would hurt anything. If you'd like to meet me out there tomorrow afternoon while Dad's downtown...?"

"Would we?" we all shout.

"I haven't any skis," says Ronnie.

"I'll loan you mine!" I offers. "But what if your Dad should find out? He gave us strict orders...!"

"Well," considers Ronnie, starting up the steps. "I suppose the worst he could do would be to put you off again."

"He wouldn't be hard on us if Ronnie was along," encourages Tommy.

"Okay!" I decides. "We'll be there, Ronnie! From now on – you're one of the gang!"

Ronnie's face actually beams. Then he takes an anxious look up the stairs.

"If I don't get home with these groceries...!" he says, "Mother'll have the police looking for me."

"You leave it to us," I calls after him as he runs up the steps. "We'll make a skier out of you!"

And the second Ronnie's disappeared in the house, we all start to dancing jigs in the snow, with Mack patting himself on the chest and declaring: "I guess I put it over, eh ... what? Got Ronnie to take us back on the old hill! And say – maybe we were wrong. If we give this bird half a chance he may not turn out a mamma's boy after all!"

The next afternoon we don't feel quite so gay. It's stopped snowing and the skiing ought to be swell but the thoughts of what Mr. Turner might do and say if he ever got wise that we were on the hill again without his permission has made us kind of shy and nervous. We're not so sure that even Ronnie's being there will help any in case...! In fact, Eddie suggests that maybe Mr. Turner would blame us for inveigling Ronnie into skiing and using the forbidden hill. Inveigle is a terrible sounding word and, while we're crazy to ski, we're not wild to ski into any more trouble.

"Besides," points out Carl, "if Ronnie should get a bump like we all do, once in a while, we're the guys who'll have to answer for it."

"It's quite a responsibility all right," admits Mack, "but I say it's worth the risk. We certainly can run as fast as Mr. Turner."

"Not if he sees us first," I warns, "so we'd better keep our eyes peeled. My old pair of skis ought to be good enough for Ronnie to learn on, don't you think?"

"Sure," rejoins Tommy. "He'll probably break 'em anyway – hit a tree or something."

"Aren't you cheerful?" I razzes. "Well, that's not going to happen if I have to go down the hill ahead of him and bend the trees out of the way!"

There's a familiar figure sitting on a fallen log and waiting for us when we climb over the fence and sneak up the hill behind the Turner house. Ronnie jumps up when he spies us, as tickled as a kid, who's about to try something he's never done before.

"I – I thought maybe you wouldn't come."

"Ronnie – we are here!" says Mack, officially and solemnly. "Your lesson is about to begin!"

"But first," breaks in Tommy, "how many miles is your father from here?"

"He's downtown," reassures Ronnie. "He's hardly ever back before five o'clock."

"Then I guess the coast is clear," says Eddie.

"It is – straight down the hill," I replies, meaning something different. "But you got to watch out for the creek and the fence on the sides. Here's your skis, Ronnie. You shove your feet into the harness like this."

Ronnie is all eyes. He lifts up his feet and lets me fix them onto the long strips of hardwood.

"You – you're not going to send me down this steep hill first off, are you?" he asks, plenty nervous.

"No, of course not. We're going to let you ski around on top of the hill here, where it's flat ... and get used to the thing. Stand up now and see how you feel."

Ronnie straightens up and looks down at the funny contraptions on his feet. He lifts one ski up and tries to take a step forward. It turns sidewise and plops down on top of the other ski. Ronnie's legs get crossed and he sits down ker-plunk. We grin and Ronnie looks worried.

"Aren't these skis a little too long for me?" he inquires. "Are you sure they're my size?"

"Skis don't come in sizes," I informs. "You lifted your foot too high. It's a sliding motion – like this." And I demonstrates.

"It's easy, isn't it?" says Ronnie, and untangles himself.

"Sure!" encourages Mack, "when you get onto it – it's like falling off a log ... or a cliff ... or anything...."

Ronnie stares at Mack a minute and then glances toward the brink of the hill.

"I couldn't get started downhill without wanting to, could I?" he questions.

"If you did, we'd grab you," I tells him. "Now try it again. Move your right foot forward. Keep your body inclined just a bit. That's the way. You look just like a skier now! Doesn't he, fellows?"

"Exactly!" they agree.

"Don't move and spoil it!" directs Mack who can't help making sport of things.

Ronnie looks kind of bewildered.

"Go ahead," says I. "Don't mind what that boob says. He's a bum skier anyway."

"I am, am I?" challenges Mack.

And down he goes over the hill, making the first tracks in the glistening snow. It's breathless to watch him as he gains speed, whizzes across the old Strawtown Pike and up the embankment where he comes to a stop. He's a black dot to us now as he turns to wave his hands and then start the long journey back.

"That's wonderful!" breathes Ronnie. "Oh, if I could only do that!"

"You've got to creep before you can ski," I instructs. "Don't get impatient. A good skier wasn't built ... I mean – made – in a day. We'll come out again ... that is ... if your Dad doesn't stop us."

"Dad's never had any time for sports," explains Ronnie. "He's been too busy. He thinks young men should ... er ... expend their energies on more worthwhile things...."

"Well, I ... er ... don't exactly agree with him," says I. "But, of course, we can't all think the same."

"All work and no play," recites Tommy, winking at the rest of us, "makes Dad a dull boy."

"He means 'any Dad'," I hastens to explain. "Now you just ski along beside me till you get the hang of this. Then we'll try a little slope back here which I'm sure you can safely ... er ... negotiate."

"Safely – what?" Ronnie asks.

"Jim means," defines Tommy, getting back at me, "a slope you can safely descend without any untoward incident...."

"Oh!" says Ronnie.

We spend a good hour, Ronnie and me, getting him familiar with having skis on his feet. Meanwhile the rest of the guys are having a swell time skiing down the hill and I'm commencing to think that I'm the martyr to the cause, being crazy to do some real skiing myself.

"How about it?" I ask, finally, "do you feel like you can go it alone?"

"It's quite simple now," says Ronnie. "Do you mean you think I'm ready to ski down the hill?"

The question gives me a chill. Skiing on a plane surface and skiing downhill is as different as walking in broad daylight and skating in the dark with roller skates.

"You'd better stick to just what you're doing for a couple days," I advises. "You're getting along swell."

"I feel quite confident," replies Ronnie. "This is mostly a matter of balance ... something I've always been good at. I walked our clothes line once. Everything would have been all right if it hadn't busted."

"Yes," says I, "Most things would be okay if something didn't happen. But you use your own judgment, Ronnie. If you think you're ready to go down the hill, it's up to you. Only don't blame me if you suffer any ... er ... minor accident."

"How could I blame you?" Ronnie wants to know. "I'm awfully grateful for all you've taught me. This is the most fun I've had in months ... maybe years...."

"That's fine," I replies. "Here's hoping you keep on having fun."

"That's why I want to go down the hill," declares Ronnie. "I imagine that would give me a real sensation."

"It's the big thrill in skiing," Mack puts in, being eager to see Ronnie make his first attempt. "Just follow my tracks, Ronnie, if you decide to go down, and you can't go wrong!"

"I – I believe I'll do it," says Ronnie, after taking a deep breath. "It's a long ways down. I probably won't be able to ski back up the hill. That looks a lot harder."

"Aim for that embankment across the Pike," points out Mack. "See if you can beat my mark."

"Oh, I couldn't do that first off," returns Ronnie, modestly. "I'd be satisfied if I could tie it. I imagine my momentum will be about the same so I should travel about as far."

"There's no doubt about it – you'll travel!" assures Tommy.

"If this works out all right," says Ronnie, "I'll have my Dad see me do it and maybe he'll change his mind about letting you fellows use the hill. Of course, he mustn't know that you've taught me. He's to think that all these tracks are mine."

"Ronnie," says I, "my hat's off to you. You're a regular sport. And what's more – I admire your nerve."

"Oh, this doesn't take nerve," disparages Ronnie. "It just takes skill."

"Well, have it your own way," says Mack, and we all stand around to watch the take-off.

"Feet together," I directs, feeling shaky inside. "Lean forward a little more. That's it!"

"Goodbye, fellows!" calls Ronnie, as he moves toward the spot where the hill slopes down, eyes glued ahead.

"Goodbye!" we shout.

It sounds to me like we're saying goodbye for a long time. There's a sickening feeling comes in the pit of my stomach as Ronnie suddenly disappears over the brow of the hill and shoots down. Say – have you ever ridden in a roller coaster? Well – you zip down a steep hill on skis and tell me which gives you the biggest heart throb. In a coaster you can at least hold onto the rod and sit tight. On skis you've got to hold yourself just so or you may find yourself flying through space and landing hard enough to jar your wisdom teeth.

"So far, so good," says Mack, when Ronnie's halfway down.

"I don't care to look," I rejoins, getting panicky. "I never should have let him gone!"

"He's doing swell!" cries Tommy. "Oh – oh, no! He's not doing so good now! He's veering to the right. He's off the course. He's heading for the fence!"

"Good grief!" I exclaims and takes a look. "Sit down, Ronnie!" I yells, making a megaphone of my hands. "Sit down – quick!"

But Ronnie doesn't hear me. He's too wrapped up in his own problem.

"Oh, my gosh!" gasps Eddie, "that tree!"

How Ronnie missed a big oak, I don't know. He just shaves it and goes on, right through a clump of underbrush and down a steep grade toward the fence, his body weaving back and forth as he's fighting to keep his balance.

"Look out!" I screams, and then it happens.

Ronnie hits the fence ker-smash and goes right on over, doing the niftiest frontward somersault you ever saw, and landing head first in a snow drift with only his skis sticking out. We're all of us so petrified that we stand there a couple seconds, not knowing what to do or say. Then we see Ronnie's feet kick and his head come out of the snow.

"I'll bet he's hurt!" I cries. "I'm going down to him!"

As I'm strapping on my skis, though, the fellows bust out laughing.

"What's so funny?" I demands.

"He's waving at us!" roars Tommy, "he thinks that's great stuff! I don't think he's hurt a bit!"

I stand up and stare and we all wave back. Ronnie starts trying to climb the fence with his skis still on, but he finds this doesn't work so good, so he takes 'em off. And when I'm sure he isn't hurt, I take to laughing myself. Honest, I haven't seen such a funny spill since I can remember. Talk about innocence abroad! The way Ronnie has gone down the hill, so sure he has known all he needed to know about skiing!

"So you're laughing at my boy, eh?" says a big voice behind us.

Wow! We just about freeze in our tracks! As we turn around, there's Mr. Turner, so mad he can hardly see straight. How long he's been standing there, we don't know, but it's probably been plenty long enough. And now we're going to catch it!

"My wife thought something was up," says the man who owns the hill, "so she phoned me and I came home. This is what you do behind my back, is it?"

"It was your son's idea," explains Tommy, who's scared green. "He wanted us to teach him how to ski...."

"So this is the way you do it – start him down this big hill?"

"I told him he'd better not try it," says I.

"When I want my son to know anything, I'll teach him!" booms Mr. Turner. "You boys aren't going to make a laughingstock of him! I used to ski when I was a boy and I...."

"You?" Mack exclaims, unbelievingly.

"Yes, me!" thunders Mr. Turner. "And Ronald could do what I used to do with a little practice. Loan me those skis, young man, and I'll show you a thing or two!"

Mack, open-mouthed, passes his skis over. Ronnie, meanwhile, is struggling to get back up the hill. He can't make it on skis and is in snow up to his waist. His dad kneels down and slips his feet into the straps as we gaze at him, darn near paralyzed. What can we say? Mr. Turner is boiling mad ... so mad that he gets one ski on backward. He kicks it off and turns it around.

"Excuse me, Mr. Turner," breaks in Tommy, "but hadn't you better come back here on the hill? Don't put your skis on while you're on the slope. You might start off before you're ready. You know, skis don't have any brakes...!"

"Are you telling me something about skis, young man?" is Mr. Turner's rejoinder.

"I'm trying to," replies Tommy, backing off, "but I guess it doesn't matter much. You'll find out soon enough."

Mr. Turner glowers.

"Careful, Dad!" cries Ronnie, who comes panting up the hill. "It's not so easy as it looks!"

"Stand back, son!" orders Mr. Turner, and stands up suddenly. The incline starts him moving and off he goes – before he's ready.

"Dad!" yells Ronnie, but there's none of us near enough to catch him.

Mr. Turner gives one anxious glance behind him, and almost falls over backwards as he swoops downward. What's worse – he hasn't had a chance to steer himself and he shoots off the straight-away at once, going more and more to the left.

"He's heading for the creek!" we all cry. "Sit down, Mr. Turner! Sit down!"

When you sit down it helps slow you up and you can usually manage to stop although you may roll over a few times. But it's better than running into something by a whole lot.

"Maybe he'll jump the creek!" speculates Mack. "It's only about fifteen feet across!"

"I don't think my Dad was ever on skis before!" says Ronnie, worriedly. "He thinks anything a boy does is easy."

We groan at this, though I'm willing to believe that Mr. Turner has had some experience with skis which he hasn't thought worth mentioning until this moment. It's even steeper down the left side of the hill than it is down the center where we've made our course, and Mr. Turner is going like the wind when he gets to the bottom. We can tell that he sees the creek and is trying to figure out how he can avoid it. He tries to move his skis to the side and make a turn but nearly upsets. Thirty feet from the creek he lifts one ski off the snow and desperately attempts to swing sidewise. Instead he criss-crosses his skis, tangles up his legs, sits down with a smack, and goes sliding right on, clawing and scraping until he clears the bank of the creek and sails out over the water to land ker-splash in the middle.

"Oh, boy – and is that water cold!" shivers Mack.

"He sure showed us something!" murmurs Tommy.

Say – if we were to be tanned the next minute, we can't help screaming at this. It's twice as funny as Ronnie's high dive what with Mr. Turner sitting in the creek, with the water up to his neck and one ski still clamped to his foot. He doesn't stay there long, though. He flounders about till he can stand up and wades ashore, climbing up into the snow which must feel warm to him in comparison to the icy water.

"Ha, ha, ha!" laughs Ronnie. "Dad didn't do as well as I did, did he?"

Man, oh man! Is this a surprise? Here we've just begun to feel bad for laughing outright at Ronnie's father and Ronnie busts a rib himself. That makes us feel better ... but Mr. Turner's coming up the hill, leaving the skis behind, so mad the water almost turns to steam on him.

"We'd better beat it!" advises Mack.

"No, fellows! Stay here!" pleads Ronnie.

"We've got to stick!" I orders. "We can't run out on Ronnie now!"

So we stand our ground, expecting to get our heads taken off the minute Mr. Turner gets to us. He's a sorry looking sight as he clambers up the hill, falling down a couple times in the snow when he loses his footing. Mr. Turner's hanging onto his dignity, though, for dear life ... trying his darnedest to preserve it. He's been humiliated in the eyes of his son and before a bunch of fellows who've come from the best homes in town, if I do say it. But all I can think of is what my Dad told me about doing business with Mr. Turner, in warning me not to make him sore. And now I've gone and done it!

"Gee, Dad!" says Ronnie, when Mr. Turner, puffing hard and teeth chattering, reaches the top of the hill. "If you knew how funny you looked!"

"I'm c-c-cold!" answers Mr. Turner. "This is no l-l-laughing m-m-matter! You b-b-boys had no b-b-business...."

"I'm sorry, Mr. Turner," I apologizes, thinking of my father and hoping to straighten things out.

"S-s-sorry, n-n-nothing!" stammers Mr. Turner. "You'll b-b-be t-t-telling this all over t-t-town...!"

"Sure they will," says Ronnie. "It's too good to keep."

Mr. Turner glares furiously. "W-w-when I w-w-want your opinion, son, I'll ask f-for it!" he returns.

Have you ever been so nervous that you can't keep your face straight even when you're scared? That's the way we feel and we commence to snicker again, one fellow starting off the others. It's some comical sight, Mr. Turner, shaking like a wet rag on a clothesline.

"I've g-g-got to be g-g-getting to the h-h-house," he says. "B-b-boys, p-p-please d-d-don't s-s-say anything about this! K-k-keep m-m-mum!"

It's so funny to hear Mr. Turner trying to talk that Mack laughs right out.

"Maybe," suggests Ronnie, taking his father's arm, "if you'd let the boys use the hill...?"

"Yes!" takes up Mr. Turner, giving us an appealing glance. "If I'll l-l-let you use this h-h-hill for a s-s-slide, w-w-will you b-b-boys keep this quiet?"

We look at one another and are we happy? There's a nodding of heads and I says: "That's a bargain, Mr. Turner! Nobody hears about this if we can play on the hill!"

"M-m-my w-w-word is my b-b-bond," says Ronnie's Dad. "C-c-come on, Ronald, b-b-before I s-s-suffer from exposure!"

"Goodbye, fellows!" calls Ronnie, and winks. "I'll be seeing you soon!"

"Goodbye, Ronnie!" we shout after him, deciding right then and there that he's a regular guy in the making.

That night, when my Dad finds where I've been he says, "How come?" and my answer is: "Oh, Mr. Turner just decided, if he didn't let us use the hill, that everybody in town would think he was all wet...."

"I don't quite understand," my Dad replies, but that's nothing – because no one, outside of our bunch, understands to this day.

HEROES by Odd Børretzen
Translation by Ingrid Christophersen

Odd Lunde Børretzen (1926 – 2012) was a Norwegian author, illustrator, translator, and one of Norway's most significant text writers, folk singers and artists. This piece is from The World of my Childhood.

In the world of my childhood we were seriously into hero worship. The heroes might excel in different ways, but they were always men.

Of course, they might be skiers or ski jumpers who won the Holmenkollen ski race. In the Teddy cigarette cases there were pictures of famous horses. After all they were someone's heroes too and they collected these pictures. The pictures were quite expensive because they were rare. It was only Kristian's mother (she was really a witch) who smoked Teddy. She was the only lady in my childhood who smoked. The men smoked a pipe or chewed tobacco and spat. In the train station waiting room there was a brass spittoon beside the electric heater. Expert spitters could sit as far as four or five metres away and spit into the spittoon. Actually, they never made it, but nearly.

Other heroes were Willy the White Clad Pilot from Africa, Dennis the Menace and Asterix. And of course, the football team that beat Germany in the Berlin Olympics in 1936. We listened to the match on the wireless. My brother had memorised the entire commentary.

"Ahhh, we are leading, we are leading two nil. Fransen to – eh – Martinsen who was brilliantly positioned but sent the ball to Isaksen who netted it. We are – eh – two nil up. This is the sensation of the day here in Berlin. The spectators cannot believe their own – eh – eyes. They are stunned. Norway is leading two nil. 39 minutes. We are leading – eh – two nil".

Then of course there were the skaters. Oscar Mathisen obviously. He had won so many medals that he was weighed down by them. He had medals all over this chest and down his legs. He was photographed from the front but I'm sure he had medals all down his back and even on his bum. Well done him for walking around with all those medals which must have rattled at every step. And Ivar Ballangrud who won the World championships and took three Olympic gold medals. And Sonja Henie, but she wasn't really a hero, she was a lady.

But our greatest heroes were the Polar explorers. Dad had books about the Polar explorers. One of the books was even called "A hero". On the jacket was a picture of a Polar explorer with skis and a fur jacket. He was struggling through a snowstorm. The wind was so strong that his face was quite distorted.

My brother and Kristian were making preparations for a trip to the North Pole. My brother was Fridtjof Nansen and Kristian was Hjalmar Johansen. I wanted to join them. I wanted to be Roald Amundsen. But my brother said that Amundsen never joined Nansen. "Amundsen never went to the North Pole," my brother said, "he only went to the South Pole and that was an awful lot easier as it was downhill." "And anyhow it was much warmer on the South Pole because it gets warmer and warmer the further south you go." Kristian said. "It was only Nansen and Johansen who went to the North Pole. Alone. They had dogs with them," my brother said. "You can be the dogs," he said. And so it was.

When my brother and Kristian came home from school one day we started skiing north. Nansen led. He was followed by Hjalmar Johansen. They carried rucksacks and packed lunches. I walked at the back with the toboggan and was dogs. The first part was easy, over the fields; they were flat and sometimes downhill. But down by the Grorud burn we encountered pack ice. It was a bloody battle. We fought on. "Don't give up Johansen," my brother said. "You're not an old woman." Actually, it was worse for the dogs for they had to pull the toboggan in the soft snow and of course dogs don't have skis. "Don't give up Johansen," Nansen panted, on his last legs. When Nansen said don't give up to Johansen for the third time, Johansen got angry. "My skiing is just as good as yours," he said.

When we reached 86° North we camped in the icy wilderness, under a tree, and ate our picnic. When we had eaten, Hjalmar Johansen said. "Now we must kill the dogs. We can't take them any further. That is what the RSPCA says." So, then they killed me and I was left in the snow while Nansen and Johansen fought on to 86° 12'. I lay in the snow and was dead dogs for quite a long time. It got rather cold, so I went home and had some hot chocolate in the kitchen. It must have been on a Saturday because afterwards I listen to the children's hour on the wireless.

I INVENT SKIING by Swaine Wolfe

Swaine Wolfe is a documentary filmmaker and a novelist who employs fable forms and mystical elements to promote respect for the natural world. As a boy, Wolfe lived on ranches in Colorado and Montana. As a youth, he worked in copper mines and listened to the stories of his co-workers. Wolfe also worked as a logger, another experience that he has said changed his view of the world.

Several days after I fell in the hayloft trying on the skis, I was feeding Joe his oats. I brushed, patted and nuzzled him. Instead of putting the saddle on, I untied him, climbed up into the loft, and slid the two long skis into the manger then crawled down and carried them through the barn into the corral. Joe stood in the doorway and watched me work my galoshes into the straps. Then I pointed the boards toward the low end of the corral and slid a short distance waving my arms before falling over. Joe watched me do this four or five times, each time with the same result. After another try, I managed to go the length of the corral. My minimal progress was concluded against the corral poles. The whole business seemed pointless, particularly my futile attempt to negotiate the lumpy ice. I decided to try the pasture. At least it would soften the fall.

I shuffled along in the pasture snow for a while, wondering how old Gardner managed to ski down and back from the store. Unless he had a horse to pull him, he must've used sticks to push himself along. Sticks to push, but there were no sticks in sight. The world was under snow. I closed my eyes and mentally searched through all the ranch buildings, looking for sticks the right size. I saw them in the milk barn.

I got out of the skis, went to the barn, fetched two worn-down brooms, returned to the pasture, wiggled a foot into each ski and pushed off with the brooms. I knew Joe was watching all of this. He stood in the doorway of the horse barn and saw me glide across the pasture getting smaller and smaller until I reached the slope down to the river. Gradually I sank down and down, until all he could see was my head, and I was gone. With every push of the brooms, I could feel his eyes on my back. I had betrayed my horse.

The slope to the river was smooth. The water was frozen over and strong enough to carry the elk who'd made a trail across the ice. I followed near the trail to the opposite bank and tried to push uphill with the brooms. That didn't work, so I took the skis off and slid down into the elk trail.

All winter a small herd of elk had been coming down single file out of the trees, through the deep snow and along the edge of a broad, open slope that spooned out into a wide meadow. The elk followed along the far edge of the meadow to a gully, then down to the river where they crossed the ice to make early-morning raids on our haystacks.

I carried my skis and brooms over my shoulder and followed the elk trail up the mountain and into the trees. Once I was in the fringe of trees, high up on the slope where it was steepest, I made stairs in the snow, climbed out of the trail and slipped my galoshes into the leather loops. I pushed myself through the trees with the brooms until I found a spot that gave me a straight shot to the meadow. Straight was important. Once I had some speed, those long boards had tendencies of their own. The snow packed under my galoshes made leaning into a turn dicey. If I tried, my heels slipped off the boards, and I was in the snow. When a tree approached, falling down was the only alternative to a smashed skull. My objective was to stay upright, get up to speed in the steep drop through the trees and then shoot straight down the mountain toward the open meadow as fast as I could go. I spent a lot more time floundering in snow than shooting down the mountain. Each time I fell meant an exhausting struggle to locate the skis. Too often, one of them would sail down the slope into the meadow. This went on until dusk.

Several weekends later, I was flying, moving faster than I had on Joe, even at a dead-out run. Making sharp turns on the long skis never worked but coming off the slope, I learned to make long, slow arcs through the meadow. At the end of my glide I'd find the trail, take the skis off and head up into the trees.

For several days a cold wind had blown the light powder off the slope and toward the river leaving a soft crust on the surface. The snow was the fastest ever. My crashes were magnificent. The skis skittered over the crust and across the meadow. I had to dig around to find my brooms. The snow couldn't support my weight without skis and I had to swim. I didn't make many runs. I spent too much time regrouping and climbing up the mountain.

After a particularly stunning crash that buried skis, brooms, my red cap, tore two buttons off my wool coat, and packed snow down my boots, pants, and neck, I retrieved my stuff and tromped back up the trail. When I got to my exit point, I was sweating and the snow was melting. I climbed out of the trail and took my time skiing over to the downhill run. By the time I was ready, my pants were starting to freeze and my feet ached.

I decided to cut across the hill toward the river. It would be easy. I didn't want to go fast in the cold air and I didn't want to crash again. I just wanted to get home and get warm.

The sun was going down as I slipped over the hill. The river was right below me when I began falling through the snow. The fall took long enough for me to think about what was happening. I was sinking through fine powder, falling down and down through bright, white snow into dim, gray snow. I was immersed in powdery snow. When I stopped falling, there were no broken bones, no crunch, no sound. I didn't land, I just stopped falling. I could still breathe. I was elated.

Years before Sam owned the ranch, someone had dug into the hillside for gravel to fill log-box pylons for a bridge whose skeleton still haunted the river. Fine, blown snow had filled the dugout to the top. I had skied off the edge of the excavation and fallen through the powder all the way down to the riverbank. All I had to do was push my way forward, and there was the river.

I crossed the ice and skied home, happy and oblivious to freezing feet and stiff pants. I kicked the skis off near the barn, ran across the road and up the hill to the cabin, full of excitement, primed to tell everyone about the amazing thing. Before I got to the door, I heard Mother screaming. When I opened the door her back was to me and Sam was sitting on the floor, his hands over his ears, staring up at her with his dead face.

My elation evaporated. Mother whirled around, her expression caught between anger and confusion. In her rage, she'd forgotten about me. For a moment I thought she was trying to figure out who I was. She said, "Where's your cap?"

I wanted to tell about falling through the snow, but this was not the time. I reached up and felt my head. I'd forgotten about the cap. I stared back at her. There wasn't much I could say. I realised my clothes were frozen, and I was cold.

Sam was still sitting on the floor. I was shivering. Mother told me to get my clothes off. One moment I'd been running, excited, oblivious. Then, except for the shivers, I could barely move my legs. Mother stoked up both fireboxes and started heating pots of water.

I sat down to pull my galoshes off. Then Sam was up and bellowing at me to take my clothes off outside.

He didn't want snow on the floor. Mother picked up a pot of still cold water and threw it at him. He was slow to duck. She soaked him and I scrambled for the door. Mother yelled something at Sam. After a moment the door opened and Sam thrust a blanket at me. "Here." His voice boomed up the canyon and bounced back. "Here, here. Take it, take it, I'm freezing."

She'd soaked him from the top down. He was still wearing his long johns and socks. I started laughing. When he came after me, he couldn't get traction. I still had my boots on. We circled the house twice to Mother's pleas to stop. Sam would've caught me, but he kept falling down. He finally cooled off, stopped, and stood in the snow glaring at me. I hesitated, not knowing if he was just getting his breath or if the chase was off. Evidently the cold and the burst of oxygen let him get a grip. We all went inside. Mother stretched a line across the cabin and hung up our wet clothes.

I took a bath standing in the galvanized tub in front of the stove, which was stoked until the top turned reddish orange. You couldn't just stand there and bathe. The side away from the stove froze. The side closest burned. You had to keep turning, reaching down with a wash rag to grab some soapy water. I had to have taken several baths that winter, but that was the one I remember. In the summer, I swam in the irrigation ditch or the river.

We must have eaten dinner that night. I imagine us standing, each in his own corner. Mother silent, Vicki humming, Sam brooding and I would've been keeping an eye on Sam.

I dreamed about wet wool coats hanging in bundles from the rafters in a large barn. It was cold, and my breath was steamy. The coats were beginning to freeze – a little crunchy on the outside and soft and wet on the inside. Sam was chasing me. I could duck under the coats but he kept bumping against them. They made a soft thudding sound… risk, risk, risk… like a dog thumping his tail on plush carpet.

In the morning, I woke in the dark, felt for the right clothes hanging from the line and got dressed. Everything was dry but the coat. I got my light jacket and an extra sweater out of the chest and went down to milk the cows. I missed my cap. Dozens of critters would find it in the spring. They would sniff, paw, and peck at the wad of red wool caught in the sage. Bits of that cap would find their way into a hundred burrows and nests, and comfort generations of baby mice, moles, and chickadees.

Some weekends I skied down to the river and explored along the banks. The skis were quieter than Joe and not as threatening to animals, other than deer. Once a small white animal stood on a log near its burrow and watched. It might've been a mink. I stopped, and we studied each other.

Deer were more timid. My voice scared them, but if I whistled, wheezed, and made slight sucking and clicking sounds, they would become curious and watch and wait.

On warmer days the soft snow absorbed sound and the quiet allowed animals to focus their attention. They weren't distracted by a thousand little sounds, bits and pieces of light off leaves or things moving in the shadows. Things that wanted to eat them couldn't hide as well against the snow.

Bound in my black wool coat, galoshes crammed into the leather loops attached to those ridiculously long skis, pushing myself through the snow with brooms, I must have been a comic sight. But I wasn't ashamed of my outfit. I'd never seen skiing. Mother and Sam were the only ones watching, and they never saw me shoot through the trees and come apart in several directions across the slope. It had occurred to me that a ski with sharp edges would cut into the snow and let me make turns. Of course, I'd have to find a way to bind my feet to the skis so I could lean or twist without falling. Ski boots, shorter skis with metal edges, and aluminium poles; none of these things entered my vision. I was determined to master a sport no right-minded fellow would bother with… downhill skiing on cross-country boards without bindings, with cow-barn brooms for poles.

In a few more weekends, I would have drilled more holes through the skis to make better bindings. I'd have used leather strips from old harnesses and added buckles. I needed to screw metal brackets into the wood so I could twist the skis with my feet. I'd also have to find something better than the brooms, which packed up with snow until they were icy stumps on a pole.

I soon forgot my plans for the ultimate ski. For Christmas, I got skis with bindings, boots, and poles and a new jacket. Maybe Mother and Sam felt sorry for me or were afraid someone would see me, but most likely it was simply a moment of love. I certainly felt loved. I was nearly delirious.

Comstock Hill was near the cabin. It was much steeper than the elk run across the river and it was treacherous. A road cut diagonally across the hill down to Taylor Road near the cabin. I'd avoided Comstock because there was nowhere to stop. At the bottom there was the Comstock road, Taylor Road, a barrow pit and a five-strand barbwire fence. I wouldn't have survived on the long boards.

Christmas morning in front of the cabin, I practised turns and sliding stops on my new skis. It was warm and the snow was soft and forgiving. Mother, Vicki, and Sam watched from the porch. I was showing off and paid the price several times. Vicki shouted and giggled. Mother smiled. Sam watched.

I'd made a few runs near the cabin then moved farther up the hill and came down where there was a shallow depression left from an old ditch. Things seemed to blur for an instant and I felt a little dizzy. Then everyone was cheering, even Sam. They were shouting, "Do it again, do it again." When I asked what happened, they said I'd made a complete somersault. They thought I'd done it on purpose and were amused when I admitted I hadn't.

The air turned cold and drove them inside. For the rest of the day I settled into learning about my new skis. The sharp edges and spring-loaded bindings were great inventions. As I made a sharp turn into a stop, one thing was going through my mind – I could tackle Comstock, because I could stop before I got to the roads and the barbwire fence. My parents were unaware that they'd just handed me the implements with which to kill myself.

By the time I started up Comstock a crust had formed on the snow. I had to kick holes through, making ladder steps all the way to the top. It was cold and clear. I could see far up the canyon to where the cliffs closed in on the river. Below the ranch, steam rose over the bridge where the ducks swam in the open river. Near the road at the bottom of the hill, smoke drifted up from the tin chimney of our cabin. The world was silent.

I stomped a flat place in the snow, set the skis down, then stepped into the bindings and levered them down tight on the fancy boots. I'd momentarily suspended my fear of gravity and pain. No one was daring me. No peers pressuring a fragile ego. This was a boy overcome by newfangled stuff and a craving for speed. The dim voice of reason was saying, "Don't do this," but the boy wasn't listening.

I lifted one ski and pointed it down. Then the other. Within seconds, I was in free fall. The mountain dropped out from under me and shot by in a blur. The speed, the icy crust and my lack of weight made turning impossible. I would have fallen and slid headfirst to the bottom.

The five, tightly stretched strands of death waited below. There were no trees to avoid. It was a straight shot to the bottom. To survive I would have to clear the Comstock road, land on Taylor Road to straighten out, clear the barrow pit, and hit the fence absolutely upright, all five strands at once.

That is exactly what happened. It was quick. The fence knocked the wind out of me and sprang me back into the barrow pit. For a moment I couldn't breathe. I was staring up at blue sky, listening to the fence twang all the way to the bridge.

Nothing was broken. The barbs left two small tears in my new jacket. I must have come out of my boots because I've a vague memory of looking for my skis. Staying upright was my only contribution to the accident of my survival and even that seemed like a thought projected onto the landscape.

I never knew how Mother and Sam were able to afford skis. They fought about money and never, ever bought anything that wasn't necessary. It was a brutal time. Buying the skis had to have been a desperate act – an attempt to undo everything that had gone bad. A lot more than me was riding on those skis. Maybe that's why I never told them about Comstock.

CHAPTER 2
COMPETITIVE SKIING

INTRODUCTION by Ingrid Christophersen

There are stories in this chapter telling of a 50-kilometre cross-country race and a slalom race. There is also an article from an 1843 newspaper from Tromsø, Norway, reporting on a ski race (and bar military races on skis), probably the first ever. 'The God of Skiing' by Peter Kray is a fascinating mixture of fact and fiction, real and imagined characters. The Prince von Hohenlohe spoken of is real and he once came and trained with my club on the Tignes glacier.

The fictional slalom race from the book 'The Downhill Racer' by Oakley Hall, is one we all find quite *quaint*. The book was first published in 1963 and compares today's alpine ski racing with that of nearly 60 years ago. From the old-fashioned, antiquated, out of the ark, it shows the pace of innovation and improvement of equipment.

At the start of my racing career in Norway at 8 years old, my skis were super long and up to an outstretched arm over the head. The bindings were the old cable type Kandahar bindings, and the steel edges were screwed on in sections. If one section came off, the whole edge would rip off. I wore plus four and red woollen stockings. Fast forward to 2020. Skis, bindings, boots, ski stoppers, poles, helmets, goggles, protection equipment, catsuits, back protectors… today, the paraphernalia of a ski racer is strictly controlled by FIS (International Ski Federation). So too are the courses, the make and specification of slalom poles, how they are set, vertical drop of hills, combination of gates etc. All are specified and must be strictly adhered to. In my day, we went into the wood and cut poles or used bamboo in three different colours; red, blue, yellow, topped by red, blue or yellow flags.

Que Vadis I wonder – the present televised World Cup is looking a bit stale and jaded. Do we need a new formula?

THE FIFTY KILOMETRE by Karsten Alnæs

Karsten Alnæs (1938) is a Norwegian author, historian and journalist. He worked as a journalist and taught at the Norwegian School of Journalism.

This story has been translated by Ingrid Christophersen.

When I caught sight of Arne's face on the ski trail, between the pine trees, right in front of me, ten kilometres from the finish, I suddenly realised that here was the fifty-kilometre Olympic Champion.

I got up from the bonfire where I had been sitting with the other lads and in spite of some haziness following night duties and all the hanging around, it was crystal clear what was about to happen. Despite the fact that Arne was at that very moment only lying third and that there was an extraordinary tough Finn and two Russians ahead of him, we heard the reporter on the transistor. Hoarse and spluttering he reported that now, just now, the fastest man on the course was Arne Huken.

Magical words, we understood the hidden clues: ten kilometres left of the deadly fifty-kilometre, and the fastest man on the course.

As in a flash of lightening, I realised that Arne would win. The powers above were about to realise what he and his father had been dreaming about for twenty years. Yes, all the time and energy they had invested. Yes, even life itself… if I can use such an expression.

"He'll win," I cried.

"Sit down," one of the others answered. "Sit down and take it easy, anything could happen, they have another ten kilometres to go."

But both he and the other weary faces around the fire wore a serious, anxious expression. They realised that I might be right. That a sensation might be about to happen. That of the four Norwegian fifty-kilometre skiers, the one that no one had much confidence in could win. What no one thought could possibly come to pass – *Arne Huken winning the Olympic fifty-kilometre.*

Expressions of devotion spread over the faces of my mates when they turned to look at me. Not only were Arne Huken and I classmates, not only had we grown up together in a small town in the County of Buskerud, not only had his sister been my sweetheart… I was Arne Huken's friend. That was the reason the other three had met him at a small reception two days before the fifty-kilometre. And before they realised that the miraculous, what no one had imagined, might come to pass.

The guys knew that I, an intellectual, had quite a critical and mocking attitude towards Olympic ski races. I had allowed my colleagues to lure me away from the Institute of Social Anthropological and History of Ideas to Austria and spend the night in a forest in the Alps, under the stars, the day before the fifty-kilometre. I was here as an observer of the public's carnival-like behaviour, not to take part in the usual sporting hysteria which characterises Norwegian spectators.

But I must admit that as I caught Arne's eye, as he was skating towards me, I felt that this moment was divine, not just in my life but in the history of the nation.

That is why I ran up the steep slope, by his side, which rose above us close to where we sat. I shouted, yelled, hollered hurrah and felt that, as I ran on beside him the ghosts of the night retreated. I lost control and felt pulled along by a wave that took me all over the place, just not where I had wanted to go in life.

And a thought rushed into my hot and befuddled brain that this was Arne's reward for the boring, deadly life he and his father had led ever since he was seven years old, when his father, the sad owner of an electric goods shop in the town market, had decided that his son would fulfil his own old dream – that of winning the Olympic fifty-kilometre.

Arne was not intelligent enough nor did he have enough imagination to oppose his father. He'd lost his mother at a young age and so had no one he could confide in, but passionately followed his father's bidding. He forsook play in the back yard or by the river, trips in the forest, apple scrumping in the autumn, football on the pitch, chasing the girls. He succumbed to systematic workouts and early bedtimes and turned his back on the forbidden life which we both gloried in and came a cropper over.

How I remember his zombie attitude to life. The servile obedience, the kind, polite and thankful manner with which he treated his father. The rather empty and sad look when, in the summer, he strapped on his roller skis.

After secondary education he enrolled in the sports college and left town. From the age of fifteen he trained two hours every day, had his own trainer when he was sixteen and lived a life without alcohol, nicotine or all-night parties. All was goal-oriented, aimed at the future and an immortal fifty-kilometre.

Puberty came and went without problems or complications. When he was twenty-two, he met a female biathlete. She played the role of intimate sweetheart when a year later he made his international breakthrough and came second in a World Cup race.

That spring he won a few minor races and started the new winter season by winning yet another international race.

But then progress came to a halt. Arne Huken became the hope that went out like a light. He fought his way to a few fourth places, won a few minor races in Northern Finland during the next few years, but never became what we mean by a winner and was thus never World or Olympic Champion.

Arne Huken lacks the 'winner instinct' the sports journalists wrote. He lacks the 'devil-may-care' attitude. He never manages to light that last deciding spark which makes one's body explode beyond its ability and the spectators to float enraptured above the pine trees.

This prompted the selection committee of the Norwegian national teams to exclude him from the team at several large competitions and this year, an Olympic year, at the age of thirty, he was a nobody.

The journalists were therefore surprised when he was chosen for the fifty-kilometre. This was caused by illness and lack of form from some of the other athletes. He should not have been at the start, but he was lucky, Arne Huken.

So, he turned up in the Olympic village together with his somewhat exhausted father and the female biathlete, who was no longer a biathlete, but who for some reason or other still followed him around.

Because from my point of view, Arne Huken was not really what we mean by a proper boyfriend, he exuded no erotic charisma, was interested in nothing outside of cross-country skiing, was uneducated and had no profession and no political affiliation. He was ignorant and boring and his sole role in life was that of a fifty-kilometre skier.

However, there was one exception. He wanted to play one role to perfection, the role of friend. He needed a counterpart for that performance, and for this he had chosen me.

Thus, I was pulled onto the stage because Arne Huken thought of me as a friend and for me that was fateful.

But it was only when I ran up the hill beside Arne that I understood the meaning of it all. Only then did it dawn on me the reason behind my journey, and that the history of ideas and anthropology were only an excuse.

I was not at all an observer of the public. I had been drawn into the whirlwind because the forthcoming Olympic Champion considered me his friend, his only friend I have to say.

"You are my friend," he said every time we met. And he repeated, "you are my best friend."

And extraordinarily I answered, "you are my friend, Arne. You are also my friend."

We never had much more to say to each other. We smiled sheepishly because we both knew that it was a myth. Why it was a myth to him, I do not know. But it was a myth to me because, amongst other things, I think the fifty-kilometre is one of the most irrational things a human being can do.

Not only does such activity lead to lack of breath, heart palpitations and a feeling of stress; your mouth tastes of blood, your urine is full of albumen and your body aches for days afterwards. A fifty-kilometre is nothing but ongoing suffering. Stupid voluntary torture, which banishes all sane thinking and leads nowhere. In a nutshell, it is one of the most horrible things a person can ever undertake.

That someone who calls himself my friend can dedicate his life to something like that, illustrates brilliantly how meaningless my own existence is.

In our country however, it is considered the greatest happiness to win Olympic gold in the fifty-kilometre. I think I can say that such an achievement towers over all else. Personally, I feel such an event suits Finns better as they fought the Winter War, or Russians who have languished in Siberia, rather than we Norwegians who have gone soft owing to the warm Gulfstream which washes up against our coast.

But on the contrary, we seem to value this self-inflicted agony more than we do a well-tuned violin. Like Italians are besotted by opera, we are besotted by the fifty-kilometre. This besottedness grabbed me as I ran up the hill like a madman, a taste of blood in my mouth, dizzy, legs suffering from lactic acid, but not caring a jot about it, in spite of my constitution suffering from an overindulgence of alcohol and nicotine which I should have taken into consideration.

Forgotten were my, not so few, personal defeats. Forgotten were the self-denials and sacrifices to the unknown human being, 'my best friend' whose life would not change owing to what was happening.

Youth, the miserable youth, was in the past, ahead lay the lonely middle age and the even lonelier old age.

None of this was in vain because at this very moment he was demonstrating that in his body lay a hidden demonic soul, a phantom concealed from all, even to me, but which in a few minutes would strike the earth like lightning.

I was filled with gratitude towards him. He had pulled me into this moment as I ran, gasping and screaming, ecstatic, mouth tasting of blood, beside him.

But Arne heard nothing. He skated up the hill with strong strides, isolated inside his own muscles, deaf to my shouts of joy, blind to the wonder and the impossible.

It was I, the onlooker, the sarcastic sceptic, who understood what was happening. I felt that I had always had this premonition, somewhere deep inside me, that this is how it would end.

But Arne attacked the hard-packed snow with his poles and skated away. I was left standing, crying, watching his back disappear up the steep hill.

THE DOWNHILL RACERS by Oakley Hall

Oakley Hall (1920 – 2008) was an American writer who has emerged mainly with wild romance novels. In particular, his 1958 novel 'Warlock' is one of the classics of this genre today. Many of the skiing sequences from the film 'The Downhill Racer' were filmed in Wengen in 1968 with Robert Redford as one of the racers and Gene Hackman as their trainer.

I C writes: I supplemented my ski school salary by signing up as an extra – great fun – and even sat next to Robert Redford – unintentionally on his part – for dinner in a Wengen restaurant.

It was snowing again as we climbed the slalom course on Cannon. Gusts of wind came down the mountain and blew the snow in startled flurries. The hill was a maze of red, blue, and yellow flagged poles, and the ascending line of racers twisted slowly up alongside the course. We individually memorised the combinations of gates as we climbed, deciding where to go high or low, where to go for speed and where to check. The trickiest part of the course was near the bottom where there was a sidehill hairpin leading into a three-gate flush and an offset H. Then there was a jog through two closed gates and the short schuss to the finish.

Skis on my shoulder, poles in my left hand, setting my boots in across the fall line to grip here where the hill was steep, I stopped when Karl Neuer, ahead of me, paused to study a combination. Snowflakes floated down and melted on my face and lay like tiny lace doilies on the sleeve of my parka and the gloved hand gripping the tips of my skis. Karl Neuer and Franz Beck were two Austrians who were teaching at Stowe and racing in the eastern starts.

Neuer muttered in German and plodded on. He had won the giant slalom but had fallen yesterday in the downhill and had no chance for the combined. Leary had won the downhill, Franz Beck had been a close second, and I an even closer third, but anyone in the first ten except Neuer still could win the combined by winning big in the slalom. In the first seed for the North Americans were Leary and me, the Austrians, a hot young Canadian named Markle, Benny Mclnemy and Joe Hammond (from last year's FIS team), Tom Boyd, (who had been in the last Olympics as well as the FIS), Jackie Samuelson, (who had also been in the last Olympics), and Harry Butler, (who was new on the circuit but had made a good record last year).

Weekend skiers stopped along the course to watch us as we climbed, and from time to time the snow lightened and T-bars were visible against the lacy snow-covering of the trees. I kept yawning. Everyone has his own way of reacting to a race, and though in slalom there is none of the fear of speed that is present in the downhill, there is tension enough. Leary was always very nervous until just before starting time, but I would go around yawning all morning, drowsy, unable to concentrate. People would seem a blur, everything too complicated to cope with – until my number was called at the top. Then the adrenalin would flow as though a faucet had been turned on and I would have to fight my nerves like trying to push a cat into a paper bag.

At the top of the course, racers and officials were crowded around the starting gate. Racers were tying on their numbers, filing edges, warming up, or merely waiting. The bright colours of sweaters and racing parkas, pants and toques, were muted and watered-looking in the white-on-grey day and the falling snow. Leary was pacing up and down to keep his legs limber. My own legs felt dull and weak.

Only the first fifteen or twenty gates were visible, their colored blobs of flags hanging limp. Below that, the course whitened into obscurity. The gatekeepers were taking up their positions and side-slippers packed the new snow that had fallen. Someone was testing the phone connection in a mechanical voice. From time to time a racer, to relieve the tension and warm up, would take off down alongside the course and crank off four or five tight turns, while the rest of us watched appraisingly. I closed my eyes and, moving a finger like a metronome, recited the order of the gates to myself. Near me, Tom Boyd and Jackie Samuelson were talking together in a relaxed fashion. They were both wearing their Olympic sweaters. Racers who'd made an Olympic squad always seemed to wear some piece of Olympic gear, as though to remind the rest of us that they'd made the Winter Games… what had we done? On the other side of me Bill Birks was unmusically singing:

> *"Downhill racers sing this song, doo-dah, doo-dah,*
> *Downhill course is goddam long, oh, doo-dah-day!"*

No one ever sang at a downhill start; there you waited and suffered silently. The slalom mood was more relaxed. But there was a sudden, swifter beat to my heart as the starter yelled, "Clear the course!" The gatekeepers took up the cry, echoing it down the hill. A gust of wind fluttered the flags. Leary came over to stand with me and we watched the first forerunner start down. He made smooth, stylish turns, not trying for speed. When the second forerunner went down, the snow had let up a little and we could see more of the course.

The first racer, Joe Hammond, burst out of the slot with a flurry of poles. He had been a downhill wonder once, but he had never come back after a broken leg.

Karl Neuer ran second; he skated, rowed with his poles, banged past the flagged gates, and worked for every fraction of a second. "Three in the slot, four on deck, five in the hole?"

I was five. My stomach rose six inches and hung there queasily. There were sharp, aching flutters in my legs. I moved up above the starting gate and waited there, flexing my knees. The loudspeaker at the bottom boomed Joe Hammond's time, distant and hollow, quarrelling with its echo – "59.6."

The starter counted down for McInemy, who leaned out of the slot, "five… four… three… two… one…

Go!" Mclnemy started down, and Franz Beck, in his white ear band, threaded his way into the gate.

"Four in the slot, five on deck." The Canadian boy, Markle, face lost behind his goggles, spat out his chewing gum and came up behind me, Leary behind him. Neuer's time was 53.8. There was cheering down below. "Good grief," somebody said.

Suddenly the T-bars and the weekend skiers were clearer, and the trees beyond them stood in puddles of blue shadow. The sun had broken through. When the starter began his count-down on Beck I had a moment of panic as the succession of the gates went blank in my mind's eye. I closed my eyes and gritted my teeth and summoned them back. "Go!" the starter said and I slid into the slot Beck had vacated. He had started faster than Neuer, too fast, I thought. Coming out of the fourth gate he had to check, throwing out a sheet of snow. He took the fifth gate off balance, one of his skis jerked up, but he recovered.

The starter touched my shoulder and said, "Roche?"

"Ho."

"Get set."

I pulled my goggles down over my eyes, leaned out and set my poles. He began to count.

"Time for number three, Mclnemy, North Conway -fifty-seven and four-tenths seconds."

I flexed my knees to the rhythm of the starter's counting.

"Go!"

I drove myself out with my poles, breathed explosively, "Hanh!" so I would not forget and hold my breath, and went down fast through the first series of gates, which presented no problems, taking the last of them so close the small of my back brushed the upper bamboo. There was a scrape of steel edges on ice as I cut hard around. My downhill ski slipped, then held, and I drove with my poles; drive! and drive! and a step up with the uphill ski and weight it and bring up the other, and drive! again. High through the next gate and skate once − too fast! too fast! I ran the tails of my skis out in a snow-plow for an instant, smacked them together and cranked around but still too fast. Just in time my edges bit and came around but off balance now − no!

I got my balance back as though the protest had done it, and now two open gates; shoulder in past the bamboo, around hard again; drive! drive! drive! with poles stabbing and the burn of snowflakes on my chin. Twist the right shoulder through this gate, and around and left shoulder through the next; out of the comers of my eyes now the banner at the bottom fluttering FINISH and the blink of the holes cut to let the wind through. I cursed out loud as my skis almost went out from under me driving through the next, closed, gate, but my ankles strained to cut the edges in, and driving with my poles again I dropped into the offset hairpin. Now the final flush. Elbows in and narrow, I steered the tips of my skis two inches to the right, a little to the left, shaving bamboo gates and into the H. Careful here! The tails of my skis cracked a gate, but I kept my balance, and there was the consciousness that from the number of close calls I'd had I must be making fast time. I ducked through the H, jogged once more, tucked, and schussed down to the finish, where the big banner hung limply now, as though holding its breath. At the last instant I came erect and flung my poles out ahead of me to break the beam of the electric timer, swept into the outrun and jarred to a stop.

There was applause from the people standing around the roped-off outrun. Panting, I pushed the goggles up on my forehead and moved slowly over to where Neuer, Beck, and McInemy stood by the timing shelter.

"You looked fast so far, Jack," McInemy said. "Good run." Beck made a saluting gesture, and Neuer put out a gloved hand to shake mine.

"Very good run, Jock."

"Thanks. Yours too." Hearing my name, I turned and waved at Anne, Brown, and Alice Beard. Markle was on course now. My stomach fluttered as the loudspeaker came to life. "Time for number five, Roche, Norden, California – fifty-three and five-tenths." There was a cheer. Karl Neuer banged a fist on his thigh. I grinned toward Anne and Brown, who were clapping. Markle shot out of the hairpin into the last flush. He hooked a tip on a pole, tottered, almost recovered, got off balance again in the H. He was falling for the last twenty-five yards, but he didn't hit the snow until just before the finish and plowed across in a tangle of arms and legs, skis and poles, to laughter and applause. But he had made a good run. A ski patrolman went over to help him up. Then Leary was on the course, the speeding dark blur of his body seeming to leap from gate to gate.

"He's going to be fast or can-up," McInerny said in his know-it-all way. Neuer muttered, "Too fast comes," and Beck spoke to him in German. The loudspeaker announced Markle's time: 54.8.

I heard Brown cry, as though Leary could hear her, "Slow down, Chris!" He didn't slow down. His movements had a jerky, half-completed look; but there was something heartbreakingly sure about him. He checked so hard before a flush he was lost in a spray of snow, and I thought he had fallen. But he hadn't fallen. Brown cried out again, "Go, Christy!"

"He is very excellent, your friend," Neuer said to me solemnly. "But sometimes foolish."

I nodded and watched Leary sweep out of the offset hairpin. He started through the flush down the fall line, twisting his shoulders like an awkward but enthusiastic dancer, each shift of weight giving him just enough deflection of line, shouldering past the bamboo poles so that they vibrated behind him. He slammed across the finish and deep into the outrun before he stopped. There was cheering and clapping and whistling, and now I didn't look toward Anne and Brown. McInemy didn't have to inform us that this was the fastest run, but he did anyway. Leary poled over to us, grinning arrogantly, eyes alight, panting. I cleared my throat and said, "Great run."

"Great run, Christy," McInerny said. "Best time so far." Neuer held out a hand to shake Leary's. Beck and Leary shook hands. Leary leaned on his poles and grinned up at the loudspeaker. You arrogant bastard! I thought. It seemed a long time before the announcement came. "Time for number seven, Leary, Colorado Springs: fifty-two and eight-tenths."

The cheering broke out again, and McInemy slapped Leary on the back. "Oh, hell," Leary said, grinning. "I thought I could bust fifty-two." He moved over toward Brown and Anne, stopping to shake hands with people along the way. Karl Neuer was watching him sourly, and I realized that I must be wearing the same expression. Above us the finish banner cracked and bellied in another gust of wind. I turned to look up the hill. The racer on course had missed a gate and was climbing frantically back up to it.

It seemed to me then that it was hopeless. That had been the best slalom run I had ever made. Leary had put out just a little more, borne down on the accelerator a little harder, and made mine not only a second, but second-rate. I had beaten him in slalom in training races and I had beaten him in the Gibson at North Conway. But this was the North Americans, the first try-out race, and he won the important races. What I wanted more, much more, than to beat him in slalom or giant slalom, was to beat him in a downhill, but now that seemed even more hopeless.

His time on that run was the best of the day. On the second run Beck and Tom Boyd beat him, but his total time was good enough to win the slalom, and with his first in the downhill, and fourth in the GS, he won the combined going away. I surprised myself by backing into third place in the combined behind Beck. It was fine to take a third in the first selection race and better than I had dreamed of doing last year. But there was no joy in it for me just as there would have been no joy for me either, in a second.

THE GOD OF SKIING by Peter Kray

The God of Skiing, a breakthrough novel by award-winning journalist Peter Kray, is being celebrated as the most accurate, action-packed, soul-stirring book ever written about the sport of skiing. A mix of fact and fiction – but the fiction is pretty accurate! I am indebted to Peter Kray for allowing me to reprint this chapter from his book – which was only published in 2014.

In Denmark scientists used carbon dating on a ski discovered in Greenland to reveal that the single board was at least 1,000 years old. They said the 85-centimetre plank, made from larch, was a common tool for winter travel used by the Norsemen who in 980 A.D. somehow first crossed the cold open sea. Older skis have been found in Mongolia, Norway, Finland and Sweden. There are Chinese cave paintings of hunters on skis thought to be more than 2,000 years old. The ski predates Christ, and in some regions, even the wheel.

But the modem birthplace of the sport is Kitzbuehel, where the Hahnenkamm, alpine skiing's most famous rollercoaster, is run every year. Begun in 1931, the race down the steep white throat of the Streif has only ever been interrupted by drought or war. The entire World Cup was built around the drama of the Mausefalle, and the shudder when you first drop down that face like a man falling by the window.

When the Frenchman asked me to watch 'The Race' with him, I felt as if he were inviting me to Mecca, and there were offerings I should bring or old clothes I should wear.

We had talked about starting a magazine together and had become friends in the little pleasures we took in the particulars of travel – a glass of wine with lunch in Italy, or the quality of German beer. I remember how his face lit up when they gave us the Mercedes Kompressor at the rental desk in Munich because they didn't have the car we had reserved.

On the Autobahn he kept pushing it faster whenever the speed limit signs above the road were clear.

"Ahh" he smiled. "I have a mee-stress now."

He had the face of a sunburned badger, like one of those retired athletes on the side-line watching the score. He had a big strong nose, a shaggy head of pepper hair and sleepy blue eyes that lit up when it was his turn to lead the conversation, which he adored.

He said, 'T-e long-eng is too Ameri-can,' when I told him about the story I wanted to tell. "You pee-pull all-ways talk about what isn't t'ere."

The adrenaline of gravity was still on our faces like coffee with Schnapps from skiing all afternoon. We drank yellow glasses of cold Pilsener at the hotel outside of Oberndorf and decided we would make a movie about the World Cup season. "We wheel call it t-e Alpine Cir-cus," Jean-Marc said with boozy authority. "It wheel show what we fee-yul."

The highlight would be of the Hahnenkamm: behind the scenes with the coaches pacing in long parkas and foreshadowing shots of the slope like an icy slide straight to oblivion; the Austrian soldiers grooming the course with crampons on so they don't fall off the edge of the earth. And the orange fencing down the Streif like a luge to the first gate covered with the 'yellow line' from the piss of fear.

By the time the racers reach the first gate they are going 70 miles per hour. The name of each winner, the flag of his country and the year he won is painted on the gondolas. Buddy Werner, 1959, was the only American for more than 40 years. So when we thought we would follow three racers for our movie, I insisted one be an American – Daron Rahlves or Bode Miller. Jean-Marc wanted one to be French, and of course, an Austrian, like Maier.

"But the French are no good."

His thick face flushed. He looked around the room.

"Swiss?"

"They're fading. It would be better if we could find an Italian."

"Italian?!" Jean-Marc exclaimed and looked at his big dark hands. He had given up smoking only weeks before. "Merde."

The crowds filled the streets. The bars are open all night, and more than 100,000 people took the bright red trains up from the cities, from the farms with their tall, grey über-Abner bumpkin hats, red and white painted faces and cases of Zipfer Bier. Most of them didn't even bother to get a room, staying warm on the beer and the glühwein as whole families, mom, dad and the kids all got drunk together.

But they were good drunks, so we hardly saw any fighting. We would film that too, how skiing was their national pastime and their birth right in the cold speed, the crosses on the peaks and the endless road of snow. We would film the finish lines and high-speed crashes where the racers are into the nets like splaying, unfortunate fish. And in the starting house where it's the cold and the nerves at the same time and there is always the idea of an ocean somewhere far below.

We would make gods out of wind and wine and the history of candy-coated towns with blue walls and warm windows, a beautiful eternity forever lost in the perfect faces of passing women, and that sound of our boots on the cobblestone.

"Austria is t-e heart t-at's all-ways beat-ing!" the Frenchman said and pounded his fist against his chest. "Eet is a love song now."

The next day we stopped at the top of the gondola where there is a small museum with posters and photos and a restaurant with big glass windows that look toward the valley where the racers were all sitting by the fire. It was the first day of training and there were half-eaten plates of sausage and bread, half-empty bowls of cereal, little espressos that went untouched and songs that kept starting and stopping. From a few tables away we could smell their fear.

"I would say good luck," the Frenchman said. "But t-ey would not hear."

"The training's even harder," Prince Hubertus von Hohenlohe told us when we went out looking for former racers to interview. "Because you still have to ski the course, and there's nothing to win, and more to lose."

Von Hohenlohe was a Mexican-Austrian prince and part-time rock star. He had thick black sunglasses and a Mexican flag on the back of the black parka he wore. His beautiful blonde girlfriend was as fine as fresh snow. Each turn of her head revealed another discovery of her white smooth-skin, and she held a cigarette as if it were breathing on its own.

"May I light that for you?" Von Hohenlohe said the organisers might as well canvas the mental hospitals to try and find skiers to forerun the course – to 'set the line' down the frozen groomed face for the racers to follow. He told us about being on the World Cup and the last time he raced at Kitzbuehel. The two skiers he was traveling with were a Swiss who had skied for eight campaigns and was thinking of retiring, and an African from Senegal.

"What do you think is cheaper?" the Swiss racer asked Hubertus. "The hotel in Wengen, or the hospital in Kitzbuehel?"

"But the downhiller from Senegal did come," Hubertus smiled. It was a flashbulb smile. "He didn't know enough to be scared." He said they were like pirates off the train, with their bags, their bright coats and the bottle of wine they shared. They stopped at every bar. It took them seven hours to make it to the hotel. But that couldn't stop the morning and on the gondola they hardly spoke a word. Hubertus said he was curious to notice how his friend was getting so pale. "It was a transformation, really. He did not look well."

They stood against the fence to watch the training runs, catching their breath as the first racers came by, dropping away like marbles. And as the Senegalese kept getting paler, he suddenly turned to von Hohenlohe and demanded, "Do you believe in God?"

"Of course," Von Hohenlohe replied. "I am a Christian."

Then the next racer came, with the battered fabric and desperate scratch of skis as he disappeared down the Streif, on his way to the stark sudden drop of the Mausefalle, where he would have to fight with all his body to resist the forces of gravity and velocity trying to pull him sideways off the hill.

He flew like they all do, like an awkward reluctant bird toward the steep face of the Steilhang. Into some certain disaster or glory waiting far below. The Senegalese was white as a ghost. He asked Von Hohenlohe, "But does God believe in you?"

THE FIRST SKI RACE 1843

A little-known episode in the history of modern skiing took place in the Arctic city of Tromsø when, in 1843, the world's first skiing competition took place…

It is known that already in prehistoric times the peoples of the Arctic used skis for transportation, hunting and maybe even for entertainment. The Norse sagas offer several passages of both Norwegians and Sámi skiers aptly flying and even at times fighting over the winter snow. If skiing remained for the most part a Scandinavian and Siberian phenomenon for the longest time, it ultimately spread over the whole world mainly as a sport and entertainment form. What is often overlooked is where this outward phenomenon started and the answer is, unsurprisingly enough, the Arctic North.

In the 17th and 18th century skis began to be used more systematically in the armies of the Scandinavian countries, especially in Sweden. During military training, skiing exercises were sometimes organised and the idea of skiers competing to reach a goal as fast as possible was born. Such exercises were however confined to the garrisons and civilians were still largely unconcerned with such contests. This all changed in March and April 1843 when the world's very first civilian skiing competition took place in Tromsø, the largest Norwegian city North of the Arctic circle.

The race had been organised by the local priest, teacher and journalist Otto Theodor Krogh who was the editor of the local newspaper Tromsø Tidende. Being responsible for the paper's content, Krogh simply wrote a short announcement in his paper and called for people to gather by the city hall, on the 21st of March for a race over the town's hill and back. A race that Krogh estimated would last around 40 minutes and was to be 'a true Norwegian game'. The fact that Krogh used such words and did not bother to describe the concept of the race further would seem to indicate that the concept of a ski race was already well-established among the locals who might very well have organised informal skiing races among friends and family for example, for quite some time already. But the competition in question is the oldest officially organised race we have any evidence about.

The race of the 21st of March was followed by two additional ones, showing that the initial competition must have been quite popular. The names of the people who won these first three skiing races were unfortunately not conserved. However, it is known that the winner of the second race was a barrel maker and that the third winner was a shoemaker of Kven origin. Kvens was (and still is) the name used to designate the Northern Finns who emigrated from Finland to North Norway in the 18th and 19th century. It was also noted that this Kven skier had quite a singular technique and skied using two ski poles. Indeed, in the Middle Ages and the early modern period, the traditional way to ski was to use a single, rather long and thick ski pole (which sometimes was also used as a weapon). The article in the Tromsø-Tidende paper about this mysterious Kven notes that using two poles was the traditional way of skiing among Kvens, insinuating that the practice of using two poles was still quite novel to be noteworthy of inclusion in an article.

It would thus seem that not only was this 1843 skiing tournament the first of its kind in the world, but also introduced the concept of double pole skiing to the wider world. This 'discovery' however took time to be fully accepted by skiers, especially in the more southerly parts of Norway where skiing using only one pole was still the norm by the 1880s. The now largely forgotten first skiing competition held in Tromsø in 1843 was, as with many things coming from the Far North, well ahead of its time but most definitely deserves to be more widely known, not only in the Arctic, but all over the world!

CHAPTER 3

HUMOUR

VENI VIDI VIKING

WINTER SPORTS BY ERIC THE RUDDY, THE LAST BUT NOT THE LEAST OF THE VIKINGS

A short extract from 'Veni, Vidi, Viking', a humorous guide on how to misbehave in Norway, commissioned by the Norwegian National Travel Agency and written by R I Christophersen (my father).

There are two varieties: first, the standing variety, such as skiing (for experts) and skating (ditto); and, secondly, the sitting variety such as tobogganing, sleighing, and skiing and skating (for beginners).

Skiing is as old as the hills and probably a bit older. Like most things it may have been invented by the Chinese, who probably pronounced it Ski-Hing, but there is no real evidence to support this (though one learned scholar has suggested that the Word 'Chinese' is really a corruption of 'Ski-Knees').

As a sporting spectacle, however, it originated in the province of Telemark some time in the 19th century when an intrepid farmer whizzing down a mountain side shot over the edge of a baby precipice and performed, quite unexpectedly, the first ski jump in modern times. He survived to tell the tale and was so surprised that he had to have another go. His fame spread, and the very next winter he was invited to Christiania, the capital of Norway, where, on a replica of his own pet precipice, he performed his daring leaps before a vast crowd of some forty citizens of the town. His pet precipice grew more formidable every year, until today it stands at Holmenkollen (pronounced Home and Colonial) where it strikes terror into the hearts of unsuspecting visitors. Ski jumping is the favourite sport of the adolescent Norwegian, and it is surprising how many of them survive. The steepness of the landing slope determines the length of the jump. Theoretically there is no limit to the distance you can jump, provided you have the nerve to take off. N.B. Parachutes are not allowed.

Having invented this sport, the Norwegians usually walk off (or rather ski off) with vast quantities of trophies and trinkets at such jolly, get-togethers as the Winter Olympics.

LAKE WOEBEGONE DAYS by Garrison Keillor

Garrison Keillor is an American author, storyteller, humourist, voice actor, and radio personality. Keillor created the fictional Minnesota town 'Lake Wobegon', the setting of many of his books, including 'Lake Wobegon Days', hilarious short stories of the goings-on in small-town America. Every story starts with the words: It has been a quiet week in Lake Wobegone.

WINTER

Christmas, years later. I got five dollars from Grandma, a big raise from the one dollar she gave to little kids and bought a bottle of Jade East cologne with it, the kind Chip Ingqvist used, the name of which I found out by making fun of him for smelling like rotten fruit. "It's Jade East," he said, smiling his superior Ingqvist smile. "It's what they wear at the U."

With a splash of it on my neck and wearing the new Christmas sweater, I headed for the skating rink after supper, feeling like I was cut out for romance. I was sixteen. Six feet, three inches tall and I walked with a peculiar springing stride, like a pogo stick, which sometimes I looked behind me and saw a little kid imitating. The Jade East was supposed to take care of that and also, I tried to saunter.

The town was buried in three feet of snow. Downtown was dark except for the Sidetrack where a red sign flashed 'BEE BEE BEE' inside the strips of orange and green neon around the front window. The lamp over the door made a cone of light, as if the step were a stage and Mr. Berge might emerge, sway back and forth, and say, "O what a noble mind is here o'erthrown!", but only Ronnie came out. He pulled his collar up and his stocking cap down and headed the other way. It was so cold, he got small as he walked, contracting his middle, like a turtle pulling himself in.

So still on a cold night. I could hear his boots crunch in the snow, could hear a car not quite starting a long way away, and then the door slamming when the guy got out and him hitting the hood with his fist. The volume of the world was turned up so the air molecules hummed a deep bass note. If the fire siren went off it would knock a person into the middle of next week. The moon rose over the frozen lake; the light seemed to come out of the snow. Buried in three feet of light. And colours jumped out, hundreds of lovely shades of shadows, browns and greys and blacks. If a woman with bright red lipstick appeared, a person would fall over backward.

On this cold night, the skating rink was a carnival. The music I could hear when I left my house and now, I saw the long 'V' of coloured lights hung out across the rink from the warming house. Its windows blazed white. Pairs of skaters flowed counter clockwise in a great loop to 'The Blue Skirt Waltz,' and little kids buzzed around the big slow wheel as it turned. I looked for the girl I loved who I had met the night before.

She was older, eighteen or nineteen, and had worn bright lipstick and sat down beside me in the warming house and slowly unlaced her leather boots and took them off and then her socks. My face turned red. In the Age of Imagination, before the Age of Full Disclosure, the removal of any article of clothing was inspirational. She was a cousin of the Ingqvists, up from Minneapolis for Christmas break, and had a way about her that set her apart. Her hair, for example, was jet-black and cut short as a man's. She wore short skirt and tights, but unlike other girls whose tights were lumpy from long johns, hers were tight. She leaned against me and said, "Got a cigarette?" No girl asked me that before, because I didn't smoke, but for her sake, I said, "Yeah, thinking I might have one – it certainly was worth a look, and who would say no at a time like that? – then said, "Oh, I just remembered. I forgot mine at home." She said, "Oh, well. I think I got two in my purse." She offered one to me. I didn't smoke, but then I was young, I'd been held back, it was time to get started on these things, so I said, "Thanks." She gave me the book of matches. As

I lit one and held it toward her mouth, she held my hand to steady it, and although I knew that you didn't make babies this way, two hands together holding a match, I thought it must be similar. We took deep drags and blew out big clouds of smoke, then she leaned back and inhaled again, and I leaned forward and put my head between my knees. Not sick exactly, I was simply appreciating it more than most people do. I was sixteen, I experienced everything deeply.

This night she was there again, sitting on the bench against the wall, with my friend Jim who was not smoking but who was inhaling her smoke as deeply as he could. "Dorene's from Minneapolis," he told me. I ignored him. "I got to show you something," I told her. "Whenever you're done here."

As we walked up the hill toward Main Street, I wasn't so sure what I could show her in Lake Wobegon that would be interesting, so I made up a story about a woman named Lydia Farrell who had lived here in love with the memory of a boy who had drowned. I picked out Florian Krebsbach's house as the home where Lydia spent fifty years in solitude, cherishing the few brief moments she spent with young Eddie before his boat overturned in a sudden storm. The moral was that we must seize our few bright moments and live deeply. It surprised me how easily I did this and kept her interested. We walked up to the Ingqvists, both enjoying Lydia's sweet sad life, and then she asked me if I skied. I said, "Sure." I never had, but how would I know I couldn't unless I tried? So, the next afternoon, I was squeezed next to her in the back seat of the Ingqvists' Lincoln, Chip driving, eight of us in the car, going goodness knows where.

Unbelievable to me, being in the same car with Ingqvists and that whole Ingqvist crowd, sharp dressers in those Norwegian ski sweaters you couldn't find in town and who never had asked me before so much as to come in their house. But Dorene, who was even finer than they, had seen something in me. She was from Minneapolis but had spotted some personal quality of mine that other people had never seen, and I was determined not to let her down. I imagined her turning to me with a smoky Minneapolis look and saying, "Kiss me," and so had practiced kissing, using my thumb and forefinger as practice lips. I had also gone to the library and skimmed through a book about skiing. I felt prepared to do either one.

A long drive during which they all talked about college and how much harder it was than high school. "You have to study six or seven hours a day," Chip said. I said I didn't think it was so hard. They laughed: "What do you know?" I said I'd read a lot of college books. "Like what?" "A lot of different things," I said. Dorene held my hand. She said, "It isn't hard for everybody. Some people have a harder time in high school, then they do real good in college."

I was grateful for that, but by the time we got to where we were going, I was much less confident about everything. It was dark. A plywood Swiss chalet sat between two spruce at the end of parking lot and beyond it, strings of lights ascended a hill much steeper than what seemed possible in Minnesota. (Maybe we were in Wisconsin.) They got their skis off the car carrier. I was going to say, "'That's all right, you go ahead, I feel like I'm coming down with something. I'll just wait in the building, I'll be okay. You go ahead" – and then she put a pair of skis and ski poles in my hands and said, "Let's go," so I went. I put on the skis, which she refastened so they wouldn't fall off and showed me where to stand, next to her, holding hands and the big wheel groaned in the wheelhouse and the bench came up behind and scooped us up and we rose into the dark. "I can't ski," I said; she said, "I know." We kissed. We slid off at the top and I staggered after her to the edge of the precipice where Chip Ingqvist stood, adjusting his binding. He grinned at me and flung himself off. She told me to relax, stay loose, bend my knees, and if I lost my balance to just sit down – and she jumped over the edge and I did too, and followed her down in a series of short rides. Skiing, sitting down, skiing. I lost momentum in the sittings so at the bottom where other skiers flashed across the flats to the chalet and plowed to a stop, I had to walk. She was gone when I got there. I sat in the chalet for an hour with some people from Minneapolis who hoped they could make it to Colorado in February, then she appeared, limping. She twisted her ankle while getting off the lift and had made the long trip down in pain. I examined it as if ankles were my specialty, a top ankle man called in from Minneapolis. "Can you walk on it?" I asked. She said, "I don't want to sit in here with all these people feeling sorry for me," so we went to the car, her arm around my neck, mine around her waist. We sat in the car for a while. After a while, I said, "I never did this before," but she seemed to be aware of that.

NOTES FROM A BIG COUNTRY by Bill Bryson

Bill Bryson OBE (1951) a prolific, terribly funny, and hugely knowledgeable author from Des Moines, Iowa. My favourite books are the 'Life and Times of the Thunderbolt Kid' and 'One Summer'. Here is a short extract from 'Notes from a Big Country'…

FUN IN THE SNOW

For reasons I cannot begin to understand, when I was about eight years old my parents gave me a pair of skis for Christmas. I went outside, strapped them on, and stood in a racing crouch, but nothing happened. This is because there are no hills in Iowa.

Casting around for something with a slope, I decided to ski down our back-porch steps. There were only five steps, but on skis the angle of descent was surprisingly steep. I went down the steps at about, I would guess, 110 miles an hour, and hit the bottom with such a force that the skis jammed solid, whereas I continued onward and outward across the patio in a graceful rising arc. About 12 feet away loomed the back wall of our garage. Instinctively adopting a spread-eagle posture for maximum impact, I smacked into it somewhere near the roof and slid down its vertical face in the manner of food flung against a wall.

It was at this point I decided that winter sports were not for me. I put away the skis and for the next thirty-five years thought no more about the matter. Then we moved to New England, where people actually look forward to winter. At the first fall of snow they cry out with joy and root in cupboards for sledges and ski poles. They become suffused with a strange vitality – an eagerness to get out into all that white stuff and schuss about on something fast and reckless.

With so many active people about, including every member of my own family, in an attempt to find a winter pastime, I borrowed some ice skates and went with my two youngest to Occum Pond, a popular local spot for skating.

"Are you sure you know how to skate?" my daughter asked uneasily. "Of course I do, my petal," I assured her. "I have been mistaken many times for Jane Torvill, on the ice and off."

And I do know how to skate, honestly. It's just that my legs, after years of inactivity, got a little over excited to be confronted with so much slipperiness. As soon as I stepped onto the ice they decided they wanted to visit every corner of Occum Pond at once, from lots of different directions. They went this way and that, scissoring and splaying, sometimes getting as much as 12 feet apart, but constantly gathering momentum, until at last they flew out from under me and I landed on my butt with such a wallop that my coccyx hit the roof of my mouth and I had to push my oesophagus back in with my fingers.

CHAPTER 4
ARCTIC AND ANTARCTIC EXPLORATION

FRIDTJOF NANSEN by Ingrid Christophersen

The world knows Roald Amundsen, the man who beat Captain Scott to the South Pole. Few people know much about Nansen, but in my eyes he towers above Amundsen. Amundsen wanted to be first, his was always a race for a prize. Fame and fortune were more important to him than exploration and science. Here is an article I wrote for the DHO Journal in 1999.

It is Nansen who should be given all the honour and glory for having popularised skiing and brought it to the attention of the general public. The 'King of Sports' he called it, and how right he was. I fell out of my cradle hearing about him and his marvellous deeds. When I talk about him to non-Norwegians I am astounded that so few know his name. Nansen was a scientist, an explorer, a philanthropist, a statesman and an ambassador. He was also a ladies' man, and courted Lady Scott while her husband was busy trying to beat that other Norwegian, Amundsen, many miles away from England! We all know how that contest ended.

Nansen's original research into the nervous system of amoeba, is still used today. He was the first President of the League of Nations and was sent by the League to Russia to relieve the famine in the 1920s. He invented the Nansen passport for displaced persons, was Norway's first ambassador to London – after the separation from Sweden – and was a Nobel Peace Prize Laureate. But most importantly, he was an explorer. He crossed Greenland on skis, from East to West in 45 days. His book, 'On Skis Across Greenland', caused a tremendous stir and admiration in Europe, and was the foundation of the modern sport of skiing. He sailed his ship the Fram into the pack-ice north of Siberia, and let it drift for three years to establish the existence of a cross polar cap current. After many months bogged down in the ice he left his crew and set off on skis with one other man to try and reach the North Pole – not knowing, as we do today, (this was in 1893) that the North Pole does not sit on solid land but is surrounded by pack ice which constantly shifts and breaks up, producing hummocks and open leads and impossibly tortuous terrain.

The two spent a winter under the hull of their tiny upturned kayak but, having killed all their dogs for food, and short of provisions, they turned for home and were miraculously intercepted by an eccentric Englishman, who was exploring the Arctic in a comfortable yacht. They had reached 83°13.6 North, 7 degrees short of the North Pole. Norway's multi Olympic gold medallist Vegard Ulvang followed in Nansen's ski tracks in 1992 and only by listening to his tale of hardship and toil and complete exhaustion do we understand the utter heroism of Nansen and his team with their old-fashioned heavy equipment, different technique and very different basis for fitness. They knew nothing about nutrition or how to prevent scurvy. He had no radio with which to call for instant supplies. What a man!

TALES OF ENDURANCE by Fergus Fleming

This piece about Frithjof Nansen is taken from 'Tales of Endurance' by Fergus Fleming, detailing gripping accounts of great feats in the history of Arctic exploration. None more gripping than the account of Nansen's attempt to ski to the North Pole. Fergus Fleming has written four critically acclaimed books on exploration. He is Ian Fleming's nephew.

In 1888, almost on a whim, a young Norwegian neuroscientist named Fridtjof Nansen decided to become the first person to cross Greenland on skis. The casual ease with which he completed the task changed his life. Abandoning his studies, he began to raise funds for an expedition to the North Pole – an expedition, as he explained to would-be sponsors, that would be unlike any other. He proposed not to fight the Arctic as others had done, but to go (quite literally) with the flow. Noting that debris from De Long's 'Jeannette', which had sunk off Siberia in 1881, had washed up on the shores of Greenland, he concluded that an east-west current ran beneath the ice. Therefore, if he set a ship in the pack above Siberia it would eventually be deposited in the Atlantic, having traversed the Arctic Ocean and possibly, even, having touched the North Pole. His plan met with approval, the money was raised, and on 24 June 1893 he left Christiania (modern Oslo) aboard the 'Fram' on a journey that would change the face of polar exploration and make him one of the greatest celebrities of the age.

The Fram was no ordinary vessel. Rounded at prow and stern, and in cross-section shaped somewhat like an egg, it was constructed specifically for Arctic travel: if squeezed by the ice it would simply pop up and rest on the surface. It also contained a generator that could be driven by wind power, a store of provisions so varied as to supply whatever magical ingredient was necessary to fend off scurvy, plus a 600-volume library to provide intellectual stimulus during the five years the journey was expected to last. There was the usual collection of compasses, chronometers, pendulums, reels of line for sounding the ocean floor and a host of other instruments – for, as Nansen swore, the Fram's voyage was primarily scientific. But there were other items too, none of which had an obvious scientific application: some portable paraffin stoves by the name of 'Primus' that were 600 per cent more efficient than standard coal or oil-fuelled models; a stock of skis to suit every snow condition; several light and flexible sledges designed by Nansen himself; a new type of conical tent, also designed by Nansen, which could be erected and dismantled in seconds; and a couple of kayaks similar to the Inuit versions he had encountered in Greenland but with watertight compartments in the bows. In addition, the Fram carried a team of dogs.

This supercargo was included for one reason only: if the Fram did not reach the North Pole Nansen intended to jump ship and ski there. On 25 September 1893 the Fram entered the ice north of the Lena Delta and began its long voyage west. Everything worked to perfection: the ship rose from every nip as it had been designed to do, the crew were not attacked by scurvy, the wind generator did its job faultlessly – everything was fine. Caught, initially, in the triangular drift that had bedevilled Weyprecht and De Long, the Fram worked its way slowly north.

The months passed, the crew became bored and complacent, the ship's doctor began to dabble with drugs. The inaction made Nansen furious: 'Can't something happen?' he wrote in his journal. But nothing did happen, beyond the occasional ice squeeze, from which the Fram emerged, as always, intact. During the first long winter Nansen roamed the pack, peering ever northwards.

On 15 January 1894 he saw a flat icescape that stretched to the horizon and, for all he knew, to the Pole itself. 'It might almost be called an easy expedition for two men,' he wrote: Throughout that year he prepared for the forthcoming odyssey. The sledges and kayaks, which had been packed in kit form were assembled. The skis were treated with Stockholm pitch and, after much moody perusal, Nansen selected a travelling companion. His name was Hjalmar Johansen, a dour but capable drifter who, before signing on as a stoker, had been among other things a prison warden and an international gymnast. On 14 March 1895, with the Fram sitting slightly above the 84th parallel – a record north for a ship – Nansen and Johansen departed for the Pole.

Nansen's plan was scary. He and Johansen would ski north with a couple of dog teams hauling their kayaks and supplies for 100 days. As the food ran out they would feed the dogs to each other and then, when they had gone as far they could, they would retreat to Franz Josef Land, where they hoped to meet a whaler. If no whaler was to hand they would paddle – and maybe sail, for Nansen had equipped his kayaks with bamboo masts – to Norway. It was 350 nautical miles to the Pole, another 500 back to Franz Josef Land and yet another 1,000 to Norway. To call the proposed journey foolhardy would have been an understatement. It was a monumental gamble, involving unsupported travel in one of the world's coldest and most unpredictable climates, across an unexplored ocean riddled with potential hazards, with an escape route so uncertain as scarcely to merit the name.

Initially it looked as if the gamble would pay off. The ice was smooth and the two Norwegians swept over it at an unprecedented rate covering 20 miles per day for the first week. By 29 March they were at a record north of 85° 09′. If conditions held good and they continued at the same pace they would be at the top of the earth within a fortnight.

Conditions did not hold. During the second week they encountered rough ice interspersed with leads of open water. The tents, which had been made of light material for ease of transport, provided chilly shelter, despite the use of the Primus stoves. At the same time the pack started drifting south and in the course of five days they made only 50 miles. By 8 April they had crossed the 86th parallel and Nansen called a halt. It was just conceivable that they would reach the Pole if they carried on, but if they did they would never return to tell the tale; as it was, their provisions were barely sufficient to last them back to Franz Josef Land. They allowed themselves a congratulatory feast of 'lobscouse, bread-and-butter, dry chocolate, stewed whortle berries, and a hot whey drink', before crawling into the tent in preparation for the trek home.

Extraordinarily, the ice that had given them so much trouble during the last ten days was now a flat plain over which they sped south as rapidly as they had travelled north during that first halcyon week. On 13 April however, Johansen found that his chronometer had stopped. Of itself this was no cause for worry; both men carried a chronometer and, as had happened in the past, if one stopped all they had to do was reset it against the one that still ticked. But when they came to do so they discovered that Nansen's chronometer had stopped too. The consequences were potentially disastrous: without knowing the exact Greenwich Meridian Time to which their chronometers had been set in Christiania, they could not calculate their longitude. Without knowing their longitude, they could not chart their east-west progress, and unless they could do that they would be unable to steer accurately for Franz Josef Land. Hesitantly, Nansen reset his chronometer to what he thought was the right time, but with a deliberate eastward bias so that when they hit the latitude of Franz Josef Land all they had to do was march west until they reached safety. Even so, without knowing when the timepiece had stopped he had no idea if the exaggeration was sufficient. If it was not, and they arrived at the correct latitude but to the west of Franz Josef Land, they would walk until they either starved or fell into the Atlantic.

On that same day Nansen also found he had left their compass behind at the last stop. He skied back to fetch it, leaving Johansen on his own. A follower rather than a leader, Johansen was immediately struck by doubts. Would Nansen fall through the ice? Would he be able to find his way back through the wilderness? If he did not return what would Johansen do next? Johansen's description of his wait is a terrifyingly evocative description of Arctic solitude. *'Never have I felt anything so still,'* he wrote. *'Not the slightest sound of any kind disturbed the silence near or far. The dogs lay as if lifeless with their heads on their paws in the white snow, glistening in the gleaming sun. It was so frighteningly still. I had to remain where I sat and I dared not move a limb. I hardly dared to breathe.'* When he heard the swish of Nansen's skis he was overcome with relief – testimony both to the loneliness of their position and the power of Nansen's presence.

Nansen's was, indeed, a gigantic personality. Tall, fit, single-minded, possessed of tremendous drive and supreme self-confidence, he conquered everyone he met with sheer force of charisma and intellect. Yet, at the same time, he was prone to dark mood shifts in which he identified with ancient Norse gods. Inspirational on first acquaintance, overpowering on prolonged contact, dangerous in confined spaces, Nansen was not a man with whom one dealt lightly.

Johansen found him self-centred, humourless, 'unsociable and clumsy in the smallest things; egoistic in the highest degree'. Then again, Johansen was a born complainer, physically strong but psychologically weak, who depended upon the guidance of others. (He would later become an alcoholic, whose directionless career ended in suicide.) Probably this was why Nansen chose him for the North Pole journey in the first place. He could not brook a travelling companion who might voice opinions or, unthinkably, question his decisions. And firm decisions were needed if they were ever to get home.

On 4 June, at 82° 17′ N, Nansen judged Franz Josef to be 25 miles distant. It was a guess, of course, because nothing was certain now the chronometers had stopped. In recent days their progress had been pitifully slow, hampered by poor weather, uneven ice and open leads. On 3 June they had travelled less than a mile. On the bright side, they were now so far south that they could augment their diminishing supplies by shooting seals, walruses and polar bears.

But having enough to eat was of little use if they could not find their way home. *'Here we are then,'* Nansen wrote during a blizzard, *'hardly knowing what to do next. What the going is like outside I do not know yet, but probably not much better than yesterday, and whether we ought to push on the little we can, or go out and try to capture a seal, I cannot decide.'* In the event they did both and on 24 July they saw land. The trouble was, it was not like any land on their maps. As described by Julius von Payer in 1873, the northernmost point of Franz Josef Land, Cape Fligely, looked nothing like what rose from the sea before them. Had they reached Franz Josef Land or an undiscovered island to its west? They no longer cared.

Shooting their last dogs, they abandoned their sledges and took to the kayaks (damaged during the long journey, but repaired hastily with candle wax) and paddled towards what had to be at least interim salvation. It was 146 days since they had left the Fram. The island on which they landed in early August 1895 was part of Franz Josef Land, and as they made their way through the archipelago they met more and more territory that accorded with their maps. There were no whaling ships in the vicinity however, and by the end of the month, as the weather began to deteriorate, Nansen realised they would have to spend the winter in the Arctic. They therefore set up camp on a desolate and uncharted spit of land and resigned themselves to a long, cold wait.

The shelter in which they intended to survive the winter comprised a three-foot-deep trench surrounded by a parapet of stones, roofed with walrus hides on a ridge pole of driftwood. Before the cold came in earnest they were able to shoot enough polar bears, seals and walruses to see them through the season. Then, their larder amply stocked, they crawled into what they called 'The Hole' and resigned themselves to an imprisonment that would not end until the arrival of spring. The situation was not life-threatening: they had enough meat to keep starvation and scurvy at bay. The blubber on the carcasses provided fuel to cook their meals, melt snow into drinking water, and give them light. But life was dull, uncomfortable and unhygienic. The diet made them constipated and after a while, gave them piles. In the absence of washing facilities they were reduced to scraping the grease from their underwear and adding it to the blubber lamps. They had nothing to do except talk, read over and over again Nansen's navigational tables (the only printed material they possessed) and, when those stimuli were exhausted, sleep. For Nansen the enforced stillness presented an opportunity to reflect upon Scandinavian mythology. For Johansen it was a time of undistilled loneliness: the only sign that he existed as a person rather than an adjunct to his leader's ambition came when Nansen addressed him in the familiar tense for the first time in the entire journey. In this manner they passed eight long months in a snow-covered ditch on a strip of land whose existence was unknown to anybody save themselves.

On 19 May the ice cleared and they resumed their journey. But within a month they were struggling. On 12 June Nansen had to swim after their kayaks when they drifted into the sea while he and Johansen took bearings from an iceberg. On 13 June both vessels were fatally punctured by a pack of irate walruses. Dragging the craft on to yet another strip of uncharted land, they spent four days over the repairs and then, as they were about to re-embark, Nansen heard dogs barking. Johansen listened closely, but said it was nothing: just seabirds, he assured his commander. Nansen was insistent, and skied inland to investigate. The decision saved both their lives.

Nansen and Johansen were not the only people on Franz Josef Land during the winter of 1895-6. A

British expedition under Frederick Jackson had been at Cape Flora throughout the season. When Jackson was alerted by a team member to an unusual human outline on the ice he pooh-poohed it. "Oh nonsense," he said, "it is a walrus, surely?" Like Nansen however, he thought it best to make sure. So, he too, donned his skis. If nothing else the trip would be good exercise. What he found was not a walrus but a black, greasy, shaggy haired, foul-smelling creature whom he took at first for a shipwrecked Scandinavian whaler.

Yet something about the man's bearing seemed familiar. As Jackson drew closer, he realised that the ragamuffin looked remarkably like a Polar fundraiser he had met at the Royal Geographical Society four years previously. When their skis were almost touching, Jackson put a name to the memory. "Aren't you Nansen?" he asked. On a par with Stanley's 'Dr Livingstone, I presume?' Jackson's understated query was one of the great moments of 19th century exploration. It was sheer luck that the only two parties in Franz Josef Land that year had bumped into each other. No fiction writer could have contrived such an encounter, each group initially dismissing the other as a chimera until, driven respectively by curiosity and desperation, their leaders came together in the heart of the Arctic. And what made their meeting so incredible was the fact that Nansen and Johansen had spent three quarters of a year in 'The Hole' while, just around the corner, Jackson and his men had been quartered in fully provisioned, wooden-hutted splendour. If not for the walrus attack, Nansen and Johansen might never have known there were other explorers in the region and would have perished in their battered, leaky kayaks. As Jackson wrote: *I can positively state that not a million to one chance of Nansen reaching Europe existed, and that but for our finding him on the ice, as we did, the world would never have heard of him again.* He was so amazed by the encounter that when Johansen was also rescued, he refused to let either man change their clothes so that he could take staged photographs of their arrival.

Jackson's support ship arrived on 25 July and by 9 September the two Norwegians were home. Here they learned that the Fram had completed its drift and had arrived intact at Spitsbergen. Nansen's theories had been proved correct, his rash adventure to the Pole had ended without casualty, and he had proved indisputably that the best means of Polar exploration was by skis and dog sled, carrying the lightest, most efficient equipment and taking as few team members as possible. Beneath the mountains that circled Christiania, smoke belched from yachts, tugs and steamers as every available ship, private or public, came to greet them. Nansen was invited to dine at the royal palace and two months later published a 300,000-word account of the expedition. Well written, with photographs, drawings and colour illustrations by Nansen himself, the two-volume journal was a bestseller. When the British mountaineer Edward Whymper reviewed it he wrote: *almost as great an advance as has been accomplished by all other voyages in the nineteenth century put together... He is a Man in a Million.*

Here is advice from Nansen regarding skis and ski equipment, based on his journey across Greenland in 1888.

NANSEN OVER GREENLAND – SKI AND SKILØBNING

The expedition I am about to describe owed its origin entirely to the Norwegian sport of 'skiløbning.' I have myself been accustomed to the use of 'ski' since I was four years old, every one of my companions was an experienced skiløber, and all our prospects of success were based upon the superiority of ski in comparison with all other means of locomotion when large tracts of snow have to be traversed. I therefore think that I cannot do better than set apart a chapter for the description of ski and the manner of their use, since so little is known about the sport outside the few countries where it is practised as such, and since a certain amount of familiarity with it and its technical terms will be necessary to the full comprehension of some part of the narrative which follows.

It is of course, not unnatural that those who have never seen the performance should be surprised to learn that a man can – by the help of two pieces of wood, shaped for the purpose – progress as rapidly over the surface of the snow as he really does.

Ski then, are long narrow strips of wood, those used in Norway being from three to four inches in breadth, eight feet more or less in length, one inch in thickness at the centre under the foot, and bevelling off to about a quarter of an inch at either end. In front, they are curved upwards and pointed, and they are sometimes a little turned up at the back end too. The sides are more or less parallel, though the best forms have their greatest width in front, just where the upward curve begins. Otherwise they are quite straight and flat, and the under-surface is made as smooth as possible. The attachment consists of a loop for the toe, made of leather or some other substance, and fixed at about the centre of the ski with a band which passes from this round behind the heel of the shoe. The principle of this fastening is to make the ski and foot as rigid as possible for steering purposes while the heel is allowed to rise freely from the ski at all times.

On flat ground the ski are driven forward by a peculiar stride, which in its elementary form is not difficult of acquirement, though it is capable of immense development. They are not lifted, and the tendency which the beginner feels to tramp away with them, as if he were on mud boards in the middle of a marsh, must be strenuously resisted. Lifting causes the snow to stick to them, so they must be pushed forwards over its surface by alternate strokes from the hips and thighs, the way being maintained between the strokes by a proper management of the body. The ski are kept strictly parallel meanwhile and as close together as possible, there being no resemblance whatever, as is sometimes supposed, to the motion employed in skating. In the hand most skiløbers carry a short staff, which is used partly to correct deficiencies of balance, but by the more skilful chiefly to increase the length of the stride by propulsion. In many country districts this pole often reaches a preposterous length. In some parts, a couple of short staffs are used; one in each hand, by the help of which, on comparatively flat ground, great speed can be obtained. When the snow is in thoroughly good condition the rate of progress is quite surprising considering the small amount of effort expended. As much as eight or nine miles can be done within the hour, while a speed of seven miles an hour can be maintained for a very considerable length of time.

Uphill the pace is of course very much slower. Here also, the practised skiløber has great advantages over all others. Here the ski must be lifted slightly, as the snow sticking to them counteracts the tendency to slip backwards. If the gradient is steep, various devices may be employed, the most effectual and characteristic being that shown in the annexed illustration.

The ski are turned outwards at as wide an angle as the steepness of the slope renders advisable and are advanced alternately one in front of the other. The track left in the snow should resemble the feather-stitch of needlewomen. This method requires some practice and cannot be employed if the ski are above a certain length, as the heels will then necessarily overlap. By its means, a slope of any gradient on which the snow will lie may be ascended quickly and easily, but the position is somewhat too strained to be maintained for long. Another and easier, though much slower way, is to mount the hill sideways, bringing the ski almost, if not quite, to a right angle with the slope, and working up step by step. Or again, especially on the open mountain, the skiløber will work his way upwards by tacking from side to side and following a zigzag course, taking instinctively the most advantageous line of ascent. In any case, if he is up to his work he will cover the ground quickly and without undue exertion, and, as a matter of fact, as Olaus Magnus wrote in 1555, *'there is no mountain so high but that by cunning devices he is able to attain unto the summit thereof.'*

Downhill, the ski slide readily and are left to themselves, the one thing necessary being to maintain the balance and steer clear of trees, rocks, and precipices. The steeper the slope the greater the speed, and if the snow is good then the friction is so slight that the pace often approaches within a measurable distance of that of a falling body. The author of 'Kongespeilet', an old Norse treatise, was speaking not altogether at random when he described the skiløber as outstripping the birds in flight. He declared that nothing which runs upon the earth can escape his pursuit.

Of all the sports of Norway, skiløbning is the most national and characteristic, and I cannot think that I go too far when I claim for it, as practised in our country, a position in the very first rank of the sports of the world. I know no form of sport which so evenly develops the muscles, which renders the body so strong and elastic, which teaches so well the qualities of dexterity and resource, which in an equal degree calls for decision and resolution, and which gives the same vigour and exhilaration to mind and body alike. Where can one find a healthier and purer delight than when on a brilliant winter day, one binds one's ski to one's feet and takes one's way out into the forest? Can there be anything more beautiful than the northern winter landscape, when the snow lies foot-deep, spread as a soft white mantle over field and wood and hill? Where will one find more freedom and excitement than when one glides swiftly down the hillside through the trees, one's cheek brushed by the sharp cold air and frosted pine branches, and one's eye, brain, and muscles alert and prepared to meet every unknown obstacle and danger which the next instant may throw in one's path? Civilisation is, as it were, washed clean from the mind and left far behind with the city atmosphere and city life; one's whole being is, so to say, wrapped in one's ski and the surrounding nature. There is something in the whole which develops soul and not body alone, and the sport is perhaps of far greater national importance than is generally supposed.

Nor can there be many lands so well fitted as ours for the practice of skiløbning, and its full development as a sport. The chief requisites are hills and snow, and of these we have indeed an abundance. From our childhood onwards we are accustomed to use our ski, and in many a mountain valley, boys and girls too for that matter, are by their very surroundings forced to take to their ski almost as soon as they can walk. The whole long winter through, from early autumn to late spring, the snow lies soft and deep outside the cottage door. In such valleys, and this was especially the case in former times, there are few roads or ways of any kind, and all men and women alike, whom business or pleasure takes abroad, must travel on their ski. Children no more than three or four years old may often be seen striving with the first difficulties, and from this age onwards the peasant boys in many parts keep themselves in constant practice. Their homes lie, as a rule, on the steep slope of the valley-side, and hills of all grades are ready to hand. To school, which is generally held in the winter season, they must go on their ski, and on their ski they all spend the few minutes of rest between the hours of work, their teacher often joining them and leading the string. Then too, on Sunday afternoons comes the weekly festival, when all the youths of the parish, boys and young men alike meet on the hillside to outdo one another in fair rivalry and enjoy their sport to the full as long as the brief daylight lasts. At such times the girls are present as spectators, notwithstanding that they too know well how to use their ski, and that many a good feat has been done here now by Norwegian lasses and gone unrecorded.

Such is the winter life of the young in many of our mountain valleys. The boy has scarcely reached the age of breeches before he knows the points of a pair of ski: what a good bit of wood should look like, and how to twist a withy to make himself the fastenings. Thus, he learns early to stand on his own legs and his own ski, to rely upon himself in difficulty, and grows up to be a man like his father before him. May our sport long be held in honour. May its interests be cared for and advanced as long as there remain men and women in the Norwegian valleys!

But it is especially for the winter pursuit of game that ski are an absolute necessity in Norway as well as the North of Europe generally and Siberia. And it is in this way that most of the clever skildløbers of country districts have been formed.

In earlier times it was a common practice in Scandinavia to hunt the larger animals, such as the elk and reindeer, during the winter upon ski. When the snow was deep the skilful skiløber had no great difficulty in pursuing and killing these animals, as their movements, as compared with his, were naturally much hampered. It was an exciting sport however, and often required considerable strength and endurance on the part of the hunter, as well as a thorough familiarity with the use of ski. Now however, these animals are protected during the winter, and all pursuit of them is illegal. Doubtless there is still a good deal of poaching done in this way, especially in the case of elk, in the remoter forests of Sweden and Norway.

Nowadays the Norwegian peasant has most use for his ski in the less exciting pursuit of the ptarmigan and willow-grouse, large numbers of which are shot and snared upon the mountains. The snaring in some districts is especially remunerative and is often the only channel through which the poor cottagers can attain to the rare luxury of a little ready money. The hare is also sometimes thus hunted and shot, the bear turned out of his lair or intercepted before he has finally taken to his winter quarters, and an occasional lynx or glutton pursued. It is, of course, on ski too that the nomad Lapps follow and destroy their inveterate enemy, the wolf.

Ski must be considered as being first and foremost instruments of locomotion, and therefore the speed which can be attained in an ordinary way across country must be regarded from a practical point of view as the most important branch of the sport. Though the jumping is always the most popular part of the programme, yet at our yearly meetings equal or greater weight is attached to the long race, for, it must be explained, the chief prizes are given for combined proficiency in the separate branches.

It must not be thought that skiløbning is a sport which develops the body at all unequally. On the other hand, there can be few forms of exercise which perform this task so uniformly and healthfully. The upper part of the body and arms come into constant use as well as the legs; the arms particularly by the help of the pole. This is especially the case if two poles be carried, a practice which is common among the Lapps, which has been adopted of late years in the Christiania races, and which was followed by us during our crossing of Greenland.

I have already given some idea of the speed to which a strong and clever skiløber may attain. But so much depends upon those two most uncertain quantities; the nature of the ground and the state of the snow, that nothing like an absolute standard can be fixed. If the conditions are moderately favourable, a good man should be able to cover from sixty to seventy miles in the course of a day's run.

The longest race hitherto brought off in Norway was held at Christiania in February 1888. The distance was 50 km, or 31 miles 122 yards, twice over a 25 km course, which was laid out over hilly ground of a very variable character and included all kinds of difficulties calculated to test the competitors' skill. The race was won by a Telemark peasant in 4 hrs. 26 min. without much pressure on the part of his rivals. A much longer race, no doubt the longest on record, was that organised by Barons Dickson and Nordenskiold at Jokkmokk, in Swedish Lapland, on April 3 and 4, 1884. The winner was a Lapp, Lars Tuorda, thirty-seven years of age, one of the two who had accompanied Nordenskiold on his Greenland expedition and had then done a great feat on the ski on the inland ice. The distance on this occasion was 220 km, or nearly 136 English miles. It was covered by the winner in 21 hrs. 22 min., rests included. The second man, a Lapp of forty, was only 5 sec. behind the winner, and of the first six, five of whom were Lapps, the last came in 46 min. after the first. The course was for the most part level, being laid mainly over the frozen lakes, and the snow must have been in a very favourable condition.

QUOTES ATTRIBUTED TO NANSEN:

"If any sport deserves the name 'king of sports' then in truth it is skiing. Nothing hardens the muscles nor makes the body so strong and supple; nothing promotes quick thinking and nimbleness like it; nothing sharpens the will nor makes the mind so fit as skiing. Can you think of anything more health-giving or natural than to strap your skis on and take off into the woods on a bracing winter's day? Can anything be more beautiful than nature buried in metres of white snow, softly sprinkled over forest and hill? Could anything be more liberating or exciting than when, swift as a bird, you rush down the forest-clad mountains while the winter air and the pine boughs whistle round your cheeks and eyes, mind and muscles are taut, ready to negotiate every obstacle which at any moment might be thrown across your path? It is as though the entire terrestrial atmosphere is washed out of your mind and left far behind, you and your skis and nature are one. Not only your muscles but your mind too is expanding. Would that this sport, this time-honoured custom, would develop and flourish as long as there are men and women in snowy climes."

"It is better to go skiing and think of God, than go to church and think of sport."

"You are one with your skis and nature. This is something that develops not only the body but the soul as well, and it has a deeper meaning for a people than most of us perceive."

"I know no form of sport which so evenly develops the muscles, which renders the body so strong and elastic, which teaches so well the qualities of dexterity and resource, which in an equal degree calls for decision and resolution, and which gives the same vigour and exhilaration to mind and body alike. There is something in the whole which develops soul and not body alone."

"…those wonderful, long, steep mountain sides, where the snow lies soft as eiderdown, where one can ski as fast as one desires… From the tips of the skis… the snow sprays knee-high, to swirl up in white clouds behind; but ahead all is clear. You cleave the snow like an arrow… you just have to tense your muscles, keep your body under control, and let yourself wing downwards like an avalanche."

SCOTT & AMUNDSEN by Roland Huntford

Amundsen skied better than he wrote. Scott wrote better than he skied. Having walked to the South Pole and back Amundsen wrote: *'we cannot report privation or danger or major hardship'*. He lacked self-dramatisation. He had a gift for making things seem easier than they were and thus it was that Scott, the loser, became the hero. But it was all down to the mighty ski! The following extracts are from Roland Huntford's book Scott and Amundsen and clearly show their different attitude to skis and skiing.

Roland Huntford (1927 in Cape Town) is British Polar historian, journalist and author. He gained international fame through his biographies on the Polar researchers Roald Amundsen, Robert Falcon Scott, Fridtjof Nansen and Ernest Shackleton. He has also written a comprehensive history of skiing – 'Two Planks and a Passion'. Roland Huntford would visit us in Oslo while researching his books on Polar Exploration and my father is credited in his book Scott and Amundsen. He has kindly given me permission to quote extracts from the book.

AMUNDSEN DECIDES TO MAKE A STAB AT THE NORTH POLE:

On his way to London at the end of January 1909, to lecture on his forthcoming expedition to the R.G.S., Amundsen had to change trains at Lübeck, in Northern Germany. There he chanced to meet a Norwegian ski team travelling to Chamonix, in French Savoy for a demonstration. In the historic Nordic disciplines of ski jumping and cross-country, the Norwegians were still the undisputed masters. Between trains Amundsen entertained his countrymen at the station restaurant. The conversation, not unnaturally, turned to his expeditions, past and future.

"Do you know," said one of the team, a lithe, dark-haired, moustachioed figure, with a glint in his eye. "Do you know, it would be fun to be with you at the North Pole." He spoke in a rich country brogue. He happened to be one of the finest living skiers, a man called Olav Bjaaland.

"Indeed?" was Amundsen's reply. "Well, if you really mean it, I think it could be arranged. Just look me up in Christiania when you get home from Chamonix. But think it over carefully. It won't only be fun."

This is how Bjaaland told the story afterwards. His motives for asking Amundsen were mixed. Of course, being a Norwegian, he had the customary desire to emulate Nansen. But also, here was a way of seeing the world and being paid for it. At the age of nearly thirty-six, he was now making his first visit abroad. Chamonix and the North Pole were both part of the great outside. To him, both seemed merely variations on the same theme; ski races both, with the North Pole perhaps a little bit more fun.

Before the fortuitous encounter at Lübeck station, the two had never met, although each knew of the other through the headlines. In 1902, Bjaaland had won the Nordic combination of ski jumping and cross-country at Holmenkollen, the annual races in Nordmarka; to this day the classic event in Nordic skiing, and which then did duty for Olympic honours.

In 1908, at the age of thirty-five he came second in the fifty kilometres race there.

Bjaaland was more than just a ski champion. He came from Morgedal in Telemark, the cradle of modern skiing. It was the men of Morgedal who turned skiing, which had existed as transport in Scandinavia since the Stone Age, into the sport we know. They invented jumping and downhill skiing. Their dialect has given us the word slalom, literally, 'the course down the meadow'. They developed the two turns dubbed 'Telemark', after their home, and 'Christiania', after the capital. They laid down the foundations of modern technique.

Bjaaland was of the pioneer generation that brought skiing out into the world. He was a farmer and a Montagnard. He was a violinist and wanted to be a professional musician but felt he lacked the proper talent. He was a skilled carpenter. A violin and ski maker, and he worked in wrought iron too. He was a bit of an artist, a bit of a poet, a bit of a child, a bit of a jester. And he had in the very highest degree the natural dignity and ceremoniousness traditionally associated with his native Telemark. He was a natural aristocrat. Amundsen discerned these qualities. When Bjaaland returned to Morgedal from Chamonix in February, he had joined the expedition.

Cook and Peary both claim to have reached the North Pole, Cook in 1908 and Peary a year later. Scott now announces that he is heading for the South Pole and Amundsen decides to challenge him but tells no one of his plan, not even his own crew. When he sets off from Christiania in 1910 the world thought he was en-route to the North Pole.

Having decided on his base and his route, Amundsen set about analysing Shackleton's performance, in order to learn from his mistakes. It is much harder to learn from success than from failure, and nothing illustrates Amundsen's calibre better than his refusal to be mesmerised by Shackleton's dazzling performance. He had the perception to see behind to the near disaster which loomed throughout, and which was the real lesson to be learned.

Shackleton had taken risks on a monumental scale. He had cut his rations to the bone. Depots were too small, too few, and too sketchily marked. Reaching them in time, a matter of life and death, was often a close-run thing. To Amundsen it was a vivid demonstration of the vital necessity of generous margins of safety.

From Shackleton's experience, Amundsen deduced that the fight for the Pole would be a ski race writ large. Indeed, Shackleton admitted this himself afterwards in a lecture. "Had we taken ski on the southern journey and understood how to use them like the Norwegians," he said, "we would presumably have reached the Pole."

So Amundsen, whilst he might admire the dashing buccaneer and the leader that was Shackleton, had no desire to emulate his methods. The heroic struggle that made such good reading, was in reality, a warning. In transport, Shackleton was an example of what to avoid. It was not only that, misled by his Discovery experience, he had eschewed skis, but man-hauling, by then outmoded and discredited outside England, had once more been the backbone of the deed. Dogs, though taken, were misjudged, and wrongly handled. The more Amundsen studied Shackleton's approach, the more he believed that he was on the right track.

He took nothing for granted and was indefatigable in his attention to detail. For example, he rejected existing snow goggles, having his own made up after a pattern of Dr. Frederick Cook's. He insisted on designing special skis, for in the basic tool of his enterprise he saw the grand necessity of adaptation to a purpose. Like any skier worth his salt he was cheerfully obsessed by equipment. Skis were then, not the laminated confections we know, but laths of solid wood, and the main controversy was on kind, origin, grain, age, seasoning. Nor were the proportions stabilised. Amundsen ordered a model, something between a jumping and cross-country ski. It was extremely long – about eight feet – and narrow for its length. This, Amundsen believed, was what the Antarctic required. The length was to bridge the widest possible crevasses. By giving a large bearing surface it avoided breaking snow bridges or thin crust and sinking into loose snow. Such a ski, reproducing the characteristics of a cross-country racing model in a more robust form, is easy to run on, because resistance is lowered. Also, it is stable, holds a straight course, and puts less strain on the legs in keeping them steady. Other refinements were a narrow waist and a deep flared tip to ride over drifts and extract the last ounce of advantage in sliding – and hence saving energy and precious food. For material, Amundsen chose hickory. It was heavy but strong, elastic, close grained, kept water out, held wax, and seemed to act best in low temperatures.

He had the wood bought in Pensacola nine years before, so he was sure of its quality.

The one drawback to these skis was their length which made them fiendishly difficult to turn. But this would only have to be paid for on the descent from the plateau, at the most a hundred miles out of 1,400. The waste of energy on that score would be infinitesimal by comparison with the savings on the rest.

Like any skier, Amundsen was preoccupied with boots and bindings. He chose the tensioned heel bindings then coming on to the market because by giving efficient control, they saved energy. A boot had to be designed that was longitudinally rigid enough to be used with the bindings, and also with crampons on ice slopes, while flexing easily to allow the heel to be raised, and avoiding the constriction and frostbite associated with stiff footwear in low temperatures.

An unconventional boot with leather soles and canvas uppers was adopted. It was enormous, to provide space for several socks and inner soles. Bindings, too, were imperfect. Amundsen began a frustrating process of development lasting, with various setbacks, for almost two years, and not finished until the last moment in the snows. In the end, he settled for the Huitfeld binding, an early form of heel strap, with Hoyer-Ellefsen snap levers.

SCOTT'S PREPARATIONS

When, at the beginning of March, Scott went to Norway for the motor trials, he also took the opportunity to buy furs and sledges. In Christiania, on the way to Fefor, he met Nansen, who now had the British strategy revealed to him.

Nansen did not particularly like Scott – although he definitely did like Kathleen who accompanied her husband – but, in the Greek sense, he was a man of charity, who could not stand coldly by and watch a fellow human being apparently bent on self-destruction.

Scott's plans (insofar as they existed) were absurd. His irrational mistrust of dogs, his reliance instead on horses and his faith in the yet unproven capacities of petrol engines in cold weather, all seemed an invitation to disaster. Nansen felt he had to save Scott from himself; at the same time a Norwegian Polar apprentice needed unobtrusive help.

This was Tryggve Gran who, at the age of twenty, had started organising an Antarctic expedition of his own. His Polar interest had been started by Captain Victor Baumann, who had been with Otto Sverdrup on the second Fram expedition. Gran had met Baumann during a brief spell as a Norwegian Naval cadet.

But it was Shackleton who inspired Gran to act. Gran had met him when he came to Norway in October 1909 and heard him lecture in Christiania on his journey almost to within sight of the Pole. "For an hour and a half I seemed to be nailed to my seat. In words and pictures, I seemed to experience reality's fairy tale. Indeed, the Antarctic was the place where Norwegian skiers could make history".

Before Shackleton left Christiania, Gran had an interview with him. I asked him straight out if he would advise me to go South on my own initiative, young as I was, and without any other experience than I had acquired at sea and in the mountains as a skier. Shackleton's answer made my heart hammer violently against my ribs. "Listen here, my young friend," he said "I will not advise you to do it but give my frank opinion. Provided you can get enough experienced men to get your ship down to the Ross Barrier, your youth is anything but a handicap." And Shackleton continued: "An English expedition under Captain Scott is in preparation and will presumably start next summer. It is necessary to act quickly. You can count on a cheque from me."

Shackleton must have been unusually off his guard when he so patently encouraged a total stranger to compete with Scott; he did not often reveal to outsiders the resentment he felt against his rival. Possibly he was carried away by his reception in Christiania, with the first snows of winter, a torchlight procession and an emotional oration by Amundsen. 'Nowhere have hearts beat more warmly for you,' ran a passage that touched Shackleton, 'and perhaps no assembly has been better qualified to judge of your undertaking.'

Gran, an impressionable young man, was fired by the same scenes, and by the encounter with Shackleton. He went away and ordered a ship. He was rich enough to indulge his whims. He began gathering companions. In January 1910, he visited Nansen to discuss his plans.

Nansen was worried by what he heard. Gran's boat was about as big as a fishing smack – ludicrously small for the Antarctic. And at the age of twenty, Gran was exceptionally young even to be thinking of leading his own expedition. Yet it was not just his youth and inexperience that worried Nansen. Gran was not untried. He had been intended for the Navy which, in Norway, meant twenty-one months' sea service on merchant ships before becoming a cadet. Between the age of sixteen and eighteen Gran had shipped before the mast on sailing ships; crossed the Atlantic several times and had been shipwrecked on the Norwegian coast. In between he had been ski-touring in the Norwegian mountains. But Nansen knew his own countrymen and in Gran he recognised (as Gran himself would willingly admit) a bit of Ibsen's Peer Gynt; that personification, indeed caricature, of something quintessentially Norwegian: the man of the grand gesture, confusing day-dream with reality; too often tragically inconsequential before great events.

Gran had given up the Navy when he seized on the idea of an Antarctic expedition. It was not the happiest background for the enterprise. All this, and much else besides, Nansen understood. The question was: how to dissuade Gran from pursuing his enterprise?

To tell him not to would almost certainly have disastrous effects. Setting a devious little scheme in train, Nansen offered to introduce Gran to Scott; Gran was delighted. He was raised at a stroke, as it were, to the company of recognised explorers. Nansen arranged the meeting at Hagen's, the shop where Scott was going to buy his sledges.

Hagen's was a large ski and sporting goods manufacturer, internationally famous for fitting out expeditions. Shackleton and Amundsen patronised it. Among Christiania skiers the shop was a favourite haunt, crammed with the paraphernalia of winter sports, heavy with the acrid scent of Stockholm tar and its nostalgic associations with waxing skis in mountain huts on frosty mornings.

Nansen had a particular reason for this mise en scène. Scott's unreasoning aversion to skis – another outcome of the Discovery expedition – seemed to Nansen crass stupidity. He hoped that exposure to the seductive ambience of skiing equipment en masse, aided by some judicious propaganda, would overcome it. So, all three men went down to Hagen's and browsed among the sledges and the skis. At a suitable moment, as Tryggve Gran recollected in after years, Nansen turned to Scott and said, "Now you're going to take ski with you. Shackleton didn't take ski and (he) told me when he had lunch with me if he had known how to use ski he would have reached the Pole. He would have done!"

This showed considerable percipience; Nansen had divined Scott's Shackleton fixation. Or had Kathleen Scott told him? "But remember, it's no use having ski unless you know how to use them properly. You ought to let a Norwegian show you." "Well, if you can point out a man who can show me," says Scott, "I would be very thankful to you." So, Nansen knocked me on the shoulder and said, "Well, Gran, can't you do it?" And I said, "With the greatest pleasure."

So, next morning Gran caught the train with Scott to Fefor. Gran was deeply conscious of his role as exponent of the noble art of skiing. A horse and sleigh took Scott's party from the railway station at Vinstra up to Fefor. When they reached the snow at the foot of the first rise, Gran jumped off the sleigh, put on his skis and, as he says, "soon grasped that Scott was impressed" at the way he managed to keep up all the way to the top.

Next day, the motor sledge, which had been sent ahead, was put through its paces on the frozen lake outside the hotel. At the controls sat Bernard Day, Shackleton's motor mechanic, the first Antarctic driver. Men from the Wolseley motor company, which had made the engine, were there to watch. So too was Skelton, now engineer commander, busy with the application of the first diesel engines to British submarines but still, at Scott's urgent appeals, finding time to supervise the manufacture and testing of the sledge.

Soon after breakfast the mountain silence was shattered by the splutter and pop of an early petrol engine; across the snow the monster crawled, cheered to the echo by the little crowd of holidaymakers. People clambered on the sledge, hung on, and were pulled along behind on ski. This miracle lasted exactly a quarter of an hour. Without warning there was a sharp crack and the sledge stopped dead, like a horse refusing a fence, throwing Day head foremost into the snow. An axle had broken. That was Gran's opportunity to show what ski could do. Time was short; Scott had to return to London. Repairs could only be done by a workshop in the valley. Carrying the pieces on his back, Gran swished off down on ski in best racing style. Scott could scarcely believe his eyes, when Gran returned after five hours, having skied some ten miles, running down and climbing 1,000 feet, with the repaired axle, a load of twenty-five pounds, on his back.

The axle was replaced and all afternoon the sledge triumphantly clattered to and fro; pulling three tons at four and a half miles per hour. At that rate it would clear the Barrier in fifty-five running hours from McMurdo Sound. Scott was in splendid humour. Gran recalled how they were skiing across the lake when Scott suddenly stopped and asked me if I would consider postponing my own Antarctic plans and follow him South instead. I thought I had heard wrongly, and it was only when Scott explained that now, for the first time he realized what ski, properly used, would mean to him and his expedition, that I grasped that my ears had not being playing me tricks.

It is entirely characteristic that, ten years after Scott began his Antarctic work, he had finally gone to source and seen skiing in its homeland. Widely regarded as a Polar expert, until he went to Fefor he had never seen ski properly used. He had floundered, the first, into the heart of the Antarctic; but Gran was the first accomplished skier he had seen in action.

Gran was an able skier of the all-round Nordic kind; good at jumping, cross-country and, in moderation, downhill. He had, besides the gift of showing off without seeming to, an ability to be a bit of an actor: exactly what was needed to make an instant impression on Scott – and his wife.

Gran showed what could be done with two sticks; how they made sliding effortless and climbing almost a pleasure. This was the revelation that converted Scott. He had never before seen two ski sticks in action but used only the obsolescent single pole. Gran also demonstrated other refinements; chiefly stable boots and bindings giving proper control over the skis.

With the fervour of the convert, Scott now invested with quasi-miraculous attributes the implements which, a few hours before, he had totally rejected. Gran's dramatic performance had been admirably timed. Scott had been plunged into despondency by the breakdown of the sledge; the elation following the repair simply magnified the uncertainties now brought to his attention. Skelton's final report enumerated over sixty mechanical faults, any one of which would be enough to cause a breakdown. There was no time for more snow trials before going into action. Skis now appeared as a providential insurance: the extra kind of transport which, added to motors and animals must get him to the Pole.

SCOTT WAS NOW ON HIS WAY TO THE ANTARCTIC, AMUNDSEN SUPPOSEDLY TO THE ARCTIC

Amundsen, having reached Madeira in the Fram, at last reveals to his crew the change of plan. His goal is the South Pole and his aim to get there before Scott.

"Now," Amundsen continued, "it was a question of racing the English."

"Hurrah," shouted Bjaaland. "That means we'll get there first!"

They were the first words spoken; relieving the tension a little. Bjaaland was naturally thinking as a ski champion, used to winning, looking on the South Pole as a cross-country ski race, longer and harder than any other, but still, basically a ski race. And, as everybody knew, the Norwegians were better skiers than the English.

THE BASE AT FRAMHEIM

11th February: The dogs pull magnificently, and the going on the barrier is ideal. Cannot understand what the English mean when they say that dogs cannot be used here. 13th February: Today we have had a lot of loose snow... For us on skis it was the most magnificent going. How men (on foot) and horses are going to get through in these conditions I cannot understand, not to mention an automobile. The Thermos flask is a splendid invention. We fill it every morning with boiling chocolate and drink it piping hot at noon. Not bad for the middle of the Barrier.

15th February: A fine performance of our dogs this: 40 geographical miles yesterday – of which 10 miles with heavy load and then 51 miles today – I think they will hold their own with the ponies on the Barrier.

The skis were right, the dogs were right, and very soon Amundsen discovered that he had got the order of running right as well. First came Prestrud, alone, as forerunner to give the dogs something to follow, a lesson from the North-West Passage! Next came Helmer Hanssen with the leading dog team and steering compass, followed by Johansen, also with a compass. Last came Amundsen, with spare compass and sledgemeter. The latter was the device for measuring distance run, consisting of a bicycle wheel with a revolution counter, running in the snow and attached to the back of the sledge.

THE RACE WON – ON THE WAY BACK

Day and night had now lost their meaning; even the date was a matter of confusion. 'Just as well we can remember the year,' as Amundsen put it. After a suitable rest, they were up again at one a.m. for the descent of the ice falls. Amundsen was quite calm. What he had once climbed, he could presumably descend. In any case, he was not afraid of physical danger and he happily lacked the tortured imagination that suffers in advance.

Before starting he stood for a long time intensely contemplating the wild mountain setting, as if trying to etch it on his memory. Over the summit of Mount Ole Engelstad, lay a little cirrus cloud [he wrote], gold-edged in the morning sun. And over there lies [Mount Don Pedro Christophersen] partly illuminated, partly in the shade. If only I could paint!

The little caravan set off. Bjaaland, still forerunner, was the first to reach the edge of the upper ice falls. Between his skis he was abruptly presented with the vertiginous sight of empty space and an apparently disconnected runout far below. It is the sight that betokens something special in the way of slopes and brings butterflies to the stomach. Once more the sledges were braked by ropes round the runners, and they all, men and dogs, launched themselves over the top.

It was (in Amundsen's words), a good day for us skiers. Loose snow, so that the ski sank about 2 inches: iced and grainy so that the ski glided as if on an oiled surface... The loose snow gave control. The one slope steeper than the next... We whizzed down. A wonderful sport.

To Bjaaland, 'The skiing was wonderful. I had many good runs and raced with the Captain.'

This is the spirited language of skiing as a pleasure, the language of The King's Mirror celebrating the skier who 'triumphs over the bird in its flight or the greyhound in its stride.' Amundsen, Bjaaland and probably Hassel were enjoying themselves; there was every reason why they should. They had perfect spring snow. The descent from the Plateau had become sheer pleasure; a long ski run which they were qualified to appreciate. Their light-heartedness makes a contrast with Scott's puritanical earnestness. Did Scott enjoy him-self at all?

But Amundsen was a master of understatement. His casual phrases mask an extraordinary performance. This was a downhill run of Alpine proportions and these men were unused to Alpine conditions. Their background was Nordic; they lacked specialised Alpine technique and equipment.

Without fixed downhill bindings, they were handicapped by long skis, difficult to turn. Nonetheless they overcame the obstacles, swinging down in wide Telemark and Christiania turns, stick-riding when the slope was too steep. They ran a tremendous slalom between crevasses, round the pits, seracs and abysses of the Axel Heiberg's monstrous cataracts of ice, albeit down the course marked on their way up.

Amundsen and his men arrived back in Framheim on January 26th, 1912.

SCOTT, WILSON AND BOWERS, HAVING REACHED THE SOUTH POLE ONE MONTH AFTER AMUNDSEN, DIED IN THEIR TENT, 11 MILES AWAY FROM THEIR LAST DEPOT – 'ONE-TON DEPOT'.

Scott would have to answer for the men he had lost. Shackleton would have the last laugh. That was something Scott could not face. It would be better to seek immolation in the tent. That way he could snatch a kind of victory out of defeat. Wilson and Bowers were persuaded to lie down with him and wait for the end, where the instinct of other men in like predicament was to keep going and fall in their tracks. For at least nine days they lay in their sleeping bags, while their last food and fuel gave out, and their life ebbed away.

They wrote their last letters, believing they would be found some day. That indeed was the argument that Scott probably used to persuade Wilson and Bowers to lie down and wait in the tent. If they had fallen in their tracks, they and their records would have been lost. In the tent, they would have a chance of being found, and their tale saved from oblivion.

Wilson and Bowers penned a few hasty, poignant, private notes. Scott, however, had been preparing his farewells for some time. The earliest was dated March 16th, to Sir Edgar Speyer, the expedition's treasurer: "I fear we must go". Scott had already given up.

QUOTES BY SCOTT:

ROBERT FALCON SCOTT ON SKIS AND SKIING...

And here I should like to explain my attitude towards ski, more especially as since Nansen's journeys it has been very generally thought that they have revolutionised the methods of Polar travel. I have mentioned in former chapters how delighted we were with our ski practice, and I have also called attention to an incident where some officers were able to push on with a journey because they possessed ski. The latter is really an extraordinary exception, and it is still more extraordinary that it should have been our first experience of Antarctic travelling. It naturally biased us all in favour of ski, so that although a few remained sceptical, the majority thought them an unmixed blessing. Bit by bit however, the inevitable truth came to light: it was found that in spite of all appearances to the contrary, a party on foot invariably beat a party on ski, even if the former were sinking ankle deep at each step; while to add to this, when the surface was hard, ski could not be used, and had to be carried as an extra weight and great encumbrance on the sledges.

I C writes:

I really cannot finish this tiny stroll through skiing history without mentioning Trygve Gran, (Scott's Norwegian ski expert) who later was the first to fly across the North Sea (on the day World War One broke out and so no one got to hear about his feat). In 1922 he was planning to fly to the North Pole. He was interviewed about this 50 years later and these were his words: '*We planned to fly to the North Pole, crash land the plane and ski from there to Greenland.*' Then he added, in order to further substantiate the plan. '*We were all three quite fit in those days.*'

CHAPTER 5
FROM A LONG TIME AGO

Kongespeilet THE KING'S MIRROR

A text in Old Norse from around 1250, an example of speculum literature that deals with politics and morality. It was originally intended for the education of King Magnus Lagabøter, the son of King Håkon Håkonsson, and it has the form of a dialogue between father and son. The son asks and is advised by his father. The King's Mirror is considered 'one of the chief ornaments' of Old Norse literature.

Son Now that I am permitted to choose a topic for entertainment, it occurs to me that I have asked too little about Ireland, Iceland, and Greenland, and all the wonders of those lands, such as fire and strange bodies of water, or the various kinds of fish and the monsters that dash about in the ocean, or the boundless ice both in the sea and on the land, or what the Greenlanders call the "northern lights," or the "sea-hedges that are found in the waters of Greenland.

Father I am not much disposed to discuss the wonders that exist among us here in the North, though my reason may be rather trivial: many a man is inclined to be suspicious and think everything fiction that he has not seen with his own eyes; and therefore I do not like to discuss such topics, if my statements are to be called fabrications later on, even though I know them to be true beyond doubt, inasmuch as I have seen some of these things with mine own eyes and have had daily opportunity to inquire about the others from men whom we know to be trustworthy and who have actually seen and examined them, and therefore know them to be genuine beyond question. My reason for bringing up this objection is that a little book has recently come into our country, which is said to have been written in India and recounts the wonders of that country. The book states that it was sent to Emmanuel, emperor of the Greeks. Now it is the belief of most men who have heard the book read, that such wonders are impossible, and that what is told in the book is mere falsehood. But if our own country were carefully searched, there would be found no fewer things here than are numbered in that book which would seem as wonderful, or even more so, to men of other lands who have not seen or heard anything like them. Now we call those things fiction because we had not seen them here or heard of them before the coming of that book which I have just mentioned. That little book has, however, been widely circulated, though it has always been questioned and charged with falsehood; and it seems to me that no one has derived honour from it, neither those who have doubted it nor the one who wrote it, even though his work has been widely distributed and has served to amuse and tickle the ear, seeing that what is written in it has always been called fiction.

Son Of course I cannot know how widely our talks will travel either in our days or later; and yet, with your permission, I will again ask the pleasure of hearing further speech concerning those matters that we might think strange in other lands, but which we know are surely genuine. And we need not be so very sceptical of this book which is said to have been written in India, though many marvels are told in it; for there are many things in our own country, which, though not strange to us, would seem wonderful to other people, if our words should fly so far as to come thither where such things are unheard of. But if I should express surprise at any of those tales that are told in that book, it seems to me not least wonderful that manikins are able to subdue those great winged dragons which infest the mountains and desert places there, as the book tells us, and tame them so completely that men are able to ride them just as they please like horses, fierce and venomous beasts though they are said to be and not inclined to allow men in their neighbourhood, still less to be tamed and to do service.

Father Both such and many other tales are told in that book which seem so marvellous that many express their doubts about them; but it seems to me that there is no need to compare the wonders that are described there with those that we have in our own country, which would seem as strange to men yonder as those that you have just mentioned seem to us. For it must be possible to tame wild beasts and other animals, though they be fierce and difficult to manage. But it would seem a greater marvel to hear about men who are able to tame trees and boards, so that by fastening boards seven or eight ells long under his feet, a man, who is no fleeter than other men when he is barefooted or shod merely with shoes, is made able to pass the bird on the wing, or the fleetest greyhound that runs in the race, or the reindeer which leaps twice as fast as the hart. For there is a large number of men who run so well on skis that they can strike down nine reindeer with a spear, or even more, in a single run. Now such things must seem incredible, unlikely, and marvellous in all those lands where men do not know with what skill and cleverness it is possible to train the board to such great fleetness that on the mountain side nothing of all that walks the earth can escape the swift movements of the man who is shod with such boards. But as soon as he removes the boards from his feet, he is no more agile than any other man. In other places, where men are not trained to such arts, it would be difficult to find a man, no matter how swift, who would not lose all his fleetness if such pieces of wood as we have talked about were bound to his feet. We, however, have sure information and, when snow lies in winter, have opportunity to see men in plenty who are expert in this art.

The next story by Jan Ove Ekeberg, is from his book *I Sverdets Tid, – At the Time of the Sword* – a thriller from the period of the Norwegian Civil War in the 12th and 13th century. It tells the story of the journey of the two-year-old Haakon Haakonsson, heir to the Norwegian throne, who was carried by the Birkebeiner, in mid-winter, from Lillehammer to Østerdalen to Trondheim, a long and perilous journey over treacherous mountains and through forests – Birkebeiner because they wound birch bark round their feet and legs. This journey is commemorated by the famous annual cross-country ski race Birkebeinerrennet. The course is 54 km and crosses two mountain ranges. The competitors must carry a backpack weighing no less than 3.5 kg – to replicate the weight of the young king.

Translation by Ingrid Christophersen.

BIRKEBEINERFERDEN FROM KONGEDRAPENE by Jan Ove Ekeberg

Jan Ove Ekeberg (1954) is a Norwegian author, journalist and TV news anchor. He was a Fulbrigth scholar and has a Master's degree in political science from the University of Minnesota.

It was late at night by the time they arrived at Graathen. No more than 15 men had accompanied Sigurd, and of those, several were injured.

Torstein Skeivla welcomed them and assisted the wounded to settle in a barn where he kept his sheep over winter. The heat from the animals kept the barn warm and Torstein found some skins for them. Torstein's wife boiled up some reindeer meat and the men ate and drank from the warm stock.

Sigurd, Digre and some of the men followed Torstein into the small room. Inga was inside nursing the small boy on her lap and one of Torstein's daughters was feeding Haakon with some watery gruel. The boy swallowed as best he could and burped loudly. The men laughed and the wee one leered, satisfied and full.

Now he scrutinised Sigurd curiously. This was the first time Sigurd had seen the heir apparent. Like his father his eyes were big and blue. The powerful jaw would in time resemble King Sverre's.

Torstein studied the wee one and his mother, who he had saved on the ice. He had got them under cover and into a warm bed where they both fell asleep immediately, exhausted and frozen. But when Inga woke up she had demanded that he fetch the county sheriff, and in a hurry. Torstein had immediately strapped his skis on and rushed down to the valley. Now he questioned Sigurd about the wee one. "There's not much of him at the moment, but I am not wrong in thinking that this is as promising a lad as I have ever seen. His mother has not said much about him, but he is no doubt the son of the sheriff?"

Sigurd found himself thinking of Guttorm. His dead body. Then the thought of Solveig loomed large in this thought. His yearning for her struck him hard and he wondered what would happen to her and Sunniva if Galen continued up Norddalen. But he pushed the thought away. Perfidious Solveig.

Sigurd answered Torstein in a loud voice so everyone in the room could hear him.

"No, this boy is of better lineage than that. You are nursing Norway's future King. Young Haakon is son of King Haakon, and the grandson of King Sverre. No one in this country is of such ancient lineage and more equipped to be king than this boy, who is now in his second winter." His voice was unnecessarily loud. When he started talking about the young boy the room fell silent. Sigurd felt tired, but there was no time to rest making sure that the pursuers did not catch up with them.

Sigurd looked towards Torstein. "How far is it over to Østerdalen, if we were to leave this evening?" Torstein shook his head, "you won't make that now. Should it cease to snow it takes at least two days by foot to cross over the mountain. There are only paths and they will be snowed in, so the horses are not of much use. No, I could not advise that."

Sigurd never answered, he deliberated for a while. Then he again looked over at Torstein.

"I have been told that you cross the mountain as swiftly as a reindeer, both in summer and in winter. How long would it take you, if you travelled alone, with just the infant in your arms?"

Torstein immediately grasped what it was Sigurd wanted him to do.

"If the Sheriff desires it then I will take him over tonight. There is a hay barn at Skramstad. I can be there by dawn. With such precious goods I will not stop other than for the boy's own sake."

Sigurd was sitting in a heavy log chair in front of the open hearth. The flames were throwing out heat. Torstein sat on a stool to the side of him.

"I have several pairs of good skis. You can come with me Sheriff Sigurd. Together we can carry the boy over the mountain."

Sigurd shook his head slowly.

"I am afraid I would only keep you back Torstein. I will wait here and see if more of my men turn up and if we can get them over the mountain. But I want you to take the chap who is sitting over there."

Torstein followed his glance over at a youth who was sitting on the floor close by.

"The son of the farmer at Skrukka is the best skier in my bodyguard. You will have someone to help carry food and weapons while you carry the boy."

Sigurd raised his voice a fraction. "What do you say to that Skjervald? Are you capable of accompanying Torstein over the mountain in this blizzard?"

Skjervald blushed lightly but pulled himself together and answered in his most manly voice,

"I will accompany him as far as I can and if he feels I am keeping him back he must go on. I will find my own way down the mountain."

Torstein had to laugh and Skjervald blushed even more.

But he soon had other things to think of. Torstein came into the room with two pairs of skis and asked Skjervald to look them over and make sure everything was in order. The skis were broad, such as are good when the snow is soft and deep. A long strip of otter fur was fixed to the running surface of the skis; the fur enabled forwards gliding but prevented sliding when kicking off. Sigurd noticed that Torstein had cut a steering groove down the middle of the skis, as was the custom nowadays.

The boots, made of thick, double reindeer skin, came to a point at the front in what looked a bit like a curled dog's tail. This was threaded through a strong leather strap at the front of the binding. When the strap was tightened the boot stayed put.

Torstein produced a pole which was a mixture of a ski pole and a spear. There was a grip below the spear point and a leather thong through which to thread one's hand. At the bottom there was a large basket, well suited for soft snow. Torstein proudly announced that he himself had designed the pole and that it was adequate to ward off bear.

While Torstein and Skjervald made skis and outfits ready, Inga dressed Haakon and smeared him with bear fat against the cold. The boy turned up his nose at the rancid smell. But he never cried. Then they dressed him in woollen clothes: trousers, shirt, socks and hat.

It surprised Sigurd that they found clothes that fitted the boy so well, until he realised there were so many children in the room and so no doubt Torstein and his wife had clothes to fit all sizes.

They stopped dressing him then and Sigurd wondered if he might not be cold in the blizzard.

"He will be wearing this too. I have carried all my own in this."

Torstein appeared with a papoose made of reindeer skin, shaped like a short, fat sausage. Inga settled the boy in the papoose. She had not muttered a word about taking her son out into a blizzard. Sigurd was sure she thought it was for the best. Torstein fastened the papoose over his shoulders and then pulled it round to his chest. In this way he could see the boy at all times. He held a shield in front of the papoose to shelter the boy from the wind.

They were ready.

Skjervald was so keen to get going he could hardly hold back. It was still snowing hard and blowing a gale and they disappeared quickly into the distance. Skjervald was leading, followed by Torstein and little Haakon. Sigurd went into the house and was about to fall asleep when he heard people approaching. Several men slept on the floor in the small hall. Sigurd called to them and ran out into the sheep barn to wake the men who were sleeping there.

"Get up and arm yourselves – there are people coming."

The men were exhausted but nevertheless armed themselves in haste and quickly left the barn. About fifty of their own men arrived. Many of them wounded. The worst were taken to the hall, the others crowded into the sheep barn.

Sigurd would have liked to have seen many more. He consoled himself with the thought that the farmers and the king's men could have fled in all directions, but he knew many must have died. His thoughts went to Kalv who lay dead in the snow, like his father had one time. Sigurd thought about two young boys, but neither Arnljot nor Gaute were among the men.

Until they were close up to it the hay barn was difficult to detect. The snow had ceased but was drifting and the barn lay in a small depression and was nearly snowed under.

Sigurd thought they were lucky to have walked on to it; they needed to rest. For two days they crossed over the mountain with little food and no possibility to slow down. Three of his men were left behind, lying in the snow. A woman was with them. Inga was skiing and had coped better than most of the men. Now she glided down the last little hill to the barn. Sigurd had told her that she should follow them to Nidaros in the spring; she would never survive the mountain in this weather. But she said her son needed his mother and that her brother had taught her to ski.

A large shape loomed out of the barn. Inga ran the last bit. It took Sigurd a bit longer to reach them, he was on foot, but he saw how Torstein held the child Haakon up to his mother.

"It was snowing so hard all night that we could only give him snow to suck on."

Inga held the child against her bosom and smiled up to the man who had now saved her son twice; once on the ice when he also saved her, and now in the blizzard over the mountain.

When Sigurd reached them, Torstein turned to him and continued talking about what a strong heir apparent he was.

"Skjervald chewed the reindeer meat for him and he swallowed several big pieces. Only when we reached the barn later in the day were we able to concoct some gruel for him. It is as though he thrives on the life of a soldier. We never heard any whining." Torstein chuckled happily and turned to Skjervald.

"We never heard anything Skjervald, did we?"

The young boy smiled broadly and nodded to Inga and Sigurd.

"He will be as good a skier as anyone when he becomes king." Sigurd realised that Skjervald was proud as punch to have carried the son of a king over the mountain and he did not appear tired at all.

"But until that day when you will teach Haakon child to ski, Skjervald, we must all protect him. You must descend into the valley and find out if the farmers there are peacefully inclined towards us." Sigurd had hardly spoken the words before the young king's man set off down the hill towards the farms. There were still open rapids in the large river, which was meandering below them.

Not long thereafter Skjervald returned and informed them that he had met only peaceful farmers, many of them who knew his father, the farmer from Skrukka. Sigurd raised his voice so all could hear him.

"We will go down and seek lodgings and food. Many of you are tired and the weather clearly will not let up."

Most of the men stood outside, the barn was so saturated with body heat that it had started to drip from the roof.

"I think Child Haakon and his mother could do with a roof over their heads." Inga's face was streaky with exhaustion, but he had to admire her for her courage. Sigurd saw that Torstein was preparing to return home.

"I would like to cross the mountain again Sheriff and see to my own." Sigurd stretched out his arm and touched Torstein's shoulder.

"You do not realise Torstein Skeivla what you have done to safeguard this country. And God willing I will make sure that he who you carried over the mountain will thank you for it."

"You must also thank Skjervald who cleared the track over the mountain for Child Haakon. He is a better skier than I am; I am no longer so young." Sigurd looked at Skjervald, his entire body was smiling. Several of the men standing around slapped the young king's man on the shoulder.

"And those words Torstein, are the best thanks Skjervald could ever get. After this feat his name will be renowned amongst the King's men."

LORNA DOONE by R D Blackmore

Lorna Doone is a romance of Exmoor, a novel by English author Richard Doddridge Blackmore, published in 1869. It is a romance based on a group of historical characters and set in the late 17th century in Devon and Somerset, particularly around the East Lyn Valley area of Exmoor. Blackmore experienced difficulty in finding a publisher, and the novel was first published anonymously in 1869 in a limited three-volume edition of just 500 copies, of which only 300 sold. The following year it was republished in an inexpensive one-volume edition and became a huge critical and financial success. It has never been out of print. This is the first mention of skiing, albeit in a rather convoluted way, in English literature.

It must have snowed most wonderfully to have made that depth of covering in about eight hours. For one of Master Stickles' men, who had been out all the night, said that no snow began to fall until nearly midnight. And here it was, blocking up the doors, stopping the ways, and the watercourses, and making it very much worse to walk than in a sawpit newly used.

Of the sheep upon the mountain, and the sheep upon the western farm, and the cattle on the upper burrows, scarcely one in ten was saved; do what we would for them. And this was not through any neglect (now that our wits were sharpened), but from the pure impossibility of finding them at all. That great snow never ceased a moment for three days and nights, and then when all the earth was filled, and the topmost hedges were unseen, and the trees broke down with weight (wherever the wind had not lightened them), a brilliant sun broke forth and showed the loss of all our customs.

All our house was quite snowed up, except where we had purged a way, by dint of constant shovellings. The kitchen was as dark and darker than the cider-cellar, and long lines of furrowed scollops ran even up to the chimney stacks. Several windows fell right inwards, through the weight of the snow against them; and the few that stood bulged in and bent like an old bruised lanthorn. We were obliged to cook by candlelight; we were forced to read by candlelight. As for baking, we could not do it, because the oven was too chill and a load of faggots only brought a little wet down the sides of it.

That night, such a frost ensued as we had never dreamed of, neither read in ancient books, or histories of Frobisher. The kettle by the fire froze, and the crock upon the hearth-cheeks; many men were killed, and cattle rigid in their head-ropes. Then I heard that fearful sound, which never I had heard before, neither since have heard (except during that same winter), the sharp yet solemn sound of trees, burst open by the frost-blow. Our great walnut lost three branches and has been dying ever since; though growing meanwhile, as the soul does. And the ancient oak at the cross was rent, and many score of ash trees. But why should I tell all this? The people who have not seen it (as I have) will only make faces and disbelieve; till such another frost comes; which perhaps may never be.

I believe it was on Epiphany morning, or somewhere about that period, when Lizzie ran into the kitchen to me, where I was thawing my goose-grease, with the dogs among the ashes – the live dogs, I mean, not the iron ones, for them we had given up long ago, – and having caught me, by way of wonder (for generally I was out shovelling, long before my 'young lady' had her nightcap off), she positively kissed me, for the sake of warming her lips perhaps, or because she had something proud to say.

"You great fool, John," said my lady, as Annie and I used to call her, on account of her airs and graces; "what a pity you never read, John!"

"Much use, I should think, in reading!" I answered, though pleased with her condescension; "read, I suppose, with roof coming in, and only this chimney left sticking out of the snow!"

"The very time to read, John," said Lizzie, looking grander; "our worst troubles are the need, whence knowledge can deliver us."

"Amen," I cried out; "are you parson or clerk? Whichever you are, good morning."

Thereupon I was bent on my usual round (a very small one nowadays), but Eliza took me with both hands, and I stopped of course; for I could not bear to shake the child, even in play, for a moment, because her back was tender. Then she looked up at me with her beautiful eyes, so large, unhealthy, and delicate, and strangely shadowing outward, as if to spread their meaning; and she said, "Now, John, this is no time to joke. I was almost frozen in bed last night; and Annie like an icicle. Feel how cold my hands are. Now, will you listen to what I have read about climates ten times worse than this; and where none but clever men can live?"

"Impossible for me to listen now. I have hundreds of things to see to: but I will listen after breakfast to your foreign climates, child. Now attend to mother's hot coffee."

She told me that in the 'Arctic Regions', as they call some places a long way north, where the Great Bear lies all across the heavens, and no sun is up, for whole months at a time, and yet where people will go exploring, out of pure contradiction, and for the sake of novelty, and love of being frozen – that here they always had such winters as we were having now. "It never ceased to freeze," she said; "and it never ceased to snow; except when it was too cold; and then, all the air was choked with glittering spikes; and a man's skin might come off of him, before he could ask the reason. Nevertheless, the people there (although the snow was fifty feet deep, and all their breath fell behind them frozen, like a log of wood dropped from their shoulders), yet they managed to get along, and make the time of the year to each other, by a little cleverness. For seeing how the snow was spread, lightly over everything, covering up the hills and valleys, and the foreskin of the sea, they contrived a way to crown it, and to glide like a flake along. Through the sparkle of the whiteness, and the wreaths of windy tossings, and the ups and downs of cold, any man might get along with a boat on either foot, to prevent his sinking."

She told me how these boats were made; very strong and very light, of ribs with skin across them; five feet long, and one foot wide; and turned up at each end, even as a canoe is. But she did not tell me, nor did I give it a moment's thought myself, how hard it was to walk upon them, without early practice. Then she told me another thing equally useful to me; although I would not let her see how much I thought about it. And this concerned the use of sledges, and their power of gliding, and the lightness of their following; all of which I could see at once, through knowledge of our own farm-sleds; which we employ in lieu of wheels, used in flatter districts. When I had heard all this from her, a mere chit of a girl as she was, unfit to make a snowball even, or to fry snow-pancakes, I looked down on her with amazement, and began to wish a little that I had given more time to books.

But God shapes all our fitness, and gives each man his meaning, even as he guides the wavering lines of snow descending. Therefore I fell to at once, upon that hint from Lizzie, and being used to thatching work, and the making of traps, and so on, before very long I built myself a pair of strong and light snow shoes, framed with ash and ribbed of withy, with half-tanned calf-skin stretched across, and an inner sole to support my feet. At first I could not walk at all, but floundered about most piteously, catching one shoe in the other, and both of them in the snow drifts, to the great amusement of the maidens, who were come to look at me. But after a while I grew more expert, discovering what my errors were, and altering the inclination of the shoes themselves, according to a plan which Lizzie found in a book of old adventures.

And this made such a difference, that I crossed the farmyard and came back again (though turning was the worst thing of all) without so much as falling once, or getting my staff entangled.

But oh the aching of my ankles, when I went to bed that night; I was forced to help myself upstairs with a couple of mopsticks! and I rubbed the joints with Neatsfoot oil, which comforted them greatly. And likely enough I would have abandoned any further trial, but for Lizzie's ridicule, and pretended sympathy; asking if the strong John Ridd would have old Betty to lean upon. Therefore, I set to again, with a fixed resolve not to notice pain or stiffness, but to warm them out of me. And sure enough, before dark that day, I could get along pretty freely: especially improving every time, after leaving off and resting. The astonishment of poor John Fry, Bill Dadds, and Jem Slocombe, when they saw me coming down the hill upon them, in the twilight, where they were clearing the furze rick and trussing it for cattle, was more than I can tell you; because they did not let me see it, but ran away with one accord, and floundered into a snowdrift. They believed, and so did everyone else (especially when I grew able to glide along pretty rapidly), that I had stolen Mother Melldrum's sieves, on which she was said to fly over the foreland at midnight every Saturday.

Upon the following day, I held some council with my mother; not liking to go without her permission, yet scarcely daring to ask for it. But here she disappointed me, on the right side of disappointment; saying that she had seen my pining (which she never could have done; because I had been too hard at work), and rather than watch me grieving so, for somebody or other, who now was all in all to me, I might go upon my course, and God's protection go with me! At this I was amazed, because it was not at all like mother; and knowing how well I had behaved, ever since the time of our snowing up, I was a little moved to tell her that she could not understand me. However, my sense of duty kept me, and my knowledge of the catechism, from saying such a thing as that, or even thinking twice of it. And so I took her at her word, which she was not prepared for; and telling her how proud I was of her trust in Providence, and how I could run in my new snow shoes, I took a short pipe in my mouth, and started forth accordingly.

SERAPHITA by Honoré de Balzac (1799-1850)

Honoré de Balzac (1799 – 1850) was a French author, who, together with Flaubert was regarded as the founding father of realism in European literature. His large output of works, collectively entitled 'The Human Comedy' (La Comédie Humaine) consists of 95 finished works, stories, novels and essays and 48 unfinished works. How extraordinary that he should write about a fjord in Norway. He is of course wrong about the violent surf keeping the fjords unfrozen in winter. No, that is the Gulf Stream, a sort of permanent Marshall Aid from Florida to Norway.

The winter of 1799-1800 was one of the most severe ever known to Europeans. The Norwegian sea was frozen in all the fjords, where, as a usual thing, the violence of the surf kept the ice from forming. A wind, whose effects were like those of the Spanish levanter, swept the ice of the Strom-fjord, driving the snow to the upper end of the gulf. Seldom indeed could the people of Jarvis see the mirror of frozen waters reflecting the colours of the sky; a wondrous site in the bosom of these mountains when all other aspects of nature are levelled beneath successive sheets of snow, and crests and valleys are alike mere folds of the vast mantle flung by winter across a landscape at once so mournfully dazzling and so monotonous. The falling volume of the Sieg, suddenly frozen, formed an immense arcade beneath which the inhabitants might have crossed under shelter from the blast had any dared to risk themselves inland. But the dangers of every step away from their own surroundings kept even the boldest hunters in their homes, afraid lest the narrow paths along the precipices, the clefts and fissures among the rocks, might be unrecognisable beneath the snow.

Thus, it was that no human creature gave life to the white desert where Boreas reigned, his voice alone resounding at distant intervals. The sky, nearly always grey, gave tones of polished steel to the ice of the fjord. Perchance some ancient eider duck crossed the expanse, trusting to the warm down beneath which dream, in other lands, the luxurious rich, little knowing of the dangers through which their luxury has come to them. Like the Bedouin of the desert who darts alone across the sands of Africa, the bird is neither seen nor heard; the torpid atmosphere, deprived of its electrical conditions, echoes neither the whirr of its wings nor its joyous notes.

Besides, what human eye was strong enough to bear the glitter of those pinnacles adorned with sparkling crystals, or the sharp reflections of the snow, iridescent on the summits in the rays of a pallid sun which infrequently appeared, like a dying man seeking to make known that he still lives. Often, when the flocks of grey clouds, driven in squadrons athwart the mountains and among the tree-tops, hid the sky with their triple veils Earth, lacking the celestial lights, lit herself by herself.

Here, then, we meet the majesty of Cold, seated eternally at the pole in that regal silence which is the attribute of all absolute monarchy. Every extreme principle carries with it an appearance of negation and the symptoms of death; for is not life the struggle of two forces?

Here in this Northern nature nothing lived. One sole power – the unproductive power of ice -reigned unchallenged. The roar of the open sea no longer reached the deaf, dumb inlet, where during one short season of the year Nature made haste to produce the slender harvests necessary for the food of the patient people. A few tall pine trees lifted their black pyramids garlanded with snow, and the form of their long branches and depending shoots completed the mourning garments of those solemn heights.

Each household gathered in its chimney corner, in houses carefully closed from the outer air, and well supplied with biscuit, melted butter, dried fish, and other provisions laid in for the seven-months winter. The very smoke of these dwellings was hardly seen, half-hidden as they were beneath the snow, against the weight of which they were protected by long planks reaching from the roof and fastened at some distance to solid blocks on the ground, forming a covered way around each building.

During these terrible winter months the women spun and dyed the woollen stuffs and the linen fabrics with which they clothed their families, while the men read, or fell into those endless meditations which have given birth to so many profound theories, to the mystic dreams of the North, to its beliefs, to its studies (so full and so complete in one science, at least, sounded as with a plummet), to its manners and its morals, half-monastic, which force the soul to react and feed upon itself and make the Norwegian peasant a being apart among the peoples of Europe. Such was the condition of the Strom-fjord in the first year of the nineteenth century and about the middle of the month of May.

On a morning when the sun burst forth upon this landscape, lighting the fires of the ephemeral diamonds produced by crystallizations of the snow and ice, two beings crossed the fjord and flew along the base of the Falberg, rising thence from ledge to ledge toward the summit. What were they? human creatures, or two arrows? They might have been taken for eider ducks sailing in consort before the wind. Not the boldest hunter nor the most superstitious fisherman would have attributed to human beings the power to move safely along the slender lines traced beneath the snow by the granite ledges, where yet this couple glided with the terrifying dexterity of somnambulists who, forgetting their own weight and the dangers of the slightest deviation, hurry along a ridge-pole and keep their equilibrium by the power of some mysterious force.

"Stop me, Seraphitus," said a pale young girl, "and let me breathe. I look at you, you only, while scaling these walls of the gulf; otherwise, what would become of me? I am such a feeble creature."

"Do I tire you?"

"No," said the being on whose arm she leaned. "But let us go on, Minna; the place where we are is not firm enough to stand on."

Once more the snow creaked sharply beneath the long boards fastened to their feet, and soon they reached the upper terrace of the first ledge clearly defined upon the flank of the precipice. The person whom Minna had addressed as Seraphitus threw his weight upon his right heel, arresting the plank (six and a half feet long and narrow as the foot of a child) which was fastened to his boot by a double thong of leather. This plank, two inches thick, was covered with reindeer skin, which bristled against the snow when the foot was raised and served to stop the wearer. Seraphitus drew in his left foot, furnished with another "skee," which was only two feet long, turned swiftly where he stood, caught his timid companion in his arms, lifted her in spite of the long boards on her feet, and placed her on a projecting rock from which he brushed the snow with his pelisse.

"You are safe there, Minna; you can tremble at your ease."

CHAPTER 6
SKI JUMPING

INTRODUCTION by Ingrid Christophersen

The Holmenkollen Ski Jump has been at the heart of Norwegian skiing for over 100 years. The first ski jumping competition took place in 1892 when 12,000 spectators were present. The longest jump was recorded at 21.5 metres. The current record is 144. It is by no means the largest ski jump in the world (at Vikersund, another Norwegian ski jump, they jump over 253 metres!), but Holmenkollen is world-famous and represents an international symbol of ski jumping and ski sports generally. 'Holmenkollen Day', which is held annually in March, is regarded as Norway's 'other' National Day, with thousands of spectators and a wonderful atmosphere. The 'Holmenkollen roar' unites the crowd across the whole social and cultural spectrum. From the grandstands to Gratishaugen (literally the free-of-charge hillock) alike, you may hear the cheers of the crowd as the ski jumpers set off down the in-run. Oslo inhabitants often walk all the way up from Oslo to Holmenkollen and carry picnics, drinks and warm clothes in their rucksacks.

I have translated the following three short stories.

THE SKIER by Mikkjel Fønhus

Mikkjel Fønhus (1894–1973) was a Norwegian journalist, novelist and short story writer. Fønhus' stories are often set in the wild, featuring animals and animal behaviour.

The mass of spectators on the small frozen lake and standing along the hill know little about what is happening on a day like this at the top of the tower.

They see the tower against the sky and the skiers detaching themselves from the summit as they come sailing and floating downwards. But they know no more than that. For up there no one is allowed entry unless they are wearing a bib on their chest and their name features on the programme amongst the hundreds of the country's toughest young men.

Halstein Kvisslo wandered up alongside the tower, his jumping skis on his shoulder.

The competition was about to start, but time enough to have a cup of coffee. This was served in a small house built under the tower, towards the top end. He entered.

The sound of two Primuses whistling. On one was a huge kettle, on the other a saucepan for washing-up water, into which the women dipped the used cups to rinse them. Three competitors were standing by the table drinking and eating packed lunches from their rucksacks. The coffee was free, and in the hut they could leave clothes and rucksacks while they were competing.

People came and went. The coffee women poured out a cup for Halstein and when he had finished and had eaten his Danish pastry, it was time to wander up to the top of the tower.

It towers over him. A huge concoction of long, slender planks, intertwined, upholding and supporting each other, upwards and upwards, he had to crane his neck to see the summit.

There are stairs. Hundreds of them, one after the other. They traverse their way to the top and the footsteps against the rungs resonate eerily and strangely. The entire framework absorbs the sound and turns it into music.

The forest on each side recedes and recedes as he climbs upwards. And when he reaches the top, at the penultimate take-off point, where today's start has been set, then he sees the top of the trees below him. He realises that he is as high as the steeple of the Holmenkollen chapel just down the way. He remembers how it affected him the first time he was up here and was about to take off; he was anything but an experienced ski jumper then, three years ago. Now he has conditioned himself and just about manages.

Many of the jumpers are already lined up, skis on, the early bib numbers at the front, in a row or abreast, according to their bibs.

Halstein relives the special atmosphere at the top of the tower before the start. There is something strange, in total contrast to life along the hill and down on the lake. Down there is the sound of thousands of voices, a bustle quivering through the air, oddly far away, although it is so close. Up here it is quiet, piously quiet, in spite of the number of people. And it feels as though the crowd down there is unthinking, indifferent; they bawl and hoot and one knows that they are chatting each other up, eating chocolate and drinking from their hipflasks – as though all this was just a joke. They don't give a damn for the person up here on the tower. Here, it feels deadly serious, as though one were waiting on an uncertain verdict. Some are maybe a wee bit scared before take-off, scared about hurting themselves. After all, anything can happen from the moment the skis start to slide and until they come to a stop, but the majority are frightened of their position, of the public. Because this famous hill has a reputation, it is sinister, unpredictable, and few feel completely confident.

And there is something peculiarly obsessive in the air, something that quivers though body and soul. It comes from those thousands out there, the music, the flags, from the jump silently waiting… the boys are quiet.

"It's difficult to be favourite, Enger," someone says. "Now you'll know how I felt last year."

"Yes," says Enger and smiles slowly.

Someone tries to make a joke… "so how many degrees are you intending to incline yourself today, Halfdan?"

"I forgot to work it out this morning," Halfdan answers, sullenly. The joke does not ignite, no one is laughing.

The music stops. The King is on his way.

From up here in the tower the public standing along the hill is not visible. But down on the frozen lake the crowd appear to be a continuation of the forest on the hill in the background. And the human forest undulates and rocks, as in a light breeze. Everywhere the dark human mass is interspersed with white blobs, the myriad of faces. The turning area blasts an oblong opening through the tightly packed, live crowd, the horseshoe shaped area edged with red cloth – a flame-red circle round sun kissed snow. And above it all is a restless, muffled murmur, a surging, flowing sound, voices and laughter from fifty thousand people.

But up here on the tower, now that the music has stopped playing, the atmosphere is increasingly solemn. This is when it counts.

Up the steps through the tower a skier appears. His steps can be heard, one after the other. He reaches the take-off point where the top take-off covers the lower one like a roof and there is no snow on the floorboards. He makes a noisy entrance and the dry wood rattles when he puts his skis down.

"Aren't they going to start a few royal anthems down there?" says one. But not even that attempt at jolliness hits the spot. Everyone knows that the guy who spoke was just trying to shore himself up.

But one distinct sound can be heard up here through the heavy silence these five or ten minutes before the start: skis being stamped and slid against the snow to test the glide. As if. Everyone knows how their skis slide, but nevertheless, not everyone can stand still. They lift one ski, then the other; there is something restless about this constant stamping and sliding noise, something impatient and restless.

"I'll be damned if I find more than one who isn't nervous here, and that is me!" A wee barrel-shaped bloke at the back of the queue quips to his neighbour and his rosy face is content, bursting with mirth and it appears that he is just voicing the truth about himself.

At the edge of the take-off, where the in-run starts to nosedive, is a grey-bearded, grey-headed man, wearing a windcheater and carrying a programme. It is he who will send them off. Just behind him is his assistant, standing by a telephone. Suddenly, somewhere from the hill, clearly through the noise of the crowds, which has noticeably calmed down: Hip, hip, hip. And the hurrahs wash over the hill and the lake.

The King has arrived.

But when the royal anthem booms out nothing else is heard. Fifty thousand people stand quietly and up on the tower not even a ski is moving. The grey-headed man bares his head.

And it all affects Halstein so deeply, his chest is tight, and his throat swells up. And he knows that what makes him feel this way, what makes him so quiveringly sensitive, is the excitement, because he is not really frightened. It merely affects him like that when the royal anthem starts up and suddenly thousands stand still and join in. He wonders if the others feel that way too.

But when the music and the singing finishes everything changes, suddenly and violently.

A bugle call pierces the calm, a simple worldly sound, no touch of celebration, it is cold, unmelodious and unfeeling. And the first competitor slides off, slides, slides faster and faster, sinking, bent over, sinking down, faster and faster, he is nearly at the jump, he is there, bends down further, rushes out into thin air, waving his arms like a bird, sinks away as into an empty abyss – and is gone.

Everyone is waiting, a few seconds. Then a wave of sound reaches them from below, thousands of hurrahs – the skier lands.

A few seconds, three more seconds, and the skier rushes out onto the sunlit, oblong flat out on the lake, out to the red-lined horseshoe. He leans to one side, turns, stops and stands still.

The Holmenkollen ski jumping competition is launched.

And after that it is as though a machine had been set in motion. The grey-bearded man on the tower, holding the programme, calls the skiers forward… "12 ready," he says and number 12 advances, ready to launch. "13 prepare!" says the man and number 13 gets ready. His assistant at the telephone repeats the orders down to the hill.

"14 ready! – 15 prepare."

"14 ready! – 15 preparing," the man on the phone repeats.

By now the fiery atmosphere has loosened up a bit and those who are waiting talk among themselves. The man who is sending the skiers off has a sharp, dry, business-like voice and the speed, the regular interval, is as it were a countdown, a sort of office job.

"17 ready! – 18 prepare."

The atmosphere is no longer solemn, there is no church-like silence. It is a relief. And Halstein takes the opportunity to recount a story for a couple who are competing for the first time: a few years ago, Bersvingen from Telemark fell in the second round and lost his grip on the Royal Cup. When he stood up, somewhere down the hill and walked over to a friend he said: "when I fell you can eat your hat that dad smashed the wireless to smithereens!"

Halstein has some time to wait for his turn.

What a wonderful view from up here.

Ahead and below, to the east, the south and to the west, the country spreads out. The Oslo Valley and the surrounding hills of Grefsenåsen and Ekeberg, the Oslo fjord, the hills around Bærum. Nothing blocks the view, high up here.

But he is not only contemplating the landscape. He is envisaging the four years that have passed since he separated from his father at their Paradis cabin to travel to the town down there and take a job in Bratteby's sports shop.

He remained there. He was now a townie.

But life had not been quite as gilded as he had once thought. The salary is reasonably OK, he works far less for the same amount than what he did at Kvisslo farm. Now he could, if he so desired, have a few rooms and some furniture like Edvard Straume. He could afford a telephone, all that appeared so attractive to him those four years ago, when he returned at night from the forest and hardly had time to rub the wood resin off his fingers.

But now he knows that there is nothing special about that, he has learnt that those are not the things that make life more or less pleasant.

To be well-known and talked about looks far more glamorous from the outside than when you are in the middle of it. It becomes a habit; no longer does a delightful quiver pass through your body when you see your name in large print and your picture in the newspaper – like it did the first time. It becomes a habit. But for many also a demand. And when you can no longer satisfy the demand, then it does no one much good.

Halstein has managed these years, to remain pretty much at the front of the prize list, albeit he has never managed to carry the torch quite as high as he did the first winter. His room in the boarding house is starting to look like a jeweller's shop.

But he has started to see his skis in a different light to how he did when he sat at home in Åkroken and read about the big guys in the newspapers and he thought, if I could ever become that much of a guy that I could shake hands with the ski king 'Bakke'.

The point is that he has started to read a lot, and books make you see yourself from the outside.

He has been contemplating the skier Halstein Kvisslo a lot.

Every winter, when the ski season starts, he takes his leave. But not only that. He has arranged things in such a way that he can take a month and a half leave of absence from his job. During this time he is exclusively a skier. He visits Årkroken only once a year, at Easter, otherwise he has no time.

But he contemplates from time to time if, instead, you used your holiday to go home and help your old father (who is nearing seventy) with the harvest? Or, if you used the month and a half leave of absence in the winter to help haul timber.

Halstein reproaches himself but knows jolly well that it is of no use. Every winter, when Nordmarka turns white, the passion in him ignites anew. The ecstasy of competing that he experienced so intensively during the Fifties is something he must revisit again and again. It is like some infection that has attacked his mind and body and which he cannot rid himself of and which in fact he doesn't really want to get rid of anyhow. In some ways, it might be an advantage, in other ways a loss.

If he were to spend less time and money on the sport, he would help his parents with money, but nothing much has come of that.

But this passionate sporting life has protected him against town life. He refuses all that pulls his body down. He is a complete teetotaller. And women… well he hopes he has done with them. Kari Bratteby cured him of that.

Halstein looks at all the boys around him on the tower. He knows many of them. And some of them have gone through what he has experienced – that skis enabled them to veer away from the path that was so conveniently carved out for them. They buckled on their skis and disappeared forever from home, from their local district and family, some for the better, others for the worse.

He spots the back of Viggo Zakariassen, the railway man from Trøndelag who rose to become a famous skier and rich ski-wax manufacturer. Now he has established himself big time in town. Without skis he might have remained forever at the railway's goods office.

His best friend, Vestem, also from Trøndelag, is not here this year. He is now a ski trainer in Germany and has just married the daughter of a rich businessman in Munich. Rumour has it that he has been made a partner of the firm. But when he left Inherred he was a farm labourer.

Ola Skåre in the checkered sweater over there, son of a newspaper editor on the west coast, has harvested no riches either on the cross-country courses or on the jumping hill. He came to Oslo to continue his education at the commercial college but left and started skiing instead. He never did enjoy education. His father gave him an ultimatum that he either returned to the commercial college or there would not be a penny forthcoming.

But Ola started working for a construction company, and that is where he has been for three years. He lives in a small maid's room and scrimps and saves month after month, in spite of making a good living. But you need a fair amount of savings, because he takes time off from Christmas to the end of March just to ski. He reads nothing but sports newspapers and sports articles. He starts training in the summer, mile-long walks in Nordmarka every Sunday. In the autumn he often runs 50 miles on a single Sunday, in rough country and with a rucksack. "I live for sport," he says.

And what about Simon Enger over there? His father is a blacksmith in a provincial town. Simon worked in the smithy with his father and brother. But then he became a famous skier, and a rich factory owner in his hometown sponsored him just as he had with other skiers from the area.

For this factory owner is possessed by a certain ambition on behalf of the town; the town must at all cost attract attention in the skiing world. He has more or less educated Simon and two other skiers. He pays a large part of their expenses and that must be costing many thousands a year.

Simon starts training towards the end of summer and goes on until Christmas when the competitions are about to start. The last competitions he takes part in are often alpine, at the mountain hotels, when spring has sprung in the lowlands. And at last Simon returns to his father and the smithy. But by then he needs a few months' holiday. Simon Enger. Title: Skier, Occupation: Skiing

And when Halstein compares himself to Simon he feels that his two months in the winter pale in comparison.

But last winter a local newspaper announced that 'Kvisslo was up for compulsory auction'. His father was no longer able to keep up with the interest payments. How that announcement must have tormented his father. He who had always taken pride in the fact that no one would lose as much as a penny for his sake, was now depicted in the newspaper as someone unable to be trusted. That night, when the papers arrived at Kvisslo, must have been a sleepless night for his father.

The compulsory auction at Kvisslo went the way of all auctions that had been announced up the valley during those last years. No one wanted to bid and his father got his farm back for a cut down price. He is now better off than before. But he and his wife sit alone, old and worn out. Tørres, the brother, has obtained a temporary post as a teacher this winter. And he will never return for good.

"So, I'll be here on my own, Halstein." Halstein envisages his father sitting on the side of the logging road above the Paradis cabin, when he said that, his head bowed. All the years since that moment that is how he has visualised him.

And round about him on the tower are many who did not behave like he did, who did not leave home for good with their skis and abandon those left behind, to a sad loneliness.

Boys from every part of the country are standing here; young, thin, sinewy, red-cheeked or weather-beaten faces. One chap arrived here straight from the farm, another from a factory, an office, and in a few days they will be back where they came from. Another hews the cabin wall with his woodman's axe, takes a few days' time off, and the day after tomorrow he will be back at the pine tree, making the chips fly. For all these guys this trip is a jolly and refreshing diversion from work, despite having just a bit of bread and butter and a sausage in their rucksacks and not being able to afford anything but a coffee and milk at the hotel. They do not spend two or several months of the year rushing around a cross-country course, adorned with red ribbon, or travelling from ski jump to ski jump where there is music and flags and a crowd cheering them on. Their title is not merely skier, their work is not merely skiing. Skis are just a happy, exciting get-together from time to time. A wild song about young force and a healthy competitive spirit.

These boys are all around him. Young Norway with shining eyes depicted against a backdrop of a cold winter sun and brilliant snow.

But far down there, far away, lies the big town, covered in a grey, gloomy haze. That is where the heir to Kvisslo lives.

And Halstein knows that he will stay there. That is just how towns are.

"57 ready! – 58 prepare."

Halstein checks the bindings for the last time, making sure they are secure. Grabs the bottom of his sweater and pulls it down. It is nearly his turn.

"59 ready!"

He advances, to where the run-in starts to fall way. He holds on to the handrail, looks down, waiting for the signal. Ahead of him is the run-in. A long descending sweep. The tracks are clearly visible. A trail straight as an arrow. A man by the side of the jump is holding a red flag, now it is resting on the jump. And out on the lake, the dark, undulating, live forest and through the air crackling trumpet music and the trembling, indeterminable din from the crowds. They are expecting him. They look at their programmes. They are waiting for Halstein Kvisslo.

The trumpet bays, cold, unmelodious, feelingless. The pennant on the jump is raised.

He wrenches the hand away that has hold of the handrail, makes one, two, three small jerks with his skis to increase speed. Then he is off.

And he senses how the whistling around the skis increases, becomes siss, siss, siss. The air is blasting around him, hissing around him. He bends down, his eyes are following the tracks made by earlier skiers, and at the same time fastened on the jump. He sinks, sinks, ever more furiously, and the world is no more, his entire being is focused on this one thing, the take-off, stay forwards, don't fall …

Siss, siss, siss, there is no other sound in the whole world now. The din from the public is silenced. He crouches a bit – now!

The whistling under the skis ceases suddenly, the skis clear the jump.

He is floating in space…

THE FLIGHT by Dag Helleve

Dag Helleve (1951) is a Norwegian teacher and author, born and living in Voss. He is a nature conservation enthusiast and writes about music, nature and politics. His published books are both fiction and non-fiction.

There is a smell of hot dogs and mustard in the air. Lars Petter stops in front of the hot dog stand. The queue snakes around the corner. Two ten-year-olds are at the back of the queue. They jump in the air and make soft landings in the snow.

"Hi, Lars Petter. You'll beat them today, won't you?"

Lars Petter tosses his head and one of the boys comes running towards him.

"Buy me a hot dog with mustard. And keep the rest."

Lars Petter unzips his back pocket and fishes out a yellow ten-crown note which he gives the boy.

"I'll be waiting over there with the others."

The boy rejoins the queue – he's smiling.

Lars Petter saunters over to a group of three or four young boys. He lifts his ski jumping skis off his shoulder and puts them down on the snow in front of him. The others turn towards him. They all have jumping skis. One of the boys, a sturdy little chap says, "Gosh you really hit the take-off during the trial rounds. I saw the lift it gave you and yet you hung on in there right to the end. It was over the hill record."

"Yeah, but trial rounds don't count. There's no point going all out when it doesn't count." This comes from a tall, brawny youth with curly blond hair. Lars Petter never answers. He pulls his blue hat with the white band back over his neck revealing his dark hair.

"Give me a smoke." Lars Petter turns towards a wee skinny chap who is wearing the same type of sweater which Lars Petter is wearing, blue with a white neck.

"I've only got this one. The pack is in my jacket." The brawny boy smiles.

"You'll lose the little fitness you have left." Lars Petter regards him while blowing smoke rings into the air. "We'll talk after the race."

The wee scrawny chap reaches out his hand for the cigarette. "I calm myself down with a cigarette before the race. Engan did that too. I saw him once in the Balberg Hill. One cigarette before he went up to jump and five times 19 style in both rounds."

A loudspeaker scratches, and the speaker asks the athletes in the junior county championships to make their way up to the tower.

The boys lift their skis onto their shoulders and start walking up. Lars Petter is the only one who remains standing. He looks towards the hot dog stand. No boys. They must be around the corner. He approaches the hatch. He shivers. He takes out a pair of white gloves from the pocket of his blue ski pants. Closes the zip, makes a few jumps on the snow.

"Hi, aren't you going up?"

A man wearing a fur cap comes over to him. He is a celebrated former local ski jumper, and now the chairman of the jumping section in the sports club.

"You know how much today counts. County championships. The first step on the way to the top. And that's where you are heading. Don't forget. You can be two or three in a local race, but when it really counts the aim is to win, so you need to be on your way up now. Calm and concentration before you set off is all important. I know what I'm talking about, I've been there. I was always first up to the top and always first on the podium."

The boy with the hot dog comes running along. His mates are just behind him. He is out of breath.

"I just couldn't get here any quicker. The queue was so slow. And then they ran out of mustard, and only had ketchup, which I didn't want, but then they found some mustard after all."

Lars Petter is toying with the idea of taking his white gloves off but is bold enough to keep them on. He hoists the skis on to his shoulder and starts walking. He takes a bite of the hot dog. It is lukewarm.

People have started arriving. Children on toboggans. Dogs. Fur caps and mittens. Red noses and ears. Thermos flasks. Picnics with goats' cheese and mutton sausage. Lars Petter walks on up. The hill rises above him. He walks along the well-trodden path in front of the judges' tower. There they are. Five honourable men. Furnished with sharpened pencils and the judges' card. Judge Roy Bean is at the head. The hardest of them all. The poor blighter who fails to execute a Telemark on landing. Double penalty, virtually on par with a fall. Roy Bean had competed with both Falkanger and Bergmann.

Lars Petter glances up at the judges' tower. One man wearing a huge fur hat stands out from the other four. Roy Bean was given the name after he had been across the pond for a few years. Told everyone that he had been in a Western film. Played the notorious judge *Roy Bean*. He only had one comment and that was 'hang him'.

Lars Petter arrives at the steps leading to the take-off tower. Breathes heavily three times. Kicks the snow off his boots and starts the ascent. Walks slowly. Hears the familiar sound of boots on the snow-covered woodwork. Feels the faint tremor of the boards. Always notices this when a race is on. Otherwise never thinks about it.

Halfway up the stairs, on the step where there is a small hole from a knot he gouged out when he was small, he moves the skis over on to the other shoulder. Does this at the same place every time. His body feels hot. He feels his legs leading him up to the top of the tower. Sees the others swinging their arms across their chests to keep warm.

Ski jumper with bib 15 is about to set off when Lars Petter arrives. That's the Nyrud chap, alias 'The Crow'. He talks non-stop. Tries to be clever. In nine out of ten jumps Lars Petter knows that Nyrud flaps over the knoll like a crow. But the tenth time is more like the soaring of an eagle. His first-round jump was the soaring variety. In fact, he is lying in second place, followed by Jonsbråten and in front of Lars Petter.

The sound of a hoarse trumpet can be heard from the take-off point. Nyrud bends down. Fiddles with his bindings. Stares straight into the air. Lars Petter notes his white face. Then Nyrud kicks off and crouches down. Lars Petter watches him. Sees the blue-clad shape increase speed as he approaches the take-off point and launches into the air. Lars Petter hears the buzz from below. Cheering and shouts. The Crow has done it again. A monster jump, longer than the first-round jump. First time ever he has managed two during a competition. There is low murmuring from the other jumpers in the tower.

The next guy is ready. The green flag is raised. Lars Petter looks over to the hill on to the other side. Dark, heavy pine forest. Open clearings where logs have been dragged out. Below small snow-laden sheds, red barns and white farmhouses. Between forest edge and valley floor hurdles stretch out like pencil strokes.

Lars Petter lets his eyes rest on the landing area. He cannot remember ever having seen so many people. Another ski jumper disappears over the jump. Lars Petter gets ready. Puts his skis carefully down on the snow. Does not want to spoil the running surface. He waxed and dribbled a layer of Paraffin Special. He wriggles his right foot into the binding. Always starts with the right foot. Pushes the buckle down. Lifts the foot forwards. The binding functions as it should. Just tight enough. He repeats the procedure with the left foot. Breathes slowly. Feels the excitement inside. The sinking feeling. He is unaware of his surroundings. Far away he hears the crowd around the outrun. He puts on the white gloves. Checks the bindings for the last time. Straightens his hat. Two more to go and then it is his turn. The excitement inside increases. He feels the power. Knows that in a few moments he will be flying over the knoll, in the air, the highest enjoyment possible. Repeats again and again, "it is OK, it is OK."

He moves one place to the side. One to go. It's Jonsbråten. His name is called. He bends over and checks the bindings one last time. Straightens his hat. Breathes in deeply. Grabs the railing and pulls himself out. Crouches down immediately. His hands in front. Gathers speed. Tears roll down his cheeks. Stretches forward just before the take-off. The jump is approaching.

THE YOUTH OF TODAY by Johan Collet Müller Borgen

Johan Collett Müller Borgen (1902–1979) was a Norwegian author, journalist and critic. His best-known work is the novel 'Lillelord' for which he was awarded the Norwegian Critics Prize for Literature in 1955.

I still dream – with unutterable horror – of the time I jumped 17 metres on skis.

It was a sunny February day at Lille Heggehullet. The school's hierarchy had taken up their positions down the hill and the jump had been decorated with flags. The teachers exposed themselves to reduced authority by appearing in tartan pants and behaving like human beings. The sun gave me no joy, life no hope. I was standing at the top of the hill.

I did not look back at youth nor forward to old age. All I saw was the off-white lip of the jump and a sea of humanity far below. The girls' school on the other side of the road had the day off too.

A bugle call sounded from death's threshold. My stomach disappeared, I trembled all over, as cold as the snow which was about to gobble me up. I remained standing and just refused to go. Heads turned up the hill, but I remained standing. The bugle call sounded again. Where is he, why is he not coming? Next…

I started to slide helplessly downhill. With panic, I regretted my 15-year-old life which had, on the whole, been devoted to wickedness. I prayed: *If only one was sure of dying, float for a short while in space and then disappear without fear. No one would laugh then, someone in the girls' school would grieve – lower fifth.*

I still shiver while I write this. The white lip took shape. I saw the tracks leading to the jump's edge. I saw the flash from Fatty's pince-nez. Oh Fatty – I do know die Angst, die Axt, die Bank, die Angst, die Angst, die Angst…

But at the Odnes Hill, in Fluberg, two young girls jumped close to 50 metres. Nothing strange about that. That is how things are done nowadays. A young girl buckles on her skis, positions herself at the edge of a precipice and floats away, out into space. 'And then on top of that some actually land on their feet and ski on at a dizzy speed', was the comment of a Danish description talking about the Holmenkollen ski jumping competition.

Firm as a rock the young girls ski down the hill, pull up under the stands, take out the powder puff, indulge in a bit of repair work, in order to increase their loveliness – and God knows they are already lovely.

We are not ashamed. We can only claim that we are old, and times have changed. Generations follow on. We can even quote old ski legends who never jumped past 30 metres and maintain that that was not the point of skiing. The point was to get out into the great outdoors, to enjoy Mother Nature, carrying with us two sandwiches, one with ham and the other with cheese.

And with the calmness afforded by that acknowledgment, we slowly glide through the beautiful scenery, and take great pleasure therein. But it was a dream to float through space and in a flash see mountain ridge behind mountain ridge, distant forests and fields. Young girls experience that nowadays.

CHAPTER 7
MÜRREN

INTRODUCTION by Ingrid Christophersen

The next two stories are about Mürren. Why Mürren? Surely, Wengen, on the other side of the Lauterbrunnen valley is more attractive, has better ski runs and is host to the world famous Lauberhorn race, which at 4.5 km, is the longest and most demanding downhill course on the World Cup circuit? And Wengen is the home of the DHO – Downhill Only Ski Club, founded in 1925. My club. Alas, the Kandahar Ski Club in Mürren is one year older, founded in 1924. In February 1925, British skiers in Mürren came over to visit the British skiers in Wengen. They were challenged to a ski race. Wengen already had the cog railway to Scheidegg, could ascend in comfort and descend at their leisure. No such uphill transport existed in Mürren. The Wengen Brits hastily concocted some paper bibs, DHO written large with a little man on skis, displayed prominently on their chest, and up they all went to Scheidegg. If the Kandahar had won the race I would have told you, but I honestly do not know!

The first story is one of Ian Fleming's most famous James Bond thrillers. In the book, the action actually takes place in and around St.Moritz, but the film was shot in Mürren and Lauterbrunnen and the Schilthorn is universally known as 'Piz Gloria'. I was an extra in this film, great fun, but no credits! The annual Inferno race starts just below the summit of the Schilthorn. This is the race Christopher Matthews so thrillingly writes about in 'The Amber Room', the second story in this section.

ON HER MAJESTY'S SECRET SERVICE by Ian Fleming

Ian Lancaster Fleming (1908–1964) was an English author, journalist and naval intelligence officer.

There are currently 39 officially licensed James Bond books authored by six writers since 1953. The first and most famous 14 were written by Ian Fleming, spawning worldwide Bond media, including films, comic strips, comic books, and video games. The excerpts below are from 'On Her Majesty's Secret Service' and the film based on the book was filmed in Mürren and Lauterbrunnen.

The telephone on the desk buzzed like a trapped wasp. Bond looked at it. He picked up the receiver and spoke through the handkerchief across his mouth.

'Ja?'

'Alles in Ordnung?'

'Ja—'

'Also hör zu! Wir kommen fur den Engländer in zehn Minuten. Verstanden?'

'Is' recht.'

'Also, aufpassen. Ja?'

'Zu Befehl!'

At the other end the receiver went down. The sweat was beading on Bond's face. Thank God he had answered! So, they were coming for him in ten minutes! There was a bunch of keys on the desk. Bond snatched them up and ran to the front door. After three misfits, he had the right one. He tried the door. It was now only held by its air-pressure device. Bond leaped for the ski-room. Unlocked! He went in and, by the light from the reception room, found his skis. There were sticks beside them. Carefully he lifted everything out of its wooden slot and strode to the main door and opened it. He laid the skis and sticks softly down in the snow, turned back to the door, locked it from the outside, and threw the keys far away into the snow.

The three-quarter moon burned down with an almost dazzling fire and the snow crystals scintillated back at it like a carpet of diamond dust. Now minutes would have to be wasted getting the bindings absolutely right. James Bond kicked one boot into the groove of the Marker toehold and knelt down, feeling for the steel cable that went behind his heel. It was too short. Coolly, unhurriedly, he adjusted the regulating screw on the forward latch and tried again. This time it was all right. He pressed down on the safety latch and felt it lock his boot into the toehold. Next, the safety thong round the top of his boot that would keep the ski prisoner if the latch sprang, which it would do with a fall. His fingers were beginning to freeze. The tip of the thong refused to find its buckle! A full minute wasted! Got it!

And now the same job on the other ski. At last Bond stood up, slipped the gloves over his aching fingers, picked up the lance-like sticks, and pushed himself off along the faint ridge that showed the outlines of yesterday's well-trodden path. It felt all right! He pulled the goggles down over his eyes and now the vast snowscape was a silvery green as if he was swimming under sunny water. The skis hissed smoothly through the powder snow. Bond tried to get up more speed down the gentle slope by langlaufing, the sliding, forward stride of the first Norwegian skiers. But it didn't work.

The heels of his boots felt nailed to the skis. He punted himself forward as fast as he could with his sticks. God, what a trail he must be leaving – like a tramline! As soon as they got the front door open, they would be after him. Their fastest guide would certainly catch him easily unless he got a good start! Every minute, every second was a bonus. He passed between the black outlines of the cable head and the Berghaus. There was the starting point of the Gloria Run, the metal notices beside it hatted with snow! Bond didn't pause. He went straight for it and over the edge.

The first vertical drop had a spine-chilling bliss to it. Bond got down into his old Arlberg crouch, his hands forward of his boots, and just let himself go. His skis were an ugly six inches apart. The Kannonen he had watched had gone down with their boots locked together, as if on a single ski. But this was no time for style, even if he had been capable of it! Above all he must stay upright!

Bond's speed was now frightening. But the deep cushion of cold, light powder snow gave him the confidence to try a parallel swing. Minimum of shoulder turn needed at this speed – weight on to the left ski – and he came round and held it as the right-hand edges of his skis bit against the slope, throwing up a shower of moon-lit snow crystals.

Danger was momentarily forgotten in the joy of speed, technique, and mastery of the snow. Bond straightened up and almost dived into his next turn, this time to the left, leaving a broad S on the virgin mountain behind him. Now he could afford to schuss the rest down to the hard left-hand turn round the shoulder. He pointed his skis down and felt real rapture as, like a black bullet on the giant slope, he zoomed down the 45-degree drop. Now for the left-hand corner. There was the group of three flags, black, red, and yellow, hanging limply, their colours confused by the moonlight! He would have to stop there and take a recce over the next lap. There was a slight upward slope short of the big turn. Bond took it at speed, felt his skis leave the ground at the crest of it, jabbed into the snow with his left stick as an extra lever and threw his skis and his right shoulder and hips round to the left. He landed in a spray of snow, at a dead halt. He was delighted with himself! A Sprung-Christiana is a showy and not an easy turn at speed. He wished his old teacher, Fuchs, had been there to see that one!

He was now on the shoulder of the mountain. High overhead the silver strands of the cable railway plunged downwards in one great swoop towards the distant black line of the trees, where the moonlight glinted on a spidery pylon. Bond remembered that there now followed a series of great zigs and zags more or less beneath the cables. With the piste unobscured, it would have been easy, but the new snow made every descent look desirable. Bond jerked up his goggles to see if he could spot a flag. Yes, there was one away down to the left. He would do some S turns down the next slope and then make for it.

As he pulled down his goggles and gripped his sticks, two things happened. First there came a deep boom from high up the mountain, and a speck of flame, that wobbled in its flight, soared into the sky above him. There was a pause at the top of its parabola, a sharp crack, and a blazing magnesium flare on a parachute began its wandering descent, wiping out the black shadows in the hollows, turning everything into a hideous daylight. Another and another sprayed out across the sky, lighting every cranny over the mountainside. And, at the same time, the cables high above Bond's head began to sing! They were sending the cable car down after him!

Bond cursed into the sodden folds of his silk handkerchief and got going. The next thing would be a man after him – probably a man with a gun! He took the second lap more carefully than the first, got across to the second flag, turned at it and made back across the plunging slope for the series of linked Ss under the cables. How fast did these bloody gondolas go? Ten, fifteen, twenty miles an hour? This was the latest type. It would be the fastest. Hadn't he read somewhere that the one between Arosa and the Weisshorn did 25? Even as he got into his first S, the tune of the singing cable above him momentarily changed and then went back to its usual whine. That was the gondola passing the first pylon! Bond's knees, the Achilles heel of all skiers, were beginning to ache. He cut his Ss narrower, snaking down faster, but now feeling the rutted tracks of the piste under his skis at every turn. Was that a flag away over to the left? The magnesium flares were swaying lower, almost directly over him. Yes. It looked all right. Two more S turns and he would do a traverse schuss to it!

Something landed with a tremendous crack amidst a fountain of snow to his right! Another to his left! They had a grenade-thrower up front in the cable car! A bracket! Would the next one be dead on? Almost before the thought flashed through his mind, there came a tremendous explosion just ahead of him and he was hurled forward and sideways in a Catherine wheel of sticks and skis.

Bond got gingerly to his feet, gasping and spitting snow. One of his bindings had opened. His trembling fingers found the forward latch and banged it tight again. Another sharp crack, but wide by twenty yards. He must get away from the line of fire from the blasted railway! Feverishly he thought, the left-hand flag! I must do the traverse now. He took a vague bearing across the precipitous slope and flung himself down it.

It was tricky, undulating ground. The magnesium flares had sailed lower and there were ugly patches of black shadow, any of which might have been a small ravine. Bond had to check all of them and each time the sharp Christie reminded him of his legs and ankles. But he got across without a fall and pulled up at the flag, panting.

He looked back. The gondola had stopped. They had telephone communication with the top and bottom stations, but why had it stopped? As if in answer, blue flames fluttered gaily from the forward cabin. But Bond heard no bullets. The gondola would be swaying on its cable. But then, high up above him, from somewhere near the first flags on the shoulder, came more rapid fire, from two points, and the snow kicked up daintily around him. So, the guides had finally got after him! His fall would have cost him minutes. How much lead had he got? Certainly, less than ten minutes. A bullet whanged into one of his skis and sang off down the mountain. Bond took a last gulp of breath and got going again, still left-handed, away from the cable railway, towards the next flag, a distant dot on the edge of the shadow thrown by the great Matterhorn-shaped peak of Piz Gloria, which knifed up into the spangled sky in dreadful majesty.

It looked as if the run was going to take him dangerously close to the skirts of the peak. Something was nagging at his mind, a tiny memory. What was it? It was something unpleasant. Yes, by God! The last flag! It had been black. He was on the Black Run, the one closed because of avalanche danger! God! Well, he'd had it now. No time to try and get back on the Red Run. And anyway, the Red had a long stretch close to the cables. He'd just have to chance it. And what a time to chance it, just after a heavy fall of new snow, and with all these detonations to loosen up the stuff! When there was danger of an avalanche, guides forbade even speech! Well, to hell with it! Bond zoomed on across the great unmarked slope, got to the next flag, spotted the next, away down the mountain side towards the tree line. Too steep to schuss! He would just have to do it in Ss.

And then the bastards chose to fire off three more flares followed by a stream of miscellaneous rockets that burst prettily among the stars. Of course! Bright idea! This was for the sake of watchers in the valley who might be inquisitive about the mysterious explosions high up the mountain. They were having a party up there, celebrating something. What fun these rich folks had, to be sure! And then Bond remembered. But of course! It was Christmas Eve! God rest ye merry gentlemen, let nothing ye dismay! Bond's skis hissed an accompaniment as he zigzagged fast down the beautiful snow slope. White Christmas! Well, he'd certainly got himself that!

But then, from high up above him, he heard that most dreaded of all sounds in the high Alps, that rending, booming crack! The Last Trump! Avalanche!

The ground shook violently under Bond's skis and the swelling rumble came down to him like the noise of express trains roaring through a hundred tunnels. God Almighty, now he really had had it! What was the rule? Point the skis straight downhill! Try and race it! Bond pointed his skis down towards the tree line, got down in his ugly crouch and shot, his skis screaming, into white space.

Keep forward, you bastard! Get your hands way in front of you! The wind of his speed was building up into a great wall in front of him, trying to knock him off balance. Behind him the giant roar of the mountain seemed to be gaining.

Other, smaller cracks sounded high up among the crags. The whole bloody mountain was on the move! If he beat the gigantic mass of hurtling snow to the tree line, what comfort would he find there? Certainly, no protection until he was deep in the wood. The avalanche would snap perhaps the first hundred yards of firs down like matchsticks. Bond used his brain and veered slightly left-handed. The opening, the glade cut for the Black Run, would surely be somewhere below the last flag he had been aiming for. If it wasn't, he was a dead duck!

Now the wild schuss was coming to an end. The trees were rushing towards him. Was there a break in the bloody black line of them? Yes! But more to the left. Bond veered, dropping his speed, gratefully, but with his ears strained to gauge the range of the thunder behind and above him. It couldn't be far from him. The shudder in the ground had greatly increased and a lot of the stuff would also find the hole through the trees, funnel itself in and pursue him even down there! Yes! There was the flag! Bond hurtled into a right-hand Christie just as, to his left, he heard the first trees come crashing down with the noise of a hundred monster crackers being pulled – Christmas crackers! Bond flung himself straight down the wide white glade between the trees. But he could hear that he was losing! The crashing of the trees was coming closer. The first froth of the white tide couldn't be far behind his heels! What did one do when the avalanche hit? There was only one rule. Get your hands to your boots and grip your ankles. Then, if you were buried, there was some hope of undoing your skis, being able, perhaps, to burrow your way to the surface – if you knew in your tomb where the surface lay! If you couldn't go down like a ball, you would end up immovable, a buried tangle of sticks and skis at all angles. Thank God the opening at the end of the glade, the shimmer of the last, easily sloping fields before the finish, was showing up! The crackling roar behind him was getting louder! How high would the wall of snow be? Fifty feet? A hundred? Bond reached the end of the glade and hurled himself into a right-hand Christie. It was his last hope, to get below the wide belt of trees and pray that the avalanche wouldn't mow down the lot of them. To stay in the path of the roaring monster at his heels would be suicide!

The Christie came off, but Bond's right ski snarled a root or a sapling and he felt himself flying through space. He landed with a crash and lay gasping, all the wind knocked out of him. Now he was done for!

Not even enough strength to get his hands to his ankles! A tremendous buffet of wind hit him and a small snowstorm covered him. The ground shook wildly and a deep crashing roar filled his ears. And then it had passed him and given way to a slow, heavy rumble. Bond brushed the snow out of his eyes and got unsteadily to his feet, both skis loose, his goggles gone. Only a cricket pitch away, a great torrent of snow, perhaps twenty feet high, was majestically pouring out of the wood and down into the meadows. Its much higher, tumbling snout, tossing huge crags of broken snow around it, was already a hundred yards ahead and still going fast. But, where Bond stood, it was now silent and peaceful except for the machine gun fire crackling of the trees as they went down in the wood that had finally protected him. The crackling was getting nearer! No time to hang about! But Bond took off one sodden glove and dug into his trouser pocket. If ever he needed a drink it was now! He tilted the little flask down his throat, emptied it, and threw the bottle away. Happy Christmas! he said to himself and bent to his bindings.

He got to his feet and, rather light-headed but with the wonderful glow of the Enzian in his stomach, started on the last mile of finishing schuss across the meadows to the right, away from the still hurtling river of snow. Blast! There was a fence across the bottom of the meadows! He would have to take the normal outlet for the runs beside the cable station.

It looked all right. There was no sign of the gondola, but he could now hear the song of the cables. Had the downcoming car reversed back up to Piz Gloria, assuming him to have been killed by the avalanche? There was a large black saloon car in the forecourt to the cable station, and lights on in the station, but otherwise no sign of life. Well, it was his only way to get off the run and on to the road that was his objective. Bond schussed easily downwards, resting his limbs, getting his breath back.

The sharp crack of a heavy-calibre pistol and the phut as the bullet hit the snow beside him pulled him together. He jinked sideways and glanced quickly up to the right, where the shot had come from. The gun blazed again. A man on skis was coming fast after him. One of the guides! Of course!

He would have taken the Red Run. Had the other followed Bond on the Black? Bond hoped so, gave a deep sigh of anger, and put on all the speed he could, crouching low and jinking occasionally to spoil the man's aim. The single shots kept on coming. It was going to be a narrow shave who got to the end of the run first!

Bond studied the finishing point that was now coming at him fast. There was a wide break in the fence to let the skiers through, a large parking place in front of the cable station, and then the low embankment that protected the main line of the Rhätische Bahn up to Pontresina and the Bernina Pass.

On the other side of the rails the railway embankment dropped into the road from Pontresina to Samaden, the junction for St Moritz, perhaps two miles down the valley. Another shot kicked up the snow in front of him. That was six that had gone. With any luck the man's pistol was empty. But that wouldn't help much. There was no stuffing left in Bond for a fight.

Now a great blaze of light showed coming up the railway line, and, before it was hidden by the cable station, Bond identified an express and could just hear the thudding of its electro-diesels. By God, it would just about be passing the cable station as he wanted to get across the track! Could he make it – take a run at the low embankment and clear it and the lines before the train got there? It was his only hope!

Bond dug in with his sticks to get on extra speed. Hell! A man had got out of the black car and was crouching, aiming at him. Bond jinked and jinked again as fire bloomed from the man's hand. But now Bond was on top of him. He thrust hard with the rapier point of a ski-stick and felt it go through clothing. The man gave a scream and went down. The guide, now only yards behind, yelled something. The great yellow eye of the diesel glared down the tracks, and Bond caught a sideways glimpse of a huge red snow-fan below the headlight that was fountaining the new snow to right and left of the engine in two white wings. Now! He flashed across the parking place, heading straight at the mound of the embankment and as he hit, dug both his sticks in to get his skis off the ground, and hurled himself forward into the air. There was a brief glimpse of steel rails below, a tremendous thudding in his ears, and a ferocious blast, only yards away, from the train's siren. Then he crashed on to the icy road, tried to stop, failed, and fetched up in an almighty skid against the hard snow wall on the other side. As he did so, there came a terrible scream from behind him, a loud splintering of wood, and the screech of the train's brakes being applied.

At the same time, the spray from the snow-fan, that had now reached Bond, turned pink! Bond wiped some of it off his face and looked at it. His stomach turned. God! The man had tried to follow him, had been too late or had missed his jump and had been caught by the murderous blades of the snow-fan! Mincemeat! Bond dug a handful of snow off the bank and wiped it over his face and hair. He rubbed more of it down his sweater. He suddenly realised that people were pulling down the windows in the brilliantly lit train above him. Others had got down on the line. Bond pulled himself together and punted off down the black ice of the road. Shouts followed him – the angry bawls of Swiss citizens. Bond edged his skis a little against the camber of the road and kept going. Ahead of him, down the black gulch of the road, in his mind's eye, the huge red propeller whirred, sucking him into its steel whirlpool. Bond, close to delirium, slithered on towards its bloody, beckoning vortex.

Bond, a grey-faced, lunging automaton, somehow stayed upright on the two miles of treacherous Langlauf down the gentle slope to Samaden. Once a passing car, its snow-chains clattering, forced him into the bank. He leaned against the comforting soft snow for a moment, the breath sobbing in his throat. Then he drove himself on again. He had got so far, done so well! Only a few more hundred yards to the lights of the darling, straggling little paradise of people and shelter!

The slender campanile of the village church was floodlit and there was a great warm lake of light on the left of the twinkling group of houses. The strains of a waltz came over the still, frozen air. The skating-rink! A Christmas Eve skaters' ball. That was the place for him! Crowds! Gaiety! Confusion!

Somewhere to lose himself from the double hunt that would now be on – by SPECTRE and the Swiss police, the cops and the robbers hand in hand!

Bond's skis hit a pile of horse's dung from some merry-maker's sleigh. He lurched drunkenly into the snow wall of the road and righted himself, cursing feebly. Come on! Pull yourself together! Look respectable! Well, you needn't look too respectable. After all, it's Christmas Eve. Here were the first houses. The noise of accordion music, deliciously nostalgic, came from a Gasthaus with a beautiful iron sign over its door. Now there was a twisty, uphill bit – the road to St Moritz. Bond shuffled up it, placing his sticks carefully. He ran a hand through his matted hair and pulled the sweat-soaked handkerchief down to his neck, tucking the ends into his shirt collar. The music lilted down towards him from the great pool of light over the skating rink. Bond pulled himself a little more upright. There were a lot of cars drawn up, skis stuck in mounds of snow, luges and toboggans, festoons of paper streamers, a big notice in three languages across the entrance: 'Grand Christmas Eve Ball! Fancy Dress! Entrance 2 Francs! Bring all your friends! Hooray!'

Bond dug in his sticks and bent down to unlatch his skis. He fell over sideways. If only he could just lie there, go to sleep on the hard, trodden snow that felt like swansdown! He gave a small groan and heaved himself gingerly into a crouch. The bindings were frozen solid, caked, like his boots, with ice. He got one of his sticks and hacked feebly at the metal and tried again. At last the latches sprang and the thongs were off. Where to put the bloody things, hide their brilliant red markings? He lugged them down the trodden path towards the entrance, gay with fairy lights, shoved the skis and the sticks under a big saloon car, and staggered on.

The man at the ticket table was as drunk as Bond seemed. He looked up blearily: 'Zwo Franken. Two francs. Deux francs.' The routine incantation was slurred into one portmanteau word. Bond held on to the table, put down the coins, and got his ticket. The man's eyes focused. 'The fancy dress, the travesty, it is obligatoire.' He reached into a box by his side and threw a black and white domino-mask on the table. 'One franc.' He gave a lop-sided smile. 'Now you are the gangster, the spy. Yes?' 'Yeah, that's right.' Bond paid and put on the mask.

He reluctantly let go of the table and wove through the entrance. There were raised tiers of wooden benches round the big square rink. Thank God for a chance to sit down. There was an empty seat on the aisle in the bottom row at rink level. Bond stumbled down the wooden steps and fell into it. He righted himself, said 'Sorry,' and put his head in his hands. The girl beside him, part of a group of harlequins, Wild Westerners, and pirates, drew her spangled skirt away, whispered something to her neighbour. Bond didn't care. They wouldn't throw him out on a night like this. Through the loudspeakers the violins sobbed into 'The Skaters' Waltz'. Above them the voice of the MC called, 'Last dance, ladies and gentlemen. And then all out on to the rink and join hands for the grand finale. Only ten minutes to go to midnight! Last dance, ladies and gentlemen. Last dance!' There was a rattle of applause. People laughed excitedly. God in Heaven! thought Bond feebly. Now this! Won't anybody leave me alone? He fell asleep.

THE AMBER ROOM by Christopher Matthew

Christopher Charles Forrest Matthew (1939) is a British writer and broadcaster. He is the author of 'Now We Are Sixty', inspired by the poems of A. A. Milne in the book 'Now We Are Six', and the chronicler of the life and times of the hapless hero, Simon Crisp, in 'Diary of a Somebody'. After Oxford he taught in a girls' finishing school in Switzerland and worked as an advertising copywriter before becoming a full-time writer in 1970.

The Diabolo race described here is of course the Inferno in Mürren which Matthews clearly knows well. Start at Schilthorn 2970m. Finish line Lauterbrunnen 800m. Difference in Altitude 2170m. Length of course 14.9 km. The Inferno was organised for the first time in 1928 by a group of 'ski-crazy' Brits. Today it is the largest amateur ski race in the world.

"Come on!"

Miles grabbed her arm for a second time and the three of them stumbled towards the tunnel. They were almost at the entrance when there was a cry from Anna as she slipped on a patch of ice and fell heavily. Miles turned and started to haul her to her feet.

Gunfire echoed once more through the cave. Bullets cracked and smacked and zinged off the rocks like a swarm of mad maybugs. At first Miles couldn't make out where they were coming from. Then he saw him. He was standing, silhouetted in the doorway of the Room, his blond hair orange under the flames, legs bent, ski-suited body crouched as he steadied the gun in both hands.

"Charlie Bishop!" shouted Miles. "He's got Alex's gun! Come on, move!"

They had a twenty second start on him, if that.

The first stretch was short and they were round the left-hand bend and out of sight in no time. But from then on, the tunnel ran straight most of the way until it curved round to the right again and into the home stretch. The lighting, though adequate for their purposes, was far from ideal for someone trying to hit a moving target at over a hundred feet with an automatic weapon.

"When we get round the bend, don't run in a straight line," Miles told them. "Keep zigzagging. And keep low. And for Christ's sake, keep going!"

There was no sign of Bishop by the time they reached the end of the straight section. Perhaps something had happened to him in the cave: someone had tried to stop him, or he'd gone back to help or he'd slipped on the ice. Ducking low, they rounded the bend. Miles was afraid the fireplace might have closed after they'd gone.

He'd never been so glad to see light at the end of a tunnel.

They made their way cautiously into the clubhouse, but it was as silent and deserted as when they'd left it. Miles tried to swing the fireplace shut, but it seemed to be locked open. If there was a release lever, they didn't have time to look for it now.

Anna and Andrew were already out on the terrace, blinking against the unaccustomed glare. Miles ran out and slammed the door behind him. He grabbed the end of one of the heavy tables and pulled it across the doorway.

"Now what?" Anna asked.

"Andrew, you run like hell to the cable car. Go straight to Willi Graf's and wait for us there. Go!"

Andrew grabbed the hand rails beside the steps, swung himself down on to the snow and disappeared out of sight round the side of the building.

"Us?" said Anna. "What are we going to do?"

"Put your boots on! Quick!"

They were next to the door where Charlie had put them, hinged wide open like baby birds waiting to be fed. Their helmets lay beside them.

"Why?"

"Do as I say. And your helmet."

It took only a few seconds to kick off their moccasins, step into their Raichles and snap them shut.

"Come on! The skis are just down here." Miles grabbed her hand and pulled her towards the steps.

"But the Totenkopf run starts from way over there. We'll never get there in time." She pointed across the hillside to where the figure of Andrew could be seen scrambling his way along the path towards the cable car.

"Who said anything about the Totenkopf?" said Miles.

It suddenly dawned on her what he was saying. "The Diabolo? You must be joking."

"We don't have to go down it," he said. "Just pretend. We'll ski down to the start and mingle with the crowd. Bishop'll never recognise us in our helmets and goggles. With our numbers we'll look just like any other racers. Come on! Let's go!" They stumbled down the steps, threw their skis flat on the ground and stamped into them. They pulled their goggles down and looked round for their poles.

"Gloves," said Anna. "Damn! They must be still in the clubhouse. Never mind."

Miles grabbed his poles, pushed his hand through the straps, jumped his skis round and pushed off. Anna was only seconds behind. There was a large crowd milling around near the start. Some were doing last-minute exercises: deep knee bends, swivelling their trunks with a pole held behind their necks, lifting their legs up and down. Others were crouching, eyes shut, hands moving in front of their faces as they travelled the course in their imaginations. Most were just standing about, shuffling their skis on the snow, waiting for the starter to announce their number over the tannoy.

Miles looked back up the hill. Bishop was already out on the terrace, grasping the rail and scanning the slopes.

"He's up there," said Miles. "Follow me! Don't look round!"

Taking care not to tread on other people's skis, they manoeuvered their way through the crowd until they found a small space near the announcer's table. Miles glanced up. Bishop was still there. Then people started stumbling out on to the terrace behind him – in ones and twos at first, but then in a steady stream. Soon there were dozens of them out there, hands on knees, coughing and gulping in mouthfuls of fresh air.

"Why should he want to kill us?" Anna said. "We're not the ones who killed his brother or set fire to the Room. What's the point? It's all over."

"In Bishop's mind, we're as guilty as Alex. If it hadn't been for us, Alex would never have found the Room. God knows how many millions this'll cost the movement. And, of course, Bishop knows perfectly well that the first thing I'll do when I get to a telephone is to ring my newspaper. If I were him. I'd want to kill me."

"*Fünf..vier…drei…zwei…eins…los!*"

With a shout of encouragement from the waiting competitors and a clang of cowbells, the next pair set off down the first straight.

The tannoy crackled: '*Achthundertundzwanzig. Achthunderteinundzwanzig.*"

"Eight twenty and eight twenty-one," said Anna. "Four more to go till they get to us. What are we going to do?"

"I'll go and tell them we're not feeling well. Stay here."

"Hurry!" She looked nervously up at the terrace. "Miles, wait! He's not there!"

"What?"

"He's not on the terrace anymore. He's disappeared!"

"He's probably gone inside. Perhaps he's gone back to help people out of the tunnel. Stop worrying. We're safe as long as we stay here."

"What if he's gone after Andrew?"

"He won't have."

"How do you know?"

"It's us he's after. He wouldn't know Andrew if he saw him."

"*Achthundert und zweiundzwanzig. Achthundertunddreiundzwanzig.*"

"English bastard!"

The German racer loomed out of the crowd, blue eyes blazing, jaw thrust forward, closely followed by his tall, blonde companion. He seemed to have acquired another pair of skis since their last meeting, though not a new race number.

"Saved by the bell!" said Miles.

He had untied the tapes at his side and almost had the thing over his head when the man grabbed him by the front of his anorak.

"Wait! I'm just giving it to you, you silly sod," Miles told him.

"My ski!" the man shouted. "You pay!"

"Oh, for God's sake!" snapped Miles. "You've got insurance cover, haven't you?"

"*Achthundertundvierundzwanzig. Achthundertundfünfundzwanzig.*"

"Look, I'll sort it out with you later," said Miles. "Take the numbers and go. You'll miss your turn."

"Miles!"

"What?"

"He's coming!"

"Who?"

"Charlie Bishop!"

"Oh, for God's sake! Let go of me, you stupid man! Take your bloody numbers and go! Go on! Go away!"

"He's on skis!"

"What the hell's he doing on skis?"

"Skiing. What do you think?"

"I meant..."

"You pay!" the man roared again. "My ski! Very expensive!"

"He's coming this way."

"Stand still! Don't move!"

"For God's sake, Miles!"

"*Achthundertundsechsundzwanzig. Achthundertundsiebenundzwanzig.*"

"Those are our numbers," Anna wailed.

"Go and tell them we've scratched," Miles told her.

Anna began to push her way towards the starting officials. The German assumed the worst.

"But that is my wife's number! She cannot race!"

"She's not racing. Don't you understand?" Miles shouted at him. "Neither of us is. She's just going to tell them. Take your number and go, for God's sake, or you'll miss your turn!"

But the man's English wasn't up to all that detailed explanation. As far as he understood the situation, he'd been pushed out of the race; on top of which he'd lost a ski and there was no doubt in his mind who was going to pay for it all.

Holding Miles's anorak with one huge fist, he brought the other back and swung. Miles saw it coming a mile off and ducked. He didn't have time to let go of his poles, so he put a left and a right into the man's stomach while still holding them. The effect was extremely satisfying.

The man doubled up, winded.

His wife ran forward and put an arm round him. She looked up at Miles, her face drawn with hatred.

"English bastard!" she screamed.

Miles looked across at Charlie Bishop. He was standing at the edge of the crowd, peering across at the absurd little drama that was being played out near the starting gate. He started to push his way towards them.

"Come on, Anna. Quick, quick!"

"Where?"

"They've called our number!"

"We can't possibly!" she said.

"We've got to!" said Miles.

"I don't believe this is happening!" said Anna, as she slid after him.

Somehow, they managed to scramble through the gap in the ropes in time and into the starting stalls.

"*Fünf...vier...drei...zwei...eins...los!*"

"Ski in my tracks," Miles called out to her as they came out of the gate. "Make the same turns I make. I won't go too fast. You won't come to any harm."

"English bastard!"

The roar followed them down the valley, like the frustrated bellow of a mythical monster when a victim escapes its clutches.

The 'Diabolo' course begins easily enough with a long, straight schuss, followed by a high-banked, left-hand turn leading out on to a wide, steep valley. An expert would take it straight, but it allows the amateur plenty of room for short, swinging turns down the fall-line.

Miles hadn't put on skis since the day of the avalanche, and Anna looked rusty too, but the snow at the top was soft and lightly pisted, flattering their techniques and making every turn a pleasure: especially so, given the numbers of spectators in their big scarves and heavy overcoats and fur-lined boots who watched them from behind the orange ropes at the top.

Having negotiated the steep face of the valley, Miles checked and slowed and called over his shoulder. "You all right?"

"Fine," she shouted. "Except I can't feel my hands."

"They'll warm up."

"I hope I do."

She had nothing to apologise for. Miles wished now he hadn't said anything about following in his tracks. She was perfectly capable of making her own.

The bottom of the valley gradually levelled out and the course swung in a big, gentle S before straightening out into another long schuss down to a narrow path that curved to the right, following the contour of the hill. The two skiers ahead of them looked like insects crossing a white eiderdown.

As he carved his way round the first bend of the S, Miles looked back up the valley, expecting to see the next pair behind them, crossing the ridge. As amateurs who hadn't even entered, they were both skiing strongly and well; but the Diabolo traditionally attracted a large, daredevil element that only slowed and turned when it was absolutely necessary, and if he was going to be overtaken by a couple of local speed merchants Miles wanted to be prepared for it. It didn't surprise him, then, to see that the first one to come over the top was taking the valley straight. The odd thing was that there was only one.

"What is it?" Anna called out.

"Nothing," Miles called back. "We're doing well."

He looked up again as he swung right. The solitary skier was in a low crouching position, with both poles tucked under his armpits, and moving very fast. He straightened slightly and Miles recognised the pale, blue ski suit. It wasn't carrying a race number.

"He's right behind us!" Miles shouted, "We're going to have to get moving!"

"Well, move then!" Anna shouted back.

Miles tucked low. The K2's reputation for gliding was well deserved. The schuss was pretty badly rutted by this stage in the race and Miles was wary of catching an edge. Yet the skis moved beautifully over the uneven surface and held their line effortlessly the whole way, barely slowing when the path rose slightly at the end.

"We can probably stay ahead of him if we keep this up."

They were both breathing hard by the time they'd skated across the little col where the Schwarzegg run joins from the right, and Miles's thigh muscles were beginning to feel the strain. He'd also lost all feeling in his hands. His palms looked like two slices of raw meat. He'd have given anything to stop for a moment to ease the burning in his legs and rub some circulation back into his hands. He looked across at Anna but she showed no signs of flagging.

"Are you all right?" he called back.

"You don't have to keep asking!" she yelled.

Hundreds of spectators lined the hill below the Schwarzegg lift. None of them could possibly have known that, of the fifteen hundred skiers who were to barrel past them that morning, there were two who were skiing, literally, for their lives. One careless slip, one badly caught edge, one moment off-balance and it would be the last run of the day. Or any other day.

From here, the Diabolo course followed the long traverse above the Stockli drag lift that led to the Gun Barrel. Miles remembered it very well. It was the way he had come down from Pauli's restaurant that afternoon. He was hardly likely to forget it. More of a worry to him now, though, was the fact that ahead was the longest stretch of the course that was out of the range of spectators. If Bishop caught up with them here...

Glancing over his shoulder, it looked to Miles as if they had made up a bit of ground since the bottom of the valley. They had almost reached the end of the traverse by the time Bishop crossed the col.

"We're doing fine," Miles shouted as they powered their way through the half-powder, half-cut-piste of the Lion's Teeth Ridge.

The entrance to the Gun Barrel came quicker than he had expected. He remembered there was a bend to the right at the top of the steep path that zigzagged down below the pass, but he had been skiing well within himself that afternoon. Today, there was a certain degree of recklessness in his skiing, engendered by a euphoric, and quite unjustified, feeling of invulnerability. Experience should have taught him to recognise the danger signs.

The bend took him completely by surprise. He saw the little row of flags. He checked hard, throwing a cloud of snow out over the valley, but he'd left it just too late. The momentum threw him sideways. He fought desperately to recover his balance, swayed a couple of times and then toppled headfirst over the edge.

The slope below was only a few degrees off the vertical. He threw his arms out in front of him, but there was no way he could stop himself sliding towards the path thirty feet below. He tried to swing his legs round in the hope of getting some purchase with his skis, but they had become tangled, and in that position there was nothing he could do about it. It was a situation in which he knew only too well that anything can happen. If his bindings didn't come undone soon, he'd be lucky to get out with anything less than a twisted knee. The new snow helped to slow his progress but even so, he was bound to come down hard on the path, and his wrists and arms were going to take the brunt of the impact.

He was almost on top of the path when he felt the bindings release. Miraculously, both feet came out at the same time. He jammed the balls of his hands deep into the snow and at the same time threw the lower part of his body sideways and downwards. The path rushed up to meet him.

"Hell's bloody teeth!" he shouted.

He wasn't in a completely upright position when he met the path, but he was upright enough to be able to use his knees to absorb most of the shock before pitching sideways into the soft snow at the side. He lay there for a moment, dazed and winded. He could hear Anna's voice calling down.

"Are you all right?"

"Fine," he groaned.

Seconds later she was bending over him anxiously.

"I'm all right, honestly," he said. "Where are the skis?"

They had come to rest, tips down, in the soft snow just above the path. Using their poles, they managed to hook them out and drag them down on to the path. Miles brushed the bindings clean and placing one hand on Anna's shoulder, banged the snow from his boots. They were seconds well spent. He couldn't risk them releasing in the middle of a turn further down.

Anna led the way down the hairpins. Though still very shaky, he managed to make the turns without mishap. Soon the rhythm started to return and the speed built up again. Check, compression, extension, and round. Check, compression, extension, and round. Even so, it came as no surprise that, by the time they'd reached the last bend and the safety of the open gully that led to the Blumen Saddle, Bishop was already halfway down the hairpins.

The Diabolo is one of only two downhill races in the world that include a section of uphill skiing, and the scramble over the Saddle tests tired leg muscles more than anything else on the course.

Bishop was schussing fast down the gully as they herring-boned the last few steps to the ridge. But he was no longer crouching with his ski poles under his armpits: he was skiing upright and trailing both poles in his left hand. In his right was the Stechkin.

Out of doors it hardly made any sound at all, and if it hadn't been for the puffs of snow around their heels, they might not even have realised that he was firing it.

"Christ!" croaked Miles through a throat that ached from hard breathing. "We're like sitting ducks up here!"

"Why didn't we take the Blumen run? The village is only two minutes from here."

"He'd have seen us," said Miles. "We've got to go on a bit. Find a place where we'll be out of sight and our tracks won't be spotted. There are woods just below Niederwald. We'll try and lose him there." The thought had not escaped his mind that the last time he had strayed from a marked piste and tried to beat his own path home it had ended in disaster. Nor that there was a good outside chance that it might happen again, and that this time there would be no last minute reprieve.

A long easy traverse took them to a point halfway down the Niederwald run. Cheered on by a sprinkling of spectators they carved a couple of long turns down the prettiest section of the blue run, then swung right, took the short, knee-pounding bumps of Molly's Meadow pretty well straight and, after dodging through a narrow strip of wood, emerged next to the Eigerhubel-Grützi railway line.

Now the course was lined two or three deep with spectators, waving and yodeling and clanking cowbells, urging the racers to even greater speeds and more daring deeds.

Miles didn't think he could keep going much longer. The strength was draining from his legs by the second. Every turn now was an effort and he must have bruised a rib in the fall because, every time he breathed in, he felt a sharp stabbing pain in his left side that took his breath away before it was halfway into his lungs.

Blood was running down his ski poles.

Here would be as good a place to leave the course as any. They could disappear round the back of the crowds without Bishop realising. He might just assume they had made ground, and ski on. Miles looked to his right for possible gaps in the lines of spectators. But the path suddenly began to steepen, his speed built up again, and no sooner had he spotted a gap than it was gone. To stand any chance of escape, he would need to slow his speed drastically. Now. Just thinking about it had lost him valuable seconds. Glancing over his shoulder, he realised that Bishop was less than fifty yards behind them and closing fast. The crowd, in the hope of witnessing a brief moment of drama, cheered them on to greater efforts.

"Faster!" Miles yelled to Anna.

"I can't!" she yelled back.

"Try!"

"I am trying!"

And then a small child walked across in front of them. She wore a tiny white ski suit and a pink bonnet tied under the chin with a ribbon, and pink woolly mittens, and pink snow boots. She looked like the Easter Bunny. Having appeared from nowhere about twenty yards ahead and taken a few steps, she stood there uncertainly in the middle of the track. Had she remained there Miles could have gone round her, but she suddenly lurched to the right. Miles shouted, "Look out!" and veered to his left. The child's mother chose that moment to make a daring rescue bid. Somehow Miles managed to squeeze through the gap between the mother and the line of spectators, but, skiing immediately behind him, Anna's view had been partially blocked. She had no time to react. The mother had bent down and was scooping the child up when she saw her. Anna swerved to the left and in her anxiety to avoid hitting her she caught an edge and went hard down on to her left side. She slid helplessly for another ten or twelve yards before a ski tip caught one of the marker poles and she spun round and finished up lying on her back, in the middle of the track, with her skis lodged amongst the spectators' feet.

Miles edged hard left and right and side-slipped to a stop. He stood there, leaning on his poles, fighting for breath, powerless to do a thing, watching as Bishop skied straight at her. Knees bent, head low, poles jutting out behind him, he seemed to be aiming his ski tips straight at Anna's head.

Miles dredged up his last reserves of breath and let out a single high-pitched yell. "No-o-o!"

It was enough to break Bishop's concentration. He looked up and at that moment his skis wandered to the left: perhaps only by a few inches, but it was enough. There was a faint click as his right boot clipped

Anna's helmet, but his eyes never wavered for a second from the figure of the man standing in the middle of the course in front of him. The man who knew too much and would tell all. The man who had to die if the movement was to live.

Miles swivelled his skis round, pointed them down the fall line and pushed as hard as he could, and again, and again. But, by the time his K2s were running, Bishop's tips were almost overlapping his backs and he could practically feel the man's breath in the gap under his helmet. He could hear the sound of a pocket being unzipped as Bishop reached for the gun.

But the crowds were thick all the way to Niederwald, and beyond. Miles gambled that he would hold his fire until they came to a stretch of the course below the railway, out of the spectators' range.

There was less than a second between them as they turned sharp right and plunged through the little tunnel under the line. Miles heard a metallic scrape and a curse and guessed Bishop had misjudged the width and caught the edge of a binding against the side.

Then he was through and out and zigzagging his way steeply down between deep moguls.

Miles was skiing on automatic pilot. If he'd thought for a second about what lay below him, fatigue and despair would have overwhelmed him and a bullet in the back might have come as a relief. But he didn't think. He just skied.

He was halfway down the mogul field when he remembered where he was. It was the section of the course he'd spotted coming up on the train the previous morning. The bit where it turned sharp left to Grützi. Where his palms had started sweating...

Now he could see the flags marking the route, and the stretch of red netting. A race marshal in an orange anorak had been positioned at the side of the track to wave people through, just in case...

Bishop was still at the top of the mogul field when he saw Miles turning to the right and the official running after him, shouting and trying to beckon him back. He skied the field fast, poles clenched in one hand, gun in the other. As he approached the turn, the official ran forward, his arms spread wide, shepherding him in the other direction. Bishop fired a short burst and the official's head exploded against the Blumenhom.

Miles glanced quickly down to his left. It looked like a perfect deep-powder slope: except he knew that, just beyond it, just out of sight, the powder ran out... He wondered if Bishop knew it too. He thought probably not. He sat back on his skis and let the tips ride free. The snow was so deep and so cold, it flew over his shoulders. And then he saw where the snow ended. It was less than fifty yards away. He glanced back. Bishop was closing fast. And then Miles realised. It wasn't because he was a good powder skier, precisely the opposite. On the piste he was as fast and technically proficient as any good amateur, but like many good piste-bashers he couldn't cope with the deep stuff. The technique wasn't there. He was one of those who just kept going and hoping for the best.

Bishop fired another burst, but again the shots went wide.

Miles was desperately close to the edge now. The far side of the valley was almost in view, but he showed no sign of slowing. Neither did Bishop. Now Miles could feel the snow giving slightly under his skis. He was less than ten yards from the edge when he made his turn. Technically speaking, it should have been impossible. But Miles was due for a spot of good luck, and Bishop wasn't. By the time he realised his mistake, it was already far too late. Sailing out into space, his despairing cry mingled with the croaking of the crows as they wheeled and glided like black undertakers against the brilliant white of the Blumenhom.

CHAPTER 8

SKIS IN WARFARE

INTRODUCTION by Ingrid Christophersen

We were all brought up on *The Heroes of Telemark* – the film about the raid on the heavy water plant in Telemark in Norway. Kirk Douglas was one of the *heroes*. Well, my father trained the real heavy water heroes in Aviemore in Scotland before they were dropped into Norway in 1942, so I knew all the heroes and met them often as a young girl growing up in Norway. According to my father, the film *The Heroes of Telemark* was exactly how it did *not* happen. He used to say, "sex, in the war," they must be joking!

Allied High Command was aware of German scientists conducting experiments for the purpose of building an atom bomb. These experiments needed heavy water in large quantities. The Allies were themselves in full swing experimenting with the production of atom bombs, and it was blatantly clear to them that whoever first acquired such a weapon would win the war. Norway had been occupied by Germany in April 1940; Vemork, near Rjukan in Telemark, was the site of the heavy water plant. A group of 4 Norwegian commandos, code name 'Grouse', were parachuted into Norway in the autumn of 1942, on to the Hardanger Plateau. They were to prepare a landing place for two gliders, pulled by two Halifax planes. On the assigned date the gliders never arrived. Only one Halifax returned to Scotland, the other Halifax and both gliders crashed, the crews taken out and shot by the Germans. The Norwegians faced overwintering on the Plateau, living off wild reindeer and nothing much else. In February 1943 a second lot of Norwegian commandos, code named 'Gunnerside', were parachuted on to the Hardanger Plateau, met up with Grouse and in February '43 the combined company, 9 in all, descended down to the heavy water plant in Rjukan, dismantled the production and escaped without a shot being fired. It was surely one of the most audacious raids of the entire war. All but one of the boys, a local, skied over to Sweden, to safety. The Hardanger Plateau swarmed with Germans, trying to catch them. The local chap offered the Germans his services tracking the *bad* Norwegians. He knew the area very well! I love the thought of one of the chaps being paid for looking for himself! If you want to learn more about this most exciting episode buy the DVD, *The Saboteurs*, a four-hour film, superb and could not be more accurate. Wonderful skiing sequences. A website link: https://www.atomicheritage. org/history/operation-gunnerside will give you an excellent short résumé of this courageous operation.

Here is a short section from the book, *The Heavy Water Raid* by Jens-Anton Poulsson, which I have translated.

THE RACE FOR THE ATOM BOMB by Jens Anton Poulsson

Jens Anton Poulsson was one of the Heroes of Telemark; the group of Norwegian saboteurs who dismantled the heavy water plant in Rjukan in 1943 in order to prevent the Germans from winning the race for the atom bomb. Two films have been made of this most exciting and audacious sabotage operation. One is very inaccurate and stars Kirk Douglas. The other is very accurate, recently made by a Norwegian/Swedish consortium and is entitled, 'The Saboteurs'.

The extract below is from JA Poulsson's book *The Race for the Atom Bomb* and has been translated by Ingrid Christophersen.

CHRISTMAS EVE 1942

One day in November 1942 a tall, pale, bearded chap carrying a rifle on his back, comes skiing over the ice at Store Saure. Mist envelops the mountain peaks.

I trudge along laboriously. The snow is sodden and clings to my skis. I halt, wipe the sweat from my face, curse and continue northwards over the ice. I turn in towards the inlet at Vesle Saure Lake and drag myself the last metres up to Svensbu hut where I unfasten my skis.

I take out a small axe and a hacksaw from the rucksack and go to work on the padlock. I catch sight of a piece of turnip lying near the door. It is water-logged and mouldy, but I eat it anyhow and savour it with delight. We have lived on soup this past week. Soup and reindeer moss plus a tiny bit of oatmeal and I feel undernourished and weak. Lord only knows I need to kill a reindeer.

Soon the padlock succumbs to the hacksaw but the door lock needs an axe. The axe handle breaks, and I continue with my knife. The lock won't budge.

Suddenly a fit of temper grabs me. I snatch the rifle and blow the lock out with two shots: two shots out of a total of ten precious cartridges. The canoe inside the hut is badly damaged. I carry the canoe out and start scrounging around for food. All I find is a handful of oatmeal and a bottle of cod liver oil.

The visitors' book lies in a drawer. I leaf through it and smile mournfully. I recognise the names and find my own entry from the summer of 1940. 'En route home from Langesjå to Lien. Have come for a bite of food and to leave the canoe behind'.

Those were the days. I close the book, bolt the door and continue slowly towards Grasdalen. But I have decided to use Svensbu as a base.

23rd December. The day before Christmas. The first fair weather and frost for many weeks. We are hungry and listless. The only food available is a few grains of oats and a fermented trout. Tomorrow is Christmas Eve. Not much of a Christmas Eve.

My skis glide easily over the ice. It feels good, having stamped around in mushy snow day after day. I am on my way to Stordalsnuten to look for game. Suddenly I freeze and yank the binoculars to my eyes. By Jove! There's a huge herd to the north side of Grasdalen. They are moving slowly towards Angelbutjønn.

Where is the wind blowing from? It is dead calm, but the clouds are moving in from the west, it appears. I need to get myself over Hålahovd and to the eastern side of Angelbutjønn Tarn in order to position myself downwind.

I set off. Weariness disappears, conked-out accumulator forgotten. I am gripped by hunting fervour. Soon the animals disappear out of sight. I continue steadily. The ground is undulating; a small depression leads eastwards towards the tarn.

I halt, unfasten my skis and crawl up behind a large boulder on the edge of the hollow. The animals have settled down near the tarn. Some feed, some have come to rest on the ice. A smaller herd is foraging far up in Angelbuhovd. I'm bound to have problems, there is no cover for stalking the herd; flat plateau towards the east and south and to the North West, where the terrain is good, the herd would get wind of me. I glance around and wait. But the herd is in no hurry, more animals lie down, it is high noon. They won't come much closer.

Time passes, it is cold and I am frozen. I can wait no longer. I start stalking. All goes well and I take up position behind some low ridges and small knolls. I will need, imperceptibly, to advance over exposed terrain, but my anorak is white. If I can only reach the small mound over there the range should be more of less good enough.

Then suddenly a couple of animals become aware of me. They take flight and immediately the entire herd is up and away, making for Grasdalen. They disappear behind a hillock.

I suddenly feel tired and dejected and tearful and swear loudly. To hell, what do I do now? Follow the herd – that won't achieve much. I glance up to the animals still in Angelbuhovd. They are feeding peacefully. I will try that lot.

I push straight on. The animals are reasonably high up on a plateau over a steep climb and I lose sight of them. I have no idea what the wind is doing up there. The light puffs are coming from every direction. I will have to cross my fingers.

When I arrive at the steep section I unfasten my skis and plod heavily on. I turn round and see my tracks in the snow, like a long, thin line which disappears in the distance. I expect to reach the herd any moment and inch forwards the last metres.

There they are! The animals have advanced a bit and I need to get closer to get a shot. They are restless. I am up on my knees to get a clean shot and fire, aiming at the closest animal. The range is about 200 metres. Nothing happens.

The herd runs in front of me. I fire again, twice, at two separate animals. Missed! The herd, about 30 deer, heads for the highest peak and disappears in a shower of snow, leaving behind hard-packed ground.

I am a lousy shot and in despair but when I reach the spot where the animals were feeding, I spot blood in the snow. There is in fact blood in three different tracks. It's those damned military non-expanding bullets. Bloody cartridges.

I carefully follow the trail of blood up the hill. After only 100 metres I find an animal lying in the snow. It tries to get up; I aim again and shoot but miss. Another shot, then – bull's eye!

The animal is a good-looking female. I snigger and laugh. By God, there'll be meat after all. I track the herd some more, but it is by now a long way off and the wounded animals appear to be hanging in there. I turn. I would never normally fire at an animal if I were not reasonably certain of killing it, but this is no sporting sortie. At stake is our very existence and the success of our mission. I drink some blood straight from the stomach cavity and then skin and quarter the animal. My rucksack and skis have been left behind and I need to retrieve them.

Then I load up and leave the remainder in a heap. But I forget to cover the carcass with the skin and when Claus returns the next day to recover the meat ravens have made a mess of it. I am soon retracing my own ski tracks. The going is excellent, and I move at a rattling pace. The day is wearing on and the sun is gilding the mountain tops. The cold creeps in, the rucksack is heavy, and I am tired but happy.

The herd from this morning is back on Angelbu tarn. They are unaware of me until I am close by. Then they dash off in a solid mass, hooves creaking, leaving behind hard-packed snow.

Towards evening I am back at Svensbu. I make as though nothing has happened. The lads don't quiz me; they are used to my returning empty-handed. But after a while Arne walks over and lifts the rucksack off the floor, it is obviously heavy. He smiles. We all smile. Life is not too bad after all; Christmas Eve is saved.

It is Christmas Eve. Silence has descended and we listen to some Christmas carols on the wireless. We have no loudspeaker but Haugland has deposited his earphone on a plate and we can just make out the music from where we sit round the table.

We are deep in thought and memories from happy childhood Christmases flood in. Perhaps we feel a little sorry for ourselves. Or are we thinking of our nearest and dearest and wondering how they are coping. Maybe we feel that, in spite of all, we are lucky to be alive. Free men in a country where Gestapo might and terror rule. Perhaps we are grateful for being able to celebrate Christmas, with something to eat and a Christmas tree on the table. Might the cause of our silence be gratitude to our Maker?

We gaze at the Christmas tree. Not a big deal and not really a Christmas tree but just a 30 – 40 cm high juniper twig. Decorations were made by cutting stars and other stuff from the radio telegraph operator's writing pad. We even sacrificed a single candle stub.

We are jolted out of our own sad thoughts by the radio being turned off. Even on Christmas Eve we cannot afford to waste more power. The accumulator must be spared for more important things, viz. our daily radio contact with England. It is the vital nerve in our existence and decisive for the success of our mission.

Someone starts to sing. Not Christmas carols: we are quite frankly fearful of our own feelings. No, we sing 'She'll be coming round the mountain when she comes' and other songs we sang in Scotland. Four bearded, unkempt chaps, miles away from civilisation, the wind howling round the bothy walls and a sprinkling of snow pushing through the flimsy door and settling on the floor in a fine coating.

We are well. We have eaten and are more replete than we have been since we left England in October.

Food is what has concerned us most. For a long time now our diet has been pretty meagre. Provisions brought from England, bar some coffee and a few other things, were consumed long ago. The fortnight before Christmas we had taken to eating reindeer moss to eke out our small supply. We were undernourished and listless. A three to four-kilometre ski tour was an effort. To ski 10 or 20 kilometres, as we often had to, was a matter of willpower. Willpower was what counted, nothing else.

I hunted every day without success. Soon our food had all but run out. We were not looking forward to Christmas.

And then suddenly, all our food worries are over and Christmas Eve 1942 sees us replete and satisfied, having eaten reindeer in every possible variety. Soup and blood, boiled and fried meat, liver and tongue. We are happy. Our Christmas present was what we were most in need of: food.

THE FINNISH WINTER WAR
Introduction by Ingrid Christophersen

I C writes: Although this is not strictly literature, it has been included in this anthology to show the importance of skis and skiing in warfare.

Russia invaded Finland on November 30th, 1939. Thus, started one of the most dramatic wars in modern history. Largely overshadowed by the conflicts of World War 2, nevertheless, this was one of the most brutal struggles fought by heroic Finns against a blundering and unprepared horde which outnumbered them by fifty to one. The subsequent ceasefire signed on March 13th, 1940 came as a total shock to the Finns, and the harsh terms of the ceasefire was received with disbelief. The Finnish repulse of the Soviet invasion helped persuade Hitler to attack Russia in 1941. It also had the effect of Stalin being compelled to reform the Red Army, which enabled them to hold their own. The effect of two murderous regimes turning on each other cannot be overstated. Without the Finnish Winter War history might well have taken another turn.

I am in possession of 2 buff-coloured pamphlets, printed in March 1940 entitled, 'PERIODICAL NOTES ON THE RUSSIAN ARMY', and a footnote saying, 'not to be published or communicated and not to be taken to the front line'. My father gave these to me. As we are now 80 years away from this event, I do not think I am breaking any official secrets act by revealing some of the contents:

Finnish ski troops have been most successful, both in patrol work and in harassing operations. They have however, been thoroughly trained for operations on skis, a form of warfare which needs particular study. Russian ski units do not appear to have had a good systematic training and, in many cases, they were hurriedly improvised for these operations. On occasions, skis and skiing handbooks were issued to men who had never seen them before. Russian ski units have therefore been comparatively ineffective. It is perhaps worth noting that the Swedish troops on winter manoeuvres in 1932 suffered 25 percent casualties through skiing accidents; as an example of the mobility of ski units it may be stated that last year the crack Swedish ski unit covered 95 km in 24 hours, of which 50 km was covered in darkness.

White Death was written by Allen Chew, a retired US Air Force instructor, college professor, and writer.

WHITE DEATH by Allen Chew

Civilians were also marshalled for the grim days ahead. On 10 October the Government broadcast an appeal for the voluntary evacuation of the large towns and provided special trains and buses for that purpose. In Helsinki the University, the public schools, and the stock exchange were closed by mid-October. Air raid shelters were constructed throughout the cities to protect those workers who could not leave for the relative safety of the countryside. Prohibition was decreed – a drastic measure for the Finns! However, by late November some of these precautions were abandoned as people became accustomed to living in a protracted state of crisis.

In addition to the regular army and reserve units, the Finns mobilised their unique Civic Guards organization and its female auxiliary during the YH period. Formed by local initiative during the fall of 1917, the Civic Guards were the nucleus of the White Army in the 1918 war.

Charged with the defence of the fatherland and "its lawful social order" this voluntary organization fostered such peacetime activities as rifle and skiing competitions, mass athletics, concerts, and fund raising for arms purchases. An average of 80,000 to 100,000 members annually participated in its training programs. Their Commander-in-Chief, General Malmberg, was directly responsible to the President of the Republic, and Marshal Mannerheim was their honorary commander. A large percentage of the Guards officers were also army reserve officers. Upon mobilization, the Civic Guards served to augment the field army, as well as train recruits and to perform civil defence duties.

Another major asset was the Finnish soldier's thorough adaptation to his peculiar environment. In a land of long snowy winters and few paved roads, virtually all Finns became skilled cross-country skiers in childhood. Robust lumberjacks and woodsmen felt assured in their beloved forest, which covered some 70 percent of the country. A popular pre-war sport was "orienteering", in which competitors raced through unfamiliar woods in any season – often at night – aided only by map and compass.

The combination of forest lore and skiing ability produced deadly efficient offensive patrols which, moving silently and almost invisibly in their white snow capes, spread consternation deep behind the enemy's lines. In marked contrast, many Red Army men were terrified by the dense woods, where lurked, in their own words, *Belaya Smert*, the White Death. Politruk Oreshin wrote that Finland's "countless ridges and hills covered with forest, its lakes and marshes make it grim and gloomy." There is an undertone of awe in this description by Captain Shevenok, who fought on the Karelian Isthmus:

'No, the Finnish woods are altogether unlike our Ukraine. Tall pines stand all together in the snow like paintings. Above are branches and down below it is bare, as if you are standing not in groves but in some sort of grotto with pillars. The stars wink – frigid, still. The snow falls silently, straight in the eye. The firing of the guns sounds like a long drawn-out echo from afar, as if from a tube.'

Moreover, many of Finland's 60,000 lakes – in conjunction with marshes and rivers – channelled invading columns along narrow passageways where they were vulnerable to flanking attacks. Finnish peacetime training had stressed precisely such active defence tactics.

Even the season favoured the defenders during most of the Winter War. The long hours of midwinter darkness limited the activity of the enemy's vastly superior air force. Snow hampered his roadbound mechanized columns, while facilitating the manoeuvring of Finnish ski patrols. And the killing frost of that severe winter – lower temperatures had been recorded only twice since 1828 – caused the ill-prepared Red Army much greater casualties than it did the acclimated and survival-equipped Finns. While Red Army men froze to death by the hundreds in icy foxholes at 30 below zero, the Finns, camouflaged in the surrounding woods, were often enjoying the warmth of their inexpensive but practical twenty-man tents, heated by portable wood burning stoves.

Finnish morale was also sustained during those trying days of early December by the hope and expectation of substantial assistance from the West, however illusory this subsequently proved to be.

Finally, in those hours of peril the nation reassuringly looked to Marshal Mannerheim, a man who was already a living legend. Although divided on his political leanings, virtually all Finns shared a sound confidence in his military leadership.

EXTRACT FROM AN ARTICLE WRITTEN FOR THE WW2 MUSEUM IN NEW ORLEANS by Mitch Swenson

While high-intensity combat raged across the isthmus, up north Mannerheim had to conduct a very different kind of war. With nearly 600 miles of border and nowhere near enough regular divisions to cover it, he had to rely upon the Home Guard as the backbone of his defense. These were independent battalions of hardy citizen soldiers who knew every inch of the land, were dead shots, and accustomed to the cold. Virtually all Finns could ski, but the Home Guard specialized in fighting on skis, gliding silently out of the forest, nearly invisible in long white parkas and hoods, to rake a ponderous Soviet column with fire from their viciously effective KP/-31 submachine guns, and then vanish back into the trees.

On Nov 30, 1939, the Soviet Union invaded Finland with more than 400,000 troops. The assault was almost three times larger than the Allied landing at Normandy. Soviet Leningrad, a city of five million, by itself contained more people than the entire country of Finland. As the world's largest infantry force, the Red Army marched across the border with resolve. It looked like a decisive victory for Stalin.

Instead, the Winter War became one of the USSR's most shocking defeats. A Finnish army just a third the size of the Soviet force slowed and bloodied the invaders until a peace deal ended the war.

In the first week, the forests of Karelian Isthmus were lit up by gunfire. The Finns lacked the anti-tank ammunition needed to adequately combat Soviet vehicles and Stalin's army gained large tracts of the forest within days. One thousand Soviet tanks successfully besieged the meager Finnish brigades until Finnish engineers found a vulnerable exhaust shoot on the back end of the Red Army's T-28 tanks.

Finnish ski troopers, quick and agile in the forests, wove through the trees, using their white uniforms to remain concealed in the snow. The skiers tossed Molotov cocktails and satchel charges through the exhaust opening into the tanks' bellows, causing the vehicles to explode from the inside out.

In one instance, a Finnish ski trooper sledded close enough to pry the treads off one T-28, demobilizing the tank and allowing other Finnish skiers to plunk explosives inside.

Eventually, Finland was able to roll back the Soviets' tank advances with these drive-by ski bombings. And on Dec. 6, Stalin's army mounted a large-scale infantry invasion near the Taipale River. The Soviets, having a huge numbers advantage, plowed through the snow towards the enemy.

But the Finnish ski troopers, again utilizing their knowledge of the white and wooded landscape, expertly positioned automatic weapons that mowed down wave upon wave of advancing Soviet soldiers.

After days of slaughter, enough dead riflemen had piled up in the snowbanks that the oncoming lines of Soviets were able to take cover behind the frozen bodies. The sub-zero temperatures hardened the corpses enough to stop the Finnish machine gun rounds.

On Dec. 17, having taken heavy losses, the Soviets shifted their focus to a different area of the Finnish front known as Summa and Lahde. The Soviets used flamethrower tanks to scorch the Finnish trenches while the Finnish army fought back fiercely. It's been said that two machine gunners fired 40,000 rounds between them.

In the evenings, the Finnish ski troops counterattacked. By Dec. 21, Stalin's birthday, seven Soviet infantry divisions had been wiped out along with 250 T-28 tanks.

A bitter winter fell. Temperatures plunged to minus 40 degrees Fahrenheit. It was so cold that when a soldier was hit by a bullet and his circulation slowed, his body would freeze almost instantaneously, immortalizing his agonized posture.

Later, the Soviets entered Finland from the eastern border and walked narrow logging trails in the woods with more than 30,000 troops. Included in this line were 'aerosani' – propeller-driven snowmobiles with mounted machine guns. These snow-skimmers had been developed for delivering mail and medical aid in Siberia.

The Finnish ski troops approached the lines from the front and back and knocked out the lead and trailing vehicles, causing the middle units to become stuck. Swiftly, the Finns jumped out of the forest and further split the Soviet columns with mortars and grenades. In this way, the Finns decimated the long Soviet columns and took 1,500 prisoners.

In January both sides recessed and regrouped as the cold became unbearable. When the Soviets returned in February, they launched an all-out assault, sending 45 divisions – a total of 750,000 troops – into the forests of the Karelian Isthmus.

Two thousand artillery shells slammed into the Finnish front line. There were simply too many Red Army troops for the Finnish ski troops to dexterously out-manoeuvre their foes – and as a result Finland's army could not hold.

The Finns sent in their reserves. The fighting raged on, with Stalin's army slowly pushing back

Finland's infantry. By March 12, the Finnish ski troops were almost out of ammunition. But the next day, March 13th, 1940, Helsinki and Moscow signed an armistice. Having largely held back the USSR, Finland sacrificed some territory for an end to the fighting.

All told, it is believed that the Finnish army killed more 200,000 Soviet soldiers for a loss of fewer than 50,000 its own.

When the snow finally melted that spring, the corpses of thousands of Soviet soldiers were unearthed in the Finnish woods, each body still contorted as in its final moments of life.

CHAPTER 9
TWO NORWEGIAN NOBEL PRIZE LAUREATES

SIGRID UNDSET – AN INTRODUCTION by Ingrid Christophersen

Sigrid Undset (1882–1949) was a Norwegian novelist who was awarded the Nobel Prize for Literature in 1928. In 1924 she converted to Catholicism and her momentous medieval family sagas are heavily inspired by Catholicism. Her best-known work is 'Kristin Lavransdatter', a trilogy about life in Norway in the Middle Ages, portrayed through the experiences of a woman from birth until death. My Desert Island book would be Kristin Lavransdatter... I read it every year.

When Norway was invaded by Germany in April 1940, Sigrid Undset had to flee the country. She had been highly vociferous in her criticism of Hitler *and* National Socialism since the beginning of the 1930s . In America she became a good friend of Eleanor Roosevelt who encouraged her to write a book about Norway, a country not well known in the States. She called it 'Happy times in Norway', and it is about the Undset family. Anders, the son mentioned here, was killed early on in the war, in April 1940, during a skirmish with German troops near his hometown of Lillehammer. The book was first published in America in 1942, and was written in English by Sigrid Undset.

HAPPY TIMES IN NORWAY by Sigrid Undset

It is the custom in Norway that on Christmas Day people stay quietly at home, or go out only to be with their closest relatives. Even the skiers who swarmed over all the roads and fields, beaming with delight over the first snow of the year, kept together in family groups. Big boys, who ordinarily spend all their free time on their ski club's training ground, stay home and take a quiet morning walk with their mamma, and sometimes with grandmamma too. Fathers potter around in the fields on this day instead of going to their cottages in the mountains. They have their tiniest youngster with them, a boy or girl of two or three, who got his, or her, first pair of skis under the Christmas tree this year and today has them on for the first time.

Anders came home to the late dinner. Cheeks red, hair damp and with eyes that were dark and shining. The whole boy seemed to be aglow. He had been clear up to Nordseter.

"Three hours up, and half an hour down, and as soft as velvet, mother!" Mother knew that from now on until the last snow in the mountains became unusable sometime in the spring, Anders would think of little else than skiing. All his free time would be used for practising and every Sunday morning he would disappear with a truckload of boys bound for some ski contest to the north, or south, or east, or west. Anders had not yet reached high on the prize list. He was too thin and light, even in his own age group.

But the judges said he had fine style, and he worked hard, so he would be good in time, when he had taken on some weight. Skiing interfered with his schoolwork of course. But Mother had the same weakness as most Norwegian mothers. It was unfortunate if his marks were altogether too poor, but if the boy could keep it up until he became an outstanding skier, she would be dreadfully proud. Secretly she pasted into a scrapbook all the little newspaper clippings in which Anders's name appeared, even though it was only one of the lowest prizes he had won.

Hans had not one particle of such vanity. He went on long trips with Magne or Ole Henrik, his friends, equipped with much good food in their knapsacks. Up in the forest and on the ridges were little farms where they could buy coffee and ginger ale, before they skied down. But to ski "just to have people standing around gaping on the hill, gape at me, that's just dumb," said Hans.

On Second Christmas Day everyone in the house had to get up early, for today the guests from Oslo were arriving on the noon train. And although Mother and Thea had been working for many days to get ready for them, there were many things to arrange at the last minute.

Bø brought two cars. Mother took Tulla with her in one, for Grandmother was always so happy when Tulla came to meet her. Anders and Hans went in the other car and in the course of the journey to the station they managed to become furious enemies. Anders had a bad habit of bossing his brother and Hans did not like to be bossed by anyone. This time it was Brit they had quarrelled about.

"Anders does not have to tell me I must not tease Brit! I guess I am just as much her uncle as he is!" ·

It was still snowing hard and the place outside the station was almost impenetrable, it was so filled with buses and cars from the many hotels and sanatoriums in and around town, and with horses and sleighs from the farms. The station platform swarmed with people. Half the town was there to meet Christmas guests, and the other half whose guests had arrived Christmas Eve was down to see who was coming on the train. The hotels were almost full and still more people were expected. Many Danes always came up here at Christmas time to ski and one could tell the Danes half a mile away as large parties of them came driving down Main Street. They talked so loud and shouted and laughed; besides, they were always clad in all the colours of the rainbow – red and blue and yellow trousers and striped and flowered jerseys. But they were astonishingly good skiers, many of them, and those who were not good were at least daring and rolled down the slopes blithely.

The train was more than an hour late, the station master announced. Special trains, overcrowding, and obstacles caused by the snow along the line had made chaos of the traffic, but that too was part of Christmas. There was much jollity at the station on these occasions. Mother greeted acquaintances from Oslo and acquaintances from town, and everyone had to wish everyone else 'Merry Christmas' and agree to meet some time during the holidays. Anders and Hans forgot to quarrel and planned skiing trips with their friends and made dates with the girls for the ball at the Bank Second New Year's Day. And the snow fell faster and faster. Soon everyone looked like a snowman or a witch, and inside the railroad station restaurant the floor and tables floated in half-melted snow. People came in to pass the time over a cup of coffee and then dashed out to peer down the tracks for the train.

They neither saw nor heard it in the falling snow until it was almost upon them. Anders and Hans burrowed a way for themselves through the mass of people in order to be the first to greet Grandmother. There she stood in the window, waving, when suddenly Anders discovered Neri between his legs. And in the middle of a great snow flurry, Njord and the beagle from Victoria Hotel were engaged in savage combat. Mother and the hotel boy threw themselves upon the dogs to separate them. How it ever happened that the dogs had got out and followed them clear down to the station it was hard to say. But when Anders and Mother finally got them into the car, Hans, proud as a peacock, was already escorting the Christmas guests. It had been he, after all, who had had to find them in that crowd on the platform and show them the way to Bø's cars.

Now followed a good deal of discussion about who should sit with whom. Hans wanted to sit beside Grandmother in the car where Mother and Tulla were, but he wanted Brit beside him also. He became annoyed with Anders again, for Anders without any more ado had lifted Brit up in his arms and whisked her into the other car. Anders, naturally, was going to sit beside Gunhild, their half-sister, for she and Anders had always been the best of friends. Bø and Godfather and Aunt Signe were busy getting all the baggage arranged and all the skis tied fast on the outside of the car. Today, skis and ski poles bristled from everything on wheels. The girls – Aunt Signe' s three, and Ulla from Stockholm – tumbled in and out of the two cars and did not know where they wanted to sit or where there would be room for them. The twins, Siri-Kari and Anne-Lotte, looked pale, for they always got train sick.

Finally, the whole party was disposed of, one way or another, and Bø started off. It was almost dinnertime when they got home but Thea had nevertheless laid the tea table in the large parlour, for Grandmother always had to have tea the moment she arrived. Thea would certainly postpone dinner an hour, for she knew everyone had to speak with everyone else and there was such a lot to talk about. The children hoped that the rest of the Christmas presents would be distributed at once, but Mother said "no" to that idea. "That will have to wait," she said. "There are so many of us that it will take too much time!"

It was a whole year since all the family had been together. Grandmother had been here in the summer and the girls from Oslo had come up rather often, whenever they had a few days' vacation. Mother's sister, Aunt Signe, and her husband (whom the children called Godfather because he was godfather to Anders) had not been here since last Christmas. And Ulla from Stockholm, the daughter of Mother's other sister who was married in Sweden, was traveling alone for the first time in her life. Since she was Hans's age, seven years old, it was rather impressive, for Hans had never been allowed to travel alone even so far as Oslo. Grandmother was still rather shocked over the fact that Ulla's mother had dared to let her go so far alone – but she was beaming at the same time for now she had all her grandchildren, except Ulla's little brother, gathered round her.

Gunhild had not been here since Brit was a tiny tot who could hardly stand. Now she was over two and could both run and talk all she needed – and a little more besides. Both Anders and Hans thought it a frightful lot of fun that they were uncles and they admired their niece tremendously! To think that Brit was not in the least afraid of the two black dogs that looked so wild and were carrying on so! For Njord seemed to think he must show Grandmother how delighted he was to see her by nearly knocking her down. And all these strange children he had to bark at, so that they would have the proper respect for him, for it would be too much of a good thing if they all petted and hugged him until he had no peace! Neri flew around like the little fool he was, trying to do everything Njord did. Finally, Brit got both her fists entwined in Njord's fur, where she held on until Njord positively had to shake her loose. After that he went and lay down under Mother's writing table in the other room and Neri took refuge in Mother's lap.

The cats did not make an appearance at all when there were so many strangers in the house. They lay in Thea's bed, when they were not in the kitchen, eating, or out walking in the snow.

Thea had decorated the long breakfast table with sprigs of evergreen, candles, and flowers. It sagged under all the good Christmas food. And in the snow outside the door stood the bottles of beer, and the old brandy decanter from Great grandfather's house. Godfather was very particular that the Christmas brandy should be the temperature of the snow.

As they sat waiting for Thea to come down with Tulla, and Gunhild to come with Brit, the children ate cookies and cracked nuts, for all during the Christmas season the big old copper bowl filled with fruit and nuts and cookies stood on a table in the corner.

A telephone call for Anders… Soon he was back in the room with a rush. "Mother, would you please pack my knapsack? I must have enough food along for twenty four hours at least. That was from Nordseter Hotel… two Danes went out as it was getting dark last night and they haven't come back. Now they are asking some of the Boy Scouts to come along and look for them. It was foggy and snowing in the mountains yesterday, of course. Just like Danes to do some foolish thing like that."

Grandmother was about to protest, for Grandmother was Danish, but Anders waved her aside:

"… talk about it when I get home, grandmother. But, grandmother, lend me your pocket flashlight, will you? Both batteries are burned out in mine."

Again, Grandmother started to protest. She could not give up her flashlight! Every time she woke up at night she wanted to see what time it was.

"Mother will give you a candle and some matches, grandmother. I must have a pocket flashlight with me."

So Grandmother went to fetch her precious flashlight.

"And you, mother, you must lend me both Thermos bottles for coffee, and I ought to have a little aquavit along too, just in case we find them. But hurry up, then! The car may be here any second."

Anders stood ready, skis and all, as the truck stopped before the gate. Mother followed him out. It was rather comforting to see that all the other boys in the car were older than Anders – several of them were young men.

"Well, I know you are used to the mountains, Anders. I can depend on you to be careful and not get separated from your party."

For now the snow was tumbling down again so thickly one could not see more than a few ski lengths ahead.

"Yes. yes, mamma."

When Anders considered any remark of Mother's ill-timed, he called her 'mamma'. "Don't worry about me... Of course, you realise I probably won't be home tonight... Yes, certainly, I'll ask the hotel to give you a ring the minute they find those Danes. By the way, the mother of one of them is on the way down to see you," Anders remembered suddenly. "They asked me to tell you. It's someone you know – she's a writer, I think they said."

"Do you know her name? Didn't they say?"

"Yes, but I can't remember it. 'Swan', I think maybe. Or maybe 'Bear'. Some kind of animal anyway. Well, take care of yourselves."

Indoors, the family was still waiting for breakfast and Aunt Signe was trying to soothe the ruffled tempers. Grandmother was annoyed, for she considered Anders altogether too young to be going on a searching party; besides, why must people always pick on the Danes? Godfather was saying he did not always pick on the Danes, but they annoyed him – yes, and all the other foreigners, as well, who staged these disappearing acts in the mountain resorts every blessed winter. Why couldn't they listen to the guides who tried to make it clear to them that when there was a heavy fog, or when it was snowing, it was no time to go skiing? For then searching parties had to be made up, lumbermen and farmers had to leave their work, often for days at a time, for sometimes it took days to find a couple of lost tourists in such terrain as the mountains hereabouts, with mile upon mile of little hills and valleys running hither and thither. There ought to be notices posted at every resort that tourists who got lost must pay the searchers for the time spent looking for them. Maybe that would put an end to the nuisance. But that would probably never be done.

It has been the rule in Norway for hundreds of years that, when anyone gets lost in the forests or on the mountains, all the men in the neighbourhood go out and search for him until he is found, dead or alive. When it was one of the country people who got lost it was usually someone out on a necessary errand – someone going to or from a sæter, or crossing the mountain into the neighbouring valley, or someone out hunting or fishing, not persons out for fun. Just because tourists who did not know any better abused good old customs, people, at least in this part of the country, had no desire to change any of them. Mother had just managed to snatch a bite of breakfast when Thea came in.

"There is a lady asking to see Madam. Shall I show her into the parlour?"

The moment Mother opened the parlour door, a big, yellow-haired woman in orange-coloured sports clothes sprang into her arms. The woman's face was so red and swollen from tears that one could scarcely tell what she looked like, and she sobbed and sobbed. Mother tried to console her. "They'll find them. They always do. And it was not cold last night, and there are so many cabins and sæters in the mountains, perhaps they got indoors somewhere last night! Ah, it could have been much, much worse." The ice was still undependable in many places on the lakes up there and in such weather, it was impossible to see far ahead. But this Mother did not say. She comforted the woman as well as she could. She had realised that this was a Mrs. Jytte Hjorth, whom she had met at some congress in Copenhagen.

Mrs. Hjorth's son had just graduated from medical school; he had passed his examination brilliantly, but he felt rather tired afterward, and so Mrs. Hjorth had come up here with him so that her Egil could have a rest… And yesterday afternoon he had gone skiing with a friend.

She cried and cried. Mrs. Hjorth was a widow and her son was her only child. Mother got the fire lit in the fireplace and settled Mrs. Hjorth in a comfortable chair before its warmth. Coffee and a dainty breakfast tray helped to calm the poor woman. She had been so upset she had not tasted food since yesterday afternoon. Aunt Signe called the hotel every half hour but there was no news about Dr. Hjorth and his companion. However, in the mountains it was almost clear now and was beginning to freeze. That would lighten the work of the rescuers a great deal. The fog had sunk down into the valley. Here the weather was grey and gloomy, and in spite of the candles the parlour was dark.

At dinnertime Mrs. Hjorth decided she must go up to the hotel again. She could not endure sitting here any longer. And she did so want Mother to come along. Mother was not entirely unwilling. She was a little uneasy about Anders… All the youngsters set up a vast howl of protest when she told them.

But, they protested the Third Christmas Day, the very first whole day they were all together was the best day in the whole year. There was an extra special dinner with dancing around the lighted Christmas tree afterward, and everything! And then, in Mother's big bedroom, after they had all undressed, they would run around and play in nightgowns and pyjamas, until Mother came up and lit the candles in front of that lovely little crib Hans had! And she told stories! Now, if she and Anders were both going to be away, the whole day would be spoiled.

Aunt Signe promised that Thea and she would do the best they could for the children. Besides, they had Grandmother, Mother reminded them. All the children idolised their grandmother. She was so tiny and so dainty, with her snow-white hair and her delicate little face. Because she never petted them but talked with them as if they were as grown up and as clever as she herself, each of the boys and girls was certain that he, or she, was Grandmother's very own favourite.

Yes, that was true, Grandmother was there; that would make things as good as possible until Mother got back.

It was not cheerful at the little mountain hotel. All the men guests were, of course, out on the searching party. Sitting around in the lobbies and parlours, the women were knitting or trying to read, or playing solitaire, but they were restless. Over and over, they asked Mr. Nesheim, the owner, the same questions.

"It would not surprise me," Mr. Nesheim declared, "if we have to get out and look for some of the searchers, as soon as we have hauled in the Danes!"

Mother sat up all night with Mrs. Hjorth, sleeping when Mrs. Hjorth slept, listening when Mrs. Hjorth was not sleeping. Between times, she speculated upon where Anders was that night, and how things were with him. At nine Mr. Nesheim awakened them.

"Well, Mrs. Hjorth, now you can be happy. Your son will be here in a few hours. They found them at the southern end of Kroksjøen. Dr. Hjorth is all right, but the lawyer, Petersen, has hurt his foot, so he will have to be brought down by ski sled. By the by," he said to Mother, as he answered Mrs. Hjorth's thousand and one questions, "Anders is down in the dining room now."

Anders looked up from the platter of bacon and eggs – much too obviously casual and uninterested. "For heaven's sake, mother, are you here? Ah, you've been sitting up with that Danish lady, haven't you? No, I'm not in the least tired... We hunted down through that draw along Deep Water Creek, you know – and all around Deep Water Lake. We went to every cabin and every sæter, you see. Finally, we turned in at Ramstad's cabin. Nils and I had been sent out with two others from the hotel here, you see – a Dane, a good fellow, by the way, good on skis, and a Swede. We finally convinced them it was no use wandering around in the mountains after it had got pitch-dark, so we turned in... We lay down to sleep for a bit, and planned to start hunting down toward Hynna as soon as it got light. But then Aasen came early this morning and said they had found them. It was Aasen's party that found them, you see."

Suddenly the boy lost his mask of indifference "And, mother, do you know what? Nils and I got to go along with Aasen – Johan Aasen, you know – from the Ramstad cabin clear up to the peak above Clear Water. Out on the ice he left us, of course, but we had managed to keep up with him clear to there! Mother, you can't imagine what a swell fellow he is – Aasen –." Johan Aasen, the lumberjack from Lismarka, champion skier and prize winner at ever so many ski tournaments both at home and abroad, was the idol and hero of all the boys. The two Boy Scouts who had been on this journey with him over the mountain obviously thought the expedition in search of the vanished Danes just a lucky adventure.

"Aasen said, by the way, that the doctor – the one who is the son of that friend of yours – is a smart fellow. When he saw they were lost, he said they should burrow down in the snow and stay there until daylight. But then the lawyer went to fetch some water – they could hear a stream running nearby under the snow where they were lying – and he stepped down between two rocks and broke his ankle… Tired? Who, me? Of course not, why should I be tired?"

But just the same Anders was quite willing to drive home with Mother in the car "- if Nils wants to, that is. Otherwise, we'll ski?" But Nils also was glad to ride. They were standing out in the courtyard, the three of them, and the boys were tying their skis to the car, when a man on skis streaked past – a slim young man, light-haired, brown-skinned, with sharp light blue eyes. "Thanks for your company." His voice was low and gentle. He nodded to the boys.

"Same to you!" Anders turned to his mother. "That was Johan Aasen." His whole face beamed.

Nils got in front with the chauffeur, and Anders crawled in with Mother in the back seat. They had scarcely started to drive, before Anders began to sway toward Mother's breast. He slept. Mother peeped at Nils, but Nils too was slumped down, his head nodding, nodding…

"Tired." The chauffeur grinned. So, Mother put her arm around her big boy, so that his head should rest well against her shoulder, and sound asleep, the two Boy Scouts drove home from their first lifesaving expedition into the mountains.

SIGRID UNDSETH – FROM HER AUTOBIOGRAPHICAL WRITINGS
Translation by Ingrid Christophersen

Anine's sister arrived from Denmark to attend the Commercial College in Kristiania. Aunt Gæa was young, her cheeks were bright crimson and her crimped fringe frothed above her forehead and made her look taller than she was. When she became agitated her voice rose; she laughed loud and often. The children instinctively enjoyed the presence of such a young and lively person in the house.

They listened carefully when, at the dinner table, she related stories from the Commercial College. She clearly very much enjoyed her time there. She mimicked the teachers in Danish and gave them and her friends nicknames. She made friends as soon as she started and Ingvild thought it might be fun when she eventually herself started attending a regular school.

This winter she was not all that keen on spending time outside with the other children. She had so looked forward to the snow arriving and thought that this Christmas she would be given either a toboggan or skis. And then when Christmas Eve arrived she was given a toboggan from her parents and skis from grandfather. To top it all, her grandmother had sent her a pair of skates which had belonged to Ingvild's father when he was young.

When she emerged onto the street on Christmas Day morning, hugging all her treasures, happy as Larry, the other children immediately let her know that it was all wrong.

The skates were made of wood, painted red and mounted with a broad iron strap under the foot. No one had ever seen such skates before and they laughed and said they must be skates for cows. Not at all, daddy said, when she moaned to him – they are snow skates, and every boy in Trondheim had a pair.

Mummy had bought the toboggan. It was beautifully painted in two shades of brown and had a back support made of iron hoops. But that was totally wrong, only toddlers had back support. That just wasn't cool.

But worst of all were the skis. At that time, all Kristiania children had rather broad skis without camber, without grooves and with a steep curve. Poles were a broomstick with a hole bored into the top to secure the strap for the hand. Nobody had seen such skis as grandfather had sent his grandchildren – because even Birthe had been sent a pair but they were so tiny they looked more like knick-knacks. Grandfather had himself overseen the construction of the skis to make sure all was done according to his blueprint. They were long and narrow, and a recessed block for the foot, a deep grove underneath, a long bow, stooping at the front. But what most made them look ridiculous was the skis' narrow and curved stern. The ski pole was turned from one piece of wood, narrow at the hand hold, and the basket looked like an upside-down humming top. No one had ever seen poles like that – not in this neck of the woods anyhow.

She could not bear it. They teased her remorselessly, both at the Fastings Hills and on The Hill, for the funny skis she had been given. And when she cried to daddy, he got angry. Did she really think that anyone in Kristiania knew anything about skis? When he arrived here in town as a student the inhabitants of Kristiania had no idea whether the skis were for their feet or their bottoms – he could have died laughing when he watched them trying to ski. That they should teach someone from Østerdalen how to ski – it was too hilarious. Grandfather had once skied down Gløshaug Hill at the same time as a farmer and his cartload of hay came driving along the road below. Grandfather had jumped clean over the hay truck, the farmer and the road and had landed elegantly on the field in a shower of snow. Daddy had been watching and how he had laughed, because the farmer had halted the horse right in the middle of the road and sat there gaping. No, Ingvild, be sure of one thing, when grandfather made your skis, there won't be a girl in all of Norway who has better ones. Well, at least in Southern Norway. And if you are stupid enough to care about criticism from those who have no idea what they are talking about, then you will really disappoint me.

So, no comfort from that direction. And she was used to being teased and did not mind, within reason. But all this was just too much – everything she had been given to enable her to enjoy the outdoors was wrong and comical. And being out in the fresh air was not optional, no amount of pleading would allow her to stay at home. Beyond Fagerborggaten she discovered some tiny hills on a knoll; so she went there and skied. But it soon became boring, she was all alone and if she needed to spend a penny it was an awful long way home.

KNUT HAMSUN

Knut Hamsun (1859–1952) was a Norwegian author who won the Nobel Prize for Literature in 1920. His works span 70 years and he has been called the father of modern literature. Alas, during the German occupation of Norway he joined the Nazi party and met high-ranking German officials – even Hitler – who capitalised on the fact that this important and well-known Norwegian supported the Nazi cause. He was heavily fined after the war but owing to his great age did not spend any time in prison.

This article, in a major Norwegian newspaper, was translated by Ingrid Christophersen.

Advice regarding ski-bindings

Under this heading A. Huitfeldt has written a very funny article, which appeared in yesterday's *Dagbladet*. I have read it many times and it affects me like a ski race in good conditions.

However, I do feel that Mr. Huitfeldt is a wee bit severe when he forbids ladies to squeal when they fall, to be followed by hearty laughter. It is not all that easy to remain tight-lipped when your head is buried in a snow drift. And besides, when one collapses into uncontrollable laughter one must be allowed to squeal a bit, I think. But this is not what I want to talk about. As a veteran skier I want to try and be business-like. It is all about bindings and boots.

According to Mr Huitfeldt bindings are one of the most important items. And there will soon be a thousand different bindings, with the name of Olsen and Persen, Fossum and Stabel and Bjerknæs, and God knows what they are all called. Some bindings cost several crowns; others are just simple cane bindings.

As there is now such an abundance of bindings, I am going to suggest another one, viz., the oldest and very best I know of – no binding.

I am a native of Northern Norway. We northerners know about skis. All winter long, five, six or even seven months, our only transport is skis or a boat. No ploughs clear our roads so that that horses can get through, and there are no roads for the plough to plough. So, Northerners are quite 'au fait' with the use of skis. But a Northerner does not use bindings, or rather he uses them very rarely.

Because bindings are dangerous. If you fall with skis attached to your feet, it is easy to sprain, dislocate or break a limb. There have been cases of skiers, whose skis are fastened to them, having their eyes poked out by their own ski tips.

I have of course observed bindings in Northern Norway, used by the Laplanders when herding reindeer; and for ascending a hill, bindings may be a help. But not even the Laplanders use bindings all the time, the point being that with their type of footwear the binding is superfluous.

In Northern Norway in winter we use the so-called 'lugs' – shoes made of material, without leather soles. These lugs do not slide back and forth on the ski if only the strap is wide and tight enough. On the other hand, it is easy to quickly remove the foot if necessary. The Laps wear their native boots – 'skaller' – where the upward curving toe piece keeps the boot firmly in position under the strap. A binding is not needed. A lug or a komag or a skalle virtually glue themselves to the skies and are far steadier during a race with jumps than a leather boot with bindings. And besides, they do not pose a risk. Bindings are not always good. I have seen the Laplanders use bindings up the hill and then undo them on the descent if the terrain was unknown to them and they were frightened of falling.

I would therefore suggest that rather than buy bindings that cost several crowns, buy a pair of skaller, komage or lap lugs that might not look as good and use skis without bindings. That, in my opinion, is the best binding.

Do not use thick woollen stockings with Lapp boots, you will overheat. But rather, stuff a dry wad of grass into each shoe, senne grass is best, most of it under the heel. That way, a heel is constructed inside rather than outside the boot. [Laplanders do not wear socks. Their boots are lined with senne grass, a species of reed cut in the summer and beaten with a wooden mallet until it becomes soft and pliable, after which it is dried and tied into small bundles.] Thus equipped and wearing the outfit recommended by Mr.Huitfeldt, the ladies will be able to ski. They are allowed to fall, squeal and laugh as much as they like. After all, no one goes to a funeral on the ski slopes.

And now a few words about the skis.

It is not at all difficult to straighten up a pair of warped skis although I do not know if people here are familiar with this sort of work. The skis do not necessarily have to be made only of pinewood; skis made of pine, the so-called 'grey pine', do not glide well, and after all skis need to glide well. If one can afford it then mountain ash and birch are preferred, partly because (and especially in cold weather) they are more slippery than pine and also stronger. Mountain ash skis unfortunately have a tendency to warp, but if they are made of wood that has matured at least one summer, then one can be fairly safe. Should they too want to go off at an angle then, as I have said, they are not difficult to straighten. Mountain ash and birch skis are not heavier than pine skis.

I wanted to put this on record and at the same time thank Mr. Huitfeldt for his lively and charming article.

GROWTH OF THE SOIL by Knut Hamsun

Knut Hamsun won the Nobel Prize for Literature with this book. Here is a very short extract, translation by Ingrid Christophersen.

The winter round of work was as before; carting wood, mending tools and implements. Inger kept house and did sewing in her spare time. The boys were down in the village again for the long term at school. For several winters past they had had one pair of skis between them. They managed well enough that way as long as they were at home, one waiting while the other took his turn. Or, one standing on the back of the skis behind the other. Aye, they managed wonderfully with but one pair, it was the finest thing they knew, and they were innocent and happy. But down in the village things were different. The school was full of skis; even the children from Breidablikk, it seemed, had a pair each. And the out-come was that Isak had to make a new pair for Eleseus, Sivert keeping the old pair for himself. Isak did more; he had the boys well clad and gave them everlasting boots.

CHAPTER 10
ROMANCE AND SKIS

INTRODUCTION by Ingrid Christophersen

I certainly know about skis and romance. If your entire youth and adolescence is spent on the snow, then at some point it is inevitable that the two (falling in love and skis) come together. Norway was, in my childhood and youth, a very safe and innocent country. The vast wilderness surrounding the capital Oslo, was criss-crossed by flood-lit trails, a necessity in a country where everyone skis and where, in winter, daylight is in short supply. Not much could happen when you and your boyfriend skied home at night after an evening on the flood-lit slalom hill. Woolly gloves and hats got in the way. But it was a start and a harbinger of delights to come later in life! One boyfriend broke a leg on the way home and little 'Miss Nightingale' got him home, leaning heavily on me – and secretly quite delighted that it was a broken bone and not just a bruised shin. More important!

There are three romantic skiing stories in this chapter. I very much identify with the girls in 'The Ideal Time'!

TWO IN DECEMBER by Jirij Kazakov

Jurij Kazakov (1927–1982) was a Russian author of short stories. A brilliant stylist, he has been compared to Anton Chekhov and Ivan Bunin. Parts of the year he lived in Northern Russia, by the White Sea, and many of his short stories are drawn from these surroundings. Born in Moscow, he started out as a jazz musician but turned to publishing his stories in 1952. Kazakov emerged as a writer only thanks to the short period in recent Russian history known as 'The Thaw', but in the mid-1960s, this period gave way to stagnation in culture and public life.

He had been waiting some time for her at the station. The day was frosty and sunny and he was very pleased with everything: from the sight of the crowds of other skiers to the underfoot crunch and squeak of the fresh snow that had not yet been cleared from the Moscow pavements. And he was pleased with himself as well, with his strong ski boots, the woollen socks that came up almost to his knees, his thick, shaggy sweater and the gay Austrian peaked cap on his head; and he was particularly pleased with his skis, a fine laminated pair with excellent foot straps.

She was late, as always, and there had been a time when that would have irritated him, but now he was used to it. If one thought about it, it was practically her only fault. He had leant their skis against a wall, and as he stood there shifting lightly from foot to foot to keep his feet warm, looking in the direction from which she would come, there was no disquiet in him. He was at peace, not particularly joyous, but at peace. He was content in knowing that everything was going well at work. They all liked him there, things were fine at home, and this winter was turning out to be very nice, for here they were in December and it was more like March, with that sun and that sparkle from the snow. Most importantly, he was at one with her. The times of painful quarrels, of jealousy, suspicion, mistrust, of sudden telephone calls – with that silence at the other end, when all you hear is the other person breathing, and your heart sinks – all those were over. Praise be. All that was over and now it was different. There was quiet confidence in each other and a tender feeling; that was what they had now.

She arrived at last and he looked at her approaching him, looked at her face, her figure. "Well now," he said to her when she was near, "Here we are then…"

He took up the skis and they moved off, slowly because she had been hurrying and had to catch her breath. She wore a pretty little red hat and under it, strands of hair had escaped and fell over her forehead. Her dark eyes wandered and were a little unsteady when she looked at him, but he mainly noted that the sun had already brought out the faintest show of small freckles across the bridge of her nose.

He dropped behind momentarily to rummage in his pockets for change for the tickets. Glancing quickly at her back and legs he thought suddenly how good-looking she was and how well she wore her clothes. And the reason she came late was probably because she always wanted to be pretty for him; those wisps of hair, seemingly accidentally there, might well not be accidental at all. How touching that always was in her, her flustered preoccupation with such things.

"Feel that sun! Some winter, this, mm?" she said while he was getting the tickets. "You haven't forgotten anything, have you?"

He made a face. If anything, he had brought too much and he could feel it as his rucksack was more than a little heavy.

The carriage of the elektrichka was jammed with rucksacks and skis and was noisy with everybody shouting, calling across seats to each other, occupying their places with a great deal of disorder and a rattling of skis. The windows were cold but clear. The radiators beneath the seats diffused a dry warmth, and once the train departed it was pleasant to look out through the glass to the sunny snow and listen to the muffled tapping of the wheels under the floor.

Some twenty minutes into the trip he went out to the vestibule at the end of the carriage to have a cigarette. The glass was missing from one of the two outside doors, and a cold wind blew in noisily and the walls and ceiling were covered with a white frosting or rime. Here there was a keen odour of snow and iron, and the wheels no longer tapped but battered the eardrums, and the hum of the rails was more like a bellows.

He smoked and looked back into the carriage through the glass of the inner door, moving his glance from one seat to another and feeling a slight sense of sorrow towards the other travellers, because, so it seemed to him, none of them could possibly be as blessedly happy in the coming two days as he was going to be. He looked at the girls too, at their animated faces, and the thought of them worried him faintly and ruefully lately as it always did whenever he saw loveliness and youth passing by on another's arm and not his.

Then he saw her and grew pleased again. He thought that even here, among many young and pretty girls, she was still better than any of them. She sat looking out through the window, the soft tone of her face accentuating her dark eyes beneath their long lashes.

He too turned to look through the glassless door at the scenery, at the hoarfrost suspended and glinting in the air, and he squinted from the brightness and from the wind of their passage. Snow-covered, creaky wooden platforms flashed by, sometimes furnished with a plywood refreshment room painted blue, with an iron flue jutting up from the roof, and ascending above that a column of blue smoke. And he thought how nice it always was to sit sheltered in one of them, drinking a mug of beer and warming oneself at the stove while some passing elektrichka prolonged its thin whistle as it rushed past outside.

And, in fact, everything was just fine: what a winter this was, what happiness that he had someone to love now, that she whom he loved was sitting not far away there in the carriage, someone whose eyes you could meet knowing that it would call from her a responsive look. How good that was he knew only too well. How many nights had he sat at home alone in those times when he still did not have her. How often had he loitered aimlessly up and down streets with friends, philosophising, handing down clever judgements on the merits of some theory, or relativity or whatever – some pleasure, that! – then returned home to boredom and gloom. He even wrote verses in those days, praised by a friend who also had no girl, until that friend found one and got married.

Standing there in the vestibule, he thought how strangely people are made! He himself was a lawyer, already thirty years old, and had never done anything special, never discovered or created anything, had not become a poet or a great athlete as he had fantasised in his youth. Yet, he had plenty of reasons to be sour if he wanted, considering that nothing of the kind had turned out in his life. But he wasn't sour, his unexceptional work and the fact that he was in no way renowned did not sadden him, nor did it horrify him. Quite the contrary. He had become content and relaxed and lived a normal life, just as if he had achieved the things he once dreamt of, had achieved them and then retired from the need to pursue them any longer.

He had only one constant preoccupation now: thoughts about summer. As far back as each November he began to think about and plan, with an intentness one might almost direct towards the solving of a fateful riddle, how and where he would take his coming summer leave. That stretch of free time seemed to him so endless and yet so short. That everything needed to be considered well ahead, the most attractive place chosen early, so that there would be no mistake or mishap to mar things. He worried all winter and spring, investigating nice-sounding locations, informing himself about the countryside and the people, the means of getting there; and those enquiries and plans were perhaps even more pleasant than the actual trip and holiday.

He stood and thought about how he would go to some little stream somewhere. They would take a tent, would arrive at the imagined little stream, pump up the rubber boat – their Indian dugout – and then goodbye Moscow, goodbye to the asphalt and to the court cases and the consultations.

And then he remembered the first time they had left Moscow together. They had gone to Estonia, to a tiny little town that he had visited before on a professional assignment and had made a mental note to try to return to. And so, they went there, and he remembered travelling on the night bus, stopping at Valday, where everything was dark and the only bit of life and light was a restaurant where he had drunk a glass of vodka. Well matured Starka it was too, and it had gone to his head and he had been very happy subsequently in the bus, because she was travelling beside him, dozing through the dark night-passage, her head on his shoulder. They arrived at first light, and although it was mid-August and in Moscow it had rained incessantly, here the sky was clear, everything was bright, and the sun was rising over the white cottages with steep-tiled roofs. There was a multitude of gardens in that town, and such a sense of solitude, of peace in those streets: streets where the grass grew in curls between the cobblestones.

They settled into a clean room full of light, where on the windowsills and under the bed and even inside the wardrobe strong-smelling ripe Antonovka winter apples were being stored. There was a bustling Estonian market in the town and they rambled about picking up smoked pork fat, blocks of honey and butter, tomatoes and cucumbers, all at fairy-tale prices. And he remembered the smell from the bakeries, and the continuous cooing of the pigeons, the sound of their wings like a long splash of water when they lifted up together. And above all, she was there: so unexpected in her ways, almost a stranger yet, and at the same time someone with whom he was already in love, who was close to him. What happiness that was; and there would be more of it probably, if only there was no war.

Lately he had thought a lot about war and had loathed the prospect of it. But now, as he looked out at the glinting snow, at the passing woods and fields, and as he listened to the whine of the wind and the rails, he concluded with certainty that there would not be any war, was resolved on that as he might decide to deny the existence of death except in some sense. Because, he thought, there are moments in life when a person must put away thoughts of terrible things or about the reality of evil.

When they got out they were practically the last passengers on the train. They walked along the platform and the snow crunched loudly under their boots.

"What a winter!" she said again, narrowing her eyes from the glare. "We haven't had one like this for a long time."

They had to ski about twenty kilometres to reach the dacha: they would spend the night there, have some fun next day skiing in the surrounding country and then return home by another line. His father had a little orchard with this weatherboard dacha among the fruit trees; a small affair with two beds, a table, homemade stools and a cast-iron German stove.

He fitted on his skis, jumped up and down a couple of times, slapping his skis down hard and raising a dust of powdery snow. Then he checked her straps, and they started off. They went slowly, although the plan had been to travel more rapidly and get to the place early, warm it up with a good fire and then rest; but in such woods and open spaces as they were traversing it was impossible to hurry.

"Just look at the trunks of those aspens!" he heard her say. She had stopped. "Have you seen the colour of cats' eyes? They're just like that."

He stopped too and looked. And it was true, the trunks had a greenish-yellow tinge toward the top, indeed the colour of cats' eyes.

Everywhere there were smoky shafts of sunlight angling down through the bare canopy of the forest. In some places, remarkably, the snow had managed to hang in frayed sheets that spanned between trees, looking as it does when it hangs down from house eaves. On occasion as they passed a fir it suddenly cascaded its burden of snow, and then the relieved branches swayed up and down with a motion like the spread-out paws of some large animal.

They went on from one gently sloping rise to another. Sometimes from the top of one they saw white-roofed hamlets. Every isba had its stove going and there was a general issue of smoke, the individual columns rising into the sky and at a certain point collapsing, tendrils then floating in every direction and finally drawing together in a common mist that lightly shrouded the surrounding hills in transparent blueness. Even a kilometre or two past such settlements the smell of wood smoke was strong. It was the kind of smell that urged one to get home quickly and light a fire.

At times they cut across dung-spattered lanes, polished to a shine by the runners of sledges. And, although it was December, there was something in those lanes – whether it was the wisps of dropped hay or the bluish shadows of old wheel ruts beneath the snow – that spoke of spring and smelled of it as well. Once, on such a lane beside a village, a black horse galloped by, coat glinting, muscles ripping, ice and snow flying from under its hooves. It passed across their front with crunching tattoo and a great snorting. There too they stopped and looked on in its wake.

And next there was the uneven, untidy passing flutter of a quite worried jackdaw, and then another bird behind it hurrying after the first; while at a little distance, a magpie kept a very interested eye on the birds' curious antics. Now, what could those two be about? was the magpie's patent expression; and the humans needed to stop and consider that scene as well. Or else it was bullfinches, rocking and purring on some thistles and protruded from the snow, unconcerned by the great oscillating swings of the stems they clung to, their strong, stubby beaks scattering the dry seeds in a pattern on the snow. Seen against the white background, the finches seemed as exotic as tropical birds.

Sometimes they came across fox spoor, a continuous and sinuous line passing from tussock to tussock, from hummock to hummock until it suddenly turned sharply and disappeared into the snowy radiance. Where the route took them through copses of aspens and birches, they passed tracks made by hares or squirrels. Such signs of a mysterious nocturnal world in the frozen, empty forest and fields worried the soul, bent the mind to thoughts of nighttime, the pre-hunt samovar, to sheepskin coats and guns, to the vision of the slowly turning stars, to the dark hayricks by the side of which all those hares fed and fattened at night, and towards which foxes, sometimes first standing tiptoe on their hind legs and sniffing the air, made their own approach. The thunderous shot echoes again in the memory, and the flash, the brittle, disintegrating return from the surrounding hills, the bark of startled dogs in a nearby village …

and then the fading, glazing eyes of the stretched-out hare, frost on the thick whiskers, the warm weight of the small carcass…

Down in the valleys and gullies the snow was deep and dry and the going sometimes quite toilsome, but on the hillsides there was a frosted moiré of crusty snow, a faintly wavelike surface covered lightly with snow dust. On that, the goings up and the descents were easy. Away in the distance, on the horizon, the forested hills glowed with rosy light, the sky was blue and the fields seemed boundless.

And so they went on, legging up and gliding down, taking a rest on a fallen tree trunk, smiling at each other. Sometimes he caught her from behind and drew her to him to kiss her cold chapped lips. They hardly talked, only gave the other an occasional call: "Look over there!" or "Listen!"

True, she seemed somewhat melancholy and abstracted, and he found her lagging behind rather often, but whatever the problem was he was unaware of it, thinking that it was because she was becoming tired. On one occasion he stopped to wait for her, and when she caught up and he saw her looking at him with a strange, reproachful expression he asked carefully, knowing how irritating such a question can be to someone having to keep up with you: "You're not tired, are you?"

"Of course not!" she replied instantly. "It's just that I'm… I was daydreaming."

"Mm, looks like it," he said lightly and turned to continue skiing, but more slowly.

The sun was now lower, and only those open areas that were in the high slopes of hills still shone, while the woods, the lower ground and the gullies had for some time now begun to be infiltrated by silent blue-grey shadows. And still as before, on the endless expanse of forest and fields, among distances beyond the sight of the two skiers, in extensions of space which made their figures tiny and solitary, they skied on: he in front, she following. He took pleasure in hearing behind him the hiss of her skis and the chirrup of her poles.

On one occasion, from out of the rosy flow in the direction where the sun had set, they heard a steady throb of engines, and within a minute an aeroplane appeared, high above them. It was the only thing still bright, the sun's rays glinting from its fuselage; and to imagine the passengers sitting in their seats, thinking of their journey's end, of their arrival soon in Moscow and those who would be meeting them.

It was dusk by the time they got to their destination. They stamped their encrusted boots on the cold veranda, unlocked the door and went in. It was quite dark in the dacha and seemed even colder than outside.

She immediately lay down on a bed and closed her eyes. On the way she had become hot and had perspired and now she began to cool quickly, and she was suddenly convulsed by such a bout of shivering that she was afraid to stand up again. Opening her eyes, she saw in the darkness above her the planked ceiling, turned and saw the flame behind the seating glass of the kerosene lamp flickering and steadying; she narrowed her eyes, and instantly a medley of colours – yellow-green, white, blue, bright red, all the colours she had seen during the day – swam and blended and changed into each other before her.

He was busy getting firewood from under the veranda, carrying armfuls inside, dropping them rumbling beside the stove, crumpling paper, lighting the stove, making grunting noises, coughing from the smoke…

and she just wanted nothing and felt no happiness whatever in having come with him this time.

The stove soon grew hot and radiated warmth, and they could begin taking off their outer clothing. He took off his boots and socks, hung things beside the stove, then sat in his shirtsleeves, happy, his eyes half closed in contentment, twitching his toes and smoking.

"Tired?" he asked her. "Come on then, better get your things off."

And although she wanted to lie down there and not move, wanted to annul in sleep her melancholy and disappointment, she got up obediently and took off and hung up her coat and socks and sweater. Then she sat on the bed, her man's checked shirt freed and hanging over her slacks, her shoulders bent and her gaze on the lamp.

He slid his bare feet into his boots again, draped his coat over his shoulders and left with a bucket. She heard it striking something with as startling 'ting!' as he passed through the veranda. On his return, he filled a kettle and put it on the stove and then unpacked his rucksack, taking out and spreading its contents on the table and on the window ledge.

She waited passively for the tea, filled herself a mug, and then sat chewing buttered bread and warming her hands on the sides of the mug, sipping and looking at the lamp.

"You're quiet," he said. "Been a great day, hasn't it?"

"Yes, well… I got terribly tired today." She stood up and stretched, not looking at him. "Let's sleep."

"Good idea," he said cheerfully. "I'll just be a moment, I'll get some wood in, the place is getting cold again."

"I'll sleep alone tonight, here by the stove, is that all right?" "Don't be angry," she added quickly and dropped her eyes.

"Why, what's this?" he asked her, puzzled. And immediately he recalled her lack of spirits and her distant expression throughout the day; and remembering it he felt a sudden surge of anger and his heart beat painfully.

And suddenly too, he saw that he really did not know her at all, how she studied at that university of hers, the people she knew and what she talked about with them; she remained an enigma to him, just as at their first meeting. A stranger. And he saw that she probably thought him coarse and obtuse because he did not understand what she needed or knew what to do to make her always happy when she was with him. So that she would need nothing and no one else. And he felt a flow of shame for the whole of that day, for this pathetic little cabin, for its stove, even for some reason for the snow and the sun. And he felt ashamed for his previous contentment. Why on earth had they come? What was it all for? And where was that damned happiness people forever went on about?

"Well, if that's how you feel," he said, keeping his tone level and releasing his breath. "Sleep where you like."

Without looking at him she lay down on the bed in her clothes and covered herself with her coat. She lay there, watching the fire in the stove, while he went to the other bed and sat smoking for a while. Then he blew out the light and lay down.

He felt bitter, sensing that she was going away from him. Somehow, things were just not working out for them as far as that happiness went; but what the problem was, he did not know, and that exasperated him.

After a minute he heard her crying. He lifted himself up on one elbow and looked across the table at her. There was sufficient light from the stove to see that she was lying prone and looking sideways at the burning wood, and he could see the misery on her tear-streaked face, its sad and unsightly contortion, the trembling lip and chin and the overflowing eyes which she rubbed with her thin hand.

What was it that had so unexpectedly weighed down on her and made her unhappy on this particular day? She herself did not know. She only felt that the season of first love had passed, something new was occurring and the life she had known with him until then had grown uninteresting. She was tired of being a nobody before his parents, his aunts and uncles, his friends and her own girlfriends. She wanted to be a wife and a mother, and he did not see that and felt just fine as he was. And yet the loss of that first, chaotic time in their love, when everything was so vague and undefined, infused with mystery, with passion and novelty, that loss was also painfully saddening.

Then she started to doze off, and a girlhood fancy returned to her, a reverie which in the past had often accompanied her into sleep. It seemed that there was someone strong and manly who loved her and she loved him in turn, but to whom for some reason she kept saying "No!" And so he had gone away, a long way up in the North, and he became a fisherman and she pined. He hunted too among the sea cliffs, leaping from boulder to boulder, and he made music, went to sea to fish, and all the time he thought of her. At last she understood that happiness could only be found with him, and so she dropped everything and went to him. She was so beautiful that everyone on the way paid court to her; aircraft pilots, drivers, sailors; but she had eyes for nobody else, she thought only of him. Their meeting was to be such a wondrous event that it was even frightening to imagine. All kinds of obstacles rose up to delay that moment. And that was how she usually fell asleep, not having met him.

It was a long time since she had outgrown that fantasy or any other like it, but tonight for some reason she wanted to return to it. Yet now, as before, even as she voyaged towards him aboard a boat which she had found sailing by chance in his direction, her thoughts grew confused and she fell asleep.

Later in the night the cold awoke her. He was squatting on his heels, lighting kindling in the cold stove. He looked miserable and she felt a pang of sadness for him.

In the morning they were quiet, ate breakfast without speaking, drank their tea. But then their spirits began to return and they took up their skis and went out for a spin. They made their way up hills, then skied down, choosing ever steeper and more risky slopes.

Back at the dacha they warmed themselves by the fire and talked about nothing in particular, about daily things and the truly fine winter they were having this year. When it began to approach dusk they packed up, locked the dacha and set out for the station.

They arrived drowsy in Moscow after dark, and when he saw the first apartments and the rows of lighted windows and he became aware that they would be parting in a few minutes, he suddenly thought of her as his wife.

Well, why not? First youth was gone: the time when everything looks easy and simple and a matter of future choice – an eventual place to live in, a wife, family, whatever – that careless time had passed, he was thirty. And what was the big deal in having someone beside you, attractive and so forth, and you smug in the confidence that you could drop her at any time and pick up another just as good because you felt yourself to be a free agent. Was there any satisfaction in that feeling? Tomorrow he was going to be in consultations over cases, be drawing up appeals, statements, be confronting human miseries, including domestic ones: and at the end of the day he would go home – to whom?

And some time in the future there was his summer. That long summer, all sorts of possible trips, the boat, the tent – but again, with whom? And he wanted to become a better person, a better human being, and do all he could to make it good for her.

But when they came out of the station and into the square, with its lights and the noises of the city all around them the snow swept up and trucked away now, they both felt as if their trip, those two days together, had left no memory. They would now say their goodbyes, go in different directions, and meet again perhaps in two or three days. A workday feeling, a calm and easy attitude returned to them, and they parted as they always did, smiling hurriedly, and he did not see her home.

THE SEDUCER by Jan Kjærstad

Jan Kjærstad (1953) is a Norwegian writer. Among his numerous publications are novels, short stories, essays, picture books, and articles. He is the holder of the most important literary award of Scandinavia, the 'Literature Prize of the Nordic Council'.

BROADCAST

So, do not forget the story that starts, or continues, at the moment when he realised just what a risk he was taking; that he should, of course, have done as the stupid safety regulations said, and turned back the minute they came out into the hollow in the hills and he saw his companion raising her eyes to the huge mountain straight ahead of them. They were heading south, towards the sun which only occasionally showed itself behind the clouds, in what would normally be described as heavy going: swirling snow and several degrees below freezing. The girl ahead of him on the track turned and grinned: "How're you doing?" He tried to smile back, feeling a cold sweat breaking out the length of his spine; he had been struck, after only the first few strides, by how deeply and sincerely he still hated this invention: skis, fibreglass now, and how terribly unfit he was; each time they stopped he had the urge to cough, his lungs seemed too small, and every inch of him pulsated with his heartbeat. They were making for a place she called Heddersvann: 'a reasonable point to make for in such bad weather' and let me just say right away that in writing the following I am treading with extreme care, because it deals with one of the few spheres in which Norwegians actually can boast greater expertise than any other nation… skiing.

At one point it seemed to him that she had altered course. They passed beneath a power-line and came to the foot of a steep slope. Just at that moment the clouds parted and the afternoon sun turned the landscape into the perfect picture of Easter in Norway as presented in tempting brochures aimed at foreign tourists. Directly above them towered a relatively high peak. The girl ahead of him made the sort of neat 180-degree turn that Jonas had never been able to do, neither as a child nor now, before gliding up alongside him.

"We're going for the bloody top," she said, squinting over the top of her sunglasses.

"That one?" said Jonas, pointing to Store Stavsronuten.

"No, that one," the girl said, pointing further up at a point diagonally behind Jonas, where Gaustatoppen itself lay hidden by cloud. She gazed resolutely, almost covetously, up what in Jonas's eyes seemed a formidably steep mountainside.

"But we haven't told anybody," he said. "I mean, we said we were going to Heddersvann. And we don't have time, it's three o'clock now!"

"What is it with you?" she said. "Don't tell me you're chicken?"

"We're going for the top, I said." She had definitely altered course, was already heading uphill, as the sky clouded over again.

'Completely Gausta', Jonas thought, this being their way as kids of saying somebody was crazy: reference to Gaustad Hospital. He turned, needing to have a piss. The sight of the yellow patch on the snow made him feel like an animal, a dog. He set off after the girl, even though he knew it was madness, feeling the action beginning to tell on his upper arms and shoulders right away.

It was the week before Easter and the massive influx of people to the mountains. Jonas Wergeland had been hanging about for some days, almost totally alone, at the Kvitavatn Mountain Lodge above Rjukan, having come to a breakthrough decision, an almost perverse decision: for the first time in his nigh-on twenty-four years he was going to give the Norwegian mountains a try.

And even though, typically for him, he chose to avoid the Easter crowds, he did also cherish a faint hope of coming up with an explanation for this almost animal-like characteristic of the Norwegian race. This abrupt, almost panicky migration. This mass exodus to the mountains over the week of the Easter holidays.

There was also another, and more intriguing motive for Jonas's choice of Rjukan in particular, and it was not, as one might think, the splendid hydroelectric monuments of Vemork and Såheim – Jonas Wergeland was to remain shamefully ignorant of these almost baroque, or perhaps one should say, fantastical, buildings until the day he met an African at Livingstone in Zambia many years later. No, it was curiosity about NRK's main transmitters, set up on the tops of mountains all over Norway that had brought him to the Gausta area – I consider this worth mentioning since it casts some doubt on whether Jonas Wergeland did indeed join NRK on an impulse as sudden and random as he himself has always claimed.

The fact is that while at the College of Architecture he had come across Le Corbusier's book, 'Vers une architecture', one of the few books which he had read as avidly as the Kama Sutra of his childhood, and what Le Corbusier had written about the link between the products of modern industrial design (cars, planes, passenger ships) and architecture, had led Jonas to think of television masts – surely these too could be transformed into an exciting architectonic impulse. He envisaged them almost as church spires in a new secular era or as the minarets of some sort of media religion. In other words, he had come to Rjukan to view the mast on the top of Gausta, the only problem being that, until now, it had not shown itself, due to the miserable weather. The clouds hung around the peak like a cap and Jonas had not felt much like getting out on his skis.

When Sigrid A. had walked into the fire-lit lounge the previous evening, tall and fair, with piercing blue eyes and a distinctive nose, Jonas had immediately been aware of that soft feather, which made its presence felt in his life only occasionally, being run up his spine by an invisible hand before coming to rest in the form of a prolonged tickling sensation between his shoulder blades. But she, it must be said, had noticed him right away, too, and in a manner quite at odds with her normally shy nature she had, without a moment's hesitation, walked straight over and sat down in the chair opposite him.

Sigrid A. was that pretty rare animal, a glaciologist. She had started out by studying medicine, it's true, but had soon switched courses, recognising the great outdoors to be her natural element. No doubt there are also some who know of her as a mountaineer; Sigrid A. was, in fact, to be the driving force behind countless daring exploits in one wilderness and another, in widely diverging parts of the world, as the leader of sponsored expeditions that generated banner headlines in the Norwegian press and led, in time, to her being called upon to fulfil other tasks, as a so-called PR ambassador for Norway. A somewhat obscure, but nonetheless lucrative diplomatic post.

Sigrid A. not only felt a deep need always to be the first, but also to do things which allowed her to push her body to the limits of its capabilities as if this were a goal in itself. More than once, she had been almost shocked by what her own flesh and blood could actually stand. During her conversation with Jonas in the lounge she did not, however, mention this at all. What she did say was that she liked going for long ski trips in the moonlight, and when Jonas confessed that skiing was rather a sore point with him, she saw her chance and invited him to go skiing with her the following day.

So there Jonas Wergeland was, against all the odds – and what was a great deal more foolhardy and irresponsible, without having told anyone – heading up the hill towards Gaustatoppen in dangerously bad weather, led by a woman who could cope with three times as much as he in terms of physical endurance.

The slope was so steep that he had to take it sideways on; the gap between them grew. She stopped, turned. "Come on!" she called, a note of anger in her voice. Jonas pushed himself even harder, not so much because he wanted to show that he was a man, as because he felt like a dog, he had to obey. His arms ached, and in the grey light the snow seemed even whiter, dazzling. He was not happy, either, about this blend of hot and cold, with half of his body, the back side, soaked with sweat, while the snow and the wind threatened to turn his front to ice. She had stopped to wait for him. His nose was running; he felt thoroughly pissed off.

"I'm sorry, I can't go any further," he said, swallowing his pride. "You can do it!" she said harshly, almost contemptuously. "Come on!" She gave him a little rap on the backside with her pole.

Up on the ridge itself, the wind came at them from the north west like a bat out of hell. Crystals of ice dug in to their faces like crampons. Evening was drawing on. Jonas could not see the point in this: why they could not turn back, why they were out here defying the forces of nature when they could be sitting in front of the fire back at Kvitavatn Mountain Lodge drinking hot cocoa and playing Scrabble, or some other dumb game. It was as if she had to finish whatever she had set out to do; every inch of her radiated determination unlike anything he had ever come across before.

Jonas plodded on, his chin lowered onto his chest. Everything was white – white, white – all the contours of the landscape had been obliterated by the swirling snow. He was growing bitterly cold, particularly around his groin. Amateur that he was, he had dressed as if for a quick run across Lillomarka. He floundered on, like a dog, he thought again and again, concentrating: right pole, left ski, he thought, left pole, right ski; he saw her turn, not to look at him – it was as if she instinctively knew he was there anyway – but at the invisible sun, with a look on her face that seemed to say she was aiming not for the top of Gausta but for something much higher, much greater. He felt afraid.

Then, when they could not have been far from the top, the blast grew even fiercer or perhaps the weather simply was that much wilder up there. They trekked through a sea of whiplashes, everything was white, the earth, the sky, Jonas had slid into a sort of physical second gear; his engine was on automatic, right pole, left ski, left ski, right pole, thoughts churning around in his head willy nilly. He looked down at the strange, windswept patterns in the driving snow and was struck by a feeling of being on an unknown planet or of suddenly having uncovered Norway's innermost secret: that Norway was another planet. Jesus Christ, why couldn't they turn back, she was out of her mind, this girl; he glanced back, that's life for you, he thought, giving in to the banality, the macabre humour of the situation; you left a track on a cold and inhospitable planet, which promptly swept it away behind you.

The driving snow reached into every nook and cranny. Jonas had visions of precipices. Wasn't there supposed to be a sharp drop on either side of the actual peak, the west side especially? Right ski, left ski, right ski, left ski, he could no longer feel his arms, his face was nothing but a cold, stiff mask, numb. Sigrid A. was looking round about, she seemed quite unperturbed, as if everything were going exactly according to plan or as if she were going on instinct, steering by some in-built compass He was struck .by her strong profile, a heroic profile, tailor-made for the heads of coins, he thought, and then once again he caught a glimpse of that look on her face, as if she relished this ordeal, this self-torment, this sub-human struggle. Suddenly she pulled up next to a high snowdrift. "We made it!" she called down to him.

"Congratulations, young man! The Tourist Board hut!" Jonas refused to believe that they were saved, giggled with mild hysteria at the very idea. A snowdrift. A heap of snow. She motioned to him to follow her round to the eastern side of the bank of snow, and through the snow Jonas made out some rough stones. Had it not been for the corner of a window peeking out, he would have taken it for a cairn. But this was, in fact, the Gaustatoppen tourist hut, built of granite. Huge blocks hacked out of the mountain itself, now totally buried in snow. "Now all we have to do is hoist the flag," she said, her face glowing as if she really loved such ordeals and was almost sorry to have reached the top.

After shovelling away another snowdrift piled up against the entrance, which was hung with a mocking sign offering 'light snacks', they found that the heavy blue, metal door was open.

"Did you know about this?" Jonas said. She did not reply. Just flashed that happy smile. Another surprise awaited them. Inside, the little room was warm, it actually felt warm after the icy wind. There was a switch; the light came on. "The extension's new," she said. "It was added when the army were building up here. They laid heating cables under the cement floor, as you know."

The door to the hut itself was locked. But Jonas was more than content, ran an eye gratefully round the wood-panelled room; there was a narrow oblong window high up in the eastern wall. Some blankets were piled on a bench along with some old sleeping bags. "People sometimes spend the night here," Sigrid A. said, unpacking her little rucksack, which proved to contain a little of this and a little of that. Soon they were sitting on the bench, each with a cup of tea and sharing a bar of chocolate and an orange. Thus, as a reward almost, for all that he had gone through, for the first time ever Jonas Wergeland was treated to the experience of a typical Norwegian Easter ritual.

As the light outside the window began to wane, Sigrid A. made up a bed on the warm floor with the blankets and sleeping bags. "Well, now we've just got to find some way of passing the time," she said, giving him a look that was as much an order as a request.

They got undressed. She swore at him when she saw how few clothes he had on, not even woollen underwear; but this anger turned to pity when she caught sight of his tiny penis, which had drawn as far into itself as it could, like a collapsed telescope.

She tucked him up under the blankets, stroking it with her hand as she did so, warming it, putting her face down to it and blowing on it, taking it in her mouth, keeping it there for a long time, so long that she gradually made it rise and before too long she had climbed on top of him and guided it inside her, and Jonas felt a glorious, red-hot glow. Concentrating in one spot he felt his frozen body being thawed, as it were, by the warmth that flowed from this one spot. They lay still, that is to say, she crouched on top of him, bent over in such a way that her breasts just grazed his chest, two hot spots, a triangle of heat; and as she clenched him tightly with the muscles of her vagina. He had a marvellously tactile sensation of something tight, soft and miraculously warm, such a wonderfully delightful warmth flowing into his limbs, and it crossed his mind that this, the sum of this heat, must be what held the world together. And it was at that moment, if anyone should be in any doubt, that Jonas Wergeland truly understood what it was that he had always sought from these women: warmth. And as she slowly began to move, he could not help thinking how this sweet friction resembled two sticks being rubbed together to make fire. He vaguely remembered something about how, during their sacrificial rituals, the ancient Aryans had done just that. Kindled a fire by grinding one stick in a hole made in another stick – symbolizing, of course, the lingam inside the yoni. There was also something about this quite unbelievably delicious warmth of Sigrid A.'s vagina that made Jonas feel it was no ordinary warmth, the sort that could thaw ice, but a warmth that could actually kindle fire, a creative flame within him, make it flare up inside him, enabling him to see things, experience something akin to visions or revelations, a warmth that would extend him, lighting up new chambers within him.

She began by making love to him long and lingeringly, with a dreamy look in her eyes, as if she were planning great exploits, or as if he were a great exploit, a wide-open space in himself.

Outside, darkness had fallen, the wind howled around the walls of the hut, crystals of ice spattered against the window. He lay there, warm from head to toe, while she made love to him with greater and greater intensity, her whole body eventually working furiously as she rode him, purposefully, tirelessly, as if this too were a wilderness that she had to conquer, a peak she had to climb. She made love to him all night long, so many times that Jonas could not believe that they – or at any rate he – could go on, but she would make him rise up again, whipping him on as relentlessly as when she dragged him to the top of the mountain, making love to him so fiercely and so divinely that his whole body seemed to glow. And it was during this exhausting coupling with Sigrid A. that Jonas not only learned how much his body could stand. That he could hold out for far longer than he had imagined and that the volume of semen in his glands had not run out, even though he was crying out that it had. During the course of that pleasurable and demanding night, a new determination was also born in Jonas Wergeland, making him realise that it was time he put his experiences into some sort of order, set himself some big goal, select, as it were, a peak. And, what with the fiery glow in his body, the great, bright light of creativity in his head and the thought of the transmitter standing at the top of Gausta, right outside the window, he had the feeling that their lovemaking was being broadcast, that the image of their coupling was being beamed into all those thousands of homes.

The next morning they stepped out into the most beautiful weather. Everything, the whole, wide world, was shimmering blue and white – sparkling white – and charged with a breath-taking silence. The television mast a hundred metres above their heads glinted like one of Carl Nesjar's year-round fountains, sculpture of ice. Jonas was sure that Le Corbusier would have appreciated this sight, that Le Corbusier, like Jonas, would have been filled with awe at the thought of such a heroic project: – wild, elongated and sparsely populated country linked together by a telecommunications network. An epic undertaking, Jonas thought. And beautiful, Jonas thought, as beautiful as nature itself.

It was said that you could see a seventh part of Southern Norway from the top and it certainly seemed so. As Jonas spun round and round on his own axis, like a little kid, wide eyed and speechless, he discovered (and this he automatically put down to the events of the previous night) that suddenly this landscape meant a great deal to him. He actually felt a kind of love for these vast open spaces, these mountains. And the snow, even the snow.

He bent down and scooped it up, having to screw up his eyes against the light, and as he crouched there, hunkered down on Gaustatoppen, clutching a handful of snow, it dawned on him why so many people migrated to the mountains at Easter time: on account of the light, the dazzling light. And from that day forth, Jonas Wergeland was always to regard this as being his countrymen's finest trait: their longing for light which, not unreasonably, manifested itself at Easter time, during a religious festival. In days to come, this insight was to form the basis for his optimistic estimation of television's potential, in as much as television was a form of light, dazzling light.

The trip down was something of an anti-climax. Even though he took the slopes diagonally, crisscrossing his way down, it went so fast that his eyes were tearing behind his sunglasses; his leg muscles ached and he fell God knows how many times, slithering and bouncing. Sigrid A. was way ahead of him, executing elegant, practised Telemark swings as though she were taking part in a display and only lacked the felt hat, the homespun breeches and the traditional sweater. When he finally caught up with her at the foot of Longefonn she was standing talking to the rescue team that had been about to institute a search for them.

THE IDEAL TIME by Lars Saabye Christensen

Lars Saabye Christensen (1953), is one of the most important contemporary Norwegian authors. He has received many awards and his works have been translated into more than twenty languages. This translation is by Ingrid Christophersen.

It happened from time to time that our parents wanted to arrange some amusements for us. It wasn't really amusing. But their favourite pursuit was to organise a ski race. It was to take place on the fields at Gaustad and there were at least twice as many parents as children. They were amused. The most ardent slept in tents the night before, to watch over the track, or so they said. There was a table full of prizes, diplomas signed by three people, tiny cups and goody-bags for the runners up with bananas and jelly babies. There were no categories. We were one big family and were supposed to have fun, and so we were obliged to compete against the dwarfs and the girls.

And we were meant to ski it in a time set by our parents, a so-called 'ideal time'.

The track looped around the field, through the woods and out onto a clearing from where you could see Gaustad lunatic asylum, and all the mad people were standing in the windows cheering us on. Then the track swung back again and when we arrived at the field the fathers were waiting in their huge anoraks, waving with their woollen mittens. The mothers were brandishing Thermos flasks and picnics and sour blood oranges and rock-hard cooking chocolate.

We set off at 20 second intervals and the invention of the wittiest of the parents was to lay out various odd items along the route that we were supposed to take note of – a pair of glasses, a tie, a piece of soap or a string vest. These items were hung up on trees or lay in the snow and when we eventually reached our goal, we had report all we had seen to two serious parents who had spent the night in a tent.

So, we plodded along the track, one after the other, an awkward bunch, looking for items that had nothing to do with our surroundings, in a time that our parents had decided but that we didn't know.

That's the sort of things our parents thought of. They called it fun!

Jonny and I never won. I skied too fast and never saw a thing, Jonny was too slow and saw everything. He arrived at the finish and reported having seen empty booze bottles, cigar butts and beer tops. That made the two parents grumpy and Jonny was disqualified. But it didn't really matter. After all, who wanted to hang one of those diplomas over your bed, with a picture of Trysil-Knut, and signed by Olsen from down the road and Jacobsen from the grocery shop?

The winter we turned 13 and had been given 'Bonna' skis with red, rat-trap bindings we refused to play ball, but to no avail. Jonny called it destiny; he had looked the word up in the family encyclopaedia, so he knew what he was talking about. A damp Sunday morning we all lined up on the Gaustad fields and bibs were fastened to our anoraks, and that was just bloody hell, because we were now the oldest in our street and our reputation was at stake. A scowl from right hand temple to left hand ear lobe crossed Jonny's face and he declined all offers of oranges. My neck was sweaty with embarrassment and I rubbed Swix under the skis until they were virtually on fire. But our parents were enjoying themselves.

I started forty seconds after Johnny. He was waiting for me behind the first and biggest pine tree. I slid out of the track and allowed the rookies to overtake, their eyes popping out, their skis balled up to their knees.

"Have you seen anything?" I asked.

"Forty mad parents, 352 oranges, three cups, six diplomas and nineteen Thermos flasks," Jonny said grumpily and hauled two cigarettes out of his pocket.

We sucked on them until our tongues burnt and then flipped the butts onto the trail.

"Now the little buggers will have more to remember."

We smirked a bit more and then the last pygmy passed us with bib twenty on his chest and rusty Kandahar bindings.

"Have to catch up then," I said.

Jonny pinched his eyes together and looked sinister.

"We'll take the track to Songsvann," he said. "And then we'll go plain on to Kikut. Heh?"

And that's what we did. We stuffed our bibs into pockets and disappeared into Nordmarka. It was quite an OK feeling, to disappear into Nordmarka, decide the pace for yourself, not give a damn, change tracks, see what we wanted to see. We said nothing during the whole trip, for Jonny and I didn't need to chinwag to have a good time. It was OK. The snow conditions improved as we ascended, past Ullevålseter. After a couple of hours, we whizzed over Bjørnesjøen, poled our way over the lake and then we were sitting at Kikut, sharing a blackcurrant toddy and a chocolate bar in a hut steaming from wet snow, sweat and tobacco.

"Can't really imagine it," Jonny said suddenly. "Can't really imagine that mum and dad were sweethearts."

"I can't either," I said. "That mum and dad were sweethearts I mean."

"That they bonked," Jonny continued. "It makes me sick just to think about."

"Do you think about it?" I asked.

"No," Jonny said.

I snapped the last bit of chocolate into two equal parts.

"Actually, yes," said Jonny. "Saw a picture of mum when she was confirmed. Bloody hell couldn't tell it was her. I mean, she was quite pretty."

"I've seen a picture of dad during the war. Didn't really recognise him either."

Jonny chewed noisily, gazed down at the checkered tablecloth, slowly looked up, heavily.

"Wish I knew mum and dad better," he said.

"Know what you mean," I said.

That's when we spotted two girls from school – Vivi and Merete. We cringed slightly. There was snow in their hair, their knees were wet and there were icicles on their eyelashes. The heat in the room made their faces glow, as though flames were licking up their cheeks. Now they saw us. They bought cocoa and a metre of waffles. They came and sat at our table.

Not so easy to think of something clever to say just off the cuff. We sat and smiled and rocked and flashed glances at each other. But someone had to get the ball rolling, and that someone was either Jonny or me.

"Not very good conditions," Jonny said at last.

"What did use for you wax?" Vivi asked.

"Soft soap and Vaseline."

And the girls laughed. What would I have done without Jonny? I don't know, I just don't know.

"We were sitting here talking about our parents," I said.

Jonny's boots kicked me under the table and silence returned.

Two can shut up, that's fine, but four, that's rather exhausting.

Jonny and I looked sideways at the two girls, inspecting them. Vivi combed water out of her hair as though she had just stepped out of the shower, and I pictured it to myself, as I picture a lot, and suddenly she looked straight at me and then I pictured something else, that she too was in the race and when she got to the finish she would say: "I saw Christian's thoughts, I have won."

"Not looking forward to the maths mocks," Merete said.

"Just have a crib sheet in your stockings and go to the loo," said Jonny.

"Do they allow you to go alone?" Vivi asked.

I needed to say something. I said something.

"Go alone?" I said.

"Yeh, to the loo of course."

"The invigilator comes to the bog," said Jonny, "but he doesn't come into the cubicle. Are you mad?"

Jonny made a low chortle and stole a waffle with goat's cheese. So did I, and made a low chortle.

"Our invigilators do," Merete said. "We aren't allowed to close the door." Jonny and I looked at each other, scratched the tablecloth and breathed out slowly. It was my turn to say something.

"Do you have to; do you have to sit on the bog with an open door?"

Vivi and Merete nodded, they nodded vigorously.

We didn't say much more before we started for home. We didn't say much then either. The sky started to glow, just like Vivi and Merete's faces, when they came into the hut and we saw them before they saw us.

It was quite beautiful, but I couldn't say that. There was a lot I couldn't say, and so I didn't. But close to the Bjørnehytta hut, there was an incline, behind some tightly packed pines whose branches flopped into the snow, like a melting soft ice. There were no tracks leading to the spot, we trampled our own, just like that. We sat there, a few paces apart, Vivi and I and Jonny and Merete. I suddenly thought of Trysil-Knut, the diploma with Trysil-Knut.

"I won't win this year either," I said.

But Vivi didn't understand what I was talking about. She bent over me, she tasted of chewing gum. I'm not sure what I tasted of, Swix maybe, or maybe blood oranges and bananas, I never asked. We lay in the snow, her hand was round my neck and she was stronger than I thought, because I had seen her throw the small ball at Frogner stadium that autumn and it landed at nine and a half metres. My body stiffened, I stiffened, our tongues were stiff from the cold. Then they melted, we thawed, pushed against each other, we were in the snow, in December, my hands moved on their own. I fumbled around in her anorak pocket and found a comb, a lipstick, and orange peel, a tram ticket, and two ski ties in Norwegian colours. Then I located her breast, and suddenly she was lying under me, she twisted and made a half angel in the snow, I think she wanted to get up, but I held her down, but lost my courage.

"No," she said softly.

"No," I said.

I hadn't taken my skis off. I lay on top of her, like a ski jumper, a perfect flight but didn't dare land. I set a new hill record, for all times, but heard no rejoicing.

"No, she said," softer still.

"No," I said.

Then we all got up, all four, like sleepy animals from our hollows. I brushed the snow off Vivi's back. Jonny brushed the snow off Merete's back. We rejoined the track and continued our way home as though nothing had happened.

Vivi and Merete caught the tram from Songsvann. That was it. They tied the skies to the outside and disappeared into the carriage. We remained behind, waving to them, but I don't think they saw us.

"They'll be pissed off," said Jonny.

"Who?"

"Who? Are you off your rocker? Our parents. I'm sure they've phoned the Red Cross and the Youth Patrol."

"There'll be all hell to pay."

We raced across to the Gaustad fields, as darkness descending from the sky made the shadows along the track stretch out. Nevertheless, I saw it all, everything that was not supposed to be there, a tie, a piece of soap, a singlet, and I memorised it, I saw it all.

We sprinted into the clearing to the finish. The prize-giving table had been taken down, orange peel tidied away, the Thermos flasks closed. And where the track stopped stood four people, Jonny's parents and mine. We glided towards them, heads bent and pulse racing. We expected the worst and stopped with two snowploughs.

"Had a good day?" my father asked and thumped my back with his woollen mittens.

"Yeh," said I.

"Been far?" Jonny's father asked.

"Yeh," said Jonny. "Quite."

"Good conditions?" asked my mum.

"Good further up," I said.

"But your time is rather lousy," Jonny's mum said. "But what did you see?"

But they started to laugh before I could answer. They laughed and Jonny and I looked at each other and understood bugger all, and I was about to answer, 'soap, tram ticket, ski tie, singlet'. But Jonny was already on his way and I followed him, and behind us our parents, singing in the track, like a request programme, the first hymns, 'Behold they Stand in Robes of White'. We skied as fast as we could to no avail, they were following us, and I heard laughter, laughter and hymns.

We found Majorstuen, we found a tram and Jonny and I found an empty seat for two.

"How odd," said Jonny.

"Off their rocker," I said .

"They've gone mad," said Jonny.

"Completely crazy," I said .

"I'd have preferred a rocket," I said. "Why aren't they giving us a rocket? They always do."

Jonny pointed to something just as the tram bumped along Kirkeveien. He pointed to the Durex advert on the Vinkel building and crossed his fingers over his nose when we got to Frognerparken.

"Did you score?" he said.

"Nearly," I said.

"Me too."

"Next Saturday," said Jonny.

"Next Saturday, I said, quarter to five?"

"Ten to five."

That night I dreamt about a heart which was hanging in a thin thread from the top branch of an old pine, in the middle of a black and hopeless forest. Rusty drops dripped into the snow, making a hollow and I fell into it and I knew I could tell no one of what I saw, that was impossible. I heard my heartbeat under my pyjamas. And it was beating far too fast, as though I was in a hurry. Then I woke out of the old dream. I was skiing, with one pole and I hadn't got there, and it was a long way and I thought about next Saturday, about everything that had not happened and all I had not seen. And though I wanted it all to happen as quickly as possible, I knew that everything would take time, and that all would come slowly, slowly but surely, that my time would come.

From this story we can draw the conclusion that some things cannot be measured in ideal time.

CHAPTER 11
ACCIDENTS AND AVALANCHES

INTRODUCTION by Ingrid Christophersen

The nature of skiing accidents has changed over the years. When I was young, you broke your leg and it wasn't really a big deal. Today, with high boots and cambered ski, it's all about knees, cruciate ligaments and even collision on more crowded slopes. Skiing is faster, the pistes are smoother and invite higher speeds. In my youth, there was no such thing as a rat track, you skied on bumpy, un-pisted slopes. On the other hand, equipment such as crash helmets, ski stoppers and the quality of ski clothing go a long way towards protecting the athletic skier. Athletes competing now wear back protectors and there is talk of airbags being used in the event of a hard and fast fall. Avalanche location equipment is vastly improved, and back-country skiers can wear transceivers for faster detection. The science of releasing avalanches before they become a risk to the public has also vastly improved.

THE BELL JAR by Sylvia Plath

Sylvia Plath (1932–63) was an American poet, novelist, and short story writer. She is credited with advancing the genre of confessional poetry and is best known for two of her published collections, 'The Colossus and Other Poems' and, 'Ariel', as well as 'The Bell Jar'.

I stood at the top of the ski slope on Mount Pisgah, looking down. I had no business to be up there. I had never skied before in my life. Still, I thought I would enjoy the view while I had the chance.

At my left, the rope tow deposited skier after skier on the snowy summit which, packed by much crossing and re-crossing and slightly melted in the noon sun, had hardened to the consistency and polish of glass. The cold air punished my lungs and sinuses to a visionary clearness.

On every side of me the red and blue and white jacketed skiers tore away down the blinding slope like fugitive bits of an American flag. From the foot of the ski run, the imitation log cabin lodge piped its popular songs into the overhang of silence.

Gazing down on the Jungfrau. From our chalet for two…

The lilt and boom threaded by me like an invisible rivulet in a desert of snow. One careless, superb gesture, and I would be hurled into motion down the slope towards the small khaki spot in the side-lines, among the spectators, which was Buddy Willard.

All morning Buddy had been teaching me how to ski.

First, Buddy borrowed skis and ski poles from a friend of his in the village, and ski boots from a doctor's wife whose feet were only one size larger than my own, and a red ski jacket from a student nurse. His persistence in the face of mulishness was astounding.

Then I remembered that at medical school Buddy had won a prize for persuading the most relatives of dead people to have their dead ones cut up whether they needed it or not, in the interests of science. I forget what the prize was, but I could just see Buddy in his white coat with his stethoscope sticking out of a side pocket like part of his anatomy, smiling and bowing and talking those numb, dumb relatives into signing the post-mortem papers.

Next, Buddy borrowed a car from his own doctor, who'd had TB himself and was very understanding, and we drove off as the buzzer for walk-hour rasped along the sunless sanatorium corridors.

Buddy had never skied before either but he said that the elementary principles were quite simple, and as he'd often watched the ski instructors and their pupils, he could teach me all I'd need to know.

For the first half hour I obediently herring-boned up a small slope, pushed off with my poles and coasted straight down. Buddy seemed pleased with my progress.

"That's fine, Esther," he observed, as I negotiated my slope for the twentieth time. "Now let's try you on the rope tow."

I stopped in my tracks, flushed and panting.

"But Buddy, I don't know how to zigzag yet. All those people coming down from the top know how to zigzag."

"Oh, you need only go halfway. Then you won't gain very much momentum."

And Buddy accompanied me to the rope tow and showed me how to let the rope run through my hands, and then told me to close my fingers round it and go up. It never occurred to me to say no.

I wrapped my fingers around the rough, bruising snake of a rope that slithered through them, and went up.

But the rope dragged me, wobbling and balancing, so rapidly I couldn't hope to dissociate myself from it halfway. There was a skier in front of me and a skier behind me, and I'd have been knocked over and stuck full of skis and poles the minute I let go, and I didn't want to make trouble, so I hung quietly on.

At the top though, I had second thoughts.

Buddy singled me out, hesitating there in the red jacket. His arms chopped the air like khaki windmills. Then I saw he was signalling me to come down a path that had opened in the middle of the weaving skiers. But as I poised, uneasy, with a dry throat, the smooth white path from my feet to his feet grew blurred.

A skier crossed it from the left, another crossed it from the right, and Buddy's arms went on waving feebly as antennae from the other side of a field swarming with tiny moving animalcules like germs, or bent, bright exclamation marks.

I looked up from that churning amphitheatre to the view beyond it.

The great, grey eye of the sky looked back at me. Its mist-shrouded sun focusing all the white and silent distances that poured from every point of the compass, hill after pale hill, to stall at my feet.

The interior voice nagging me not to be a fool – to save my skin and take off my skis and walk down, camouflaged by the scrub pines bordering the slope – fled like a disconsolate mosquito. The thought that I might kill myself formed in my mind coolly as a tree or a flower.

I measured the distance to Buddy with my eye.

His arms were folded, now, and he seemed of a piece with the split-rail fence behind him – numb, brown and inconsequential.

Edging to the rim of the hilltop, I dug the spikes of my poles into the snow and pushed myself into a flight I knew I couldn't stop by skill or any belated access of will.

I aimed straight down.

A keen wind that had been hiding itself struck me full in the mouth and raked the hair back horizontal on my head. I was descending, but the white sun rose no higher. It hung over the suspended waves of the hills, an insentient pivot without which the world would not exist.

A small, answering point in my own body flew towards it. I felt my lungs inflate with the inrush of scenery – air, mountains, trees, people. I thought, 'This is what it is to be happy.'

I plummeted down past the zigzaggers, the students, the experts, through year after year of doubleness and smiles and compromise, into my own past.

People and trees receded on either hand like the dark sides of a tunnel as I hurtled on to the still, bright point at the end of it, the pebble at the bottom of the well, the white sweet baby cradled in its mother's belly.

My teeth crunched a gravelly mouthful. Ice water seeped down my throat. Buddy's face hung over me, near and huge, like a distracted planet. Other faces showed themselves up in back of his. Behind them, black dots swarmed on a plane of whiteness. Piece by piece, as at the strokes of a dull godmother's wand, the old world sprang back into position.

"You were doing fine," a familiar voice informed my ear, "until that man stepped into your path."

People were unfastening my bindings and collecting my ski poles from where they poked skyward, askew, in their separate snowbanks. The lodge fence propped itself at my back.

Buddy bent to pull off my boots and the several pairs of white wool socks that padded them. His plump hand shut on my left foot, then inched up my ankle, closing and probing, as if feeling for a concealed weapon.

A dispassionate white sun shone at the summit of the sky. I wanted to hone myself on it till I grew saintly and thin and essential as the blade of a knife.

"I'm going up," I said. "I'm going to do it again."

"No, you're not."

A queer, satisfied expression came over Buddy's face.

"No, you're not," he repeated with a final smile. "Your leg's broken in two places. You'll be stuck in a cast for months."

DR FISCHER OF GENEVA by Graham Greene

Graham Greene (1904–1991) needs no introduction. His novels 'Stamboul Train', 'The Power and the Glory', 'Brighton Rock' and 'The Heart of the Matter' are classics of British literature. Graham Greene was a Companion of Honour and a member of the Order of Merit. Of his book, 'Dr Fischer of Geneva', it is said that he manages to say more about love, hate, happiness, grief, immortality, greed and the disgustingly rich than most contemporary English novels three times the length.

I suppose there is a day in most lives when every trivial detail is held in the memory as though stamped in wax.

Such a day proved for me to be the last day of the year – a Saturday. The night before we had decided to drive up in the morning to Les Paccots if the weather proved fine enough for Anna-Luise to ski. There had been a slight thaw on Friday, but Friday night it was freezing.

We would go early before the slopes were crowded and have lunch together at the hotel there. I woke at half past seven and rang the meteo to find out the conditions.

Everything was OK though caution was advised. I made some toast and boiled two eggs and gave her breakfast in bed. "Why two eggs?" she asked.

"Because you'll be half dead of hunger before lunch if you are going to be there when the ski lift opens."

She put on a new sweater that I had given her for Christmas: heavy white wool with a wide red band round the shoulders: she looked wonderful in it. We started off at half past eight. The road was not bad, but as the meteo had announced there were icy patches, so I had to put on chains at the Chatel St Denis, and the ski lift was open before we arrived.

We had a small argument at St Denis. She wanted to make a long round from Corbetta and ski down the black piste from Le Pralet, but my anxiety persuaded her to come down the easier red piste to La Cierne.

I was secretly relieved that a number of people were already waiting to go up at Les Paccots. It seemed safer that way. I never fancied Anna-Luise skiing on an empty slope. It was too like bathing from an empty beach. One always fears there must be some good reason for the emptiness – perhaps an invisible pollution or a treacherous current.

"Oh dear," she said, "I wish I'd been the first. I love an empty piste."

"Safety in numbers," I said. "Remember what the road was like. Be careful."

"I'm always careful."

I waited until she was on the move and waved to her as she went up. I watched her until she was out of sight among the trees; I found it easy to pick her out because of the red band on the sweater. Then I went into the Hotel Corbetta with the book I had brought with me. It was an anthology of prose and verse called 'The Knapsack made by Herbert Read' and published in 1939, after the war broke out, in a small format so that it could be carried easily in a soldier's kit. I had never been a soldier but I had grown attached to the book during the phoney war. It whiled away many hours of waiting in the firemen's post for the blitz on London which never seemed to be coming, as the others played their compulsory round of darts wearing their gas masks. I have thrown away the book now, but some of the passages I read that day remain embedded in the wax, just as on that night in 1940 when I lost my hand. I remember clearly what I was reading when the siren sounded: it was, ironically, 'Keats's Ode on a Grecian Urn': 'Heard melodies are sweet, but those unheard are sweeter...' An unheard siren would certainly have been sweeter. I tried to reach the end of the Ode, but I got no further than, 'And, little town, thy streets for evermore Will silent be...' before I had to move out of the relative safety of our burrow. By two o'clock in the morning the words returned to me like something I had picked in a Sortes Virgilianae because there was a strange silence in the City streets. All the noise was overhead: the flap of flames, the hiss of water and the engines of the bombers saying, 'Where are you? Where are you?' There was a kind of hush at the heart of the destruction before an unexploded bomb was somehow set off and tore the silence away at street level and left me without a hand.

I remember... but there is nothing about that day until the evening that I can forget... for instance I remember the slight altercation I had at the Hotel Corbetta with the waiter because I wanted a window seat from which I could watch the road she would come along from the foot of the piste at La Cierne. The table had just served a previous occupant and there was a used cup and saucer which I suppose the waiter didn't want to clear. He was a surly man with a foreign accent. I expect he was a temporary employee, for Swiss waiters are the most agreeable in the world, and I remember thinking that he wouldn't last long. The time passed slowly without Anna-Luise. I grew tired of reading and I persuaded the waiter with the help of a two-franc piece to keep the table for me, and I added the promise that two of us would soon be taking a snack there when lunchtime came. A lot of cars were now arriving with skis on their roofs and quite a long queue had formed at the ski lift. One of the rescue team, who are always on duty at the hotel was gossiping with a friend in the queue. "Last accident we had was Monday," he said. "Boy with a broken ankle. You always get them in the school holidays."

I went to the little shop next to the hotel to see if I could find a French paper, but there was only the Lausanne daily which I had already scanned at breakfast. I bought a packet of Toblerone for us to eat as a dessert, for I knew that at the restaurant there would be only ice-cream. Then I took a walk and watched the skiers on the piste rouge. She was a very good skier: as I've already written, her mother had taken her out for the first time and had begun teaching her at the age of four. An icy wind was blowing and I went back to my table and read suitably enough 'Ezra Pound's Seafarer':

'Hung with hard ice-flakes, where hail-scur flew,

There I heard naught save the harsh sea

And ice-cold wave...'

After that I opened the anthology at random and reached 'Chin Shengt'an's 33 Happy Moments'. To me there always seems to be a horrible complacency about oriental wisdom: 'To cut with a sharp knife a bright green watermelon on a big scarlet plate of a summer afternoon. Ah, is not this happiness?' Oh yes, if one is a Chinese philosopher, well-to-do, highly esteemed, at ease with the world, above all safe, unlike the Christian philosopher who thrives on danger and doubt. Though I don't share the Christian belief I prefer Pascal.

'Everyone knows that the sight of cats or rats, the crushing of a coal etc. may unhinge the reason.'

Anyway, I thought, I don't like watermelons. It amused me however, to add a thirty-fourth happy moment just as complacent as Chin Shengt'an's. 'To be sitting warm in a Swiss cafe, watching the white slopes outside, and knowing that soon the one you love will enter, with red cheeks and snow on her boots, wearing a warm sweater with a red band on it. Is not this happiness?'

Again, I opened The Knapsack at random, but the Sortes Virgilianae do not always work and I found myself faced with 'The Last Days of Doctor Dome'. I wondered why a soldier should be expected to carry that in his knapsack for comfort or reassurance and I tried again. Herbert Read had printed a passage from one of his own works called 'Retreat from St Quentin', and I can still remember the gist, though not the exact words, I was reading when I laid the book down for ever. I thought this is the moment of death. But I felt no emotion. I recalled once reading how in battle when men are hit, they never feel the hurt till later. I looked up from the page.

Something was happening by the ski lift. The man who had spoken about the boy with a broken ankle was helping another man to carry a stretcher to the ski lift.

They had laid their skis on the stretcher. I stopped reading and for curiosity I went out. I had to wait for several cars to pass me before I got across the road and by the time I reached the ski lift the rescue team was already on the way up.

I asked someone in the queue what had happened. No one seemed very much interested. An Englishman said, "Some kid has fallen a cropper. It's always happening."

A woman said, "I think it's a practice for the sauveteurs. They telephone down from above and try to catch them off their guard."

"It's a very interesting exercise to watch," a second man said. "They have to ski down with the stretcher. It takes a lot of skill."

I went back to the hotel to get out of the cold. I could see just as well from the window but most of the time I was watching the ski lift because almost any moment now Anna-Luise would be joining me. The surly waiter came and asked me whether I wanted to order: he was like a parking meter which indicated that my two francs of time had expired. I ordered yet another coffee. There was a stir among the group at the ski lift. I left my coffee behind and went across the road.

The Englishman whom I had heard making his guess that a child had been hurt was now telling everyone triumphantly, "It's a real accident. I was listening to them in the office. They were telephoning for an ambulance from Vevey."

Even then, like the soldier at St Quentin, I didn't realize I had been hit, not even when the sauveteurs came along the road from La Cierne and laid the stretcher down with great care for the sake of the woman on it.

She was wearing quite a different kind of sweater from the one I had given Anna-Luise — a red sweater. "It's a woman," somebody said, "poor thing, she looks bad," and I felt the same momentary and automatic compassion as the speaker.

"Pretty serious," the triumphant man told us all. He was the nearest to the stretcher. "She's lost a lot of blood." I thought from where I stood that she had white hair and then I realized that they had bandaged her head before bringing her down.

"Is she conscious?" a woman asked and the Englishman who knew all about it shook his head.

The small group diminished in number and curiosity as people took the ski lift up. The Englishman went and spoke to one of the sauveteurs in bad French. "They think she's hurt her skull," he explained to all of us, like a television commentator translating. I had a direct view now. It was Anna-Luise. The sweater wasn't white anymore because of the blood.

I pushed the Englishman to one side. He grasped my arm and said, "Don't crowd her, man. She has to have air." "She's my wife, you bloody fool."

"Really? I'm sorry. Don't take it rough, old man."

It was a matter of minutes, I suppose, though it seemed hours, before the ambulance arrived. I stood there watching her face and seeing no sign of life. I said, "Is she dead?" I must have seemed to them a bit indifferent.

"No," one of them assured me. "Just unconscious. A crack on the head."

"How did it happen?"

"Well, as far as we can make out, there was a boy who fell up there and sprained his ankle. He shouldn't have been up on the piste rouge, he should have been on the piste bleu. She came over a rise and she hadn't much time to avoid him. She would have been all right probably if she had swung right, but I suppose she had not much time to think. She swung left towards the trees – you know the piste – but the snow is hard and tricky after the thaw and the freeze and she went right into a tree at top speed. Don't worry. The ambulance will be here any moment now. They will fix her up at the hospital."

I said, "I'll be back. I've got to go and pay for my coffee."

The Englishman said, "I do apologize, old man. I never thought..."

"For God's sake go and piss off," I said.

The waiter was more surly than ever. He told me, "You reserved this table for lunch. I have had to turn away customers."

"There's one customer you'll never see again," I told him back, and I threw a fifty-centime piece on the table which fell on the floor. Then I waited by the door to see if he would pick it up. He did and I felt ashamed. But if it had been in my power I would have revenged myself for what had happened on all the world – like Doctor Fischer, I thought, just like Doctor Fischer. I heard the scream of the ambulance and I returned to the ski lift.

They gave me a seat beside her stretcher in the ambulance and I left our car behind. I told myself that I would pick it up one day when she was better, and all the time I watched her face, waiting for her to come out of this coma and recognise me. We won't go to that restaurant, I thought, when we return, we'll go to the best hotel in the canton and have caviare like Doctor Fischer. She won't be well enough to ski, and by that time probably the snow will have gone. We shall sit in the sun and I'll tell her how scared I was. I'll tell her about that damned Englishman – I told him to piss off and he pissed off – and she'll laugh. I looked again at her unchanging face. She might have been dead if her eyes had not been closed. Coma is like deep sleep. Don't wake up, I urged her in my mind, until they've given you drugs so that you won't feel pain.

The ambulance went crying down the hill to where the hospital lay and I saw the mortuary sign which I had seen dozens of times, but now I felt a dull anger about it and the stupidity of the authorities who had put it just there for someone like myself to read. It's got nothing to do with Anna-Luise and me, I thought, nothing at all.

The mortuary sign is all that I can complain about now. Everyone, when the ambulance arrived, was very efficient. Two doctors were waiting at the entrance for our arrival. The Swiss are very efficient.

Think of the complex watches and precision instruments they make. I had the impression that Anna-Luise would be repaired as skilfully as they would repair a watch – a watch of more than ordinary value, a quartz watch, because she was Doctor Fischer's daughter.

They learnt that when I said I must telephone to him.

"To Doctor Fischer?"

"Yes, my wife's father."

I could tell from their manner that this watch carried no ordinary guarantee. She was already being wheeled away accompanied by the older doctor. I could see only the white bandages on her head which had given me the impression of old age.

I asked what I should tell her father.

"We shall know better after the X-ray."

"You think it may be serious?"

The young doctor said with caution, "We have to consider any injuries to the skull as potentially serious."

"Shall I wait to telephone till after the X-ray?"

"I think as Doctor Fischer has to come from Geneva you should perhaps tell him at once."

The implication of his advice didn't strike home to me until I was dialling. I could not at first recognise the voice of Albert when he answered.

I said, "I want to talk to Doctor Fischer."

"Who shall I say is speaking, sir?" This was his servile voice which I hadn't heard him use before.

"Tell him Mr Jones, his son-in-law."

At once the voice became the familiar Albert voice.

"Oh, Mr Jones, is it? The doctor's busy."

"I don't care if he is. Put me through."

"He told me that he was on no account to be disturbed."

"This is urgent. Do as I tell you."

"It might cost me my job."

"It will certainly cost you your job if you don't put me through."

There was a long silence and then the voice returned – the voice of the insolent Albert and not the servile one. "Doctor Fischer says he's too busy to talk to you now. He can't be interrupted. He's preparing to party."

"I've got to speak to him."

"He says as how you are to put what you want in writing."

Before I had time to reply he had broken the connection.

The young doctor had slipped away while I was on the telephone. Now he came back. He said, I'm afraid, Mr Jones, there has to be an operation – an immediate one. There are a lot of outpatients in the waiting room, but there's an empty room on the second floor where you could rest undisturbed. I'll come and see you immediately the operation is over.'

When he opened the door of the empty room I recognised it, or I thought I did, as the room where Mr Steiner had lain, but hospital rooms all look the same, like sleeping tablets. The window was open and the clang and clatter of the autoroute came in.

"Shall I close the window?" the young doctor asked.

From his solicitude you would have thought I was the patient.

"No, no, don't bother. I'd rather have the air." But it was the noise I wanted. It is only when one is happy or undisturbed that one can bear silence.

"If there is anything you want just ring" and he showed me the bell beside the bed. There was a thermos for iced water on the table and he checked to see whether it was full. "I'll be back soon," he said. "Try not to worry. We have had many worse cases."

There was an armchair for visitors and I sat in it and I wished that Mr Steiner lay in the bed for me to talk to. I would even have welcomed the old man who couldn't speak or hear. Some words of Mr Steiner came back to my mind. He had said of Anna-Luise's mother: "I used to look in other women's faces for years after she died and then I gave it up." The awful thing in that statement was 'for years'. Years, I thought, years... can one go on for years? Every few minutes I looked at my watch... two minutes gone, three minutes gone, once I was lucky and four and a half minutes passed. I thought: Shall I be doing this until I die?

There was a knock on the door and the young doctor entered. He looked shy and embarrassed and a wild hope came to me: they had made a gaffe and the injury wasn't serious after all. He said, "I'm sorry. I'm afraid..." Then the words came out in a rush. "We hadn't much hope. She didn't suffer at all. She died under the anaesthetic."

"Died?"

"Yes."

All I could find to say was, "Oh."

He asked, "Would you like to see her?"

"No."

"Shall we get you a taxi? Perhaps you wouldn't mind coming to the hospital tomorrow. To see the registrar. There are papers which have to be signed. Such a lot of paperwork always."

I said, "I'd rather finish with all that now. If it's the same to you."

COME WINTER by Evan Hunter

Evan Hunter (1926–2005), pseudonyms 'Ed McBain', 'Curt Cannon', 'Ezra Hannon', 'Hunt Collins', and 'Richard Marsten', was a prolific American writer of best-selling fiction, of which more than 50 books are crime stories published under the pseudonym Ed McBain. Hunter wrote the screenplay for Alfred Hitchcock's 'The Birds' (1962) and several later films.

The north face was cold and bleak and forbidding.

We stood on the level stretch of ground to the left of the unloading platform, waiting for Foderman and Mary Margaret to arrive at the summit, cursing the absence of a warming hut, shivering as each new fierce gust of wind blew snow ghosts into our faces. Lulled by the sunshine and balmy breezes on the other side of the mountain, we were unprepared for such a frigid assault, and improperly dressed for it. This was Vermont weather, ten below at the top, frostbite lurking if you stood still for more than a minute. Back East, we'd have worn a woollen shirt and two sweaters over our thermal underwear. We'd have zipped the linings into our parkas, put on wet pants over our regular garden variety ski pants, pulled slitted suede masks over our faces. Here in the glorious West, we trembled in our lightweight parkas, did windmill exercises with our arms, jumped up and down on our skis, blew on our hands, and decided that if Foderman and Mary Margaret did not show within the next ten minutes, we were heading down without them. They arrived thirty seconds short of the deadline. The chair ride up had numbed them to the marrow, and we waited another five minutes for them to go through the same warming up exercises we had just performed, while we grew colder and colder and more and more irritable.

It is dangerous to ski when you are cold. Aside from the obvious physical disadvantage of tight muscles and aching toes and fingertips, there is a psychological disadvantage as well. When the temperature drops below zero and the wind adds its ferocity to the already biting cold, there is an urgent need to get down to where it is warmer. A skier who is cold skis faster than he normally would, takes reckless chances he would otherwise avoid, all in an attempt to escape those howling wolves chasing the troika. He knows only that if he remains where he is, he will freeze solid to the side of the mountain. So, he will run over helpless babes and mewling kittens in his desperate headlong plunge down the mountain in search of warmth. None of which excuses Mary Margaret for deliberately breaking Foderman's leg. She was cold, we all were cold. But she was an expert skier and could have avoided the accident. The north face was everything Hollis had promised.

A full view of the difficult terrain on the chair ride up had been anything but reassuring. Wide fields of moguls blistered the sharp descent, each threatening mound looking like a concrete World War II pillbox in a frozen Maginot Line. Connecting links stitched their way brokenly across the face of the mountain, opened suddenly into icy chutes that plunged vertically into yet more fields of closely spaced moguls. The turns were abrupt and narrow, treacherously clinging to cliff faces so steep they could not hold snow, exposing instead jagged rock formations that had been thrust up out of the earth, Christ knew how many centuries before. Most of the trails appeared wind-blown and glazed with ice, flanked with deep snow waiting in ambush to catch a tip or an edge. I said nothing to Sandy on the chair ride up, and I said nothing now as we prepared to ski down. I was very frightened. I had stopped worrying about Foderman because I was honestly more concerned for my own safety. I realised, of course, that his usual technique simply would not work on this enormously challenging terrain. But I only thought of this fleetingly. I was cold, and I was frightened, and I wanted to get down to the bottom as fast as I could.

Mary Margaret was a superb skier and an excellent guide. Since she had skied the north face last year, and was familiar with it, she quite naturally took the lead now, with Sandy close behind her, Foderman and David next in the formation, and me in the rear. Foderman much to my surprise, skied with caution and control, adapting his bulldozing style to the exigencies of the situation, forcing himself to make frequent turns in answer to the demands of the mountain; he had to make turns, in fact, or he'd have gone off into space (as Hollis had put it) never been heard from since. We started down through a glade of pines through which the trail deceptively and lazily wound, coming out without warning into a wide but extremely steep slope. Mardy Margaret sliced the hill diagonally in an oblique traverse, neutralizing the fall line, gliding effortlessly down and across the face of the trail. Following her, it all seemed easy. Even Foderman had no difficulty, and I was beginning to think we'd make a good skier out of him before his stay at Semanee ended. Dogging her tracks, we reached an almost level stretch of ground partially covered with glare ice, skirted easily around the patch, carved wide turns around the bend in the trail, and came out onto a narrow passage clinging to the outer edge of the mountain with a drop on the left that fell away vertically to a jagged rock outcropping below. But Mary Margaret handled this with ease as well. The tails of her skis thrust partially out over the edge of the mountain, tips angled toward the wall of snow on her right, checking enough to control her speed but not enough to turn her or to stop her, she led us safely over the ridge and around a curve that opened onto the first wide field of moguls.

We were beginning to warm up a little, but none of us was eager to stop and bask in the sun, not with that wind still raging in over the top of each rounded mogul. Like mist rising over a fen, the snow shifted and swirled as Mary Margaret in green led the way down, again cutting the mountain in a gliding traverse, turning, traversing to the left, turning again, endlessly repeating the pattern until we reached a section of the trail protected from the wind by a gigantic spruce forest. We stopped there to catch our breath. I glanced into the forest. It was shaded and still.

"How we doing?" Mary Margaret asked.

"Good," Foderman said.

"You're a nice skier," she told him. "Everybody else okay?"

"Fine," Sandy said.

"You're all nice skiers," Mary Margaret said, and grinned broadly. There was in her voice a note of condescension, the patronising tone a master uses to a pupil. Nor had we missed her pointed equation. Foderman was a nice skier, and the three of us were also nice skiers.

"The thing that's gorgeous about this side of the mountain," Mary Margaret said, "is the variety. You never know what's coming up next. You'll see what I mean. It's really exciting."

"I love it so far," Foderman said.

"I knew you would, Seymour."

"I really do love it."

"Don't get carried away, Seymour," David said.

"He's a nice skier," Mary Margaret said.

"Yes, we're all nice skiers," Sandy said, letting Mary Margaret know she had caught the earlier appraisal of our skills, and blowing her nose to emphasise the point and to dismiss the slanderous comparison.

"Well, shall we go?" Mary Margaret asked.

The wind, lying in wait just beyond the edge of the forest, leaped across the trail as Mary Margaret led us through a deep crevasse. Walls of snow on either side of us rose to hide the sun, causing the temperature (psychologically at least) to drop another five degrees. I was beginning to understand what she meant about this side of the mountain.

There was no way of handicapping it, no way of predicting responses to secrets it stubbornly withheld. There are mountains that become boring the second time down. The skier learns the trails, establishes a rhythm that nullifies their challenge, and then can ski them effortlessly. There was no doing that on the north face. The crevasse became a narrow catwalk that became another field of moguls that became an icy chute that became a shaded glade that became an open, sun-drenched, virtually flat plain. The challenge was continuous, the mountain refused to be second guessed. I had the feeling it could be skied indefinitely without ever fully revealing its treasures.

We came across one of those tight little ridges Hollis had talked about, where the trail was barely wide enough to permit passage of both skis, and the outside drop was a sheer cliff surely leading to the very bowels of the earth. I navigated that precipitous ledge with dread certainty that I would fall off the mountain and be found below only months later, crushed and broken, when the Ski Patrol swept the trails during the spring thaw. We skied for what seemed forever on that sharply angled ribbon, Foderman hugging the side of the mountain, Sandy standing erect in defiance, I watching my outside ski for fear it would slip off the ledge and send me on my anticipated trip, David doing God knew what behind me. But at last the trail began to widen, and finally it opened onto a field of small, gently rolling hills, the far sides of which sloped gradually to the next small crests beyond. Mary Margaret, as she had done throughout, showed us the way to best enjoy this new terrain.

She skied to the top of the nearest hill, jumped, soared six feet through the air with arms akimbo like a big green bird, landed on the downside, glided to the top of the next hill and jumped again, knees bent to absorb the shock as she landed, rising again to take the next crest and the next jump, as free of gravity as though she were on the moon. We leaped from hillock to hillock, exhilarated. It was on the next stretch of trail that Mary Margaret broke Foderman's leg. He had, until that time, been skiing like an angel, keeping his place in the formation, following not three feet behind the tails of Mary Margaret's skis, fastidiously imitating each of her moves. Exuberantly, he took the jumps with each of us, and then – perhaps because he was so excited, perhaps because he was still cold in spite of all the leaping – regressed to his earlier downhill technique, and schussed the remainder of the field, passing Mary Margaret, taking the lead, and disappearing from sight around a bend at the bottom. Mary Margaret was immediately behind him, and I was behind her. I saw everything that happened. The mountain, in another of its surprises, unravelled a rather steep twisting trail some four feet wide, running through a V-like crotch bounded on both sides by angled walls of snow. Foderman, who should have known by this time that the mountain was secretive and perverse, went into the trail as if it were a continuation of the gently rolling field we had just come down. He was skiing far too fast and was not skilful enough to check his speed in such a narrow passage.

A simple snowplough check would not have worked here because he'd have had to apply pressure by bending sharply at the knees, tips pointed toward each other, and the spread heels of his skis would have struck the walls on either side of the trail, resulting in a certain fall. A better skier would have slowed himself by executing a series of short, sharp heel thrusts, exactly as Mary Margaret and I were doing. If Foderman had been behind either of us, he might have followed our example, imitated our moves, and been able to ski the passage with ease. But he was in the lead, and clearly at a loss, gaining momentum and speed, and faced with a sharp turn below which he could not possibly negotiate if he did not somehow slow down.

He resorted to a beginner's device. He sat abruptly, his fat backside thudding into the snow. Sliding down the trail on his back, knees bent, skis flat on the ground, arms and poles up and away from his body, he might have been fine if his right ski hadn't suddenly darted out from under him, the leg shooting straight up into the air. He slipped sideways across the trail, and the heel of the right ski came down hard, sinking deep into the soft snow adjacent to the sloping wall. He was now athwart the trail, head and shoulders against the left wall, elbows bent, left knee bent and left ski flat on the ground, right leg extended straight with the tail of the right ski anchored firmly in the snow. He looked rather like a railroad crossing, his leg effectively barricading the trail, his boot fastened to the ski. I suddenly remembered that Sandy had tightened the binding on that ski only two days ago, and I wondered if Foderman had since had it readjusted.

It was too late. Mary Margaret was skiing toward him. There were several things Mary Margaret could have done. She was an expert skier. She had been checking her speed all the way down the trail, and most certainly could have executed a stop now. Or she could have jumped over the barricade of Foderman's leg; his foot, firmly bound to the ski, was no more than three feet off the ground. But she lowered her head instead, bent her knees, crouched into a downhill schuss position, and raced directly for Foderman where he lay helplessly pinioned athwart the trail. A moment before she crashed into his leg, I realised she was determined to ski through him.

His scream echoed off the walls of the narrow canyon. The force of their collision sent Mary Margaret into a somersaulting roll over Foderman's body. Thrashing, flailing, she went skidding down the trail while Foderman lay screaming in agony, the splintered bones of his leg showing through the torn ski pants. He was still screaming when she rolled to a stop some twelve feet below him, unharmed.

THE HARTLEYS by John Cheever

John William Cheever (1912–1982) was an American novelist and short story writer. He is sometimes called 'the Chekhov of the suburbs'. A compilation of his short stories, The Stories of John Cheever, won the 1979 Pulitzer Prize for Fiction.

Mr and Mrs Hartley and their daughter Anne reached the Pemaquoddy Inn, one winter evening, after dinner and just as the bridge games were getting under way. Mr Hartley carried the bags across the broad porch and into the lobby, and his wife and daughter followed him. They all three seemed very tired, and they looked around them at the bright, homely room with the gratitude of people who have escaped from tension and danger, for they had been driving in a blinding snowstorm since early morning. They had made the trip from New York and it had snowed all the way, they said. Mr Hartley put down the bags and returned to the car to get the skis. Mrs Hartley sat down in one of the lobby chairs, and her daughter, tired and shy, drew close to her. There was a little snow in the girl's hair, and Mrs Hartley brushed this away with her fingers. Then Mrs Butterick, the widow who owned the inn, went out to the porch and called to Mr Hartley that he needn't put his car up. One of the men would do it, she said. He came back into the lobby and signed the register.

He seemed to be a likable man with an edge to his voice and an intense, polite manner. His wife was a handsome, dark-haired woman who was dazed with fatigue, and his daughter was a girl of about seven. Mrs Butterick asked Mr Hartley if he had ever stayed at the Pemaquoddy before. "When I got the reservation," she said, "the name rang a bell."

"Mrs Hartley and I were here eight years ago February," Mr Hartley said. "We came on the twenty third and were here for ten days. I remember the date clearly because we had such a wonderful time." Then they went upstairs. They came down again long enough to make a supper of some leftovers that had been kept warm on the back of the stove. The child was so tired she nearly fell asleep at the table. After supper, they went upstairs again.

In the winter, the life of the Pemaquoddy centered entirely on cold sports. Drinkers and malingerers were not encouraged, and most of the people there were earnest about their skiing. In the morning, they would take a bus across the valley to the mountains, and if the weather was good, they would carry a packed lunch and remain on the slopes until late afternoon. They'd vary this occasionally by skating on a rink near the inn, which had been made by flooding a clothesyard. There was a hill behind the inn that could sometimes be used for skiing when conditions on the mountain were poor. This hill was serviced by a primitive ski tow that had been built by Mrs Butterick's son. "He bought that motor that pulls the tow when he was a senior at Harvard," Mrs Butterick always said when she spoke of the tow. "It was in an old Mercer auto, and he drove it up here from Cambridge one night without any license plates!" When she said this, she would put her hand over her heart, as if the dangers of the trip were still vivid.

The Hartleys picked up the Pemaquoddy routine of fresh air and exercise the morning following their arrival.

Mrs Hartley was an absent-minded woman. She boarded the bus for the mountain that morning, sat down, and was talking to another passenger when she realized that she had forgotten her skis. Her husband went after them while everyone waited. She wore a bright, fur trimmed parka that had been cut for someone with a younger face, and it made her look tired. Her husband wore some Navy equipment, which was stenciled with his name and rank. Their daughter, Anne, was pretty. Her hair was braided in tight, neat plaits, there was a saddle of freckles across her small nose, and she looked around her with the bleak, rational scrutiny of her age.

Mr Hartley was a good skier. He was up and down the slope, his skis parallel, his knees bent, his shoulders swinging gracefully in a half circle. His wife was not as clever but she knew what she was doing, and she enjoyed the cold air and the snow. She fell now and then, and when someone offered to help her to her feet, when the cold snow that had been pressed against her face had heightened its color, she looked like a much younger woman.

Anne didn't know how to ski. She stood at the foot of the slope watching her parents. They called to her, but she didn't move, and after a while she began to shiver. Her mother went to her and tried to encourage her, but the child turned away crossly. "I don't want you to show me," she said. "I want Daddy to show me." Mrs Hartley called her husband.

As soon as Mr Hartley turned his attention to Anne, she lost all her hesitation. She followed him up and down the hill, and as long as he was with her, she seemed confident and happy. Mr Hartley stayed with Anne until after lunch, when he turned her over to a professional instructor who was taking a class of beginners out to the slope. Mr and Mrs Hartley went with the group to the foot of the slope, where Mr Hartley took his daughter aside. "Your mother and I are going to ski some trails now," he said, "and I want you to join Mr. Ritter's class and to learn as much from him as you can. If you're ever going to learn to ski, Anne, you'll have to learn without me. We'll be back at around four, and I want you to show me what you've learned when we come back."

"Yes, Daddy," she said.

"Now you go and join the class."

"Yes, Daddy."

Mr and Mrs Hartley waited until Anne had climbed the slope and joined the class. Then they went away. Anne watched the instructor for a few minutes, but as soon as she noticed that her parents had gone, she broke from the group and coasted down the hill toward the hut. "Miss," the instructor called after her. "Miss…" She didn't answer. She went into the hut, took off her parka and her mittens, spread them neatly on a table to dry, and sat beside the fire, holding her head down so that her face could not be seen. She sat there all afternoon. A little before dark, when her parents returned to the hut, stamping the snow off their boots, she ran to her father. Her face was swollen from crying. "Oh, Daddy, I thought you weren't coming back," she cried. "I thought you weren't ever coming back!" She threw her arms around him and buried her face in his clothes.

"Now, now, now, Anne," he said, and he patted her back and smiled at the people who happened to notice the scene. Anne sat beside him on the bus ride back, holding his arm.

At the inn that evening, the Hartleys came into the bar before dinner and sat at a wall table. Mrs Hartley and her daughter drank tomato juice, and Mr Hartley had three 'Old-Fashioneds'. He gave Anne the orange slices and the sweet cherries from his drinks. Everything her father did interested her. She lighted his cigarettes and blew out the matches. She examined his watch and laughed at all his jokes. She had a sharp, pleasant laugh.

The family talked quietly. Mr and Mrs Hartley spoke oftener to Anne than to each other, as if they had come to a point in their marriage where there was nothing to say. They discussed haltingly, between themselves, the snow and the mountain, and in the course of this attempt to make conversation Mr Hartley, for some reason, spoke sharply to his wife. Mrs Hartley got up from the table quickly. She might have been crying. She hurried through the lobby and went up the stairs.

Mr Hartley and Anne stayed in the bar. When the dinner bell rang, he asked the desk clerk to send Mrs Hartley a tray. He ate dinner with his daughter in the dining room. After dinner, he sat in the parlor reading an old copy of 'Fortune' while Anne played with some other children who were staying at the inn. They were all a little younger than she, and she handled them easily and affectionately, imitating an adult. She taught them a simple card game and then read them a story. After the younger children were sent to bed, she read a book. Her father took her upstairs at about nine.

He came down by himself later and went into the bar. He drank alone and talked with the bartender about various brands of bourbon. "Dad used to have his bourbon sent up from Kentucky in kegs," Mr Hartley said. A slight rasp in his voice, and his intense and polite manner, made what he said seem important. "They were small, as I recall. I don't suppose they held more than a gallon. Dad used to have them sent to him twice a year. When Grandmother asked him what they were, he always told her they were full of sweet cider." After discussing bourbons, they discussed the village and the changes in the inn. "We've only been here once before," Mr Hartley said. "That was eight years ago, eight years ago February." Then he repeated, word for word, what he had said in the lobby the previous night. "We came on the twenty third and were here for ten days. I remember the date clearly because we had such a wonderful time."

The Hartleys' subsequent days were nearly all like the first. Mr Hartley spent the early hours instructing his daughter. The girl learned rapidly, and when she was with her father, she was daring and graceful, but as soon as he left her, she would go to the hut and sit by the fire. Each day, after lunch, they would reach the point where he gave her a lecture on self-reliance. "Your mother and I are going away now," he would say, "and I want you to ski by yourself, Anne." She would nod her head and agree with him, but as soon as he had gone, she would return to the hut and wait there. Once (it was the third day) he lost his temper. "Now, listen, Anne," he shouted, "if you're going to learn to ski, you've got to learn by yourself." His loud voice wounded her, but it did not seem to show her the way to independence. She became a familiar figure in the afternoons, sitting beside the fire.

Sometimes Mr Hartley would modify his discipline. The three of them would return to the inn on the early bus and he would take his daughter to the skating rink and give her a skating lesson. On these occasions, they stayed out late. Mrs Hartley watched them sometimes from the parlor window. The rink was at the foot of the primitive ski tow that had been built by Mrs. Butterick's son. The terminal posts of the tow looked like gibbets in the twilight, and Mr Hartley and his daughter looked like figures of contrition and patience. Again and again they would circle the little rink, earnest and serious, as if he were explaining to her something more mysterious than a sport.

Everyone at the inn liked the Hartleys, although they gave the other guests the feeling that they had recently suffered some loss – the loss of money perhaps, or perhaps Mr Hartley had lost his job. Mrs Hartley remained absent-minded, but the other guests got the feeling that this characteristic was the result of some misfortune that had shaken her self-possession. She seemed anxious to be friendly and she plunged, like a lonely woman, into every conversation. Her father had been a doctor, she said. She spoke of him as if he had been a great power, and she spoke with intense pleasure of her childhood. "Mother's living room in Grafton was forty-five feet long," she said. "There were fireplaces at both ends. It was one of those marvellous old Victorian houses." In the china cabinet in the dining room, there was some china like the china Mrs Hartley's mother had owned. In the lobby there was a paperweight like a paperweight Mrs Hartley had been given when she was a girl. Mr Hartley also spoke of his origins now and then. Mrs Butterick once asked him to carve a leg of lamb, and as he sharpened the carving knife, he said, "I never do this without thinking of Dad." Among the collection of canes in the hallway, there was a blackthorn embossed with silver. "That's exactly like the blackthorn Mr Wentworth brought Dad from Ireland," Mr Hartley said.

Anne was devoted to her father but she obviously liked her mother too. In the evenings, when she was tired, she would sit on the sofa beside Mrs Hartley and rest her head on her mother's shoulder. It seemed to be only on the mountain, where the environment was strange, that her father would become for her the only person in the world. One evening when the Hartley's were playing bridge – it was quite late and Anne had gone to bed – the child began to call her father. "I'll go, darling," Mrs Hartley said, and she excused herself and went upstairs. "I want my daddy," those at the bridge table could hear the girl screaming. Mrs Hartley quieted her and came downstairs again. "Anne had a nightmare," she explained, and went on playing cards.

The next day was windy and warm. In the middle of the afternoon, it began to rain, and all but the most intrepid skiers went back to their hotels. The bar at the Pemaquoddy filled up early. The radio was turned on for weather reports, and one earnest guest picked up the telephone in the lobby and called other resorts. Was it raining in Pico? Was it raining in Stowe? Was it raining in Ste. Agathe? Mr and Mrs Hartley were in the bar that afternoon. She was having a drink for the first time since they had been there but she did not seem to enjoy it. Anne was playing in the parlor with the other children. A little before dinner, Mr Hartley went into the lobby and asked Mrs Butterick if they could have their dinner upstairs. Mrs Butterick said that this could be arranged. When the dinner bell rang, the Hartleys went up, and a maid took them trays. After dinner, Anne went back to the parlor to play with the other children, and after the dining room had been cleared, the maid went up to get the Hartleys' trays.

The transom above the Hartleys' bedroom door was open, and as the maid went down the hall, she could hear Mrs Hartley's voice, a voice so uncontrolled, so guttural and full of suffering, that she stopped and listened as if the woman's life were in danger. "Why do we have to come back?" Mrs Hartley was crying. "Why do we have to come back? Why do we have to make these trips back to the places where we thought we were happy? What good is it going to do? What good has it ever done? We go through the telephone book looking for the names of people we knew ten years ago, and we ask them for dinner, and what good does it do? What good has it ever done? We go back to the restaurants, the mountains, we go back to the houses, even the neighborhoods, we walk in the slums, thinking that this will make us happy, and it never does. Why in Christ's name did we ever begin such a wretched thing? Why isn't there an end to it? Why can't we separate again? It was better that way. Wasn't it better that way? It was better for Anne – I don't care what you say, it was better for her than this. I'll take Anne again and you can live in town. Why can't I do that, why can't I, why can't I, why can't I." The frightened maid went back along the corridor. Anne was sitting in the parlor reading to the younger children when the maid went downstairs.

It cleared up that night and turned cold. Everything froze. In the morning, Mrs. Butterick announced that all the trails on the mountain were closed and that the tramway would not run. Mr Hartley and some other guests broke the crust on the hill behind the inn, and one of the hired hands started the primitive tow. "My son bought the motor that pulls the tow when he was a senior at Harvard," Mrs Butterick said when she heard its humble explosions. "It was in an old Mercer auto, and he drove it up here from Cambridge one night without any license plates!" The slope offered the only skiing in the neighborhood, and after lunch a lot of people came here from other hotels. They wore the snow away under the tow to a surface of rough stone, and snow had to be shovelled onto the tracks. The rope was frayed and Mrs Butterick's son had planned the tow so poorly that it gave the skiers a strenuous and uneven ride. Mrs Hartley tried to get Anne to use the tow, but she would not ride it until her father led the way. He showed her how to stand, how to hold the rope, bend her knees, and drag her poles. As soon as he was carried up the hill, she gladly followed. She followed him up and down the hill all afternoon, delighted that for once he was remaining in her sight. When the crust on the slope was broken and packed, it made good running, and that odd, nearly compulsive rhythm of riding and skiing, riding and skiing, established itself.

It was a fine afternoon. There were snow clouds, but a bright and cheerful light beat through them. The country, seen from the top of the hill, was black and white. Its only colours were the colours of spent fire, and this impressed itself upon one – as if the desolation were something more than winter, as if it were the work of a great conflagration. People talk, of course, while they ski, while they wait for their turn to seize the rope, but they can hardly be heard. There is the exhaust of the tow motor and the creak of the iron wheel upon which the tow rope turns, but the skiers themselves seem stricken dumb, lost in the rhythm of riding and coasting. That afternoon was a continuous cycle of movement. There was a single file to the left of the slope, holding the frayed rope and braking from it, one by one, at the crown of the hill to choose their way down, going again and again over the same surface, like people who, having lost a ring or key on the beach, search again and again in the same sand. In the stillness the child Anne began to shriek. Her arm had got caught in the frayed rope; she had been thrown to the ground and was being dragged brutally up the hill toward the iron wheel. "Stop the tow!" her father roared, "Stop the tow! Stop the tow!" And everyone else on the hill began to shout, "Stop the tow! Stop the tow! Stop the tow!" But there was no one there to stop it. Her screams were hoarse and terrible, and the more she struggled to free herself from the rope, the more violently it threw her to the ground. Space and the cold seemed to reduce the voices – even the anguish in the voices – of the people who were calling to stop the tow, but the girl's cries were piercing until her neck was broken on the iron wheel.

The Hartleys left for New York that night after dark. They were going to drive all night behind the local hearse. Several people offered to drive the car down for them but, Mr Hartley said that he wanted to drive, and his wife seemed to want him to. When everything was ready, the stricken couple walked across the porch, looking around them at the bewildering beauty of the night, for it was very cold and clear and the constellations seemed brighter than the lights of the inn or the village. He helped his wife into the car, and after arranging a blanket over her legs, they started the long, long drive.

John Hoyer Updike *(March 18, 1932 – January 27, 2009) was an American novelist, poet, short-story writer, art critic, and literary critic. One of only four writers to win the Pulitzer Prize for Fiction more than once. Updike published more than twenty novels, more than a dozen short-story collections, as well as poetry, art and literary criticism and children's books during his career.*

THE RESCUE by John Updike

Helplessly Caroline Harris, her husband and son having seized the first chair, found herself paired with Alice Smith. Together they were struck in the backs of their knees and hurled upward. When Caroline had been a child, her father, conceited in his strength, would toss her toward the ceiling with the same brutal, swooping lurch.

Alice snapped the safety bar, and they were bracketed together. It was degrading for both of them. Up ahead, neither Norman nor Timmy deigned to glance back. From the rear, hooded and armed with spears, they were two of a kind, Timmy at twelve only slightly smaller than his father; and this, too, she felt as a desertion, a flight from her body. While she was dragged through the air, rudely joggled at each pier, the whiteness of the snow pressed on the underside of her consciousness with the gathering insistence of a headache. Her ski boots weighed; her feet felt captive. Rigid with irritation and a desire not to sway, she smoked her next-to-last cigarette, which was cheated of taste by the cold, and tried to decide if the woman beside her were sleeping with Norman or not.

This morning, as they drove north into New Hampshire, there had been in the automobile an excessive ease, as if the four of them knew each other better than Caroline remembered reason for. There had been, between Alice Smith and Norman, a lack of flirtation a shade too resolute, while on sleepy, innocent

Timmy the woman had inflicted a curiously fervent playfulness, as if warm messages for the father were being forwarded through the son, or as if Alice were seeking to establish herself as a sexual nonentity, a brotherly sister. Caroline felt an ominous tug in this trip. Had she merely imagined, during their fumbling breakfast at Howard Johnson, a poignancy in the pauses, and a stir of something, like toes touching, under the table? And was she paranoid to have suspected a deliberate design in the pattern of alternation that had her and her son floundering up the T-bar together as the other two expertly skimmed down the slope and waited, side by side, laughing vapour, at the end of the long and devious line? Caroline was not reassured, when they all rejoined at lunch, by Alice's smile, faintly flavoured with a sweetness unspecified in the recipe.

Alice had been her friend first. She had moved to their neighbourhood a year ago, a touching little divorcée with pre-school twins, utterly lost. Her only interest seemed to be sports, and her marital grief had given her an awkward hardness, as if from too much exercise. Norman had called her pathetic and sexless. Yet a winter later he had rescued his skis from a decade in the attic, enrolled Timmy in local lessons, and somehow guided his wife in the same dangerous direction, as irresistibly as this cable was pulling them skyward.

They were giddily lifted above the tops of the pines. Caroline, to brace her voice against her rising fear, spoke aloud: "This is ridiculous. At my age women in Tahiti are grandmothers."

Alice said seriously, "I think you do terribly well. You're a natural dancer, and it shows."

Caroline could not hate her. She was as helpless as herself, and there was some timid loyalty, perhaps, in Norman's betraying her with a woman she had befriended. She felt, indeed, less betrayed than diluted, and, turning with her cigarette cupped against the wind, she squinted at the other woman as if into an unkind mirror. Alice was small-boned yet coarse; muscularity, reaching upward through the prominent tendons of her throat, gave her face, even through the flush of windburn, a taut, sallow tinge. Her hair, secured by a scarlet ear warmer, was abundant but mousy, and her eyes were close-set, hazel, and vaguely, stubbornly inward. But between her insignificant nose and receding chin there lay, as if in ambush, a large, complicated, and (Caroline supposed) passionate mouth. This, she realized, as the chair swayed sickeningly, was exactly what Norman would want: a mouse with a mouth.

Disgust, disgust and anger, swung through her. How greedy men were! How conceited and brutish! The sky enlarged around her, as if to receive so immense a condemnation. With deft haste Alice undid the safety bar; Caroline involuntarily transposed the action into an undoing of Norman's clothes. Icy with contempt for her situation, she floated onto the unloading platform and discovered, slipping down the alarming little ramp, that her knees were trembling and had forgotten how to bend.

Of course, they were abandoned. The males had heedlessly gone ahead, and beckoned, tiny and black, from the end of a tunnel tigerishly striped with the shadows of birches. On whispering skis held effortlessly parallel, Alice led, while Caroline followed, struggling clumsily against the impulse to stem. They arrived where the men had been and found them gone again. In their place was a post with two signs. One pointed right to 'GREASED LIGHTNING (EXPERT)'. The other pointed left to 'THE LIGHTNING BUG (INTERMEDIATE-NOVICE)'.

"I see them," Alice said, and lightly poled off to the right.

"Wait," Caroline begged.

Alice christied to a stop. A long lavender shadow from a mass of pines covered her and for a painful instant, as her lithe body inquisitively straightened, she seemed beautiful.

"How expert is it?" The Harrises had never been to this mountain before; Alice had been several times.

"There's one mogully piece you can sideslip," Alice said. "The Bug will take you around the other side of the mountain. You'll never catch the men."

"Why don't you follow them and I'll go down the novice trail? I don't trust this mountain yet." It was a strange mountain, one of the lesser Presidentials, rather recently developed, with an unvarnished cafeteria and very young boys patrolling the trails in rawly bright jackets chevron-striped in yellow and green. At lunch, Norman said he twice had seen members of the ski patrol take spills. His harsh laugh, remembered at this bare altitude, frightened her. The trembling in her knees would not subside, and her fingertips were stinging in their mittens.

Alice crisply sidestepped back up to her. "Let's both go down the Bug," she said. "You shouldn't ski alone."

"I don't want to be a sissy," Caroline said, and these careless words apparently triggered some inward chain of reflection in the other woman, for Alice's face clouded, and it appeared certain that she was sleeping with Norman. Everything, every tilt of circumstance, every smothered swell and deliberate contraindication, confirmed it, even the girl's name, 'Smith' – a nothing-name, a demimondaine's alias. Her hazel eyes, careful in the glare of the snow, flickeringly searched Caroline's and her expressive mouth froze on the verge of a crucial question.

"Track! Track!"

The voice was behind them, shrill and young. A teenage girl, wearing a polka-dot purple parka, and her mother, a woman almost elderly, who seemed to have rouged the tip of her nose, turned beside them and casually plunged over the lip of Greased Lightning.

Caroline, shamed, said, "The hell with it. The worst I can do is get killed." Murderously stabbing the snow next to Alice's non-committal buckle-boots, she pushed off to the right, her weight flung wildly back, her uphill ski snagging, her whole body burning with the confirmation of her suspicions. She would leave Norman. Unsteady as a flame she flickered down the height, wavering in her own wind. Alice carefully passed her and, taking long traverses and diagrammatically deliberate turns, seemed to be inviting her not to destroy herself. Submitting to the sight, permitting her eyes to infect her body with Alice's rhythm, she found the snow yielding to her as if under the pressure of reason; and, swooping in complementary zigzags, the two women descended a long white waterfall linked as if by love.

Then there was a lazy flat run in the shadow of reddish rocks bearded with icicles, then another descent, through cataracts of moguls, into a wider, elbow-shaped slope overlooking, from the height of a mile, a toy lodge, a tessellated parking lot, and, vast and dim as a foreign nation, a frozen lake mottled with cloud shadows and islands of evergreen. Tensely sideslipping, Caroline saw, on the edge of this slope, at one side of the track, some trouble, a heap of dark cloth. In her haste to be with the men, Alice would have swept by, but Caroline snow plowed to a halt. With a dancing waggle Alice swerved and pulled even. The heap of cloth was the woman with the red-tipped nose, who lay on her back, her head downhill. Her daughter knelt beside her. The woman's throat was curved as if she were gargling, and her hood was submerged in snow, so that her face showed like a face in a casket.

Efficiently, Alice bent, released her bindings, and walked to the accident, making crisp boot prints. "Is she conscious?" she asked.

"It's the left," the casket face said, not altering its rapt relation with the sky. The dab of red was the only colour not drained from it. Tears trickled from the corner of one eye into a fringe of sandy permed hair.

"Do you think it's broken?"

There was no answer, and the girl impatiently prompted, "Mother, does it feel broken?"

"I can't feel a thing. Take off the boot."

"I don't think we should take off the boot," Alice said. She surveyed the woman's legs with a physical forthrightness that struck Caroline as unpleasant. "We might disturb the alignment. It might be a spiral. Did you feel anything give?" The impact of the spill had popped both safety bindings, so the woman's skis were attached to her feet only by the breakaway straps. Alice stooped and unclipped these, and stood the skis upright in the snow, as a signal. She said, "We should get help."

The daughter looked up hopefully. The face inside her polka-dot parka was round and young, its final form not quite declared. "If you're willing to stay," she said, "I'll go. I know some of the boys in the patrol."

"We'll be happy to stay," Caroline said firmly. She was conscious, as she said this, of frustrating Alice and of declaring, in the necessary war between them, her weapons to be compassion and patience. She wished she could remove her skis, for their presence on her feet held her a little aloof; but she was not sure she could put them back on at this slant, in the middle of nowhere. The snow here had the eerie unvisited air of grass beside a highway. The young daughter, without a backward glance, snapped herself into her skis and whipped away, down the hill. Seeing how easy it had been, Caroline dared unfasten hers and discovered her own boot prints also to be crisp intaglios. Alice tugged back her parka sleeve and frowned at her wristwatch. The third woman moaned.

Caroline asked, "Are you warm enough? Would you like to be wrapped in something?" The lack of a denial left them no choice but to remove their parkas and wrap her in them. Her body felt like an oversized doll sadly in need of stuffing. Caroline, bending close, satisfied herself that what looked like paint was a little pinnacle of sunburn.

The woman murmured her thanks. "My second day here, I've ruined it for everybody – my daughter, my son…"

Alice asked, "Where is your son?"

"Who knows? I bring him here and don't see him from morning to night. He says he's skiing, but I ski every trail and never see him."

"Where is your husband?" Caroline asked; her voice sounded lost in the acoustic depth of the freezing air.

The woman sighed. "Not here."

Silence followed, a silence in which wisps of wind began to decorate the snow-laden branches of pines with outflowing feathers of powder. The dense shadow thrown by the forest edging the trail was growing heavy, and cold pressed through the chinks of Caroline's sweater. Alice's thin neck strained as she gazed up at the vacant ridge for help. The woman in the snow began, tricklingly, to sob, and Caroline asked, "Would you like a cigarette?"

The response was prompt. "I'd adore a weed." The woman sat up, pulled off her mitten, and hungrily twiddled her fingers. Her nails were painted. She did not seem to notice, in taking the cigarette, that the pack became empty. Gesturing with stabbing exhalations of smoke, she waxed chatty. "I say to my son, 'What's the point of coming to these beautiful mountains if all you do is rush, rush, rush, up the tow and down, and never stop to enjoy the scenery?' I say to him, 'I'd rather be old-fashioned and come down the mountain in one piece than have my neck broken at the age of fourteen.' If he saw me now, he'd have a fit laughing. There's a patch of ice up there and my skis crossed. When I went over, I could feel my left side pull from my shoulders to my toes. It reminded me of having a baby."

"Where are you from?" Alice asked.

"Melrose." The name of her town seemed to make the woman morose. Her eyes focused on her inert boot.

To distract her, Caroline asked, "And your husband's working?"

"We're divorced. I know if I could loosen the laces it would be a world of relief. My ankle wants to swell and it can't."

"I wouldn't trust it," Alice said.

"Let me at least undo the knot," Caroline offered, and dropped to her knees, as if to weep. She did not as a rule like complaining women, but here in this one she seemed to confront a voluntary dramatization of her own possibilities. She freed the knots of both the outer and inner laces – the boot was a new Nordica, and stiff. "Does that feel better?"

"I honestly can't say. I have no feeling below my knees whatsoever."

"Shock," Alice said. "Nature's anesthetic."

"My brother will be furious. He'll have to hire a nurse for me."

"You'll have your daughter," Caroline said.

"At her age, it's all boys, boys on the brain."

This seemed to sum up their universe of misfortune. In silence, as dark as widows against the tilted acres of white, they waited for rescue. The trail here was so wide skiers could easily pass on the far side. A few swooped close, then veered away, as if sensing a curse. One man, a merry ogre wearing steel-framed spectacles and a raccoon coat, smoking a cigar, and plowing down the fall line with a shameless sprawling stem, shouted to them in what seemed a foreign language. But the pattern of the afternoon – the sun had shifted away from the trail – yielded few skiers. Empty minutes slid by. The bitter air had found every loose stitch in Caroline's sweater and now was concentrating on the metal bits of brassiere that touched her skin.

"Could I bum another coffin nail?" the injured woman asked.

"I'm sorry, that was my last."

"Oh dear. Isn't that the limit?"

Alice, so sallow now she seemed Oriental, tucked her hands into her armpits and jiggled up and down. She asked, "Won't the men worry?"

Caroline took satisfaction in telling her, "I doubt it." Looking outward, she saw only white, a tilted rippled wealth of colourlessness, the forsaken penumbra of the world. Her private desolation she now felt in communion with the other two women; they were all three abandoned, cut off, wounded, unwarmed, too impotent even to whimper. A vein of haze in the sky passingly dimmed the sunlight. When it brightened again, a tiny upright figure, male, in green and yellow chevron stripes, stood at the top of the cataracts of moguls.

"That took eighteen minutes," Alice said, consulting her wristwatch again. Caroline suddenly doubted that Norman, whose pyjama bottoms rarely matched his tops, could fall for anyone so finicking.

The woman in the snow asked, "Does my hair look awful?"

Down, down the tiny figure came, enlarging, dipping from crest to crest, dragging a sled, a bit clumsily, between its legs. Then, hitting perhaps the same unfortunate patch of ice, the figure tipped, tripped, and became a dark star, spread-eagled, a cloud of powder from which protruded, with electric rapidity, fragments of ski, sled, and arm. This explosive somersault continued to the base of the steep section, where the fragments reassembled and lay still.

The women had watched with held breaths. The woman from Melrose moaned, "Oh dear God." Caroline discovered herself yearning, yearning with her numb belly, for their rescuer to stand. He did. The boy (he was close enough to be a boy, with lanky legs in his tight racing pants) scissored his skis above his head (miraculously, they had not popped off), hopped to his feet, jerkily sidestepped a few yards uphill to retrieve his hat (an Alpine of green felt, with ornamental breast feathers), and skated toward them, drenched with snow, dragging the sled and grinning.

"That was a real eggbeater," Alice told him, like one boy to another.

"Who's hurt?" he asked. His red ears protruded and his face swirled with freckles; he was so plainly delighted to be himself, so clearly somebody's cherished son, that Caroline had to smile.

And as if this clown had introduced into vacuity a fertilizing principle, more members of the ski patrol sprang from the snow, bearing blankets and bandages and brandy, so that Caroline and Alice were pushed aside from the position of rescuers. They retrieved their parkas, refastened their skis, and tamely completed their run to the foot of the mountain. There, Timmy and Norman, looking worried and guilty, were waiting beside the lift shed. Her momentum failing, Caroline Harris actually skated – what she had never managed to do before, lifted her skis in the smooth alternation of skating – in her haste to assure her husband of his innocence.

OVER THE EDGE by Marc Paul Kaplan

Marc Paul Kaplan, author and avid skier, has written two thrilling wilderness adventures: 'Chasing Klondike Dreams' and 'Over The Edge'. The blossoming author first wrote 'Over the Edge', a great outdoors story set in Jackson Hole, Wyoming. Marc spent years in beautiful Jackson Hole, skiing and capturing the uniqueness of the area.

Matthew and crew took over a picnic table on the cafeteria deck. He had logged eight orgasmic trips down the incredible bowls, chutes, and ridges of the Jackson Hole Resort. Not bad before noon, a record for Matthew. The quality of the conditions had kept physical effort to a minimum. The Clock Tower registered 12:30. He wanted more.

"How about we head out of bounds to Rock Springs?" Jim suggested.

"Yeah, OB. Well, you guys enjoy," Ace said. "Billy's gotta be looking for me. I'm on patrol duty."

"You're takin' care of us poor beginners," Wesley said. "We appreciate your help and guidance, Ace. Maybe we'll drop a note in the suggestion box about what an excellent employee you been."

"You can do that for me," Ace said, "if you find the goddamn box. Meantime, it's been swell. I'm outta here. Gotta cover my ass."

Ace rose and picked up his skis and poles. Matthew noticed the patroller seemed to be in no hurry.

"Ain't it a little warm for goin' OB?" TJ spoke up. "It snowed over four feet top of rock-solid hard pack. Perfect conditions for slides."

"Rock Springs has lots of southern faces," Jim said. "Sun would just be getting there now. That bastard, the White Dragon's still dozing."

"Amazing how fast the mountain's getting chopped up," Matthew said. "Hell of a lot of people compared to the last couple of months. Good thing most of the tourists aren't powder hounds, or there'd be nothing left."

"Told ya," Wesley said. "In March weather gets better and the flatlanders show up. But they sure as hell ain't headin' for out of bounds and Rock Springs. Untouched."

"I don't know if were opening OB," Ace said, still standing at the edge of the circle, skis on his shoulder. Matthew grinned at Ace's reluctance to leave. Tough to go back to work with your partners headed for ecstasy.

"TJ's right," Ace said, "it's warmed up. I'll tell patrol I saw a group of guys headed over to the Springs case something happens."

"Don't say anything till we've started down," Jim warned. "I don't want Billy flying over there trying to stop us."

Matthew flashed on Billy's panicked exit from the platform with his birthday present. Billy paid a high price for being the only straight man on the mountain.

"No problem," Ace said. "Just wish I wasn't on duty."

"Come on, ya little turkey," Wesley taunted. "You been on duty all morning. What's another run?"

"Takes too long to get from the bottom of the Springs to the Tram." "Well, heaven won't wait," Jim called out, moving to his skis. Matthew's smile felt permanently plastered on his face. Matthew didn't care where they went; he just didn't want the day to end. A high tide of unqualified, unquestioned joy. Reality would return that night, but this, now, he accepted with open arms.

"Hey, Matthew," Wesley called out. "Quit smilin'. Think of your reputation."

A crow's harsh cry reverberated through the Village. The bird's shadow caught up with the giant dark scavenger on the Clock Tower. Glossy black feathers blocked the hour hand. An omen. Good or bad? Matthew laughed. Hell, his omens came wrapped in explosives.

This trip up the Tram, the view at the top of Rendezvous Peak, captured Matthew's attention. The Grand Tetons and the unbroken, white expanse of Jackson Hole's valley stretched all the way north to Yellowstone. Huge triangular Cody Peak beckoned them to the hidden treasures of Rock Springs, located just beyond the southern boundaries of the ski resort. The many runs that made up Jackson Hole surpassed Rock Springs in quality and diversity. But anything out of bounds added excitement and fresh terrain.

Matthew followed Jim's lead out of the Box, across the top of Rendezvous Bowl. He trusted Jungle Jim's years of experience in the mountains of Wyoming, even as he grew more uncomfortable with the man's apparent lack of character. Jungle Jim's relationship with Julia was so strange. And how come he lacked the discretion of his brother, the surgeon?

Matthew stopped as Jim reconnoitred. Below, shade still defined many of the short chutes and small open faces of Rock Springs Canyon. The snow would be cold and stable. But beyond the safety of the canyon, the large open Rock Springs Bowl sat seductively in the sun.

"Not a tough choice," Jim said, pointing over at the sparkling, unblemished surface. Matthew couldn't agree more.

"Been in the sun most of the morning," TJ commented. "Looks mighty good though. Shall we give it a shot?"

Jim answered by pushing forward, continuing the traverse across the first crease that defined the birth of Rock Springs Canyon. Matthew went next, bright sunshine suffusing his body with liquid warmth. A sky too blue to be real expanded Matthew's consciousness of space, beauty, and contentment. Control became an unnecessary dimension, saved for later.

Matthew stopped behind Jim at the side of a tantalizing, untouched expanse – steep, sensual Rock Springs Bowl. The free-floating promise below brought a pleasant flutter to Matthew's stomach.

"I'll go in first," Jim said, pushing off. "I'd allow ten to fifteen turns between us."

Rays of sun lit up crystals shrouding Jim's body as he swept from side to side down the exact centre of the two-hundred-foot-wide bowl.

"Right down the middle," Wesley howled in disgust. "What a Powder Pig."

Matthew forced himself to wait for the proper safe distance between him and Jim before he dove in. It wasn't easy. Then Matthew skied across the face, well to the right of Jim's symmetrical tracks. Jim had skimmed a quarter of the way down when Matthew made his first tight rotation back towards the middle. He gauged the now shorter distance to the trees lining the right side of the open run.

Whump! The semi-muffled sound of a gigantic concussion vibrated across the side of the mountain. Matthew compressed to a stop after only two turns. But the sinking sensation beneath his feet contradicted expected physics. Matthew moved when he should be stationary. Then he knew. The White Dragon.

Arms flailing, Matthew attempted to regain balance and ski off to the safety of the fir trees. Too late. A world gone horizontal and dark swallowed him. The avalanche picked up speed. Panic and fear extinguished a flash of anger at Jim's choice of runs. Then debris covered Matthew, and a crushing, intense weight drove him under.

He knew the slide rules. He focused solely on breathing. Unlike a battle, unlike a fight, time did not slow down. Just the opposite. He had options, but Matthew had been too slow to respond to the danger. He flashed through the checklist of survival.

Scream.

Too late. Besides, Wesley and TJ had to know where Matthew had headed, assuming they weren't victims also.

Drop all your gear.

Again, too late. His boots twisted out of his bindings, but the skis augured down into the heart of the cascading snow, still attached to his feet by the safety straps. Safety – the irony of that adjective wasn't lost on him, even in his desperate struggle to resurface. He did drop his poles. That freed his arms.

Swim towards the top.

Breast-stroking, head downhill, Matthew popped to the top. He gasped, gulping air, slamming his mouth shut as he rotated back into the maelstrom. Everything went black. Keep moving your arms. Now both safety straps ripped from his boots and bindings. Back on top, tumbling to the right.

Matthew had to make it to the trees. Death lay buried at the bottom beneath the tons of wet snow. Keep swimming. Under again. A solid object crushed his butt, jerking Matthew to a tentative halt.

But the force of the slide ripped him from his precarious perch. Inverted and disoriented, Matthew sunk again under the overpowering density of the avalanche. He worked to roll his body, arms flailing, until he faced downhill again. His breaststroke evolved into a frantic, spastic, acid freestyle. This time he grabbed a tree, hanging on with arms and legs.

Matthew flipped the lower part of his torso to the far side of the fir, out of the fatal grasp of the killer slide. He clung to the tree with strength only the fear of death could generate as the roar passed him by.

Numbing silence filled the space. Matthew hugged the tree. The rasping sound of his gasps competed with the retreating echoes of devastation rattling through Rock Springs. Then the screams of Wesley and TJ rippled through the solid mist and clouds hovering over the avalanche chute. Wesley appeared from the backside. He must have skied above the fractured fissure of the bowl and down between the trees along the far side. Gratitude filled Matthew. Thanks that he was safe. Thanks that Wesley had avoided disaster. "Holy shit," Wesley panted. "You're alive. You hurt bad?" "No idea," Matthew said, now that air circulated through his system. "But until I know, I'm not letting go of this tree." The Indian's face was drawn tight over his high cheekbones and tall forehead. His face reflected the horror of their near-death experience. "Wesley, you look like a white man," Matthew said. Wesley's expression reinforced the constant thought that had resonated through the frightening chaos. That had fuelled Matthew's desperate struggle, had helped pull him to the surface. The words escaped his lips. "I want to live." He looked up at his friend, the moisture of tears indistinguishable from the wet snow packed in every orifice and crease of his battered body. His moving parts still functioned. Too early for the pain from the bruises and connective-tissue damage to register. The numbness would wear off too soon. "Did Jim make it?" Matthew asked, voice trembling. Wesley's face faded from pale to grey. The pupils of his dark eyes distended, creating anxious pools surrounded by white. "I don't think so." Matthew still hung tight to the tree, his bruised arm rigid in its grip. A wave of vertigo and despair for Jim swept through him. He looked to the bottom of Rock Springs Bowl. The small, frantic figure of TJ bounced on top of tons of snow and debris, the mess solidifying into cement. Death and destruction had piled twenty feet high in an unforgiving mass. Jim would be buried near the bottom. "Jungle Jim's in the belly of the Dragon." Wesley's chiselled countenance crumbled with emotion. "Ain't no hope. Won't be able to dig him out till late spring."

Wesley pried Matthew off the fir and helped him struggle out of the tree line. Matthew stood dazed, holding onto Wesley, the sun filtering through the trees on this once perfect day. Matthew attempted one step and sunk to his waist in the deep powder. Wesley grabbed tighter, supporting Matthew, unlikely lovers during the last dance. "It's gonna be a bitch gettin' down to the Village without your skis," Wesley said. "I'll make it." Matthew nodded towards the wreckage at the base of the bowl. "If I start to whine, remind me of the alternative."

CHAPTER 12
MURDER AND SKULDUGGERY

THE RACE by Unni Lindell

Unni Maria Lindell (1957) is a Norwegian writer. She is best known for her crime novels but has also written a collection of poems and several children's and young adult books. Shel was awarded the Mads Wiel Nygaards Endowment in 1998 and the Critics' Prize for the year's best children's or youth literature.[2] *In 1999 and in 2018 she received the Riverton Prize, a literature award given annually to the best Norwegian detective story.*

This short story has been translated by Ingrid Christophersen.

She parked the small Volkswagen in the floodlit parking lot. Hers was the only car. She banged her head as she slid out of the car. "Blast!" She was too tall for such a tiny car. She was tall for a woman. Tall and elegant some might say. Feminine in a masculine way. Her face was strong and the features large and regular.

She unclipped the skis from the roof rack and buckled them on. The evening was clear and starry. The flood-lit trail was bathed in white, ice-cold light. A perfect evening. The fresh snow that had fallen the day before softened the hard trail.

The first inclines were the worst. Her thigh and leg muscles were still stiff. She stretched her long body and settled into an even, but not too fast pace up the first rise.

Best of all was the silence. Not a sound; just the cold, the dark and the flood-lit track. She was nearly always alone. That was because she always skied late at night. The time now was just before 10.30

The skis cut the cold surface and produced a lonely rhythm which thumped in time to her inner self. She relaxed.

These were the trips she had most missed when she and Tormod had spent winters in Southern Europe. Admittedly, only a couple of weeks at a time, but still... In the heat and amongst tourists, the otherwise so boring Tormod had blossomed in an undisguised rather silly way. Alcohol proliferated and he conducted loud small talk with Germans and Swedes while she looked on, sipping her drink.

Back in the hotel bedroom she could in no way avoid her conjugal duties and that alone had been a nightmare. Sometimes she even feared her violent dislike of him. He just would not get it into his head that she would rather be at home in the snow and the cold. He never understood that *down there* she could not escape from him for even a minute. At home, at least they had single bedrooms.

On the top of a rise she stopped and leant on the ski sticks. The track continued straight ahead before curving to the left and continuing down a hill. She knew the track inside-out and could ski it blindfolded. She sometimes met other skiers, but more often earlier in the evening. Many had skied here this evening, probably men in tracksuit tops with the name of a ski club on the back. Now they were at home, watching TV, having showered and with a clear conscience.

It was pleasant to feel the heat of her body in spite of the cold air. She glided forwards like a programmed robot.

She had been a bit nervous lately. No wonder, she had been a widow for only a few months. It was most noticeable at work. She might be lost in thought and then jump sky-high if someone knocked on the door or the phone rang.

Her girlfriends never understood how she had the guts to ski alone in the dark, but she had never thought of it as dangerous. She liked doing things on her own. Fear was not really something she knew much about, although, now that she was alone, she had to admit that she sometimes had an inkling about it.

She stopped for a breather. The silence wasn't exactly stifling, but it was intrusive. Her heart pounded in hard, rhythmical beats, buzzing in her ears. The pounding slowed down after a while but the buzzing continued. It sounded like the surface of skis sliding over cold snow. But she was standing still? Her scalp felt cold in spite of the woolly hat over her ears. She accelerated and pushed hard forwards.

She tossed her head and caught a glimpse of the firmament. It was large and dark. Her skis groaned against the snow surface and beat a melody in her thoughts – I'm not frightened, I'm not frightened. She had to laugh. She had never been so stupid before. But there had been a lot to do at work lately. She had worked overtime a few evenings and even taken work home. She slept badly at night. She was quite frankly overworked.

I'm not frightened, I'm not frightened. Maybe she should pause again and try and relax. No, she wasn't really tired yet.

The track continued ahead before the shallow incline down by the old fir trees. She could see the long trunks bathed in the yellow light. There was a lump in her throat which she could not swallow and her saliva was dry. She tried to think about things other than the dark and the loneliness in the woods. Tormod's face took shape in her mind. His eyes, stupid but reproachful and hard. They had been so different. She never understood why she married him. He was sixteen years older and already then he was an old man. She could not imagine that he had ever been young.

The flat in the terraced house, only quarter of an hour's drive from the flood-lit trail, had been too small for them the last years. "We don't talk anymore," he said. We are after all married. We both work all day and the in the evening you go skiing. We don't even share a bedroom.

Maybe Tormod's ghost was following her to avenge himself. Dear Lord, do pull yourself together. No one was after her. Or were they?

Suddenly she realised, she was scared stiff. And it was not only her own thoughts and imagination that scared her. The sound behind her was proof enough. She never turned around but knew it instinctively. Someone was really following her.

Cold panic crept into her warm body; blood rushed through her wrists. Her heart ached. Maybe it was just another skier who would pass her and continue on his way under the trees. But it wasn't and she knew that with all her heart.

She stopped, one second, two seconds. Her heart virtually shook. She threw her head round and her eyes caught a vision, in an instant, of the man who was following her. Immediately a scream stuck in her throat, hard and painful. My God!

Instantly she heard laughter, a greedy, booming laughter, thundering through the cold. No one was out as late as this. Not a soul. She was wet though from sweating, her legs stiffened, and she trembled. Her skis rushed through the snow like arrows.

He was quick and was about to overtake her. This was dangerous, fatal. She sobbed aloud while skiing for her life. It happened suddenly. The lights went off. The track lay in darkness; the forest was black. Her eyes still adjusting to darkness, she saw nothing, but nor did he. A low curse reached her.

She knew the track inside out, knew every corner and every hill. He did not – maybe. Now she was sobbing aloud and suddenly realised what an animal experiences when it is being hunted. She was the prey and she knew that with every fibre of her body. But at the same time she realised another thing – that the stalker was dropping back. Round the next corner was a steep hill and thereafter the track continued sharply to the right. She nearly fell at the bottom of the hill; something must have been lying in the snow, an orange peel maybe or some chocolate wrapping. Her body jolted, but she quickly regained her balance.

He fell. She heard the heavy thud just behind her.

Fear was still overwhelmingly present, but something else had appeared; a sort of ecstasy, akin to what a soldier on the scene of battle must feel when all his comrades fall around him but he runs on. Her skin was prickly. She was the mouse playing with the cat. She felt cold, she shivered. He was up again. The chase continued. She had no idea of time. For how long had this been going on? Half an hour, twenty minutes? Probably only five.

The track continued along an open field. The whiteness of the snow made it easier to see. Her legs dragged the skis forwards. She heard his breath but did not know how far behind he was. Two metres, maybe only one?

The thought of giving up made her urge her body on, beyond her capability. This new strength shot her skis forwards. She could not die now, did not want to. Tormod was dead. She was alive and she wanted to continue to live.

The field was flat and the trail a black streak ahead. Further on a small bridge crossed the river, then a short distance before the turnaround and the same way back. Then what? If she got that far? There was one possibility, but would it work? Her head was a jumble of thoughts, excitement and calculations. If… The ski tracks were deep and her skis followed them mechanically like a train on rails.

She was tired, no more strength. Hardly any. Nausea surged through her body. Her lips were swollen with frozen saliva. Her hair a tangled mass under her hat. Her breathing boomed like bellows and escaped from her mouth in hard gasps. The taste of blood accumulated like an acrid lump under her tongue. All around was quiet. The world had stopped rotating.

Her heart was the only sound. He had caught her up again. His skis were on top of hers. They pulled at them and she nearly fell. His breath was laboured but he had strength to spare – he was a man.

As a last resort she thrust her skis off the track, 10 metres short of the small bridge. The skis charged through the snow, making fresh tracks. She had acted unexpectedly. After a few seconds he was after her again. Would she make it? A few more metres. Three metres. Two, one.

She flew across the river, like an apparition. The thin layer of ice, topped by newly fallen snow, was just strong enough to hold her weight for a second, and then she was already on the other side. Ice floes disappeared in the roar of the river. And so did he. He called out whilst floundering with poles and skis in the cold water. The current carried him downstream. His head bobbed around like a small boat and dipped in and out a few times. Then he was gone.

He was gone. She was left standing with burning cheeks and the roar from the river in her ears. Her hair was full of icicles; perspiration poured off her, as did her tears. She had made it. She had made it.

The silence was overwhelming. Then the light returned. It flowed from above like liquid gold. Slowly she returned to life. Her heart no longer shook but a dull exhaustion took hold and she could hardly move.

Slowly she set out on the return trip. She walked along the riverbank until she reached the bridge. The way back was long. Very long. She worked slowly but surely. After a while she felt the eeriness from the big forest and increased her pace. At last the parking lot appeared below her and during the last descent she had regained full control of her body.

A second car was parked there, a silver BMW. Morten's car. She knew he would be there this evening. At work today they had arranged to meet at the parking lot at 10.30pm. But she had not waited for him, on purpose. She wanted a small head start. But oh God, it had been in the nick of time. At one stage she thought the whole plan would collapse. She never realised he was so fit.

Morten knew that she had killed Tormod. She had had too much to drink at an office party and in a weak moment had confided in him. She thought she could trust him. She should have known better. After all, he was a man. Since then he had taken advantage of her, humiliated her. Threatened to expose her if she did not do as he said. Twice she had been to his flat. Now that was over.

She started the Volkswagen. It was snowing again. Thin white flakes which obstructed the view. She listened to the engine, put the car in reverse and pressed the accelerator. The car refused to move, skidded, while the snowflakes descended slowly onto the windscreen.

WOLF WINTER by Clare Francis

This is my very favourite thriller, set in Arctic Norway during the '60s at the height of the Cold War. Superbly written and nail-bitingly exciting, as well as also being very accurate. The Ministry of Defence female employee, who turns out to be a traitor for the love of a Norwegian spying for the Russians, is pushed under a tram and I remember that incident very well.

Having read it my father said: "How the hell did she know so much? One wonders where Clare Francis got her information from." Clare Francis (1946) is a British novelist who was first known for her exploits as a yachtswoman. She twice sailed single-handed across the Atlantic and was the first woman to captain a successful boat on the 'Whitbread Around the World' race. Her other best-selling thrillers are 'Night Sky' and 'Red Crystal'.

PROLOGUE – NORTH NORWAY, JANUARY 1945

The night was cold and brilliantly clear. You could see for miles: peak after peak of ice-mountains rose into the dome of the sky. Jagged, crystal teeth squeezed between the deep inroads of the jet-black fjords. High in the mountains the near-full moon cast long shadows and lit the snow with transparent brilliance so that visibility was particularly good. Which was just as well for the two young men who were making a quick but properly cautious descent of the mountain known by the Lappish name of 'Goalsvarre'.

At 4,230 feet the peak was not the highest in the Lyngen Alps. There were several higher, many of which were tantalisingly unclimbed, but Goalsvarre was close to the village of Lyngseidet and convenient for the bus and ferry ride back to Tromsø. Most people, had they known of this expedition, would have considered it foolish. It was irresponsible enough to go mountaineering in the depths of a winter night, but to do so when the place was thick with Germans was asking for trouble.

But no one did know. And even if they had, the young men would have argued that winter was the best time to go mountaineering – the snow was firm and powdery – and that at sixty-nine degrees north, well within the Arctic Circle, the long hours of darkness at this time of year made night climbing more or less unavoidable. And as for the Germans – well, the Occupation had lasted five years and if one waited for it to end one might wait forever.

The descent of the upper slopes went smoothly and by seven in the morning they had regained their camp on a bluff below the main ridge and were eating a spartan breakfast. They made desultory but contented conversation. It had been a good hard climb and they had done it in record time with the minimum of equipment. Taking to their skis, they began the descent of the lower slopes. The moon was setting but the snow was vibrant with reflected starlight. Above the northern peaks the polar sky flickered with the ghostly radiance of the northern lights.

As always, Hal led and Jan followed. They travelled in silence; there was no need to speak. It was enough to hear the soft hiss of the skis on the virgin snow, and the resonant hush of the frosty air. A frozen lake discharged into an equally frozen stream; its course discernible only by a slight depression in the thick snow. As the young men followed it downward, Lyngenfjord began to open out before them; a narrow black gash between the glistening mountains. Hal gestured and they came to a stop.

From deep in the fjord rose a low hum. The two listened for a moment then skied on until they could see across the distant water to where Route 50, the German Army-built north-south highway, snaked its way tortuously down the far shore of the fjord. They paused again and stared, transfixed by the sight of a procession of glimmering pinpricks of light creeping slowly southward. "Retreat?" Jan asked, unable to keep the excitement out of his voice. "This far, anyway," Hal said cautiously. "But surely they'll keep going. They're bound to." "Well..." Hal said doubtfully. "It'll depend on the Russians."

"That's what I mean. The Russians'll chase them out!"

Hal was silent for a moment. "I hope so," he murmured finally.

The German 20th Mountain Army had been on the retreat from the Russian border for two months, dragging themselves across Finland and the top of Norway to this, the Lyngenfjord. During the retreat along the Arctic coast, the German Army had been pursuing a ruthless scorched-earth policy, evacuating civilians, burning towns and villages and destroying livestock.

For weeks evacuees had been arriving in Tromsø by coastal steamer, many of them to be sent further south. Now over a hundred thousand German soldiers of the 18th and 36th Mountain Corps were encamped at Lyngen. Hal tried to imagine what this retreat must have cost the Germans, floundering first through the forests and lakeland of northern Finland then across the vast emptiness of the high plateau until they reached this, the deeply indented coastline of northern Norway – and all in the depths of winter, on primitive roads that were often closed by avalanche and drift snow. And with the Russian Army on their heels.

It must surely rank as one of the most difficult retreats ever undertaken. Hal knew how impossible it was to move a heavily equipped army quickly, even in ideal conditions; at the age of twelve he'd had a taste for military history and had read his way through a detailed account of the Napoleonic Wars. For a while he'd even wanted to be a soldier. But then at fourteen he'd discovered the glory of the mountains, and that had spoilt him for everything else.

Now he was almost eighteen and his old ambition to be a soldier had returned. Like every other boy of his age he wanted to get hold of a decent weapon and have a shot at the Germans and force them to get out of Norway.

But would the Russians come? There were rumours: it was said the Russians were already deep within the northernmost province of Norway, named Finnmark, and advancing fast on Lyngen. But Hal doubted it. No army would risk getting trapped on this coast, hemmed in by the fjords and open sea on the one side and the mountains on the other.

No: the Russians would hold off. And the Germans, having abandoned Finnmark, would stay here at Lyngen until the bitter end. "Come," he said to Jan, and they refastened their hoods and adjusted their gloves and set off once more.

As they continued downward the night retreated a little and the outlines of the mountains lost their sharpness and became soft and blue-tinged as the winter day, which would grow to no more than a dim twilight, glimmered slowly to life. Lyngseidet came into view beneath them. Pausing, they looked down. The small village on the edge of Lyngenfjord was choked with German vehicles that hadn't been there the previous evening. "Better keep clear," Hal said.

They turned away from the village and headed towards a pass through the mountains. This led to a small fjord called Kjosen, a finger of water that almost dissected the forty-mile-long Lyngen peninsula. A narrow snow-packed road led over the pass towards the Tromsø ferry. Even this road, though far from busy, had more traffic than usual.

Hal decided it would be risky to take the bus, even if it was running, which was doubtful. Their papers were in order, but with all this activity the guards at the checkpoints might be overzealous and ask questions about the unusual amount of food and survival gear in their rucksacks. The guards were always on the lookout for young men fleeing over the mountains to Sweden to avoid Arbeidstjenesten – known as 'AT' – the so-called 'labour service' introduced by the Quisling government in a thinly disguised attempt to force Norwegians into the German Army.

Hal led the way down into the pass and, when it was safe to do so, on across the snow-packed road and up the opposite slope. Keeping high above the road and the checkpoints, they made their way along the mountainside, parallel to the road, until the pass was left behind, and Kjosen Fjord lay below and to their left, a dark gash between the steep blue-lit slopes. Along the shore an occasional farm nestled darkly in the snow, the windows blacked out, the buildings dead looking. The hillside got steeper. Hal looked up, trying to remember the formation of the hidden upper slopes. There was a hanging glacier, he knew, and at least one deep snow-filled gully: avalanche country.

Finally, they were forced to descend on to a gentler slope covered with sparse birch scrub. The road was now only a hundred yards away. Occasionally a German military vehicle sped past, throwing up clouds of snow but, screened by the scrub, the two skiers remained unnoticed, striding along in the long sliding gait of practised cross-country skiers. A valley opened out to the right. They curved into its mouth to distance themselves from the road.

Suddenly Hal stopped dead so that Jan almost ran into him.

Motionless, they listened. The air was very still. For several moments the silence was deep and unbroken. Then a muffled sound floated across the snow. A human voice.

Hal stiffened. He saw them now: a group of skiers about half a mile away, coming straight for them on a reciprocal course. There were six of them, uniformly dressed in white parkas with rifles slung over their shoulders: a German patrol. And travelling fast. Why ski-troops should be down by this road Hal couldn't imagine, but they were. And there would be no escaping them. It would be best to look casual and unconcerned when first seen. With a sigh of resignation and anger, Hal gestured to Jan and led the way forward again.

Just as it seemed the patrol must spot them, the leading soldier halted and trained his binoculars up the narrow side valley. He appeared to see something for, with a sudden movement, he grabbed his rifle and put it to his shoulder. Then, just as abruptly, he lowered it again and, beckoning excitedly to his men, led the way into the valley, skiing briskly. The opportunity was too good to miss. The moment the patrol was gone, Hal and Jan thrust rapidly forward in a rapid kick-glide movement that was almost a run and crossed quickly behind the disappearing Germans.

As he ran Hal glanced sideways. The reason for the soldiers' excitement was now clear. High in the head of the valley were two black dots, plainly visible in the blue light. Men on skis. Climbing slowly up the steep slope at the head of the valley, like two ants on a white wall. Reaching the comparative safety of a thick clump of birch at the far side of the valley mouth, the two young men paused.

Jan whispered: "Who can they be?" Hal gave a shrug. The two figures couldn't be Lapps – the Lapps were miles inland on the plateau at this time of year – and they weren't likely to be mountaineers – it wasn't exactly a popular sport. They were probably AT evaders. Hal wished there was something they could do to help, but short of side-tracking the patrol and getting themselves arrested or shot in the process, there was nothing to be done.

The Germans had now reached the head of the valley and were striking up a deep gully, climbing awkwardly and slowly. It was hard to be sure from such a distance, but to Hal's eyes the gully looked heavy with drifts, bulges and hummocks of snow. Some distance above the gully was a steep snowfield, with a thick cover of snow, smooth as a cake topping, which gleamed ice blue in the late-morning twilight.

The gully looked tricky but it was nothing to the snowfield. That looked wildly unstable. Only fools or men untrained for these mountains would have chosen that route. But the two black dots higher on the mountain knew their stuff all right, for they had bypassed the gully and were now making short work of a ridge well to the side of the pregnant snowfield. Soon they would reach the safety of the high mountains. Hal put up a silent cheer. Halfway up the gully the soldiers were making heavy weather of their climb. They had slowed down visibly and the leader was stationary, as if undecided about the route ahead.

Suddenly the silence was broken by the distant sound of a shot, echoing once, faintly, through the valley. Hal stiffened, thinking: They're mad. There was a long and deathly silence. Another shot rang out, reverberated once, feebly, and was quickly absorbed by the snow. Jan gasped audibly. A small puff of white had appeared at one side of the snowfield.

Slowly, almost leisurely, more delicate puffballs ballooned out, like cannon smoke from a broadside. The sound came seconds later, a low rumbling of distant thunder. Denser clouds blossomed out from the bottom of the snowfield which lay curiously pristine and untouched in the centre. Yet this was an illusion, for the whole face was in fact sliding, the bottom already voiding itself like some vast ponderous waterfall, a white cataract disgorging tons and tons of compacted snow into the gully beneath.

The surface of the snowfield cracked and heaved and segmented and was slowly obscured by the billowing snow which rose up and outward in a vast cloud. The six soldiers below seemed rooted to the spot. Then, as if at a signal, they moved at once, racing down the gully in jerky zigzags like insects fleeing a fire. Two figures collided and one fell. The others pressed on, their progress in the heavy snow painfully slow.

It was a race that couldn't be won. The avalanche poured remorselessly into the gully. Hal winced as the dense white cloud engulfed the first man and the next and the next, until four had been overcome. For a moment it seemed that the last two might escape – they appeared to be keeping ahead of the advancing wall – but then they too were enveloped in the rumbling cloud. A German Army truck passed by on the road behind. It did not stop. It was a full two minutes before the last thundering echo died away. A pall of blue cloud hung in the valley like morning mist.

Hal and Jan exchanged brief glances. They both knew what the other was thinking. Had the buried men been Norwegians they would have gone for help and tried to dig them out. But it was impossible to feel pity for Germans. It had been a long war and few families had suffered more than Hal's. In 1941 his elder brother had been lost at sea in a torpedoed cargo ship and a year later his father had been deported to Germany.

Without a word they turned away. Hal set off at a smart pace: the sooner they were clear of the scene the better. In the absence of anyone to blame, the Germans would doubtless arrest them. Jan made an exclamation and, calling to Hal, gestured back up the valley. Following his gaze, Hal saw with surprise that the two fugitives had reappeared. Their tiny figures were heading downhill again, back into the valley. Jan raised his eyebrows questioningly at Hal. Hal thought for a long moment. "They might need help." His words hung heavily on the air. If the men were wanted by the Germans the risks would be considerable. The penalties ranged from deportation to a forced labour camp to a bullet in the head.

There was no discussion. Hal and Jan turned and skied into the valley. A short way up the valley they stopped and waited in the cover of a thicket of dwarf birch. The figures had reached the lower slopes at the head of the valley. But instead of hurrying towards the valley mouth, they made a long traverse, heading for the vast pile of avalanched snow at the foot of the gully. Halting on top of the white burial mound, they went first one way then the other, as if searching for something.

After a while they seemed to find what they were seeking, for one moved across to the other and they both crouched in the snow. They remained in the same spot for some time, and Hal thought he could see them digging. Finally, after a good five minutes, the two figures stood up, their task apparently completed, and began to ski down the valley.

Hal let them get quite close before emerging from the thicket. The two men stopped dead. One slid an automatic weapon quickly off his shoulder.

Hal called a casual: "Good morning."

There was a long silence, then: "Who are you?"

"Friends."

They murmured to each other then moved cautiously forward until the four of them stood face to face. The two strangers were hooded and muffled, but Hal could see from their eyes that they were young, roughly his own age, he guessed. Hal decided on the direct approach. "We saw what happened. We thought you might need help." The taller of the two pulled the hood down from his mouth.

"Help? You could say that. You could tell us how to get out of this place!"

"Where are you going?"

There was a pause while the tall one eyed Hal thoughtfully. He seemed to make up his mind. "North."

Hal blinked with a mixture of alarm and admiration. Only desperate men would try such a thing. The new German lines would be almost impenetrable. And even if they got through they'd have to run the gauntlet of the demolition squads before they could hope to reach the relative safety of the Russian lines.

"Not easy," Hal said.

The tall one gave a short harsh laugh, the sound uncomfortably loud in the silent valley. "Well, we know that, my friend!"

Hal flushed. Recovering quickly, he tried to think. "All I could do is direct you to a place where there are boats. Someone might be able to take you a few miles up the coast, past the lines. Though it's an awful risk."

The two exchanged glances. "We'll give it a try," said the second one. "Anything's better than freezing up there." He indicated the mountains.

"We need food, too," said the tall one. "As much as you can find." It was the request of someone accustomed to getting what he wanted.

"You're welcome to what we've got," Hal offered solemnly.

Another German vehicle passed along the distant road. Aware that both the fugitives had highly visible automatic weapons over their shoulders, Hal added urgently, "We must get away from here."

He led the way out of the valley and along the side of the fjord, keeping as high above the road as possible. Finally the narrow strip of lowland by the shore opened out into a wide flat plain and, hugging the edge of the mountain, they curved away from the road until safely out of view of passing vehicles. They stopped and made camp, waiting for the cover of the deepening afternoon twilight.

The two fugitives ate ravenously, consuming all Hal and Jan's remaining rations. While they ate, Hal examined them. They were both about eighteen, he guessed; twenty at the most. The taller one had a handsome face, with regular features, a thatch of thick yellow-blond hair and vivid blue eyes. But what one noticed most was his taut energy: a sort of driving force that commanded attention. He talked in great bursts, as if his energy could barely be contained, and his eyes were charged with a restlessness which only fell away when he laughed; then he seemed exhilarated, almost euphoric. His friend, who was dark with a pleasant round face, was altogether quieter, appearing strangely unaffected by the day's events.

They didn't offer an explanation of how they had arrived in Lyngen or where they had come from, and Hal didn't ask. But their accent was not a local one. It was from further south, though Hal couldn't place it exactly. It was Jan who asked: "Have you come far?"

The first one shot his friend a warning glance, but too late to prevent him saying: "Trondheim."

There was an awkward pause, then the conversation switched to the avalanche. The two strangers discussed it with great amusement, even pride. With a slight shock Hal suddenly realised that it was they, and not the Germans, who had fired the shots. He stared at them, slightly awe-struck. Finally, he asked: "You meant to start the avalanche?"

"Well, we didn't mean to, exactly. But we certainly caused it!" said the tall one. He gave a brittle laugh, his blue eyes sharp and shrewd, and Hal had the feeling that he had known exactly what he was doing with those shots.

"We did well out of it too," he added. He patted the sub-machinegun propped against the rucksack beside him. "A Schmeisser," he said proudly. "Now we have one each."

"And ammo, and a knife, and new gloves, and goggles, and a warm fleece-lined cap!" his friend added, pulling article after article out of his rucksack.

"And look at this," the tall one boasted, producing a pair of field glasses, rubber-jacketed and overpainted with flaking white paint. "The Germans are very good at making binoculars. They make the best lenses in the world, did you know that?" He put the glasses to his eyes and twiddled with the focus. "Excellent!"

Hal wasn't so sure this booty was excellent at all. He murmured: "If they catch you with it..."

The tall one gave his short snorty laugh. "If we're caught, we're dead anyway!"

Hal wondered what they had done that was so serious. As if reading his thoughts, the tall one indicated his friend and said: "He beat up an officer, I, he paused, I executed one of their lot!" He said it with a bright mocking smile, as if he didn't care a damn, but his quick eyes darted straight to Hal's face, searching for a reaction.

There was a moment's silence. Hal was meant to be impressed, he realised, but he could only feel a stab of concern. When one of their number was killed the Germans always exacted terrible reprisals, executing dozens of civilians – sometimes even women and children.

The tall one sensed his dismay. "Sometimes these things have to be done," he said defensively. "We did everyone a favour, believe me. We're heroes back home. Or at least I hope so!" He laughed again. The sound was sharp and discordant in the silence. No one spoke. After a while the two strangers settled back in the snow and dozed. Hal and Jan kept watch until gathering clouds brought an early darkness. Waking the sleeping men, they packed up and set off again.

Luck was with them: the cloud thickened and they were able to travel across the flatlands with little fear of being seen. Hal led them along the wide shore of Ullsfjord until they were safely past the checkpoint at the ferry link to Tromsø. Then he explained the way to the isolated settlement where they might find a boat.

"One favour," the tall one said to Hal.

"If I can."

"Your skis. You see, one of my bindings is almost off. I can't fix it without tools, but it wouldn't take a moment in a workshop. You don't mind, do you? I'll return them or at least repay you – I promise. Though I can't say when!"

Hal's face fell in the darkness. His skis were new. It had taken him two years to get hold of some seasoned spruce and hickory, and another year to persuade the local ski maker to make the skis to Hal's own design: spruce upper with laminated hickory sole; narrow and very fast. They had proved to be everything Hal had hoped they would be, and more.

"You can't fix yours?" he asked, hoping for a miracle.

"Afraid not. And we've a long way to go."

Hal sighed inwardly and, wishing he didn't mind quite so much, bent down to remove his skis. He thrust them quickly into the other man's hand and took the damaged ones in exchange. The tall one murmured to his friend in the darkness:

"Yours all right, Petter?"

"Yes."

The four of them parted, shaking hands gravely in the darkness. On impulse Hal said, "If for any reason you can't get away and you find yourselves in Tromsø, ask for the Starheim house."

"Thanks," said the tall one in the distant tone of someone who never expects to have to take up an offer.

And then the two of them were gone, and Hal and Jan turned back along the path to the ferry and the faint hope of a bus ride home.

Two days later the news flew around Tromsø: a boat had been stolen from Ullsfjord the previous night and gunfire had been heard in the fjord. No one knew anything more. But in Hal's imagination it was only too horrifyingly obvious: the two boys had been captured and were already in Gestapo headquarters in Tromsø. The memory of his father's incarceration in the grey forbidding building on Bankgata was still vivid in his mind. It was said that everyone thrown into its notorious cells talked in the end.

His friends on Ullsfjord would be betrayed and punished, probably executed. But those fears were nothing to what he felt when he remembered he'd told the two young men his family name. His name! He couldn't believe what a fool he'd been. His mother, his sister, himself – they would all be taken and shot.

Two days passed with agonising slowness. Then another day, and another. Still the Gestapo did not come. Neither was there news of any arrests at Ullsfjord. Gradually Hal began to hope. Perhaps, despite everything, the two boys had got away.

After a month he finally allowed himself to relax and, far from minding about the loss of his lovely new skis, grew quite fond of the other pair. Not that they were any use: quite apart from the damaged binding, one ski had a long crack down the length of the grain.

Had the fellow known about the crack when he suggested the swap? Probably. But in a strange way Hal didn't mind. In the same position he liked to think he would have had the nerve to do the same thing himself.

On examining the skis closely he saw that something had been carved into the tips then scratched out. From time to time he made desultory attempts to decipher the markings. Then, several months after the German capitulation, when no harm could possibly come from knowing, he took a soft pencil and thin paper and did a rubbing. Initials, faint but distinguishable. R.B.

After that Hal put the skis in the cellar and forgot about them. Only now and again, when he was climbing in the Lyngen Alps or passing the insignificant valley off the Tromsø-Lvngseidet road, did he wonder about the skis' owner and whether he had got through. He still liked to think that he had. But, on consideration, he thought not. The Russians had stopped short many miles to the north east. It would have been an impossibly long journey across the devastation of Finnmark, and without supplies in the harshness of Arctic January. No, the fellow probably hadn't made it. Hal was sorry

We continue the story with Chapter 35. Between the prologue and this chapter is one of the most exciting stories about Northern Norway and the Cold War in the 1960s.

Berg plodded steadily forward and came to a decision. He would have to abandon Ragna. He would have preferred not to abandon her at all, of course – a promise was a promise – but she was holding him back, and he couldn't afford to waste any more of this wonderful weather.

It was eleven in the morning; the blue light was at its most intense and vivid and, though the temperature was very low, the air was clear. They should have covered a good twenty five miles by now. Instead it was a pathetic fifteen. But for Ragna he would have had a good chance of reaching the road that night. He'd been ridiculously patient, but not any longer. There should be a hut of some sort about five miles ahead, the only one for miles. It was the logical place to leave Ragna. She'd manage. At heart she was a tough girl. But not so tough that it wouldn't take her at least twenty-four hours to get to the road, or, if the weather deteriorated, a great deal longer. The trip back over the border would be no faster. Either way, he'd have enough time to get clear.

He looked over his shoulder. Ragna had stopped yet again to fiddle with a troublesome binding. He waited, gritting his teeth with exasperation. If he had any sense he'd leave her now, this minute, and she could make her own way to the hut. But, impressed at his own generosity, he waited. He hadn't forgotten the way she'd guided him to the hut last night. He was suitably grateful. And he knew that she'd tried very hard to keep up – tried too hard, in fact, and exhausted herself in the process. Perhaps it had been a mistake to tell her about the child; it had made her frantic. He waited. But this, he decided, was definitely the last time.

"Come on!" His call was absorbed by the hungry silence, a silence that was vibrant, alive, as if something menacing were taking place within it. At last Ragna stood up and started forward again. Behind her Berg noticed that the horizon was less distinct, and that some of the blue had gone out of the light.

A change – he should have known! Seized by a new sense of urgency, he started off again, momentarily forgetting Ragna, searching the landscape, looking for landmarks. Ahead, a large hill rose to his right, and beyond it another. According to the map the hut should be on the far side of that second hill. The landscape was distinctive enough for him to be fairly confident. Not like earlier in the day when the light had been dim and the rolling terrain especially deceptive. They had turned south too soon and almost lost themselves in a valley which hooked back over the border.

The blue was fading fast. Everything was turning a monotonous grey-white. Only a scattering of stunted birch stood out from the flatness, their thin branches like black latticework against the snow, while on the bare hillside boulders of dark granite, the occasional outcrop, lay exposed by the wind. He looked up and the sky was opaque with mist. The air fast losing its sharpness.

The damned weather had been too good to last. When he came level with the first hill he looked back. Ragna had fallen even further behind. In a fury of impatience he realised he would have to wait for her, if only to tell her he was going on ahead and to give her directions to the hut. While he waited, he climbed a little way up the side of the hill to make absolutely sure of his bearings in case the visibility should clamp down. He glanced back the way they had come. The rolling landscape was fast blending into a featureless expanse. Something made him pause. He stood motionless like an animal scenting the wind. He blinked to sharpen his focus. He thought he had seen something. Something that was moving.

He remained absolutely still, hardly breathing, his senses reaching out into the distance. A small dark grey dot, barely distinguishable from the mass of greyness surrounding it. He watched for several minutes. It was moving. He felt a leap of fear. An animal? Yet what sort of an animal travelled alone and didn't stop to scent the air; what sort of an animal was tall and thin and came inexorably forward with a jerky swaying movement? A man? Yet no one came up here in mid-winter, no one except the Lapps. Yet this fast-moving figure was never a Lapp – was he? He thought viciously: Who are you? Whoever, he was coming their way, and along the same route. It wasn't too difficult to imagine that he was following their tracks. Berg looked swiftly ahead, re-examining the lie of the land, then, with a jab of his sticks, skied rapidly down to Ragna.

Hal stopped abruptly as the now familiar nausea rose in his throat. The cold sweat came shortly after, followed a few agonising moments later by the violent retching which, since his stomach had long-since been empty, squeezed his guts painfully. As soon as the unpleasant business was over he sat weakly back on his skis, pulling in great gulps of freezing air, waiting for the last of the shivering and faintness to pass.

He felt confused, cloudy, and it worried him. The tight vicious band of pain round his head could be ignored, the dry heaves were merely a nuisance. Losing his grip on reality was deeply disturbing, like being partially anaesthetised, so that you were dimly aware of what was happening but unable to control it.

He pulled out his map and, frowning with concentration, tried to make sense of it. For the moment he couldn't think where he was. He backtracked mentally and realised that whole sections of the journey were a complete blank. He looked at his watch. Eleven. That should give him an idea of his distance.

He made a rough estimate, then looked around him, searching for landmarks. There was a hill, a distinct one, just ahead. On the map there were three, one after the other. He looked back and thought he saw one behind, but how far away he couldn't tell. His vision seemed to give him nothing but false readings. He took a stab at a position and hoped it was right. He would have to check on it as he went along. When, if, he remembered. Would he remember? He wasn't at all certain. His mind was playing elusive tricks, grabbing thoughts then whisking them away again so that he couldn't pin even the simplest thing down. He got wearily to his feet. His limbs felt very heavy, his brain so light it floated out of his head.

He scooped up some snow and rubbed it into his face. Wake up! Wake up! He started off again, dropping his skis into the tracks he had followed all the way from the hut at the head of Kaafjord Valley. He didn't consider stopping, not while the going was good. Stopping would be tantamount to giving up, and giving up was the one thing you never did up here.

As he got back into his rhythm a thought hovered elusively in his mind. He tried to pin it down, but it kept fluttering away. Then, peering forward into the distance, the thought finally swooped in and settled. The others. He hadn't caught sight of them yet. He must go faster or he'd never catch up. Yes, that was it: he must go faster. Lowering his head, screwing up his eyes with the effort, he pushed himself into an approximation of a run.

Rolf said, "quick! hurry!" then poled off rapidly, leaving Ragna to carry on as best she could. Hurry! She could have killed him. What did he think she'd been doing all this time? God, if anyone wanted to hurry it was her! She thought of nothing but getting to a telephone – she clung to the idea as if to a lifeline. And now he was saying hurry! Something had made him impatient. Something that had brought him down from the hillside in a rush, tight-lipped and pinched with tension. The weather maybe? She could see it was changing. That was all they needed – another storm. The thought was like torture.

Her skis back-slipped yet again. The backsliding happened on almost every stride, wasting half of each forward thrust. Wax might help, yet the only stuff she'd managed to find was useless. Rolf, of course, had no such problem. His skis were an experimental design which had built-in fish scales along the sole that gripped automatically. His skis? – she almost choked. They had been Jan's.

Then there was the problem of her right binding. If she thrust forward too hard she walked straight off her ski. And even if she was careful not to push too hard, her boot came free every few minutes anyway. She'd tried to fix it, but it was impossible without a screwdriver.

The fatigue and the sheer discomfort of the journey were nothing compared to these frustrations, which drove her into rages of despair. Rolf was poling further and further ahead. She thought: He's going to leave me behind. But he came to a stop and she saw that he was waiting. Why?

By this time she knew it wasn't likely to be out of the goodness of his heart. She struggled on, enduring the infuriating backsliding, until she finally panted up to him. Before he could say anything, she sat exhausted in the snow. He reached for her arm and pulled her roughly to her feet. "I need you to go up that hill and look for the hut while I take a good look at the map." A hut. The prospect of a short rest, some food, was irresistible. She pulled her hood down from her mouth. "There's a hut?" she asked stupidly. He gestured vaguely towards the map. She leant over and got a glimpse of a small black dot in a large neutral expanse interspersed by the occasional, blue-coloured summer stream and numbers in black, showing the hill heights. She saw that the hut was well over halfway to the road.

Rolf pulled the map away. His eyes glittered harshly over the rim of his hood. "Go as far as those rocks there." He pointed to a dark outcrop some way up the gently rising slope. "You should be able to see it from there." Another hurdle to be overcome. She nodded acquiescently. She certainly wasn't going to waste energy arguing. With Rolf it was a waste of time.

Leaning down briefly to scoop up some snow and press it into her mouth, she pulled her hood up over her chin and started off. The surface soon turned from powder to hard crust ridged with icy furrows. Despite the gentleness of the slope, her skis were soon backsliding hopelessly, and she had to sidestep.

She glanced back at Rolf. He was motionless, watching her. The outcrop was much further than it had looked. It took her a solid ten minutes to reach it. By the time she finally climbed on to it she was faint with weariness. She sat down and pressed more snow into her mouth. It didn't seem to do a lot for her thirst. She remembered Jan, or was it Hal telling her that it was bad to eat snow, but she couldn't remember why.

She looked for the hut and felt a quick disappointment. The weather was changing quite rapidly. A haze had rolled in, fading out the light and obscuring the landscape behind a soft veil of opaque mist. She could barely see the land just ahead, let alone a far-off hut.

She looked for Rolf to signal her lack of success. He wasn't in sight. Standing up, she looked right and left. No sign. She searched for a suggestion of shape or colour, she examined every faint shadow, each wind-blown boulder and exposed rock... He had vanished. Her mouth went dry, she tried to keep calm. He couldn't have gone, she would have seen him. Or would she?

Even as she combed the slope for a sight of him the mist seemed to close in around her. Creeping down from the hill above, rising up from the snow below, becoming thicker, whiter and more intensely cold, until the air itself seemed to freeze. Ice formed on her lashes and around her hood. She looked for him and felt complete disgust. It had been a trick. Of course, it had been a trick! He'd sent her up here to give himself time to get away. And she'd gone like a lamb. Rolf must be laughing himself silly.

On the brink of tears, cursing under her breath, she leant down and directed her rage at the troublesome binding, almost tearing it off in a vain and furious attempt to fix it. Her anger vented, she sank down into the snow, her shoulders sagged, she bowed her head.

After a time she pulled herself together. No point in feeling bitter or angry. Nothing had changed. She still had to get to a telephone. The only difference was that she was on her own. She only wished it didn't seem quite such a terrifying prospect. She fastened the binding as well as she could, stood up determinedly, and brushed the snow briskly off her ski trousers. She faced the encroaching mist and, suppressing a tiny twinge of panic, tried to decide on her best plan of action. There was only one, she realised: to carry on into Finland. It was the shortest route and she shouldn't have any trouble in finding her way and she'd have Rolf's tracks to guide her.

Filled with grim determination she thought: I'm going to get out of this if it bloody well kills me! And felt absurdly heartened by her own bravado. Fumbling with a mitten, she managed to get a bare hand into her pocket and find a bar of chocolate. Raw energy. She bit on it resolutely. She paused in mid-bite. In the mist below. Someone. But emerging from the north. From the way they had come.

Berg tensed and shifted position, ducking his head further down behind the boulder. Moving cautiously, he peered round it. There. A white figure, barely visible in the mist. But getting more distinct all the time. Coming fast. Following in their tracks. Who are you, you bastard? A border guard? A soldier? Maybe the abandoned Land Rover had been discovered. Maybe this was a rescue party that had been sent to save them! The thought was absurd, almost funny.

There was also the possibility that the man was completely innocent – a Lapp out hunting, or searching for his herd, or training for one of the spring endurance races that were held down south, hoping to win a prize and make his name... And yet, Lapps didn't wear white, they wore reindeer skins and distinctive colours.

"Who are you?" Berg pulled the rifle in to his shoulder, checked the magazine for the tenth time and rested his gloved forefinger on the trigger. Whatever the man's identity, he would shortly show himself for what he was. In about thirty yards he'd come to the point where the tracks stopped and turned sharply up the hill – Ragna's to continue upwards, Berg's to loop back down to the boulder, although the man in white wouldn't be able to see that. When he got to that point he would either pause momentarily and go straight on (an innocent hunter) or, he would reveal himself as a pursuer. The choice would be his. The choice whether to live or die.

Rolf, it could only be Rolf – was it Rolf? She stared uncomprehendingly: he must have backtracked, though God only knew how or why. And his clothing – Rolf had been wearing a pale anorak and dark trousers. This figure was all in white. It wasn't Rolf, it was someone else!

The figure was really shifting, his shoulders bent well forward, his body swaying from side to side as he threw his weight into his stride. At the same time his movements were strangely exaggerated, his head unusually low, as if he were tired. He was showing no signs of slowing up, and she suddenly realised he was going to carry on past.

She shouted, but her voice was feeble in the heavy air. It was possible he would pass without seeing her. Quickly, she set off down the slope on a convergent course, intending to shout again when she was a little closer. Then, abruptly, the figure stopped, and in such haste that he almost tripped over his skis. Recovering his balance, he bent to examine the snow, then, looking wildly about him, slipped his rifle off his shoulder and into his hands in one deft movement.

She guessed he had seen her tracks coming up the hill, for his head turned sharply towards her. The rifle, the defensive pose, who was he? She decided she didn't terribly care. Stopping, she raised a stick and waved it frantically from side to side. He saw her then, she could tell by the way he slowly lowered his rifle.

Skiing gently downhill she waved again, just to be sure. An arm rose and waved tentatively back, as if he couldn't quite believe what he was seeing. She called silently: "Oh I'm here all right! I'm here!" She ran into thick snow, it pulled at her feet, she flung out her arms to regain her balance.

When she looked up again a movement caught her eye. But it wasn't the waiting figure, he was still standing there. What then? It took her a moment to find it: a dark object on the periphery, something that hadn't been there before. She slowed momentarily and peered down through the frozen mist. Yes, to her right and just ahead of the man in white: a dark shape. It seemed to have appeared from nowhere. It took her a moment to work out what it was. A head, arms, the top of a man's body, strangely crouched.

Suddenly she understood and the realisation hit her like a punch in the stomach. She opened her mouth to scream, and this time it came out loud and strong, an agonised shout. She shouted again and again and thrust a stick in the direction of Rolf and begged the man in white to see. But the figure in white stood immobile, puzzled, uncomprehending. She thrust herself forward down the slope again. She screamed: "Look out! Look, out!" Then her binding came adrift and she pitched headlong into the snow.

Hal lowered his rifle, and peered up the hill. Everything was hazy. He rubbed his good eye, but the blur didn't go away. It was the mist perhaps. He knew it was misty because he could see the general whiteness and the way his breath condensed and froze in front of his nose.

Another shout came floating over the air. High-pitched, feminine. He listened in growing excitement. When the shout came again, he knew. Ragna. A lump came into his throat and he had to swallow several times. He lifted an arm and waved. If only he could see her more clearly. The shouts became shriller, almost like screams. There she was, a small grey shape suspended in a grey sea of fog. She was waving – or was she? He just couldn't tell. He rubbed his left eye again.

Yes, she was screaming and waving and... There was some meaning to all this, some significance to the noise and the strange movements. Scenting danger, he stiffened and looked about him.

Berg took a long and careful aim. This man was no innocent hunter. This man had been sent to find him. His purpose had been revealed the moment he'd reacted so violently and swung the rifle into his hands. A pro. Suspecting an ambush. How right he was! But not a very smart pro. He was standing still, mesmerised by Ragna's screams and waves. Just as Berg had hoped. Now he had all the time in the world. Holding the rifle steady in his hands, Berg shifted his elbows slightly on the boulder, sighted down the barrel, and gently increased the pressure on the trigger.

Ragna fought her way hastily to her feet. As she looked down the hill two things happened, one immediately after the other. The man in white sagged forward and a shot rang out. Ragna cried out. The man in white sank slowly on to one knee. But he wasn't finished. He raised his rifle and aimed it in Rolf's direction.

"Get him!" Ragna shrieked. "Get him!" A second shot rang out. Yes – from *his* rifle. But he hadn't got Rolf. Rolf was still there, behind the rock. A third *crack!* The man in white slowly toppled over. Ragna let out a cry of anguish. From behind the boulder Rolf stood up and began to plod towards the prone figure.

Shaking with anger, Ragna reached for her lost ski and jammed her foot into the loose binding. Digging her sticks deep into the snow she pushed off, and kept pushing and pushing, swinging all her weight into the thrust of the sticks, willing herself forward. But slow, so slow!

At last the slope steepened a little and her skis found their own momentum, and she suddenly didn't have to push any more. She'd forgotten to pull her hood up and the frozen air scorched painfully into her lungs and across her cheeks, like fine broken glass. As the ground dropped away she went faster still, wobbling dangerously on her loose ski, battling to keep it running straight. Rolf had got there. He was standing over the man in white.

She hit a patch of soft snow and lost speed. She began to pole again. Rolf was picking up the other man's rifle. For a moment Ragna thought he was going to point it at the man, maybe use it, but he hoisted it on to his back and knelt beside the immobile figure.

Almost there. Rolf became aware of her approach, for he glanced over his shoulder. The anger flowed over Ragna like a red hot sea. "You bastard! You absolute bastard!" she screamed as she came up to him. She swung a punch which glanced ineffectually off his shoulder. His kneeling body was masking the man in the snow. She pushed at him viciously. "Get out of the way! Get out!" Rolf yielded, getting slowly to his feet. "He's – extraordinary."

His voice was heavy with something like admiration. "Anyone else and..." He didn't finish but, straightening up, looked nervously about him as if he'd suddenly remembered where he was. Then, without a word, he pushed past her and was gone. Ragna looked down and saw the face of the man in the snow.

THE LIONS OF LUCERNE by Brad Thor

'On the snow-covered slopes of Utah the President of the United States has been kidnapped and his Secret Service detail massacred... only one agent has survived'. The closing lines of the book, 'Well Mr. President'. There is one thing... tells us that the President survived!

Brad Thor is a number 1 New York Times best-selling author. He has won numerous awards. Brad Thor has *served as a member of the US Department of Homeland Security's Analytic Red Cell Unit and has lectured to law enforcement organizations on over-the-horizon/future threats.*

"You guys having an awesome day or what?" asked the young liftie as Scot Harvath and Amanda Rutledge shuffled up to get on the next chairlift. He was referring to the snow that had been falling all day. "Light's kinda flat," replied Amanda. Scot had to laugh. Amanda was relatively new to skiing, but she was picking up the lingo and the idiosyncrasies of a spoiled skier pretty quickly.

"What's so funny?" she said as the lift gently hit them in the back of the knees and they sat down, beginning the ride up to Deer Valley's Squaw Peak. "You, that's what's so funny."

"Me? What do you mean?"

"Don't get me wrong, Mandie; your skiing's come a long way, but you've skied, what, maybe five or six times in your life?"

"Yeah, so?"

"And it's always been that East Coast garbage. All ice, right?"

"And?"

"Well, it's just funny to hear you complaining about the light when you are skiing on snow people would kill for."

"I guess it is kind of funny, but you've got to admit that it's tough to see anything in this weather."

On that point, Amanda Rutledge was one hundred percent correct. The snow had been falling steadily for a week. Hoping to indulge his passion for astronomy, Scot had brought his telescope on this trip. The lights back home in D.C. made it impossible to see anything in the night sky. Unfortunately, the weather in Park City had so far refused to cooperate. Today, in particular, it was really coming down. Visibility was extremely low, and the conditions worried Scot enough that he suggested the president and his daughter take the day off and wait to see what tomorrow brought. Regardless of what the head of his advance team had to say, though, the president made it clear that he and Amanda had come to ski and that's exactly what they were going to do. Unfortunately for his ski plans, the coalition the president had cobbled together to get his fossil-fuel reduction bill – the bill that signaled a financially devastating blow for the major oil companies, but would breathe long overdue life into America's alternative energy sectors – through Congress was starting to crack. The president's constant hand-holding of key 'swing' voters was absolutely necessary if he was to see his legislation through. The predicted turnover in the upcoming congressional election spelled doom for the president's pet project. The simple fact was that this bill could pass only in this session. Even though he had already shortened the length of his vacation before leaving D.C., the president was thinking about returning even earlier now. Scot understood the man's desire to get in as much skiing and quality time with his daughter as possible before returning to the capital.

"Are you dating anyone now?" asked Amanda.

The sudden change of subject caught Scot off guard and pulled his mind back from the president's problems and the weather.

"Am I dating anyone? Who wants to know?" he teased.

Blushing, Amanda turned away from his gaze, but kept speaking. "I do. I mean, you never seem to talk about anybody."

Scot started to smile again but didn't let her see. He thought she must have been building up her courage all day to ask him. Amanda had had a crush on Scot ever since he'd become part of daily life at the White House, and everybody knew it. More than once, the president had had to reprimand his daughter and remind her not to distract Scot while he was on duty. Amanda, or Mandie, as Scot called her, was a good kid. Despite having lost her mother to breast cancer only a couple of years ago, she seemed as normal as any other child her age. She was smart, athletic, and would someday grow into a beautiful woman. Scot decided to change the subject.

"That was one heck of a birthday party last night," he offered.

"It was pretty cool. Thanks again for the CDs. You didn't have to get me anything."

"Hey, it was your birthday. The big sixteen. I wanted to get you a car, but your dad's national security advisor thought that behind the wheel of your own machine, you might be too dangerous for the country. So, the Ferrari will just have to sit in my garage until we can change his mind."

Amanda laughed. "Not only were the CDs sweet, but I really appreciate the lessons today."

Before joining the SEALs and subsequently being recruited into the Secret Service, Scot had been quite an accomplished skier and had won a spot on the U.S. freestyle team. Against the wishes of his father, Scot had chosen to postpone college to pursue skiing. He had spent several years on the team, which trained right there in Park City, Utah. He did extremely well on the World Cup circuit and had been favored to medal in the upcoming Olympics. When Scot's father, an instructor at the Navy SEAL training facility in their hometown of Coronado, California, died in a training accident, Scot had been devastated. Try as he might, after losing his father, he hadn't been able to get his head back into competitive skiing. Instead, he chose to follow in his father's footsteps. After graduating college cum laude, he joined the SEALs and was tasked to Team Two, known as the cold weather specialists, or Polar SEALs.

Scot knew that it was not only his familiarity with Park City, but also his background and experience that were key factors in his being selected to lead this presidential advance team. He also knew that was why President Rutledge had agreed to indulge his daughter's request for Scot to ski on her protective detail today and give her pointers.

Amanda had been overjoyed, and despite the flat light she felt the day had been perfect. "You're an excellent student, so the lessons are my pleasure." Scot's radio crackled, interrupting their conversation. He held up his hand to let her know he was listening to his earpiece. Amanda remained quiet. "Norseman, this is Sound. Over," came the scratchy voice via Scot's Motorola. Norseman was the call sign Scot had picked up in the SEALs, which had remained with him ever since. At five feet ten and a muscular one hundred sixty pounds, with brown hair and ice blue eyes, the handsome Scot Harvath looked more German than Scandinavian. In fact, the call sign didn't derive from his looks, but rather from a string of

Scandinavian flight attendants he had dated while in the SEALs. The voice on the other end of Scot's Motorola identified as Sound, was the head of the president's protective detail, Sam Harper. Harper had taken Scot under his wing when he joined the team at the White House. The head White House Secret Service agent, whom Harper and Scot reported to, was William Shaw – call sign Fury. When you put Harper together with Shaw, you got 'The Sound and The Fury', and anyone who had ever screwed up on their watch knew exactly how appropriate that title was. Communications had been fine over the past week, but for some reason the radios had been cutting in and out today. Maybe it was the weather.

"This is Norseman, go ahead Sound. Over," said Scot via his throat mike. "Norseman, Hat Trick wants to know how Goldilocks is doing. Over." "Mandie," said Scot, turning to Amanda, "your dad wants to know how you're holding up." When then Vice President Rutledge came into office after having three times been named one of D.C.'s sexiest politicians, the hockey-inspired nickname Hat Trick, meaning three goals, became an inside joke among the people who knew him. Though Jack Rutledge found the media's focus on his looks somewhat embarrassing, he didn't object to the nick name, and so, via the Department of Defence, which issues the presidential and vice-presidential codenames, it stuck. After the president's wife passed away, word quietly spread among White House staffers that the president would not seek to return to Pennsylvania Avenue for a fourth time. The code name had turned out to be aptly prophetic.

Amanda's code name, on the other hand, was an obvious call. With her long, curly blond hair, she had been called Goldilocks for as long as anyone in the White House could remember. "I'm a little hungry, but other than that pretty good," she said. "Sound, Goldilocks is shipshape, though she'd like to get into the galley sometime in the near future. Over." "Roger that, Norseman. The lifts close to the public at sixteen-thirty; that's twenty minutes from now. Hat Trick wants to know if Goldilocks wants to keep going, or if we should wrap it up. Over." Scot turned to Amanda, "Your dad wants to know if you want to have them keep the lift open for us, or if you want to make this the last run and we'll ski back to the house?"

"My toes are getting kind of cold. I think I've had enough skiing for today. Let's make this the last run." "Sound, Goldilocks wants to little piggy. Over." "Little piggy" referred to the children's nursery rhyme where the fifth little piggy went wee, wee, wee, all the way home.

"Roger that, Norseman. Hat Trick concurs. Let's meet at the last lap. Over." "Last lap, roger that, Sound. Norseman out."

When Scot, Amanda, and their security detail reached the meeting point known as the last lap, the President, Sam Harper, and the rest of the team were already waiting for them. "Hi, sweetheart," said the president as his daughter skied up, and he gave her a hug. "How's your skiing coming along? Notice any difference now that you're sixteen?"

"Sixteen doesn't make any difference, Dad. But I have gotten better."

"Is that so?" replied the president, glancing at Scot.

"Yes, sir, Mr. President. Amanda has come a long way this afternoon. I think she could take us all down Death Chute if she wanted to," said Scot.

"Death Chute?" said Amanda. "You've gotta be nuts. I wouldn't even snowplow down that thing!" Several of the Secret Service agents laughed nervously. Death Chute was one of the most difficult of the off-piste chutes that fed back to the area where the presidential party was staying. The home the president was using was located in the ultra-exclusive ski-in, ski-out Deer Valley community known as Snow Haven. The Secret Service agents' nervousness was well founded. Death Chute required a tremendous amount of skill to navigate and would have been a nerve-racking challenge for even the best of them. Not only were there lots of rocks and steep vertical drops, but as the piste began to flatten out before dropping off again, there was a wide plateau filled with trees. Quite an accomplished skier, the president loved tackling a new chute each day on his way back to the house. He skied easy runs with his daughter in the mornings, and then they split up after lunch so he could ski the more difficult trails. The super challenging, end-of-the-day chutes he had to choose from were technically known as backcountry and not part of Deer Valley's marked and maintained trail system. Therefore, the chutes had not required a lot of work for the Secret Service to secure. All of the routes feeding into them were simply made off-limits to any other skiers. As the president's confidence grew, so did his desire to tackle harder chutes. The 'rush' he got was a rewarding way to end the day. All of the chutes he had tried up to this point were grouped in one area. Death Chute stood alone, a bit further to the east, and the Secret Service knew it was only a matter of time before the president decided he wanted to give it a whirl. The only person who could possibly have given him a run for his money on Death Chute was Scot, and he was skiing with Amanda's detail today. Amanda would take the long, easy way down, as she had all week. That was okay. The last thing the president wanted was for his daughter to get hurt. "So, honey," began the president, "what do you think? You take the high road and I'll take the low road, and I'll be sippin' hot chocolate afore ye?"

"I might beat you yet!" yelled Amanda as she gave herself a push and started shooting down the longer, yet safer of the two routes. Scot and the rest of his team smiled at the president's group and took off, quickly catching up with Amanda. She seemed hell-bent on beating her father back to the house, an impossibility unless she dropped over the rim of the bowl and shot straight down. Even with her growing skill and confidence, Scot knew she wasn't ready to tackle something that serious yet. Amanda used her poles to push herself forward and picked up more speed. One of the agents skiing to the right of Scot shot him a look suggesting, *Somebody's cruisin' for a bruisin'* – and before Scot could return the look, Amanda caught an edge and tumbled down hard. First she lost a pole and then a ski, then the other pole and the other ski.

When she finally came to a stop, her gear was scattered across thirty feet of snow uphill from where she lay. Scot caught up to her as she stopped sliding. "Impressive! If you're gonna go, go big. That's what I always say." Amanda was on the verge of tears, her pride hurting more than anything else. "That's not funny," she said, sniffling. "I'm sorry. You're right; it's not funny. Are you okay?" "What do you care?" she said, wiping the snow from her face. Scot started to laugh. "It's not funny, Scot. Cut it out!" "I know, I know. I'm sorry, Mandie. You were really flying, though. You looked good. Right up until the point you biffed. You know, we should have tagged your gear before you decided to have a yard sale."

"Stop it!" Amanda managed before breaking into a fit of laughter. "Oh, so that was a mistake? There wasn't supposed to be a yard sale today. Whoa, then I better gather up the merchandise before we upset any of the neighbours."

He told Amanda to sit still and joined Secret Service agent Maxwell, who was uphill gathering her equipment. When Scot reached Maxwell, he saw that he was staring into the distance at the presidential party making their way down Death Chute.

"Glad I'm not on that detail," said Maxwell as he handed Scot one of Amanda's skis. Scot dusted the snow out of the binding, checking for damage as he waited for the next ski. "Maxwell, the reason you're not on that detail is that when it comes to skiing, you suck."

"Fuck you, Harvath," said Maxwell as he shoved the other ski at him, confident he was out of Amanda's earshot.

"No, seriously. I heard that Warren Miller was looking to shoot a little footage of you for his next ski film. It's going to be a spin-off of that movie 'Beastmaster', only worse. He's going to call it 'Biff master'. Nothing but your wipe outs…"

"Fuck you."

"I'm not kidding. Nothing but three hours of wall-to-wall Maxwell face down in the snow."

"Fuck you."

"There'll be some of those trademark Maxwell-fully-geared somersaults, some awesome face plants... I think you could be up for an Oscar, my friend."

"Harvath, which part of fuck you do you not understand? I mean, I'm good to go on explaining either of the two words to you." Scot laughed as Maxwell lost his balance reaching over to pick up one of Amanda's ski poles. Looking off toward Death Chute, Scot, too, could see the president and his detail still making their way down.

The detail was doing a good job of keeping up with him. Everybody was right on the money. As he turned to take Amanda's gear back to her, he glanced once more at Death Chute, just in time to see the president's group near the trees and two Secret Service agents wipe out. Maxwell had already recovered and gone down to Amanda. He was handing over her poles when Scot skied up. "Well, Maxwell, it looks like the heat will be off your skiing at dinner tonight."

"What do you mean?" he asked.

"I think I just saw Ahern and Houchins bite it going into that part of the chute with the trees. But, with all the snow falling, it's hard to tell."

"At least I'm not the only one who bought it this afternoon," said Amanda as she got to her feet and dusted the remaining snow off her jacket.

"I told you," said Scot, "the end of the day is when most wipe-outs happen. You're more tired than you think, and some people push it a little too hard."

Agent Maxwell took the skis from Scot and let Amanda lean on his shoulder for balance as she put them on. "I hope nobody hit a tree," he said. "That's a good point," responded Scot as he engaged his throat mike. "Sound, this is Norseman. Do we need to send the Saint Bernards and schnapps down for Ahern and Houchins? Over."

Scot's radio hissed and crackled. There was no response. He tried again. "If either of them blew their knees, I've got a buddy here who's a great surgeon. Tell Ahern and Houchins I'll split the commission with them if they use my guy. Over."

He waited longer this time, but there was still nothing but static. "Sound, this is Norseman; we saw two agents go down. Can you give us a sit rep. Over?" Sit rep was short for "situation report." The president had probably pushed his guys just a little too far and just a little too fast for the end of the day. This really was the most common time for wipe-outs.

Ahem and Houchins were probably all right, but as head of the advance team, Scot felt responsible for every agent and wanted to know for sure.

"Sound, this is Norseman. Let's have that sit rep. Over."

Nothing.

Scot decided to change frequencies to the direct channel with the Secret Service command post. The blowing snow was beginning to pick up again.

"Birdhouse, this is Norseman, come in. Over."

"Scot, I'm getting cold," said Amanda as she snapped into her bindings.

"Quiet a sec, Mandie." Scot pressed the earpiece further into his ear, but all he got was crackling static.

"Birdhouse, repeat, this is Norseman, come in. Over." Scot waited.

"Birdhouse, repeat, this is Norseman. Can you read me? Over."

More static.

Agent Maxwell looked at Scot, who shook his head to indicate he hadn't made any contact.

"What do you think?" said Maxwell.

"I don't know, and I don't want to cry wolf to the rest of Goldilocks's detail just yet. I'll try my Deer Valley radio. If that doesn't work, then we harden up." Harden up was the Secret Service term for immediately closing ranks and body-shielding their assignment from any potential threat.

Scot tried three times to raise Deer Valley's ski patrol and then tried Deer Valley's operations station. There was no response. All of the radios were completely down. Scot let out a loud whistle, catching the attention of the rest of the detail agents, and gave the harden up command by waving his gloved index finger in a high circle the wagons motion above his head. In a matter of seconds, Amanda's protective detail had her completely surrounded. There was an incredible array of weaponry drawn, from Heckler & Koch MP5s to SIG-Sauer semiautomatics, and even a modified Benelli M1 tactical shotgun. The men's eyes never stopped surveying the area as Scot explained that he had seen two of the president's detail agents go down and all radio communication was dark. There probably was a simple explanation. Ahem and Houchins could just have wiped out, and the radios had been acting up all day, with the weather the most likely culprit, but that was not how the Secret Service was trained to think. Operating procedure dictated that they take the fastest and safest route back to the command center immediately. With the loss of radio contact, Birdhouse would already have scrambled intercept teams to recover both details as quickly as possible. But they were still a long way off. It was time to move.

Amanda saw her chance to break in and asked, "Scot, what's going on?"

"Probably nothing, Mandie, but we need to get you back down to the house as quickly as possible," said Scot. "You've done an awesome job today. I'm really proud of you. Your skiing is red hot. Now, the normal way we go home would take us a bit too long. If we ski through the bowl, I can have you sipping hot chocolate by the fire with your dad in fifteen minutes. What do you say?"

"This is about him, isn't it? Has something happened? Is he okay?"

"I'm sure he is, and the quicker we get back, the quicker you'll see for yourself. Do you think you can do the bowl with me? I'll be right next to you."

"I don't know. I think I can handle it."

"Good girl."

Scot smiled reassuringly at Amanda and gave the order to move out. The detail dropped over the icy lip into the steep bowl. The wind grew more fierce and sent sharp blasts of snow into their faces. Amanda was slow, but at least she was moving forward. It was terrifying for her, but to her credit, she was doing everything Scot had taught her – weight on the downhill ski in the turns, leaning forward into her boots and keeping her hands out in front as if she were holding on to a tray.

Even though Amanda's cautious skiing slowed them down, it looked as if they were going to make it without incident. Then the detail heard what sounded like the crack of a rifle, followed by the low rumble of a thunderhead. Scot had been around mountains too long not to recognize that sound… Avalanche!

Despite his formfitting winter assault fatigues lined with a revolutionary new weatherproof thermal composite, Hassan Useff lay in his coffin of snow and shivered. He had been one of the toughest kids growing up in his balmy, south Lebanon village and was now one of the Middle East's finest snipers, but the cold and being buried alive beneath two feet of snow were beginning to get to him. When the hideous repetition of his own raspy breathing was finally interrupted by two squelch clicks over his earpiece, the fear and cold immediately disappeared, replaced by a rush of adrenaline surging through his stiff body.

Useff tensed and released his muscles several times to relieve some of the stiffness in his joints. Cradling the high-tech glare gun in his gloved hands, he heard an almost imperceptible whine as he powered the weapon up. Two more clicks over the earpiece and he readied himself to spring from his snowy grave. Buried completely from view in several more snowy crypts nearby, Gerhard Miner and five more of his 'Lions' were about to undertake the most daring mission of their lives.

"Son of a bitch," cursed Sam Harper to himself as his ski clipped the edge of another rock. He loved skiing, but hated having to follow the president down Death Chute. He had fallen a little bit behind and was glad that several of the younger guys on the detail were able to keep up with the commander in chief. The biggest consolation of all was that Ahern and Houchins were behind him. At least he wouldn't be the last one to ski up when the party rested in the flat area among the trees before tackling the final vertical drop.

When Harper reached the beginning of the trees, everything began to happen in what, had he survived, he would have described as a split-second flash. Three final squelch clicks came over Hassan Useff's earpiece, signalling that the last members of the president's Secret Service detail were entering the heavily treed area. Springing from his icy hideaway, Useff began pulsing his glare gun as his fellow team member, Klaus Dryer, did the same twenty metres away.

The results were exactly as planned. Even with their UV-protective ski goggles, the entire protective detail, as well as the president, was dazzled. The glare guns were Russian copies of the nonlethal weapon developed by the American Air Force's Phillips Laboratory. First brought into action in Somalia in 1995, the purpose of the high-tech laser weapon was to temporarily blind and disorient an enemy. Temporarily was all Miner's team needed. Useff and Dryer's cross-pulsing in the narrow alley formed by the trees created a blinding laser funnel that the president's team couldn't escape. This included the members of the Secret Service counter-sniper unit, known as 'JAR', or 'Just Another Rifle', who were posted strategically throughout the trees along this leg of the president's run.

Completely blinded and disoriented, several agents lost their balance and wiped out before they even had a chance to come to a complete stop. Those agents who had already been in the process of slowing down and could stop, instinctively drew their weapons, but they had one major problem. They couldn't see a thing. Not knowing where their fellow agents were or, more important, where the president was, every single agent, weapon drawn or not, had been rendered not only totally useless but helpless as well.

Useff gave the 'go command' over his lip mike as he shouldered the glare gun and switched off the safety of his silenced German-manufactured Heckler & Koch MP5 submachine gun. The pleasure of being able to freely kill so many agents of the Great Satan was almost unbearable. He had already shot two Secret Service agents before the rest of the team had fully sprung from their hiding places.

As the Lions' silenced machine gun rounds drummed into the bodies of the defenceless Secret Service agents, Miner made his way toward where the president had fallen. "Harp, Harp," mumbled the president from where he lay in the snow, still blind and disoriented but alert enough to call out for the head of his protective detail as he tried to raise himself into a seated position.

Miner dropped to his knees next to him and removed the president's gloves and jacket. As he helped him sit up, he placed a copy of the Salt Lake Tribune on his chest, pulling the president's hands in so he could feel it. Instinctively, the president grabbed hold of it. Miner shot several quick Polaroids and slipped the slowly developing pictures into his pocket.

Then he took the paper away and, with a pair of trauma scissors, began to cut through the left sleeves of the president's sweater and turtleneck.

"Toboggan! Where is that toboggan?" Miner yelled.

"Harper? What's happening?" repeated the president.

"There's been an accident, Mr. President," responded Miner in perfectly American accented English.

"You need to lie back now and remain still, while we start an IV."

"Who are you? Where's Harper? What's happened to my eyes? I can't see."

"Please, Mr. President. You need to be completely quiet and completely still. My team is attending to the others. There you go. Let's just lie back. Good." Miner knew the effects of the glare gun would be wearing off soon. From his pack, he withdrew an insulated medical pouch, unzipped it, pulled out a bag of saline solution, and began an IV on the president, who continued to call for members of his protective detail and complain about his eyes.

Once the IV was in place, Miner filled a syringe with a strong sedative called Versed and piggybacked it into the IV line. The effect was almost instantaneous. The president's eyes rolled back, closed, and his body went limp.

As one of Miner's men rushed past, towing an all-white ski-patrol-style transport toboggan, Dryer made his way over to Hassan Useff. Without even turning, Useff began speaking, knowing Dryer was behind him. "This is Sam Harper, head of the president's protective detail, is it not?"

Though Harper was badly injured from his fall and couldn't see who was standing above him speaking, he knew the Middle Eastern accent didn't belong to anyone on his team. "Yeah, I'm Sam Harper, and whoever you are, you are in a lot of trouble. Give yourself up."

"Typical American arrogance. Even in the face of death," said Useff.

"Fuck you," snarled Harper as he attempted to draw his weapon.

"Once again, typical. Is nothing original in this country?" asked Useff as he squeezed off a three round burst into the career Secret Service agent and father of two's head.

Ever since Dryer had recruited Useff for this assignment, he had marveled at the man's hatred for the United States. That hate, coupled with the Lebanese man's intense religious fervor, made him perfect for this job. Hassan Useff was the only non-Swiss on the team.

As he began walking away, Useff said, "Protecting the president, he should have been the best. A pity he won't be remembered that way. The pathetic coward never even fired a shot."

When Useff had his back completely turned, Dryer withdrew an empty Evian bottle from the pack he was carrying and picked up Harper's SIG-Sauer P229. "I think the Americans might beg to differ," were the last words Hassan Useff heard before the .357 bullet, effectively muffled by being shot through the plastic bottle, ripped through the back of his skull, killing him instantly. Dryer placed the SIG-Sauer in Harper's dead hand. He then withdrew a model 68 Skorpion machine pistol with a silencer and fired indiscriminately into the bodies of the dead Secret Service agents lying around him. He blew through two more twenty-round magazines before placing the Skorpion on the ground next to Useff and shouldering the dead Muslim's glare gun and H&K.

The waters were now sufficiently chummed.

THE LONELY SKIER by Hammond Innes

Hammond Innes (1913–1998) is famous for his many thrilling stories, he wrote over thirty novels, of spies, counterfeiters, black markets and shipwrecks, which earned him literary fame and an international following. 'The Lonely Skier' was inspired by a ski course he attended in the Dolomites after the war. It is a superbly constructed and atmospheric thriller. He was a passionate sailor and wrote, in 1956, 'The Wreck of the Mary Deare', which was later turned into a film.

What are you doing today, Blair?' he asked. 'Yesterday you introduced me to a very good entertainment at that auction. Today I would like to return your kindness. I would like to take you ski-ing. It is early in the season and there is a lot of snow still to fall. We should not waste a fine day like this. Besides, the forecast is for snow later. What about coming up Monte Cristallo with me?'

'I'd like to,' I said. 'But I feel I ought to do some work.'

'Nonsense,' he said. 'You can work all this evening. Besides, you ought to have a look at one of the real mountains up here. I can show you a glacier and some very fine avalanche slopes. Your fat friend is only taking pictures of the ordinary' ski runs. You ought to take a look at the real mountains. There's good film stuff up there.'

'Really,' I said, 'I must work.'

He shrugged his shoulders. 'My God, you take life seriously. What does a day more or less matter? You should have been born in Ireland. Life would have been more fun for you.' He swung back to the piano and began thumping out one of Elgar's more solid pieces, looking at me over his shoulder with a twinkle in his eyes. He quickly changed into a gay Irish air. 'If you change your mind,' he said, 'I'll be leaving about ten.'

The others were drifting in now, attracted by the music and the smell of bacon and eggs frying. Conscious of a growing audience, Mayne switched to Verdi and began to play seriously again. Only Joe was not interested. He looked tired and liverish.

'Does he have to make a damned row so early in the morning?' he grumbled in my ear. 'Like talking at breakfast – can't stand it.' His face looked grey in the hard sunlight and the pouches under his eyes were very marked.

The mail came up, after breakfast, on the first sleigh. With it was a cable from Engles. It read: *Why Mayne Keramikos unmentioned previously. Full information urgent. Engles.*

A few minutes later Mayne came over to me. He had his ski boots on and was carrying a small haversack. 'What about changing your mind, Blair?' he said. We needn't make it a long day. Suppose we're back by three, would that be all right for you? It's not much fun going for a ski run by one's self.'

I hesitated. I did want to get some writing done. On theother hand, I couldn't bear the thought of being cooped up in the hut all day. And Engles wanted information about Mayne.

It would be a good opportunity to find out about the man. 'All right,' I said. 'I'll be ready in about ten minutes.'

'Good!' he said. 'I'll have Aldo get your skis ready. No need to worry about food. We'll get it at the hotel at Carbonin.' His eagerness was infectious. Any one less like a man who had once led a gang of deserters I could not imagine. And suddenly I did not believe a word Keramikos had said. It was too fantastic.

The Greek had just been trying to divert my attentions from himself.

As I came down in my ski suit and boots, Joe raised his eyebrows. He did not say anything but bent over the camera he was loading.

'Care to lend me that small camera of yours, Joe?' I asked.

He looked up. 'No,' he said. 'I wouldn't trust that camera to anyone. Why? Think you can get some shots that I can't? Where are you off to?'

'Monte Cristallo,' I told him. 'Mayne says he can show me a glacier and some fine avalanche slopes. I thought they might produce some good shots. It would be grander stuff than you can get down here.'

Joe laughed. 'Shows how little you know about camera work,' he said. 'It's all a matter of angles and light. I haven't been more than a thousand yards from this hut, but I've got everything. I don't need to go trapesing all over the Dolomites to get my background.'

'I wish I had your sublime self-confidence,' I said.

I suppose I had spoken with a shade of bitterness, for he looked up and patted my arm. 'It'll come,' he said. 'It'll come. A couple of successes and you'll never listen to advice again – until it's too late. I'm at the top now. Nobody can teach me anything about cameras. But it won't last. In a few years' time younger men will come along with new ideas which I shan't be able to see, and that'll be that. It's the way it goes in this racket. Engles will tell you the same.'

I left him then and went out on to the belvedere. Mayne was waiting for me there. Just a couple of successes! It was so easy to talk about it. And I hadn't even begun a script. The wood of my skis was actually warm to the touch as they stood propped against the balustrade in the sun. But though the sun was warm, it made little or no impression on the snow, which remained hard and frozen.

We started up across virgin snow until we hit the track to the Passo del Cristallo. It was not really a track – just a few ski marks lightly dusted over with a powder of snow that had drifted across them during the night. The run looked as though it was little used. 'You know the way, I suppose?' I asked Mayne.

He stopped and turned his head. 'Yes. I haven't done it this year. But I've done it often before. You don't need to worry about having no guide. It's quite straightforward until we get up near the top of the pass. There's a nasty bit of climbing to do to get to the top of it. We'll be just on ten thousand feet up there. We may have to do the last bit without skis. Then there's the glacier. That's about a kilometre. There should be plenty of snow on it. After that it's quite a simple run down to Carbonin.' He turned and plodded on ahead of me again, thrusting steadily with his sticks.

I think if I had had the sense to look at the map before we started out, I should never have gone on that particular run. It is not a beginner's run. And it looks a bit frightening even on the map. There's at least a kilometre on the way up to the glacier marked with interrupted lines, denoting 'difficult itinerary.' Then there is the glacier itself. And both on the way up from Col da Varda and on the way down to

Carbonin, the red hachures of avalanche slopes are shown falling down towards the track on every side.

As we climbed steadily upwards, zig-zagging in places because of the steepness of the entrance to the pass, I had a glimpse of what was to come. The outer bastions of Monte Cristallo towered above us to the left, a solid wall of jagged edges. To our right, a great field of snow swept precipitously down towards us, like a colossal sheet pinned to the blue sky by a single jagged peak. It was across the lower slopes of this that we were steadily climbing.

There was no track at all now. The wind whistling up the pass had completely obliterated the marks of the previous day's ski-ers. We were alone in a white world and ahead of us the pass rose in rolling downs of snow to the sharp rock teeth that marked the top of the pass. The sunlight had a brittle quality and the bare rock outcrops above us had no warmth in their colouring. They looked cold and black.

I could, I suppose, have turned back then. But Mayne had a confident air. He was never at a loss for direction. And I was feeling quite at ease now on my skis. The stiffness had worn off and, though the going was hard and I was out of training, I felt quite capable of making it. It was only the solitude and the lurking belief that we should have had a guide on a run of this sort that worried me.

Once I did say, 'Do you think we ought to go over the top on to the glacier without a guide?'

Mayne was making a standing turn at the time. He looked down at me, clearly amused. 'It's not half as bad as landing on a shell-torn beach,' he grinned. Then more seriously, 'We'll turn back if you like. But we're nearly up to the worst bit. See how you make out on that. I'd like to get to the top at any rate and look down to the glacier. But I don't want to do it alone.'

'Of course not,' I said. 'I'm quite all right. But I just feel we ought to have had a guide.'

'Don't worry,' he said quite gaily. 'It's almost impossible to lose your way on this run. Except for a spell at the top, you're in the pass the whole time.'

Soon after this it began to get very steep. The pass towered ahead of us, itself like the face of an avalanche slope. And on each side of us, we were hemmed in by real avalanche slopes that swept high above the pass to the dark crests. It was no longer possible to zig-zag up the slope. It was too steep. We began side-stepping. The snow was hard like ice and at each step it was necessary to stamp the ski edge into the frozen snow to get a grip. Even so, it was only just the inside edge of the ski that bit into the snow. It was hard, tiring work. But there was nothing dangerous about it so long as the skis were kept firm and exactly parallel to the contour of the slope.

For what seemed ages, I saw nothing of the scenery. Indeed, I did not even look up to see where we were going. I just blindly followed the marks of Mayne's ski edges. My eyes were fixed entirely on my rhythmically stamping feet, my mind concentrated on maintaining my skis at the correct angle. The higher we climbed the more dangerous it became if the skis faced fractionally down the slope and began to slide. So we progressed in complete silence, save for the stamp of our skis and the crunch as they bit into the icy snow.

'Snow's drifted up here,' came Mayne's voice from above.

'Have to take our skis off soon.'

A few feet higher up I saw the first sign of rock. It was a small outcrop, smooth and ice-rounded. Then I was up with Mayne. The slope was less now. I stood up and looked about me, blinking my eyes in the sunlight. We were standing on the rim of a great white basin. The snow simply fell away from under our feet. The slope up which we had climbed fanned out and mingled with the avalanche slopes that came in from either side. I could scarcely believe that those were our ski marks climbing up out of the basin – the tracks showed clearly like a little railway line mapped out on white paper.

I looked ahead of us. There was nothing but smoothed rock and jagged tooth-like peaks. 'That's Popena,' Mayne said, pointing to a single peak rising sharply almost straight ahead of us. 'The track runs just under that to the left.' The sun was cold – the air strangely visible, like a white vapour. It was a cold, ratified air and I could feel my heart pumping against my ribs.

A little farther on, we removed our skis. It was just drift snow here and, with our skis over our shoulders, we made steady progress, choosing the rock outcrops and avoiding the drifts.

At last we stood at the top of the pass. The main peaks were still above us. But they only topped our present position by a few hundred feet. We were looking out upon a world of jumbled rocks – black teeth in white gums of snow. It was cold and silent. Nothing lived here. Nothing had ever lived here. We might have been at one of the Poles or in some forgotten land of the Ice Age. This was the territory of Olympian Gods. The dark peaks jostled one another, battling to be the first to pierce the heavens, and all about them their snow skirts dropped away to the world below, that nice comfortable world where human beings lived. 'Wesson should bring his camera up here,' I said, half to myself.

Mayne laughed. 'It'd kill him. He'd have heart failure before he got anywhere near the top.'

It was cold as soon as we stood still. The wind was quite strong and cut through our windbreakers. It drove the snow across the rocks on which we stood like dust. It was frozen, powdery snow.

I could sift it through my gloved hands like flour. Here and there along the ridges a great curtain of it would be lifted up by the wind and would drift across the face of the rock like driven spume. There was no sign of the blue sky that had looked so bright and gay from Col da Varda. The air was white with light.

Mayne pointed to the great bulk of Monte Cristallo. The sky had darkened there and the top of the mountain was gradually being obscured as though by a veil. The sun was only visible as an iridescent light. 'Going to snow soon,' he said. 'Better be moving. I'd like to get across the glacier before it conies on thick. Later it doesn't matter. We'll be in the pass. If it looks bad after lunch, we'd better come back by Lake Misurina.'

He was so confident, and I was so reluctant to face the steep descent into that basin that I raised no objection to going forward.

Soon we reached the glacier and put on our skis. It was very little different to the rock slopes that encompassed it, for it was covered with a blanket of snow. Only here and there was there any sign of the ice that formed the foundation for the snow.

The going was much easier now. The slope was quite gentle and our skis slid easily across the snow with only an occasional thrust of our sticks. The brightness slowly dimmed, and the sky became heavy and leaden. I did not like the look of it. You feel so small and unimportant up there in the mountains. And it's not a pleasant feeling. You feel that one rumble of thunder and the elements can sweep you out of existence. One by one the peaks that surrounded the glacier in a serrated edge were blotted out.

We were barely halfway across the glacier when it began to snow. At first it was just a few flakes drifting across our path in the wind. But it grew rapidly thicker. It came in gusts, so that one moment it was barely possible to see the edges of the glacier and the next it was almost clear, so that it was possible to see the encircling crests that swept upwards to bury their peaks in the grey sky.

Mayne had increased the pace. I became very conscious of the pounding of my heart. Whether it was the continued exercise at that altitude or nervousness I do not know. Probably both.

In all that world of grey and white, the only friendly thing was Mayne's back and the slender track of his skis that seemed to link us like rope across the snow.

At last we were across the glacier. The snow was falling steadily now, a slanting, driven fall that stung the face and clung to the eyes. The slope became steeper. We began to travel fast, zig-zagging down through tumbled slopes of soft, fresh snow. It became steeper still and the pace even faster.

I kept in the actual track of Mayne's skis. Sometimes I lost sight of him in the snow. But always there were the ski tracks to follow. The only sounds were the steady hiss of driven snow and the friendly biting sound of my skis. I followed blindly. I had no idea where we were going. But we were going downhill and that was all I cared. How Mayne managed to keep a sense of direction in that murk I do not know.

I suddenly found him standing still, waiting for me. His face was hardly recognisable, it was so covered in snow. He looked like a snow man. 'It's coming on thick,' he said as I came up with him. 'Have to increase the pace. Is that all right with you?'

'That's all right,' I said. Anything so long as we got down as quickly as possible. The smoke of our breath was whipped away by the wind.

'Stick to my tracks,' he said. 'Don't diverge or we'll lose touch with each other.'

'I won't,' I assured him.

'It's good, fast going now,' he added. 'We'll be out of the worst of it soon.' He stepped back into his tracks where they finished abruptly and pushed off ahead of me again.

I was a bit worried as we started off, for I did not know how much better Mayne was as a ski-er than myself. And ski-ing across fresh snow is not the same as ski-ing down one of the regular runs. The ski runs are flattened so that you can put a brake on your speed by snow-ploughing – pressing the skis out with the heels so that they are thrusting sideways with the points together, like a snow-plough. You can stem, too. But in fresh snow, you can't do that. You adjust your speed by varying the steepness of the run. If a slope is too steep for you, you take it in a series of diagonals. You can only go fast and straight on clean snow if you can do a real Christi – and the Christiana turn is the most difficult of all, a jump to clear the skis from their tracks and a right angle turn in mid-air.

I mention this because it worried me at the time. I have never got as far in ski-ing as the Christiana turn and, if Mayne could Christi, I wondered if he would realise that I could not. I wished I had mentioned the fact to him when he suggested increasing the pace.

But soon my only concern was to keep my skis in his tracks.

We were going in an oblique run down the shoulder of a long hill. Mayne was taking a steep diagonal and we were running at something over thirty miles an hour through thick, driving snow. It is not an experience I wish to repeat. I could have followed the line of his skis on a gentler run and zig-zagged down to meet it when I got too far above his line. But that would slow my pace and I did not dare fall too far behind. As it was, the snow was quite thick in his tracks by the time I followed on. In places they were being half obliterated in a matter of seconds.

The snow whipped at my face and blinded my eyes. I was chilled right through with the cold and the speed. In places the snow was very soft and Mayne's skis had bitten deep into it. This made it difficult for me at times to retain my balance.

At the end of that long diagonal run, I found him waiting for me, a solitary figure in that blur of white and grey, the track of his skis running right up to him like a little railway. I stepped out of his tracks just before I reached him and stopped by running uphill. I looked at him and saw that he had brought himself up standing by a Christi. A wide arc of ploughed-up snow showed where he had made the turn.

'Just wanted to find out whether you were all right on a Christi,' he called to me.

I shook my head. 'Sorry!' I shouted back.

'All right. Just wanted to know. We'll soon be in the pass now.

That'll give us some shelter. I'll go easy and stick to diagonals.'

He turned and started off again. I joined his ski tracks and followed on. We reached a steeper part, made two diagonals down it, with standing turns at the end of each. Then followed a long clear run across a sloping field of snow.

It was like a plateau – like a white sloping desk-top. As I came to the edge of it, I realised suddenly that it was going to drop away sharply. I remember noticing how the edges of Mayne's ski tracks stood out against the grey void of falling snow beyond the lip. Then I was over the edge, plunging, head well down, along tracks that ran straight as a die down a long, very steep hillside of snow. I should have fallen before my speed became too great. But I had confidence in Mayne's judgment. I felt sure that the steep descent must end in a rise. Mayne would never have taken it straight otherwise. The wind pressed in an icy blanket against my face. Already I was travelling at a tremendous pace. The snow was thick and I could not see more than forty or fifty yards ahead. I kept my legs braced and supple at the knees and let myself go. It was exhilarating, like going downhill on the Giant Racer. Then suddenly the snow lifted a little. Mayne's tracks ran down into the bottom of a steep-sided little valley of snow. The opposite slope of that valley seemed to rise almost sheer. It was like a wall of snow, and I was hurtling towards it. And at the bottom I could see the flurry of churned-up snow where Mayne had been forced to do a Christi. His tracks ran on away to the right along the floor of the valley.

My heart leaped in my throat. There was nothing I could do about it but hope that my skis would make the opposite side and not dig their points in. I dared not fall now. I was going too fast. The snow slope of the opposite side of the valley rose to meet me with incredible speed. It seemed to pounce at me. I braced my legs for the upward thrust of my skis. My ski points lifted as I hit the floor of the valley. Then the snow slope beyond flung itself at me. A cold, wet world closed about me in an icy smother.

I was suddenly still. All the wind was knocked out of my body. I could not breathe. My mouth and nostrils were blocked with cold snow. My legs felt twisted and broken. I could not move them. I sobbed for the air I needed.

I fought to clear my face. I got my hand to my mouth and scraped away the snow. Still I could not breathe. I panicked and lashed out with my arms. Everywhere I felt soft snow that yielded and then packed hard as I fought against it. I realised then that I was buried. I was frightened. I fought upwards with my hands, gripped in a frenzy of terror. Then the grey light of the sky showed through a hole in the snow and I breathed in air in great sobbing gulps.

As soon as I had recovered my wind, I tried to loosen my legs from the snow in which they were buried. But the ski points had dug themselves firmly in and I could not move them. I tried to reach down to loosen the skis off my boots. But I could not reach that far, for every time I tried to raise myself in order to bend down, my arm sank to the shoulder in the snow. It was very soft. I tried to find my sticks. I needed the webbed circle of them to support me. But I could not find them. I had removed my hands from the thongs when I was fighting for air and they were buried deep under me. I scraped a clear patch in the snow around me and slewed my body round, bending down whilst still lying in the snow. It took all my energy and gave my twisted legs much pain. But at last I was able to reach the spring clip of my left ski. I pressed it forward and felt immediate release from the pain in my leg as my boot freed itself from the ski. I moved my leg about in the snow. It seemed all right. Then I did the same with the other foot. That too seemed sound.

I lay back exhausted after that. The snow fell steadily on me from above. The wind kept drifting it into the hole in which I was lying, so that I had to be continually pressing the fresh snow back in order not to be smothered. When I had recovered from the effort of freeing my legs, I began to set about trying to get on to my feet. But it was quite impossible. The instant I put pressure on the snow with either my hands or my legs, I simply sank into it. It was like a bog. I was only safe as long as I continued to lie at full length. Once I strug-gled into a sitting position and managed to grasp the end of one of my skis. With this I levered myself on to both feet at the same time.

Immediately I sank in the snow up to my thighs. I was utterly exhausted by the time I had extricated myself. There is nothing in the world more exhausting than trying to get up in soft snow and I was tired from the long run in the first place. I lay on my back, panting. My muscles felt like soft wire. They had no resilience in them. I decided to wait for Mayne. He would follow his ski tracks back. Or would they be obliterated? Anyway, he would remember the way he had come. It might be a little time yet. But he would soon realise that I was not behind him. He might have to climb a bit. How long had I been there? It seemed hours.

I lay back and closed my eyes and tried to pretend that this wasn't wet snow, but a comfortable bed.

The sweat dried on me, making my skin feel cold. The snow was melting under me with the heat of my body and the wet was coming through my ski suit. Fresh snow drifted across my face. I thought of that long steep descent that had ended so ignominiously here in the snow. And then I remembered with a terrible feeling of panic how Mayne's ski tracks had turned sharply along the floor of the valley. That flurry of ploughed-up snow! Mayne had done a Christi there. Yet only a few minutes earlier he had stopped expressly to find out whether or not I could do a Christi.

The truth dawned on me slowly as I lay there in the snow. Mayne had meant this to happen. And I knew then that he would not come back.

CHAPTER 13

THREE ENGLISH AUTHORS

THE OPENING RUN by A A Milne

Alan Alexander Milne (1882–1956) was an English author, best known for his books about the teddy bear, 'Winnie-the-Pooh' and for various poems. Milne was a noted writer, primarily as a playwright, before the huge success of Pooh overshadowed all his previous work. Milne served in both World Wars, joining the British Army in World War I, and was a captain of the British Home Guard in World War II.

With a great effort Simpson strapped his foot securely into a ski and turned doubtfully to Thomas.

"Thomas," he said, "how do you know which foot is which?"

"It depends whose," said Thomas. He was busy tying a large rucksack of lunch on to himself and was in no mood for Samuel's ballroom chatter.

"You've got one ski on one foot," I said. "Then the other ski goes on the foot you've got over. I should have thought you would have seen that."

"But I may have put the first one on wrong."

"You ought to know, after all these years, that you are certain to have done so," I said severely. Having had my own hired skis fixed on by the concierge I felt rather superior. Simpson, having bought his in London, was regarded darkly by that gentleman, and left to his own devices.

"Are we all ready?" asked Myra, who had kept us waiting for twenty minutes. "Archie, what about Dahlia?"

"Dahlia will join us at lunch. She is expecting a letter from Peter by the twelve o'clock post and refuses to start without it. Also she doesn't think she is up to skiing just yet. Also she wants to have a heart-to-heart talk with the girl in red, and break it to her that Thomas is engaged to several people in London already."

"Come on," growled Thomas, and he led the way up the hill. We followed him in single file.

It was a day of colour, straight from heaven. On either side the dazzling whiteness of the snow; above, the deep blue of the sky; in front of me the glorious apricot of Simpson's winter suiting. London seemed a hundred years away. It was impossible to work up the least interest in the Home Rule Bill, the Billiard Tournament, or the state of St. Paul's Cathedral.

"I feel extremely picturesque," said Archie. "If only we had a wolf or two after us, the illusion would be complete. The Boy Trappers, or Half-Hours among the Rocky Mountains."

"It is a pleasant thought, Archie," I said, "that in any wolf trouble the bachelors of the party would have to sacrifice themselves for us. Myra dear, the loss of Samuel in such circumstances would draw us very close together. There might be a loss of Thomas too, perhaps – for if there was not enough of Simpson to go round, if there was a hungry wolf left over, would Thomas hesitate?"

"No," said Thomas, "I should run like a hare."

Simpson said nothing. His face I could not see; but his back looked exactly like the back of a man who was trying to look as if he had been brought up on skis from a baby and was now taking a small party of enthusiastic novices out for their first lesson.

"What an awful shock it would be," I said, "if we found that Samuel really did know something about it after all; and, while we were tumbling about anyhow, he sailed gracefully down the steepest slopes. I should go straight back to Cricklewood."

"My dear chap, I've read a lot about it."

"Then we're quite safe."

"With all his faults," said Archie, "and they are many – Samuel is a gentleman. He would never take an unfair advantage of us. Hallo, here we are!"

We left the road and made our way across the snow to a little wooden hut which Archie had noticed the day before. Here we were to meet Dahlia for lunch; and here, accordingly, we left the rucksack and such garments as the heat of the sun suggested. Then, at the top of a long snow slope, steep at first, more gentle later, we stood and wondered.

"Who's going first?" said Archie.

"What do you do?" asked Myra.

"You don't. It does it for you."

"But how do you stop?"

"Don't bother about that, dear," I said. "That will be arranged for you all right. Take two steps to the brink of the hill and pick yourself up at the bottom. Now then, Simpson! Be a man. The lady waits, Samuel. The... Hallo! Hi! Help!" I cried, as I began to move off slowly. It was too late to do anything about it. "Good-bye," I called. And then things moved more quickly....

Very quickly....

Suddenly there came a moment when I realised that I wasn't keeping up with my feet....

I shouted to my skis to stop. It was no good. They went on....

I decided to stop without them....

The ensuing second went by too swiftly for me to understand rightly what happened. I fancy that, rising from my sitting position and travelling easily on my head, I caught my skis up again and passed them....

Then it was their turn. They overtook me....

But I was not to be beaten. Once more I obtained the lead. This time I took the inside berth, and kept it....

There seemed to be a lot more snow than I really wanted.... I struggled bravely with it....

And then the earthquake ceased, and suddenly I was in the outer air. My first ski run, the most glorious run of modern times, was over.

"Ripping!" I shouted up the hill to them. "But there's rather a nasty bump at the bottom," I added kindly, as I set myself to the impossible business of getting up....

"Jove," said Archie, coming to rest a few yards off, "that's splendid!" He had fallen in a less striking way than myself, and he got to his feet without difficulty. "Why do you pose like that?" he asked, as he picked up his stick.

"I'm a fixture," I announced. "Myra," I said, as she turned a somersault and arrived beaming at my side, "I'm here for some time; you'll have to come out every morning with crumbs for me. In the afternoon you can bring a cheering book and read aloud to your husband. Sometimes I shall dictate little things to you. They will not be my best little things; for this position, with my feet so much higher than my head, is not the one in which inspiration comes to me most readily. The flow of blood to the brain impairs reflection. But no matter."

"Are you really stuck?" asked Myra in some anxiety. "I should hate to have a husband who lived by himself in the snow," she said thoughtfully.

"Let us look on the bright side," said Archie. "The snow will have melted by April, and he will then be able to return to you. Hallo, here's Thomas! Thomas will probably have some clever idea for restoring the family credit."

Thomas got up in a business-like manner and climbed slowly back to us.

"Thomas," I said, "you see the position. Indeed," I added, "it is obvious. None of the people round me seems inclined – or, it may be, able – to help. There is a feeling that if Myra lives in the hotel alone while I remain here – possibly till April – people will talk. You know how ready they are. There is also the fact that I have only hired the skis for three weeks. Also, a minor point, but one that touches me rather, that I shall want my hair cut long before March is out. Thomas, imagine me to be a torpedo-destroyer on the Maplin Sands, and tell me what on earth to do."

"Take your skis off."

"Oh, brilliant!" said Myra.

"Take my skis off?" I cried. "Never! Is it not my duty to be the last to leave my skis? Can I abandon – Hallo! is that Dahlia on the sky-line? Hooray, lunch! Archie, take my skis off, there's a good fellow. We mustn't keep Dahlia waiting."

THE GLAMOUR OF THE SNOW by Algernon Blackwood

Algernon Henry Blackwood, CBE (1869 – 1951) was an English broadcasting narrator, journalist, novelist and short story writer, and among the most prolific ghost story writers in the history of the genre. Blackwood winds a tale about a man's infatuation with a supernatural winter beauty.. "Under the steady moonlight it was more than haunting. It was a living, white, bewildering power that deliciously confused the senses and laid a spell of wild perplexity upon the heart. It revealed itself through all this sheeted whiteness of snow."

That night there was excitement in the little hotel-world, first because there was a bal costumé, but chiefly because the new snow had come. And Hibbert went – felt drawn to go; he did not go in costume, but he wanted to talk about the slopes and ski-ing with the other men, and at the same time....

Ah, there was the truth, the deeper necessity that called. For the singular connection between the stranger and the snow again betrayed itself, utterly beyond explanation as before, but vital and insistent. Some hidden instinct in his pagan soul – heaven knows how he phrased it even to himself, if he phrased it at all – whispered that with the snow the girl would be somewhere about, would emerge from her hiding place, would even look for him.

Absolutely unwarranted it was. He laughed while he stood before the little glass and trimmed his moustache, tried to make his black tie sit straight, and shook down his dinner jacket so that it should lie upon the shoulders without a crease. His brown eyes were very bright. "I look younger than I usually do," he thought. It was unusual, even significant, in a man who had no vanity about his appearance and certainly never questioned his age or tried to look younger than he was. Affairs of the heart, with one tumultuous exception that left no fuel for lesser subsequent fires, had never troubled him. The forces of his soul and mind not called upon for "work" and obvious duties, all went to Nature. The desolate, wild places of the earth were what he loved; night, and the beauty of the stars and snow. And this evening he felt their claims upon him mightily stirring. A rising wildness caught his blood, quickened his pulse, woke longing and passion too. But chiefly snow. The snow whirred softly through his thoughts like white, seductive dreams.... For the snow had come; and She, it seemed, had somehow come with it – into his mind.

And yet he stood before that twisted mirror and pulled his tie and coat askew a dozen times, as though it mattered. "What in the world is up with me?" he thought. Then, laughing a little, he turned before leaving the room to put his private papers in order. The green morocco desk that held them he took down from the shelf and laid upon the table. Tied to the lid was the visiting card with his brother's London address "in case of accident." On the way down to the hotel he wondered why he had done this, for though imaginative, he was not the kind of man who dealt in presentiments. Moods with him were strong, but ever held in leash.

"It's almost like a warning," he thought, smiling. He drew his thick coat tightly round the throat as the freezing air bit at him. "Those warnings one reads of in stories sometimes ...!"

A delicious happiness was in his blood. Over the edge of the hills across the valley rose the moon. He saw her silver sheet the world of snow. Snow covered all. It smothered sound and distance. It smothered houses, streets, and human beings. It smothered – life.

In the hall there was light and bustle; people were already arriving from the other hotels and châlets, their costumes hidden beneath many wraps. Groups of men in evening dress stood about smoking, talking "snow" and "ski-ing." The band was tuning up. The claims of the hotel-world clashed about him faintly as of old. At the big glass windows of the verandah, peasants stopped a moment on their way home from the café to peer. Hibbert thought laughingly of that conflict he used to imagine. He laughed because it suddenly seemed so unreal. He belonged so utterly to Nature and the mountains, and especially to those desolate slopes where now the snow lay thick and fresh and sweet, that there was no question of a conflict at all. The power of the newly fallen snow had caught him, proving it without effort. Out there, upon those lonely reaches of the moonlit ridges, the snow lay ready – masses and masses of it – cool, soft, inviting. He longed for it. It awaited him. He thought of the intoxicating delight of ski-ing in the moonlight....

Thus, somehow, in vivid flashing vision, he thought of it while he stood there smoking with the other men and talking all the "shop" of ski-ing.

And, ever mysteriously blended with this power of the snow, poured also through his inner being the power of the girl. He could not disabuse his mind of the insinuating presence of the two together. He remembered that queer skating-impulse of ten days ago, the impulse that had let her in. That any mind, even an imaginative one, could pass beneath the sway of such a fancy was strange enough; and Hibbert, while fully aware of the disorder, yet found a curious joy in yielding to it. This insubordinate centre that drew him towards old pagan beliefs had assumed command. With a kind of sensuous pleasure he let himself be conquered.

And snow that night seemed in everybody's thoughts. The dancing couples talked of it; the hotel proprietors congratulated one another; it meant good sport and satisfied their guests; every one was planning trips and expeditions, talking of slopes and telemarks, of flying speed and distance, of drifts and crust and frost. Vitality and enthusiasm pulsed in the very air; all were alert and active, positive, radiating currents of creative life even into the stuffy atmosphere of that crowded ball-room. And the snow had caused it, the snow had brought it; all this discharge of eager sparkling energy was due primarily to the – Snow.

But in the mind of Hibbert, by some swift alchemy of his pagan yearnings, this energy became transmuted. It rarefied itself, gleaming in white and crystal currents of passionate anticipation, which he transferred, as by a species of electrical imagination, into the personality of the girl – the Girl of the Snow. She somewhere was waiting for him, expecting him, calling to him softly from those leagues of moonlit mountain. He remembered the touch of that cool, dry hand; the soft and icy breath against his cheek; the hush and softness of her presence in the way she came and the way she had gone again – like a flurry of snow the wind sent gliding up the slopes. She, like himself, belonged out there. He fancied that he heard her little windy voice come sifting to him through the snowy branches of the trees, calling his name ... that haunting little voice that dived straight to the centre of his life as once, long years ago, two other voices used to do....

But nowhere among the costumed dancers did he see her slender figure. He danced with one and all, distrait and absent, a stupid partner as each girl discovered, his eyes ever turning towards the door and windows, hoping to catch the luring face, the vision that did not come ... and at length, hoping even against hope. For the ball-room thinned; groups left one by one, going home to their hotels and châlets; the band tired obviously; people sat drinking lemon-squashes at the little tables, the men mopping their foreheads, everybody ready for bed.

It was close on midnight. As Hibbert passed through the hall to get his overcoat and snow-boots, he saw men in the passage by the "sport-room," greasing their ski against an early start. Knapsack luncheons were being ordered by the kitchen swing doors. He sighed. Lighting a cigarette a friend offered him, he returned a confused reply to some question as to whether he could join their party in the morning. It seemed he did not hear it properly. He passed through the outer vestibule between the double glass doors, and went into the night.

The man who asked the question watched him go, an expression of anxiety momentarily in his eyes.

"Don't think he heard you," said another, laughing. "You've got to shout to Hibbert, his mind's so full of his work."

"He works too hard," suggested the first, "full of queer ideas and dreams."

But Hibbert's silence was not rudeness. He had not caught the invitation, that was all. The call of the hotel-world had faded. He no longer heard it. Another wilder call was sounding in his ears.

For up the street he had seen a little figure moving. Close against the shadows of the baker's shop it glided – white, slim, enticing.

And at once into his mind passed the hush and softness of the snow – yet with it a searching, crying wildness for the heights. He knew by some incalculable, swift instinct she would not meet him in the village street. It was not there, amid crowding houses, she would speak to him. Indeed, already she had disappeared, melted from view up the white vista of the moonlit road. Yonder, he divined, she waited where the highway narrowed abruptly into the mountain path beyond the châlets.

It did not even occur to him to hesitate; mad though it seemed, and was – this sudden craving for the heights with her, at least for open spaces where the snow lay thick and fresh – it was too imperious to be denied. He does not remember going up to his room, putting the sweater over his evening clothes, and getting into the fur gauntlet gloves and the helmet cap of wool. Most certainly he has no recollection of fastening on his ski; he must have done it automatically. Some faculty of normal observation was in abeyance, as it were. His mind was out beyond the village – out with the snowy mountains and the moon.

Henri Défago, putting up the shutters over his café windows, saw him pass, and wondered mildly: "Un monsieur qui fait du ski à cette heure! Il est Anglais, donc ...!" He shrugged his shoulders, as though a man had the right to choose his own way of death. And Marthe Perotti, the hunchback wife of the shoemaker, looking by chance from her window, caught his figure moving swiftly up the road. She had other thoughts, for she knew and believed the old traditions of the witches and snow-beings that steal the souls of men. She had even heard, 'twas said, the dreaded "synagogue" pass roaring down the street at night, and now, as then, she hid her eyes. "They've called to him ... and he must go," she murmured, making the sign of the cross.

But no one sought to stop him. Hibbert recalls only a single incident until he found himself beyond the houses, searching for her along the fringe of forest where the moonlight met the snow in a bewildering frieze of fantastic shadows. And the incident was simply this – that he remembered passing the church. Catching the outline of its tower against the stars, he was aware of a faint sense of hesitation. A vague uneasiness came and went – jarred unpleasantly across the flow of his excited feelings, chilling exhilaration. He caught the instant's discord, dismissed it, and – passed on. The seduction of the snow smothered the hint before he realised that it had brushed the skirts of warning.

And then he saw her. She stood there waiting in a little clear space of shining snow, dressed all in white, part of the moonlight and the glistening background, her slender figure just discernible.

"I waited, for I knew you would come," the silvery little voice of windy beauty floated down to him. "You had to come."

"I'm ready," he answered, "I knew it too."

The world of Nature caught him to its heart in those few words – the wonder and the glory of the night and snow. Life leaped within him. The passion of his pagan soul exulted, rose in joy, flowed out to her. He neither reflected nor considered but let himself go like the veriest schoolboy in the wildness of first love.

"Give me your hand," he cried, "I'm coming ...!"

"A little farther on, a little higher," came her delicious answer. "Here it is too near the village – and the church."

And the words seemed wholly right and natural; he did not dream of questioning them; he understood that, with this little touch of civilisation in sight, the familiarity he suggested was impossible. Once out upon the open mountains, 'mid the freedom of huge slopes and towering peaks, the stars and moon to witness and the wilderness of snow to watch, they could taste an innocence of happy intercourse free from the dead conventions that imprison literal minds.

He urged his pace yet did not quite overtake her. The girl kept always just a little bit ahead of his best efforts.... And soon they left the trees behind and passed on to the enormous slopes of the sea of snow that rolled in mountainous terror and beauty to the stars. The wonder of the white world caught him away. Under the steady moonlight it was more than haunting. It was a living, white, bewildering power that deliciously confused the senses and laid a spell of wild perplexity upon the heart. It was a personality that cloaked, and yet revealed, itself through all this sheeted whiteness of snow. It rose, went with him, fled before, and followed after. Slowly it dropped lithe, gleaming arms about his neck, gathering him in....

Certainly, some soft persuasion coaxed his very soul, urging him ever forwards, upwards, on towards the higher icy slopes. Judgment and reason left their throne, it seemed, completely, as in the madness of intoxication. The girl, slim and seductive, kept always just ahead, so that he never quite came up with her. He saw the white enchantment of her face and figure, something that streamed about her neck flying like a wreath of snow in the wind, and heard the alluring accents of her whispering voice that called from time to time: "A little farther on, a little higher.... Then we'll run home together!"

Sometimes he saw her hand stretched out to find his own, but each time, just as he came up with her, he saw her still in front, the hand and arm withdrawn. They took a gentle angle of ascent. The toil seemed nothing. In this crystal, wine-like air fatigue vanished. The sishing of the ski through the powdery surface of the snow was the only sound that broke the stillness; this, with his breathing and the rustle of her skirts, was all he heard. Cold moonshine, snow, and silence held the world. The sky was black, and the peaks beyond cut into it like frosted wedges of iron and steel. Far below the valley slept, the village long since hidden out of sight. He felt that he could never tire.... The sound of the church clock rose from time to time faintly through the air – more and more distant.

"Give me your hand. It's time now to turn back."

"Just one more slope," she laughed. "That ridge above us. Then we'll make for home." And her low voice mingled pleasantly with the purring of their ski. His own seemed harsh and ugly by comparison.

"But I have never come so high before. It's glorious! This world of silent snow and moonlight – and you. You're a child of the snow, I swear. Let me come up – closer – to see your face – and touch your little hand."

Her laughter answered him.

"Come on! A little higher. Here we're quite alone together."

"It's magnificent," he cried. "But why did you hide away so long? I've looked and searched for you in vain ever since we skated – " he was going to say "ten days ago," but the accurate memory of time had gone from him; he was not sure whether it was days or years or minutes. His thoughts of earth were scattered and confused.

"You looked for me in the wrong places," he heard her murmur just above him. "You looked in places where I never go. Hotels and houses kill me. I avoid them." She laughed a fine, shrill, windy little laugh.

"I loathe them too – "

He stopped. The girl had suddenly come quite close. A breath of ice passed through his very soul. She had touched him.

"But this awful cold!" he cried out, sharply, "this freezing cold that takes me. The wind is rising; it's a wind of ice. Come, let us turn ...!"

But when he plunged forward to hold her, or at least to look, the girl was gone again. And something in the way she stood there a few feet beyond, and stared down into his eyes so steadfastly in silence, made him shiver. The moonlight was behind her, but in some odd way he could not focus sight upon her face, although so close. The gleam of eyes he caught, but all the rest seemed white and snowy as though he looked beyond her – out into space....

The sound of the church bell came up faintly from the valley far below, and he counted the strokes – five. A sudden, curious weakness seized him as he listened. Deep within it was, deadly yet somehow sweet, and hard to resist. He felt like sinking down upon the snow and lying there.... They had been climbing for five hours.... It was, of course, the warning of complete exhaustion.

With a great effort he fought and overcame it. It passed away as suddenly as it came.

"We'll turn," he said with a decision he hardly felt. "It will be dawn before we reach the village again. Come at once. It's time for home."

The sense of exhilaration had utterly left him. An emotion that was akin to fear swept coldly through him. But her whispering answer turned it instantly to terror – a terror that gripped him horribly and turned him weak and unresisting.

"Our home is – here!" A burst of wild, high laughter, loud and shrill, accompanied the words. It was like a whistling wind. The wind had risen, and clouds obscured the moon. "A little higher – where we cannot hear the wicked bells," she cried, and for the first time seized him deliberately by the hand. She moved, was suddenly close against his face. Again she touched him.

And Hibbert tried to turn away in escape, and so trying, found for the first time that the power of the snow – that other power which does not exhilarate but deadens effort – was upon him. The suffocating weakness that it brings to exhausted men, luring them to the sleep of death in her clinging soft embrace, lulling the will and conquering all desire for life – this was awfully upon him. His feet were heavy and entangled. He could not turn or move.

The girl stood in front of him, very near; he felt her chilly breath upon his cheeks; her hair passed blindingly across his eyes; and that icy wind came with her. He saw her whiteness close; again, it seemed, his sight passed through her into space as though she had no face. Her arms were round his neck. She drew him softly downwards to his knees. He sank; he yielded utterly; he obeyed. Her weight was upon him, smothering, delicious. The snow was to his waist.... She kissed him softly on the lips, the eyes, all over his face. And then she spoke his name in that voice of love and wonder, the voice that held the accent of two others – both taken over long ago by Death – the voice of his mother, and of the woman he had loved.

He made one more feeble effort to resist. Then, realising even while he struggled that this soft weight about his heart was sweeter than anything life could ever bring, he let his muscles relax, and sank back into the soft oblivion of the covering snow. Her wintry kisses bore him into sleep.

They say that men who know the sleep of exhaustion in the snow find no awakening on the hither side of death.... The hours passed and the moon sank down below the white world's rim. Then, suddenly, there came a little crash upon his breast and neck, and Hibbert – woke.

He slowly turned bewildered, heavy eyes upon the desolate mountains, stared dizzily about him, tried to rise. At first his muscles would not act; a numbing, aching pain possessed him. He uttered a long, thin cry for help, and heard its faintness swallowed by the wind. And then he understood vaguely why he was only warm – not dead. For this very wind that took his cry had built up a sheltering mound of driven snow against his body while he slept. Like a curving wave it ran beside him. It was the breaking of its over-toppling edge that caused the crash, and the coldness of the mass against his neck that woke him.

Dawn kissed the eastern sky; pale gleams of gold shot every peak with splendour; but ice was in the air, and the dry and frozen snow blew like powder from the surface of the slopes. He saw the points of his ski projecting just below him. Then he – remembered. It seems he had just strength enough to realise that, could he but rise and stand, he might fly with terrific impetus towards the woods and village far beneath. The ski would carry him. But if he failed and fell ...!

How he contrived it Hibbert never knew; this fear of death somehow called out his whole available reserve force. He rose slowly, balanced a moment, then, taking the angle of an immense zigzag, started down the awful slopes like an arrow from a bow. And automatically the splendid muscles of the practised ski-er and athlete saved and guided him, for he was hardly conscious of controlling either speed or direction. The snow stung face and eyes like fine steel shot; ridge after ridge flew past; the summits raced across the sky; the valley leaped up with bounds to meet him. He scarcely felt the ground beneath his feet as the huge slopes and distance melted before the lightning speed of that descent from death to life.

He took it in four mile-long zigzags, and it was the turning at each corner that nearly finished him, for then the strain of balancing taxed to the verge of collapse the remnants of his strength.

Slopes that have taken hours to climb can be descended in a short half-hour on ski, but Hibbert had lost all count of time. Quite other thoughts and feelings mastered him in that wild, swift dropping through the air that was like the flight of a bird. For ever close upon his heels came following forms and voices with the whirling snow-dust. He heard that little silvery voice of death and laughter at his back. Shrill and wild, with the whistling of the wind past his ears, he caught its pursuing tones; but in anger now, no longer soft and coaxing. And it was accompanied; she did not follow alone. It seemed a host of these flying figures of the snow chased madly just behind him. He felt them furiously smite his neck and cheeks, snatch at his hands and try to entangle his feet and ski in drifts. His eyes they blinded, and they caught his breath away.

The terror of the heights and snow and winter desolation urged him forward in the maddest race with death a human being ever knew; and so terrific was the speed that before the gold and crimson had left the summits to touch the ice-lips of the lower glaciers, he saw the friendly forest far beneath swing up and welcome him.

And it was then, moving slowly along the edge of the woods, he saw a light. A man was carrying it. A procession of human figures was passing in a dark line laboriously through the snow. And – he heard the sound of chanting.

Instinctively, without a second's hesitation, he changed his course. No longer flying at an angle as before, he pointed his ski straight down the mountain-side. The dreadful steepness did not frighten him. He knew full well it meant a crashing tumble at the bottom, but he also knew it meant a doubling of his speed – with safety at the end. For, though no definite thought passed through his mind, he understood that it was the village curé who carried that little gleaming lantern in the dawn, and that he was taking the Host to a châlet on the lower slopes – to some peasant in extremis. He remembered her terror of the church and bells. She feared the holy symbols.

There was one last wild cry in his ears as he started, a shriek of the wind before his face, and a rush of stinging snow against closed eyelids – and then he dropped through empty space. Speed took sight from him. It seemed he flew off the surface of the world.

Indistinctly he recalls the murmur of men's voices, the touch of strong arms that lifted him, and the shooting pains as the ski were unfastened from the twisted ankle ... for when he opened his eyes again to normal life he found himself lying in his bed at the post office with the doctor at his side. But for years to come the story of "mad Hibbert's" ski-ing at night is recounted in that mountain village. He went, it seems, up slopes, and to a height that no man in his senses ever tried before. The tourists were agog about it for the rest of the season, and the very same day two of the bolder men went over the actual ground and photographed the slopes. Later Hibbert saw these photographs. He noticed one curious thing about them – though he did not mention it to anyone:

There was only a single track.

WOMEN IN LOVE by D H Lawrence

There is not a lot about skiing in this penultimate chapter of Women in Love, *widely regarded as D. H. Lawrence's greatest novel. However, DH Lawrence is an iconic writer, one of the most important writers of the Modernist movement, I felt it needed to be included in this anthology. It is also interesting that a novel written in 1920 by the son of an alcoholic and virtually illiterate miner from the Midlands, can write about skiing in Innsbruck.*

Gerald did not come in from his skiing until nightfall, he missed the coffee and cake that she took at four o'clock. The snow was in perfect condition, he had travelled a long way, by himself, among the snow ridges, on his skis, he had climbed high, so high that he could see over the top of the pass, five miles distant, could see the Marienhutte, the hostel on the crest of the pass, half buried in snow, and over into the deep valley beyond, to the dusk of the pine trees. One could go that way home; but he shuddered with nausea at the thought of home; one could travel on skis down there, and come to the old imperial road, below the pass. But why come to any road? He revolted at the thought of finding himself in the world again. He must stay up there in the snow forever. He had been happy by himself, high up there alone, travelling swiftly on skis, taking far flights, and skimming past the dark rocks veined with brilliant snow.

But he felt something icy gathering at his heart. This strange mood of patience and innocence which had persisted in him for some days, was passing away, he would be left again a prey to the horrible passions and tortures.

So he came down reluctantly, snow-burned, snow-estranged, to the house in the hollow, between the knuckles of the mountain tops. He saw its lights shining yellow, and he held back, wishing he need not go in, to confront those people, to hear the turmoil of voices and to feel the confusion of other presences. He was isolated as if there were a vacuum round his heart, or a sheath of pure ice.

The moment he saw Gudrun something jolted in his soul. She was looking rather lofty and superb, smiling slowly and graciously to the Germans. A sudden desire leapt in his heart, to kill her. He thought, what a perfect voluptuous fulfilment it would be, to kill her. His mind was absent all the evening, estranged by the snow and his passion. But he kept the idea constant within him, what a perfect voluptuous consummation it would be to strangle her, to strangle every spark of life out of her, till she lay completely inert, soft, relaxed for ever, a soft heap lying dead between his hands, utterly dead. Then he would have had her finally and for ever; there would be such a perfect voluptuous finality.

Gudrun was unaware of what he was feeling, he seemed so quiet and amiable, as usual. His amiability even made her feel brutal towards him. She went into his room when he was partially undressed. She did not notice the curious, glad gleam of pure hatred, with which he looked at her. She stood near the door, with her hand behind her.

"I have been thinking, Gerald," she said, with an insulting nonchalance, "that I shall not go back to England."

"Oh," he said, "where will you go then?"

But she ignored his question. She had her own logical statement to make, and it must be made as she had thought it.

"I can't see the use of going back," she continued. "It is over between me and you."

She paused for him to speak. But he said nothing. He was only talking to himself, saying "Over, is it? I believe it is over. But it isn't finished. Remember, it isn't finished. We must put some sort of a finish on it. There must be a conclusion, there must be finality." So he talked to himself, but aloud he said nothing whatever.

"What has been, has been," she continued. "There is nothing that I regret. I hope you regret nothing…" She waited for him to speak.

"Oh, I regret nothing," he said, accommodatingly.

"Good then," she answered, "good then. Then neither of us cherishes any regrets, which is as it should be."

"Quite as it should be," he said aimlessly.

She paused to gather up her thread again. "Our attempt has been a failure," she said. "But we can try again, elsewhere."

A little flicker of rage ran through his blood. It was as if she were rousing him, goading him. Why must she do it?

"Attempt at what?" he asked.

"At being lovers, I suppose," she said, a little baffled, yet so trivial she made it all seem.

"Our attempt at being lovers has been a failure?" he repeated aloud.

To himself he was saying, "I ought to kill her here. There is only this left, for me to kill her." A heavy, overcharged desire to bring about her death possessed him. She was unaware.

"Hasn't it?" she asked. "Do you think it has been a success?"

Again the insult of the flippant question ran through his blood like a current of fire.

"It had some of the elements of success, our relationship," he replied. "It might have come off." But he paused before concluding the last phrase. Even as he began the sentence, he did not believe in what he was going to say. He knew it never could have been a success.

"No," she replied. "You cannot love."

"And you?" he asked.

Her wide, dark-filled eyes were fixed on him, like two moons of darkness. "I couldn't love you" she said, with stark cold truth.

"I shall be leaving tomorrow."

"We will go together as far as Innsbruck, for appearance's sake?"" he asked.

"Perhaps," she said.

She said "Perhaps" between the sips of her coffee. And the sound of her taking her breath in the word, was nauseous to him. He rose quickly to be away from her.

He went and made arrangements for the departure on the morrow, Then, taking some food, he set out for the day on the skis. "Perhaps," he said to the Wirt, he would go up to the Marienhütte, perhaps to the village below.

CHAPTER 14
PERSONAL REMINISCINGS

AN ALPINE PASS ON 'SKI' by Sir Arthur Conan Doyle

From the *London Gazette:*

Sir Arthur Ignatius Conan Doyle (1859–1930) was a British writer, who created the character Sherlock Holmes. Originally a physician, he published more than fifty short stories about Holmes and Dr. Watson.

There is nothing peculiarly malignant in the appearance of a pair of ski. They are two slips of elm wood, 8ft. long, 4in. broad, with a square heel, turned-up toes, and straps in the centre to secure your feet. No one to look at them would guess at the possibilities which lurk in them. But you put them on, and you turn with a smile to see whether your friends are looking at you, and then the next moment you are boring your head madly into a snow bank, and kicking frantically with both feet, and half rising only to butt viciously into that snow bank again, and your friends are getting more entertainment than they had ever thought you capable of giving.

This is when you are beginning. You naturally expect trouble then, and you are not likely to be disappointed. But as you get on a little the thing becomes more irritating. The ski are the most capricious things upon earth. One day you cannot go wrong with them. On another, with the same weather and the same snow, you cannot go right. And it is when you least expect it that things begin to happen. You stand on the crown of a slope and you adjust your body for a rapid slide, but your ski stick motionless, and over you go upon your face. Or you stand upon a plateau which seems to you to be as level as a billiard table, and in an instant, without cause or warning, away they shoot, and you are left behind staring at the sky. For a man who suffers from too much dignity, a course of Norwegian snowshoes would have a fine moral effect.

Whenever you brace yourself for a fall it never comes off. Whenever you think yourself absolutely secure it is all over with you. You come to a hard ice slope at an angle of 75 deg. and you zig-zag up it, digging the side of your ski into it, and feeling that if a mosquito settles upon you, you are gone. But nothing ever happens, and you reach the top in safety. Then you stop upon the level to congratulate your companion, and you have just time to say, "What a lovely view is this!" when you find yourself standing on your two shoulder blades, with your ski tied tightly round your neck. Or, again, you may have had a long outing without any misfortune at all, and as you shuffle back along the road, you stop for an instant to tell a group in the hotel veranda how well you are getting on. Something happens and they suddenly find that their congratulations are addressed to the soles of your ski. Then, if your mouth is not full of snow, you find yourself muttering the names of a few Swiss villages to relieve your feelings. 'Ragatz!' is a very handy word, and may save a scandal.

But all this is in the early stage of skiing. You have to shuffle along the level, to zig-zag or move crab fashion up the hills, to slide down without losing your balance, and, above all, to turn with facility. The first time you try to turn, your friends think it is part of your fun. The great ski flapping in the air has the queerest appearance, like an exaggerated jitterbug. But this sudden whisk round is really the most necessary of accomplishments, for only so can one turn upon the mountain side without slipping down. It must be done without ever presenting one's heels to the slope, and this is the only way.

But granted that a man has perseverance, and a month to spare in which to conquer all these early difficulties, he will then find that skiing opens up a field of sport for him which is, I think, unique. This is not appreciated yet, but I am convinced that the time will come when hundreds of Englishmen will come to Switzerland for the skiing season, in March and April. I believe that I may claim to be the first save only two Switzers to do any mountain work (though on a modest enough scale) on snow shoes, but I am certain that I will not by many a thousand be the last.

The fact is that it is easier to climb an ordinary peak or to make a journey over the higher passes in winter than in summer, if the weather is only set fair. In summer you have to climb down as well as climb up, and the one is as tiring as the other. In winter your trouble is halved, as most of your descent is a mere slide. If the snow is tolerably firm, it is much easier also to zig-zag up it on ski than to clamber over boulders under a hot summer sun. The temperature, too, is more favourable for exertion in winter, for nothing could be more delightful than the crisp, pure air on the mountains, though glasses are, of course, necessary to protect the eyes from the snow glare.

Our project was to make our way from Davos to Arosa over the Furka Pass, which is over 9,000ft. high. The distance is not more than from twelve to fourteen miles as the crow flies, but it has only once been done in winter. Last year the two brothers Branger made their way across on ski. They were my companions on the present expedition, and more trustworthy ones no novice could hope to have with him. They are both men of considerable endurance, and even a long spell of my German did not appear to exhaust them.

We were up before four in the morning, and had started at half past for the village of Frauenkirch, where we were to commence our ascent. A great pale moon was shining in a violet sky, with such stars as can only be seen in the tropics or the higher Alps. At a quarter past five we turned from the road and began to plod up the hillsides over alternate banks of last year's grass and slopes of snow. We carried our ski over our shoulders and our ski boots slung round our necks, for it was good walking where the snow was hard, and it was sure to be hard wherever the sun had struck it during the day. Here and there in a hollow we floundered into and out of a soft drift up to our waists, but on the whole it was easy going, and as much of our way lay through fir woods, it would have been difficult to ski. About half past six, after a long, steady grind, we emerged from the woods, and shortly afterwards passed a wooden cow house, which was the last sign of man which we were to see until we reached Arosa.

The snow being still hard enough upon the slopes to give us a good grip for our feet, we pushed rapidly on over rolling snow fields with a general upward tendency. About half past seven the sun cleared the peaks behind us and the glare upon the great expanse of virgin snow became very dazzling. We worked our way down a long slope and then, coming to the corresponding hillside with a northern outlook, we found the snow as soft as powder and so deep that we could touch no bottom with our poles. Here, then, we took to our snow shoes, and zig-zagged up over the long, white haunch of the mountain, pausing at the top for a rest. They are useful things, the ski, for, finding that the snow was again hard enough to bear us, we soon converted ours into a very comfortable bench, from which we enjoyed the view of a whole panorama of mountains, the names of which my readers will be relieved to hear I have completely forgotten.

The snow was rapidly softening now under the glare of the sun, and without our shoes all progress would have been impossible. We were making our way along the steep side of a valley, with the mouth of the Furka Pass fairly in front of us. The snow fell away here at an angle of from 50 deg. to 60 deg., and as this steep incline, along the face of which we were shuffling, sloped away down until it ended in absolute precipice, a slip might have been serious. My two more experienced companions walked below me for the half mile or so of danger, but soon we found ourselves on a more reasonable slope, where one might fall with impunity. And now came the real sport of snowshoeing. Hitherto we had walked as fast as boots would do over ground where no boots could pass. But now we had a pleasure which boots can never give. For a third of a mile we shot along over gently dipping curves, skimming down into the valley without a motion of our feet. In that great untrodden waste, with snow fields bounding our vision on every side and no marks of life save the track of chamois and of foxes, it was glorious to whizz along in this easy fashion. A short zig-zag at the bottom of the slope brought us, at half past nine, into the mouth of the pass, and we could see the little toy hotels of Arosa away down among the fir woods, thousands of feet beneath us.

Again we had half a mile or so, skimming along with our poles dragging behind us. It seemed to me that the difficulty of our journey was over, and that we had only to stand on our ski and let them carry us to our destination. But the most awkward place was yet in front. The slope grew steeper and steeper, until it suddenly fell away into what was little short of being sheer precipice. But still, that little, when there is soft snow upon it, is all that is needed to bring out another possibility of these wonderful slips of wood. The brothers Branger agreed that the place was too difficult to attempt with the ski upon our feet. To me it seemed as if a parachute was the only instrument for which we had any use, but I did as I saw my companions do. They undid their ski, lashed the straps together, and turned them into a rather clumsy toboggan. Sitting on these, with our heels dug into the snow, and our sticks pressed hard down behind us, we began to move down the precipitous face of the pass. I think that both my comrades came to grief over it. I know that they were as white as Lot's wife at the bottom. But my own troubles were so pressing that I had no time to think of them. I tried to keep the pace within moderate bounds by pressing on the stick, which had the effect of turning the sledge sideways, so that one skidded down the slope. Then I dug my heels hard in, which shot me off backwards, and in an instant my two skis, tied together, flew away like an arrow from a bow, whizzed past the two Brangers, and vanished over the next slope, leaving their owner squatting in the deep snow. It might have been an awkward accident in the upper fields, where the drifts are 20ft. to 30ft. deep. But the steepness of the place was an advantage now, for the snow could not accumulate to any very great extent upon it. I made my way down in my own fashion.

My tailor tells me that Harris tweed cannot wear out. This is a mere theory and will not stand a thorough scientific test. He will find samples of his wares on view from the Furka Pass to Arosa, and for the remainder of the day I was happiest when nearest the wall.

However, save that one of the Brangers sprained his ankle badly in the descent, all went well with us, and we entered Arosa at half past eleven, having taken exactly seven hours over our journey. The residents at Arosa, who knew that we were coming, had calculated that we could not possibly get there before one, and turned out to see us descend the steep pass just about the time when we were finishing a comfortable luncheon at the Seehof. I would not grudge them any innocent amusement, but, still, I was just as glad that my own little performance was over before they assembled with their opera glasses. One can do very well without a gallery when one is trying a new experiment on ski.

IN PRAISE OF SKIING by Sir Arnold Lunn

FROM *THE MOUNTAINS OF YOUTH*

Sir Arnold Henry Moore Lunn (1888–1974) was a skier, mountaineer and writer. He was knighted for 'services to British Skiing and Anglo-Swiss relations' in 1952. Through his efforts, Downhill and Slalom races were introduced into the Olympic Games in 1936, although he opposed the Winter Olympic Games of that year being held in Garmisch-Partenkirchen. He was a long-standing member of FIS (International Ski Federation). He is the author of numerous books on skiing, mountaineering, philosophy and Christianity. 'The Mountains of Youth' was first published in 1925. Bernard, his grandson, gave me kind permission to reproduce these remenicences.

Skiing belongs to a great family of sports which owe their appeal to the primitive passion for speed. Mere speed is not enough. An urchin sliding along on a scooter enjoys a finer thrill than a traveller in a modern aeroplane de luxe which averages more than a hundred miles an hour between Croydon and Paris. To secure the fine unspoiled flavour of pace you must eliminate mechanism, retain the sense of personal control, and preserve the ever-present risk of a fall.

Ski are the simplest of all the servants of speed. The pioneers carved a plank from mountain ash and attached it to their feet by a rough leather thong. A man and his horse are two personalities, but an expert ski runner and his ski form an indivisible unit. The motorist imposes his will through an elaborate mechanism of pedals and levers, but the ski seem to belong to their owner just as wings belong to the bird, so intimate is the connection, so instantaneous their response to the command of mind and body. No form of swift movement gives a sense of personal control so complete.

Skiing is at once simple and subtle. It is simple because the movement owes nothing to machinery; between the ski runner and the hillside there is nothing but the sensitive ash which responds to every change of rhythm in the slope. It is subtle because the snow is subtle. The skeleton rider soon gets to know the tricks of the Cresta. He masters the secrets of each corner, gives them all pet names, and can gossip of 'Scylla and Charybdis' with the same esoteric knowledge that a golfer displays in describing the holes of his favourite course. But the hills are never the same, and the snow is never the same. Every run is a new discovery, every snowfall a new creation.

Skiing makes demands on mind as well as on muscle. The expert must study Nature in one of her most fascinating and elusive moods. He must adapt his tactics to every fickle fancy of the snow. Each type of snow has its own temper, its own pace and its own dangers. In deep powder snow you will swing to rest by the Telemark. Crust calls for the close-cut sweep of the Christiania, as you force the whole breadth of the ski against the surface of the slope. No sport makes such instant demands on the alliance of muscle and mind.

The summer climber has, of course, to learn the habits of the snow, but he can content himself with a superficial and comparatively elementary knowledge. He need only know when snow is likely to be hard enough to bear his weight, and yet not so hard as to call for the axe, and when snow is safe or threatens an avalanche. Moreover, his decision is deliberate. He has time to think, time to examine the snow. Not so the ski runner. The wind whistles past, and only a mottled look on the snow betrays the secrets of its surface. And, until he can diagnose snow while travelling at high speed, until he can carry a compass in his head, and instinctively allow for the difference in texture, according to the orientation and the steepness of the slope, he will spend more time on his back than on his feet. The simple categories into which the summer mountaineer must divide the snow are complicated in a thousand ways for the ski runner, who must learn to recognise, diagnose and foretell a whole gamut of snow values, each of which has its own significance and its own difficulties. For the ski runner the snow is no inert mantle on the hills, the shroud which buries those dead pastures which are waiting for the resurrection of the spring. It is alive with a multiple personality. He learns to love the snow as a friend, and to wrestle with it as an enemy.

The study of snow is endless. Every month has its lessons. Spring snow differs from winter snow, and summer snow has its own secrets. '*L'amore di qualunque cosa*,' wrote Leonardo da Vinci, '*e figliulo d'essa cognitione. L'amore é tanto piu fervente quanto la cognitione é piu certa*'. And perhaps because the ski runner is forced to study snow more intimately than the mountaineer, his love for this fickle feminine surface is 'tanto piu fervente.'

The worst and best moments in skiing are often separated only by seconds. You are standing at the top of some fierce slope which you have vowed to take straight. You look at the line and observe with sick disgust that the change of gradient is abrupt at the bottom, and that the slight bump half-way down will probably send you into the air. A kind friend says: "I shouldn't take that straight," and your enemy remarks: "Oh, it's safe enough. Jones took it straight yesterday."

And then suddenly, before you quite realise what has happened, you are oft. The wind rises into a tempest and sucks the breath out of your body. A lonely fir swings past like a telegraph pole seen from an express train. Your knees are as wax, and your stomach appears to have been left behind at the top. You fight against the tendency of your ski to run apart – the inevitable sequel to undiluted funk – by locking your knees and turning your ski on to their inside edges. And now comes the supreme crisis. The run-out where the gradient suddenly changes. You throw your weight forward, and mutter "Hold it, hold it." You clench your teeth, and make strange noises as the shock drives up through your legs. Your ski quiver with the strain… and you realise to your intense astonishment that you have not fallen.

The pace relaxes. The hurricane dies away. You are drunk with the wine of speed, and you marvel at the faint heart which so nearly refused the challenge. You glory in the sense of control which you have recaptured over your ski, no longer untamed demons hurrying you through space, but the most docile of slaves. You are playing with gravity. You are master of the snow. You can make it yield like water or resist like steel. Suddenly you decide to stop. A rapid Telemark, the snow sprays upwards, and the 'slabberie snow broth', to quote an old Elizabethan, 'has relented and melted about your heeles'.

A laugh floats upwards, and you much enjoy telling your enemy that his diagnosis was correct, and that he can safely venture to take it straight. And, if he falls, your triumph is complete.

Among Englishmen skiing is a new sport, and is still regarded by many as the poor relation of mountaineering. The ski runner is still looked upon with suspicion, as a vulgar fellow who invades the sacred haunts of the true mountain worshipper, and who regards the hills only as things to slide down. An older generation of mountain lovers greeted the mountaineer with similar taunts. There may be ski runners for whom the sport is everything and the environment nothing, and there may be mountaineers who justify Ruskin's famous sneer about greased poles and their climbers, but such men are exceptional. Skiing, so far from restricting, widens the range of our mountain sympathies. The ski runner has rediscovered the spell of the lower ranges, and the fascination of the great snow highways of the Alps. Romance for the mountaineer begins among the crags and icefalls, which alone can test his courage and his craft. But there is no hill, however humble, which cannot yield to the ski-runner emotions as intense as those which the mountaineer experiences in the kingdom which is all his own. A tramp up and down a mule path has no technical interest. The views from the Faulhorn and Brevent are the common possession of the mountaineer and the ski runner, but the business of getting up and down is mere monotony to the man who is eager to pit his strength against rock and ice. To the ski runner, however, every mood of hill and hollow has its own charm, every phase of the descent its own peculiar rhythm. The boot is a coarse medium of contact, but the ski respond sympathetically to undulations too trivial to be noticed by the pedestrian, who jogs downhill unconscious of all but the crudest changes of slope, and oblivious of a thousand subtle harmonies of gradient.

An older school of mountaineers criticised their successors for their alleged indifference to the charms of snow scenery. The modern cragsman has little use for easy snow passes, and need we blame him? I confess that the memory of those snow passes that I crossed on foot resolves itself in the main into recollections of wading down through the snow under the glare of the pitiless sun. Even the noblest of snow scenery is an anti-climax after hours of great adventure among the peaks. But when every pulse is throbbing with the thrill of a swift descent on ski, the mind is alert to observe and to record a thousand delicate beauties which are missed in a weary tramp. The details of glacier passes crossed on foot are blurred in my memory, but I can recall with meticulous accuracy every phase of those snow passes which I have crossed on ski. And I remember not only the changing tactics which each slope demanded, but also the details of the surrounding country, which never seems more beautiful than when it borrows from the ski something of the ski's own magic motion.

Skiing is not in competition with other forms of mountain activity. Indeed, skiing rounds off the mountain epic, and brings back drama and interest to those regions of the Alps which have hitherto been regarded as a necessary but perhaps monotonous preface to the romance of rock and ice.

To the ski runner Scheidegg and Parsenn Furka are names to conjure with no less than Charmoz and Mont Blanc. To the ski runner indeed there is 'neither hill nor hillock which doth not contain in it some most sweet memory of worthy matters'.

I began to ski at Chamonix in 1898. My father had given me a pair of ski, and I joined a small group composed of four or five other visitors who were making some half-hearted attempts at the new sport. They were not particularly successful, and I, for one, far preferred tobogganing.

In 1900 I made my first expedition on ski, the ascent of the Scheidegg from Grlndelwald, but it was not until I went to Adelboden in the winter of 1902–03 that I really fell in love with skiing. In those days very few people skied. Rickmers did not come to Adelboden until the following winter, and it was not until he appeared that skiing became generally popular. That first season Canon Savage, Percival Farrar, and a few others whose names I have forgotten, were almost the only visitors who ever attempted even the smallest tours on ski.

We made what was perhaps the first ski ascent of the Elsighorn, and perhaps the first ski ascent by visitors of the Laveygrat. On the Elsighom I broke a ski near the summit, and had to walk down. I climbed the Laveygrat on snow which had been drenched for three days by heavy rain and frozen solid by an intensely severe frost. We carried our ski up and we carried our ski down again. The snow was so hard that our boots left scarcely any impression. Snow which rests on grass or earth is never transformed into ice, for the water trickles down into the ground. Ice only forms when snow rests on an impermeable surface such as rock. The snow we found was not ice, but it was the nearest thing to ice that I have ever seen on the lower slopes. Just below the Laveygrat I slipped down a hundred yards on my back and was only stopped by the guide, who suddenly threw himself on the ground and received the full impact of my body in his stomach.

Our primitive equipment did not make matters any easier. We used the old-fashioned Norwegian ski without toe irons, and with a curious cane contraption in place of a heel strap. Skiing boots were unknown, and I climbed in my ordinary English boots. In consequence, I always suffered intensely from cold feet. On our third expedition that winter (the Schwandfeldspitz) I took off my boots to rub my feet in the snow in order to restore the circulation. One of my boots suddenly disappeared, and slid down a thousand feet over a slope of hard-crusted snow. Luckily the guide was able to retrieve it.

I had no skiing on the first two expeditions, and very little on the third, and yet I was far from being disappointed. The ski had served their purpose. They had given me the entry to a new world, or rather to an old world in a new and strangely beautiful dress. I enjoyed good running when I could get it, but I came back from the Elsighorn, where I had scarcely skied for five minutes, drunk with the beauty of my first view from a winter summit.

Today there is a broad highway up the Hahnenmoos. Ski runners leave Adelboden after a late breakfast and walk uphill on snow beaten hard by the tramp of their predecessors. In those days one set off even for these humble expeditions with a sense of real adventure. It was all so new. The Hahnenmoos was untracked when first I saw it, and the authentic spirit of the mountains haunted the Elsighorn, which is less than 8,000 feet in height, far more than it haunts today the Concordia Hut in the very heart of the glacier world, for the Concordia can be reached in an hour or so from the Jungfraujoch Railway Station.

Let me try to recall an early visit to the Laveygrat. We started, of course, before the dawn, for familiarity had not taught us to despise the expeditions which the modern novice gaily attempts at the end of his first week on ski. The stars paled as we tramped through the village street, and as we crossed the Engstligenbach the crest of the Albristhorn blazed up in honour of the sun. The mists still hung above the sluggish stream, and though the sun would soon hunt them away, their work was done and the long night had not been wasted. Tree and shrub were ready to welcome the new day in all the incomparable livery of hoar frost.

We followed the long valley to the pass. Behind the Ammertengrat we could see rays of cold light shooting out from an invisible focus. Suddenly a diamond point burned up on the crest of the Wildstrubel. The point broadened into a glowing arc, the arc became a semicircle, the semicircle changed slowly into the full orb of the sun. But the sun seemed, for the moment, to be played out, a cold, unsympathetic disk. Minutes passed before the cold blanket of air allowed its warmth to pass. The snow at our feet, pearl-grey flecked with a tracery of shadows, suddenly sparkled into life. Our bodies relaxed in the welcome warmth. It was glorious to be among the secret places of the hills just as the sleepy folk in Adelboden were thinking of breakfast. The slopes of the Hahnenmoos had lost that jaded look which they too often wear in the glare of midday. They were fresh and clean, cooled by the little breezes which are born when the rising sun meets the mists that form by night. A cow shed whose dark rafters set off the clinging snow, a persevering fence just clear of the white smother, these were the only links with the busy summer life of this cattle-haunted Alp. All else was sleep and silence. A solitary ski track cut the even fall of the slopes, as delicate as the line of a silverpoint engraving.

We lunched on the summit, an idle, windless hour of perfect contentment. Some hours later we re-crossed the bridge above the stream. We had not swept downhill in a series of Open Christianias varied by spectacular straight runs. We had leant heavily on our sticks and executed bastard stemming turns, but we were unconscious of shame. And as we wandered back through the pines we were haunted by the lingering echoes of the descent, memories of sudden dives into sheltered glades where the ski had driven up a wave of crystals breast high. Isolated pictures detached themselves from the cinematograph of the day, a pine outlined against the turquoise sky, a cornice moulded by the wind, the great surprise of the pass, the shadows on snowfields fifty miles away, the dreamlike enchantment of the great peaks.

We were lucky in those far-off days. Romance had not deserted the lower ranges. The modern ski runner must go further afield, must invade the glacier world, to discover the magic which for us haunted Elsighorn and Hahnenmoos… 'yesterday, many years ago'.

TALES FROM MONTENEGRO by Henrik Angell

Henrik August Angell (1861–1922) was a Norwegian military officer, sportsman, and writer. He was a ski pioneer and the first Norwegian delegate to the International Olympic Committee. Henrik Angell grew up in Bergen, Norway. This extract from 'Tales from Montenegro' tells of a ski trip from Cattaro to Cetinje.

What a wonderful winter landscape that met my eyes next morning in the rays of the rising sun! The shining white peaks and the mountain sides looked marvellous. Up there it was sunny and warm. Here, in the valley below, it was still shadow and cold, minus 10-15 degrees. And the mountain air, so fresh and cold! The majestic nature invited you, just like back home.

It was Sunday morning, with peace and quiet in the mind as well as in nature. And everything was joy and harmony. You felt brisk and strong, breathing easily, feeling completely free. Before your eyes the new, unknown country opened out in the glow of the sun, in expectation – and in your thoughts you were already on your way, further and further on, over the hill yonder, across the high mountains into the unknown, the enticing, the unfamiliar.

This is the wondrous experience of travelling in unknown regions: Your imagination can work freely, you can dream, build up new impressions and put yourself in the hands of adventure. And the indescribable feeling to move on the light skis along the compact, glittering white snow, without a path, no roads, here in the foreign country, so similar to my own, and yet so different, where all is interesting to the stranger who comes here: the scenery, the people, their customs, their way of life.

Two clergymen passed by – orthodox priests. Only their long hair and beard distinguished them from other Montenegrins. They, too, carried the revolver and handchar in their belt, at the back of their heads the small, dainty, Montenegrin cap with the red crown. Their dress was like everybody else's – a soldier's uniform. I never saw such ecclesiastical physiognomies. Their long hair might remind me of certain folk high-school or seminary pupils back home, but there the comparison stopped. These were tall, erect men, strong and supple, with faces bronzed by rough weather, aquiline noses, twinkling eyes, with proud – not arrogant – and stately appearance.

They greeted me gently, in a military way, smiled at the sight of the skis and hurried on to the church in Njegusch. I recognised one of them as one of the Montenegrins who the night before had been the most keen to try my skis, and who had obtained a storm of applause after a spectacular somersault in the deep snow.

The village church bells started to chime when I finally could say goodbye to my friendly landlord and landlady. The bells sounded so merrily in the wondrously clear winter morning. They bid me welcome into the hospitable, proud Montenegro, giving their blessing to my journey.

Soon you pass another village, which is Petrowitschi, the native district of the present prince's family. You are proudly guided to the house where the prince was born. His parents were Mirko Petrowitsch and Stana Martinovitsch, poor peasants who had to work hard to make ends meet. Mirko's brother, however, was the Zika, who after the death of vladika Petar II was proclaimed prince of Montenegro under the name Danilo I.

When he was killed by an assassin in 1860 in Cattaro, his nephew Nikolai was appointed his successor. This is the present prince, Nikita. (Nikita is a pet name for Nikolai, meaning 'little Nikolai'; the prince was very young when he acceded to power.)

From the plain the new road winds in innumerable serpentines up the long side of the mountain in front of us. It is an unbroken climb of more than 1,000 feet. Fortunately, the snow was hard-packed, if it is not it is hard work to force the 'Golo Brdo' (the naked mountain) on skis. If it had not been a question of prestige, I would have taken off my skis and carried them, taking the trampled path that my guide was walking.

From the highest point of the pass, 1,274 meters, or almost 4,000 feet above sea level, you have the most splendid view. In front of you, as far as the eye can see, only snow-capped mountains, peak after peak, all glittering white against the deep blue sky. Close by, the Lovtschen dominates impressively this congealed ocean of rocks and snow. In the distant horizon over there you see the Albanian mountains, right below you the bowl-shaped valley of Njegusch with its low houses, and even further down the shimmering blue expanse of the Adriatic. It is an incomparable panorama, but wild and dreary in its desolation. In summer the scenery is somehow cheered up by the green land around the houses, the patches of fields and the strips of hayfield that have been conquered from the barren land. Everywhere you find traces of the long, tenuous and victorious struggle against greedy neighbours and an inhospitable nature.

Here they have cleared the ground and broken rocks more than in any other place. Stone walls the height of a man, here and there sticking out of the snow, revealed the existence of a small patch of field, the size of a parlour floor.

It reminded me of the patches of field in my native Lærdal and Sogn. Indeed, the mountains, the valley, the climb up to Montenegro and to some extent the people itself made me more than once think about the valleys by the fjords in the interior of Sogn. When you advance even further on the height, you see a jumble of snow-clad mountains in the south – a whole alpine range. That is the Albanian Alps in all their magnificent beauty and wildness.

Under Maranai, a 5,000 feet high mountain, you spot a greyish expanse. That is the normally smiling, blue Skutari Lake with its luxuriant environment. Now you could see nothing but grey. The Skutari Lake was frozen and partly covered by snow! You could go skating on this lake of the South.

The sound of the bells is gradually fading, and we start the descent on the other side of Golo Brdo. The skis glide quicker and quicker, we swoop downhill until we reach more level ground. We are surrounded by nothing but wild, desolate nature. There could be houses in the valley below, but they are hidden under the snow. Where the track turns, we finally see human dwellings, two rather sizable stone buildings, only the roofs are visible. It must be a 'lokanda' or a 'kan'.

We step inside and enter a room that lies in darkness because of the masses of snow covering the windows. At the fire, where several men and women are seated, we meet acquaintances from yesterday, and then there are welcome greetings and lots of questions about the last adventures. I squatted like the rest of the company beside one of my skiing friends from the night before, and we enjoyed meeting again and telling about our most recent adventures, each in his own tongue – none of us understood his interlocutor.

The phrases of greeting, however, are a must, since they are standard.

"Pomaga ti Bog!" (God bless you), says the first one. "Dobra tisreschal" (Dobra ti sreca) (I wish you luck), answers the other one.

"Kako ste, brate?" (How are you, brother?)

"Dobro, hvala Bogu! Kako ti?" (Well, thank God – and how are you?)

"Dobro, hvala Bogu. Este li zdravi? Thanks, God willing. Are you in good health?

"Iesam Bogami, hvala Bogu." (Yes, I am, God willing.)

And then the Montenegrin asks about the wellbeing of your father, mother, brothers and sisters etc. Nobody must he left out.

"Dobro, hvala Bogu!" is the answer that you hear most often.

Alter all these obligatory civilities you can expect the same questions as in any locality in the Norwegian mountain regions: Where does this fellow come from, where is he going, what is his business etc.

When we had gone through all these questions, that Jovo answered, he groped for something in the deep pockets of his trousers. It was a piece of meat that he put in the smouldering ashes. It fizzled and sputtered in there, and it was soon finished. He let the scorching hot piece of meat rotate between his two hands until it was reasonably cooled. Then it was cleaned with some strokes by the back of his hand, and with the handchar that had cut off all those Turkish noses through the years, the meat was divided between Jovo and me. It was very salty – but anyhow edible.

After a lunch like this we were fit for heading for Cetinje, and set off briskly, once more to the great enthusiasm of the locals, who had never seen that it was possible to rush along like this on the deep snow.

There were the most wonderful slopes, and in some places we made a terrific speed. A shepherd who had seen from a distance a black shape rushing down a mountainside – faster than a horse could run – almost like the flight of a bird, sooner contacted the editor of the national newspaper, 'Glas Tsernagora', to inform him that he had observed no less a person than the Devil, or at least one of his nearest kin. 'The whirl of snow in his wake looked like smoke ...! It could not have been a human being, since travelling by steam has not yet been invented!'

Fortunately, no one threw fire or steel or shot with silver bullets. To avoid shooting was especially lucky – the Montenegrins are good marksmen.

We descend the new, excellent road, you expect getting sight of Cetinje, but it still takes some time. Finally, the mountains open up, and right below you see a vast plain, surrounded by mountains in all directions. Along the slopes there are some houses, and on the opposite side of the plain: There is Cetinje! – the capital of Montenegro.

You never saw such masses of snow! There seems to be more snow down there than up here. In many places the snow reaches the level of the roofs of the houses.

My priority number one was the possibility to go skiing. I was looking for ski hills. But when l had finished this, I was almost able to begin guessing which was which among the different buildings in Cetinje based on the numerous descriptions that I had already read. There was the arsenal, there the old, famous monastery, the church, the palace, the hospital and the entire small town.

Soon you are down on the plain. For half an hour we follow a long, equally broad road with young trees on both sides and around noon we find ourselves in the main street of Cetinje.

As you will remember, it was Sunday, and the street was teeming with Montenegrins, most of them men, taking a walk. In most places it was impossible to walk two abreast because of the incredible masses of snow piled up everywhere. So far there had not been time for clearing the street, they had just managed to make a sort of sunken road in the middle and along the walls of the houses. The heaps of snow by far exceeded the height of a man, and from the street it was impossible to see the windows on the ground floor. If you went skiing up on the heaps of snow, you could peep into the first floor.

At the end of the main street you spot the façade of at big stone building. That is the hotel, managed by Vouko Vuletitsch. That is where we will put up.

ESCAPE TO THE MOUNTAINS

A MEMOIR by A M Leni Riefenstahl

Helene Bertha Amalie 'Leni' Riefenstahl (1902–2003) was a German film director, producer and actress as well as scriptwriter, editing master, photographer and dancer. She is considered one of the most controversial figures in film history. On the one hand, she is revered by many filmmakers and critics as an 'innovative filmmaker and creative aesthete', on the other hand, criticised for her work in the service of propaganda during the Nazi era. Hitler commissioned her to film his large Nazi rallies, his campaign in Poland and the 1936 summer Olympics in Munich. One feels that this book is an excuse and an apology, an attempt to justify her friendship with Hitler and the Nazi Party, as much as a memoir.

After that I had only one wish… to leave Berlin as soon as possible. I did not want to run into Dr Goebbels again or for that matter, Hitler. Christmas was only a few days off however, and since my parents wanted to spend Christmas Eve with me, I decided to remain in Berlin until then. Besides, I still hadn't finished my series of articles for Manfred George. The first few instalments had already come out in 'Tempo'. After my return from Greenland, George had asked me to write a book about my experiences on location, and he had acquired the first serial rights for Tempo. My book was published in early 1933 by Hesse & Becker in Leipzig. Its title was 'Struggle in Snow and Ice'.

One day, when I returned from shopping, I found a bouquet outside my door. The accompanying card said: 'Du-Du, I'm back again and I'm staying at the Hotel Eden.' Josef von Sternberg was in Berlin after a three-year absence. We met the next day and I found he had hardly changed at all. He told me that Erich Pommer had invited him to make another film.

Naturally, the conversation turned on Hitler and National Socialism, and I told him about our encounters. To my amazement Sternberg said, "Hitler is a phenomenon – too bad that I'm a Jew and he's an anti-Semite. If he comes to power, we'll see whether his anti-Semitism is genuine or just campaign rhetoric." Incidentally, Sternberg was not the only one of my Jewish acquaintances to say such things. Harry Sokal and others made similar comments. I realise that today, when we know about the dreadful crimes that took place during the Hitler regime, all that sounds unbelievable, especially to younger people. But it is the truth.

Sternberg wanted to see 'The Blue Light'. We drove to the Geyer printing lab in Neukolln where my film material was stored. I was eager to hear his opinion, for I knew that he was a severe critic. But I was not disappointed.

"It's a beautiful film," he said, "and you are wonderful. There is no greater antithesis than that between you as Junta in 'The Blue Light' and Marlene as Lola in 'The Blue Angel'. I made Marlene: she is my creature. Now she's an international star. And you, when are you coming?"

"I'll come as soon as I've completed the shooting for 'SOS Iceberg'. I really hope it'll be by spring." With this promise we parted after celebrating our second farewell until midnight, with lots of champagne at the Eden Bar. This separation was to last a long time.

The next day, Christmas Eve, I was still far behind in preparing for my trip to the Swiss mountains where the shooting would take several months. As I was packing my bags the doorbell rang several times with deliveries of Christmas presents. When it rang again I yanked open the door and I stared aghast into the face of Dr Goebbels, wearing an embarrassed smile. Before I could utter a word, he said, "Please excuse me, I wanted to wish you a merry Christmas and bring you a small Yuletide gift."

I let him in, and when he saw the huge wardrobe trunk he asked in surprise: "Are you going on a trip?"

I nodded.

"Will you be away for a long time?"

I nodded again.

"Where are you going. When are you coming back?"

"I'll be gone for a long time. First I'm going on a skiing vacation and then I have to do my scenes for SOS Iceberg."

In some agitation Goebbels said, "Please don't go away." When I held up my hand to ward him off, he said, "Don't be afraid, I won't get too close, but I'd at least like to talk to you now and then. I'm so alone, my wife is seriously ill. She's in hospital, and I'm afraid she may die." He said this with such a poignant expression that I almost felt sorry for him, but I was much more sorry to hear that Magda Goebbels was in hospital.

"Listen, Doctor, your place is with your wife more than ever. You should spend every free moment with her."

I could not understand this man. Goebbels was very depressed. Despondently he sat down on the couch without removing his coat. "At least tell me where you can be reached, so that I can telephone you."

"I don't know where I'll be. I'm going to a different winter resort, and I have no idea when the shooting will start."

Once he realised how hopeless his efforts were, all human quality vanished from his features. His face now looked like a mask as he handed me two small packages, muttering, "A Yuletide greeting."

When the door shut behind him, I opened his gifts. One package contained a copy of Hitler's 'Mein Kampf' bound in red leather, with a personal dedication from Goebbels. The second package contained a bronze medallion with a relief of Goebbels' head. What bad taste, I thought, to make me a present of himself.

It was good to be in the mountains again. In St Anton on the Arlberg I was able to improve my skiing with Hannes Schneider and learn the latest techniques at what was perhaps the finest skiing school in the world.

One afternoon, when I returned to the Hotel Post after skiing, the manager told me that a certain Dr Goebbels had rung me up several times. How had he tracked me down in St Anton? No sooner had I changed my clothes than I was summoned to the telephone. It was Goebbels again. I was upset, and asked him who had revealed my whereabouts to him, but he answered merely that he had called up several skiing resorts till he found me. I didn't know if I could believe him.

"What do you want from me?"

"I only wanted to find out when you'll be back in Berlin." His stubbornness was beyond belief. Coldly I said, "I won't be back for the time being, and please leave me in peace, Herr Goebbels, and don't telephone me anymore."

I hung up. My mood was spoiled for the rest of the evening.

In mid-January I travelled to Davos, lured by the Parsenn skiing area – a dream area for skiers, which surpassed all my expectations. There were miles of downhill terrain covered with powder snow and so many routes that you could pick a different one every day, each more beautiful than the last.

On the Parsenn I ran into Walter Prager, whom I had first met in St Anton. Surprisingly this young Swiss had become the Kandahar champion. He offered to train me for the Parsenn-Derby race, and skiing was even more fun with him, for he was a first-class trainer. I made progress day after day and we now trained by the clock.

Walter Prager and I developed a friendship. In time it grew deeper, resulting in a romance that lasted for two years. Oddly enough, I have never fallen in love with men who were socially, politically or artistically prominent, or who spoiled women with expensive gifts. When my mother eventually met Walter she wasn't very happy about my choice.

"What do you see in the boy?" she asked. "You never show up with an intelligent man. I don't understand you." Poor Mama, how could I explain it to her? Walter was handsome but did not make much of an impression at first. Soon, however, I was utterly entranced by his special charm, his vivacity, his personal appeal. It is not easy to make people understand sudden feelings of liking and love – not even people one is as close to as I was to my mother.

Our Swiss location shooting was delayed from week to week, but I didn't mind. I was in Davos in late January when I was surprised by the sensational news: Hitler had become Chancellor of Germany. So, he had made it. I didn't know how, for I had read no newspapers for weeks. Since there was no television in those days, I didn't watch the day of Hitler's takeover and the torchlight parade until years after the war, in old newsreels. Hitler had achieved his goal, and as Chancellor he interested me a lot less than he did before the takeover.

In early February I was finally called to location shooting at the Bernina Lodge. At the time I was still in Davos. My bags were already packed when, without warning, Udet turned up. "What are you doing here?" I asked, surprised.

"I'm calling for you," he said impishly.

"How?" I asked, nonplussed. "In your plane?"

"Of course in my plane." Udet was unbelievable. I sent my mountains of luggage on by rail and climbed into the sports plane which Udet had landed on the small frozen lake in Davos.

At take-off we almost had an accident. The area for taxiing was small and there was a stiff tail wind. Terrified, I saw that our plane was dashing straight towards the hayricks at the end of the lake. But with his innate skill Udet pulled the plane aloft just before it reached the haystacks. After a brief flight we landed effortlessly and to a warm welcome on the small icy surface of Lake Bernina, right beside our sets. I greeted Fanck and his colleagues and also the movie people who had come from Hollywood. Tay Garnett was directing the American version, in which 'Rod la Roque' was the male lead.

The ice sets were fantastic. The architects had built a genuine polar landscape containing huge ice caverns and I was pleased to see that working relationships were generally harmonious. Tay Garnett and Dr Fanck seemed to have a fine rapport. It was a real pleasure working with Garnett, although it was a pity the weather was so bitterly cold and the shooting prolonged for such a long time. Luckily, I often had long breaks, and our executive producer, Paul Kohner, was generous enough to allow me to fly to Davos with Udet on my free days. I could continue my ski training on the Parsenn, and my efforts were crowned with success. I participated in the renowned Parsenn Derby, along with the best female racers in Switzerland and, after skiing down the long run, I won second prize.

It was already May, and the shooting still hadn't ended. The ice was starting to melt, so that we had to climb further up. As a result we transferred to the Jungfrau Pass, which looms ten thousand feet high in the Berne Alps, and it was here that, most important of all, the scenes with the sled dogs were to be shot. At last, in June, the final footage of the 'Greenland' film was completed.

BOYHOOD ISLAND by Karl Ove Knausgård

Karl Ove Knausgård (1968) is a Norwegian author. He became known worldwide for six autobiographical novels, titled 'My Struggle (Min Kamp)'. He has been described as 'one of the 21st century's greatest literary sensations'.

At the start of December, three days before my birthday and two days before mum came home again, I was sitting on the toilet having a dump when the familiar sound of dad's car turning and parking in the drive was not followed by the equally familiar sound of a door being opened and closed but the doorbell ringing.

What could this be?

I hurriedly wiped my arse, pulled the chain, yanked up my trousers, opened the window above the bathtub and poked my head out. Dad was standing beneath me wearing a new anorak. On his legs he wore knee-length breeches and long blue socks, and on his feet a pair of blue and white boots, all equally new.

"Come on!" he said. "We're going skiing!"

I got dressed in a flash and went outside, where he was tying my skis and sticks to the roof-rack beside a pair of brand new long wooden Splitkein skis.

"Have you bought yourself some skis?" I said.

"Yes," he said, "isn't it great? So we can go skiing together."

"OK," I said. "Where are we going then?"

"Let's go to the west of the island," he said. "To Hove."

"Are there pistes there?"

"There? Oh yes!" he said. "They've got the best."

I doubted it but didn't say anything, got in the car beside him, how unfamiliar he looked in his new clothes, and then we left for Hove. Not a word was said until he parked and we got out.

He had driven through Hove Holiday Centre, which consisted of a large number of red houses and huts originating from the last war, most probably built by the Germans. Like the firing range which, I had heard rumoured, had been an aerodrome and like the concrete gun emplacements towering above the sea-smoothed rocks and the pebble beaches close to the edge of the forest and the fascinating low bunkers among the trees, where we used to play on the roofs and in the rooms when we were here in the afternoon on 17 May celebration days. He had driven past all this, along a narrow road into the forest which came to an end by a small sand quarry, where he stopped and parked.

After taking the skis off the roof, he came over with a little case full of ski waxing equipment he had also bought. We waxed the skis with blue Swix, which, after reading the back of one of the tubes, he said had to be the best. Apparently unfamiliar with bindings, it took him a bit longer to put on his skis than it did me. Then he put his hands through the loops on the poles. But he didn't do it from underneath so that the loop wouldn't slip off even if you lost hold of the pole. No, he put his hands straight through. That was how small children who knew no better held them. It hurt me to watch, but I couldn't say anything. Instead I took my hands out and then threaded them through again so that, if he was paying attention, he could see how it was done. But he wasn't watching me; he was looking up at the little ridge of hills above the sand quarry.

"Let's get going then!" he said.

Although I had never seen him ski before, I could never have dreamed in my wildest imagination that he couldn't ski. But he couldn't. He didn't glide with the skis, he walked as he normally walked without skis, taking short plodding steps which on top of everything else were unsteady, which meant that every so often he had to stop and poke his poles into the snow so as not to topple over.

I thought perhaps this was just the beginning and soon he would find his rhythm and glide as he should glide along the piste. But when we reached the ridge, where the sea was visible between the trees, grey with frothy, white-flecked waves, and started to follow the ski tracks he was still walking in the same way. Occasionally he would turn and smile at me.

I felt so sorry for him. I could have shouted out aloud as I skied. 'Poor dad. Poor, poor dad.'

At the same time I was embarrassed, my own father couldn't ski, and I stayed some distance behind him so that potential passers-by wouldn't associate me with him. He was just someone out ahead, a tourist, I was on my own, this was where I came from, I knew how to ski.

The piste wound back into the forest, but if the view of the sea was gone its sounds lingered between the trees, rising and falling, and the aroma of salt water and rotten seaweed was everywhere. It blended with the forest's other faintly wintry smells, of which the snow's curious mixture of raw and gentle was perhaps the most obvious.

He stopped and hung on his ski poles. I came alongside him. A ship was moving on the horizon. The sky above us was light grey. A pale greyish-yellow glow above the two lighthouses on Torungen revealed where the sun was.

He looked at me.

"Skis running well?" he said.

"Pretty well," I said. "How about you?"

"Yes," he said. "Let's go on, shall we? It'll soon be time to head for home. We have to make dinner as well. So, away you go!"

"Don't you want to go first?"

"No, you head off. I'll follow."

The new arrangement turned everything in my head upside down. If he was behind me he would see how I, someone who knew how to ski, skied and realise how clumsy his own style was. I saw every single pole plant through his eyes. They cut through my consciousness like knives. After only a few meters I slowed down, I began to ski in a slower, more staccato style, not unlike his, just not as clumsy, so that he would understand what I was doing, and that was even worse. Beneath us the white, frothy breakers washed lazily onto the pebble beach. On the rocks, in some places, the wind whirled snow into the air. A seagull floated past, its wings unmoving. We were approaching the car, and on the last little slope I had an idea, I changed the tempo, and went as fast as I could for a few meters, then pretended to lose my balance and threw myself into the snow beside the piste. I got up as quickly as possible and was brushing my trousers down as he whistled past.

"It's all about staying on your feet," he said.

We drove home in silence, and I was relieved when we finally turned into our drive and the skiing trip was definitively over. Standing in the hall and taking off our skiing gear, we didn't say anything either. But then, as he opened the door to the staircase, he turned to me.

"Come and keep me company while I'm cooking," he said. I nodded and followed him up.

In the living room he stopped and looked at the wall. "What on earth…" he said. "Have you noticed this before?"

I had forgotten all about the streak of orange juice. My surprise as I shook my head must have had a dash of authenticity about it because his attention wandered as he bent down and ran his finger over the thin line of orange. Even his imagination would hardly stretch far enough to guess it was caused by my flinging an orange at the floor just there, on the landing outside the kitchen.

He straightened up and walked into the kitchen. I sat down on the stool as usual, he took a packet of pollock from the fridge, placed it on the worktop, fetched flour, salt and pepper from the cupboard, sprinkled it on a plate and began to turn the soft, slippery fillets in the mixture.

"Tomorrow after school we'll go to Arendal and buy you a birthday present," he said without looking at me.

"Shall I go with you? Isn't it supposed to be a secret?" I said.

"Well, you know what you want, don't you?" he said. "Football kit, isn't it?"

"Yes."

"You can try it on and then we'll know if it fits," he said, pushing a knob of butter from the knife into the frying pan with his finger.

BIRKEBEINEREN by Laila Stien

Laila Stien (1946) is a Norwegian novelist, poet, author of children's literature and translator. She grew up in Rana and later lived in Finnmark, Norway's northernmost county. She has won several literary prizes. She made her literary debut in 1979 with the short stories collection 'Nyveien'.

This vignette was translated by Ingrid Christophersen.

SOUND IN MIND AND BODY

I remember the year when Roald and Jens, my husband and Rita's (we were both still married then) started an intense exercising regime.

They had decided to enter the Birkebeiner cross country race. Once upon a time Roald had been a good skier. Jens, not quite as good, but according to Roald he had potential. Roald drew up a training programme for his mate focusing on balance. Jens trained night and day. If at night he had to answer the call of nature he would hop on one foot. In addition to balance it was of course everything to do with fitness. They ran. And they ran. They were both of average build and the slight age-related rubber tyre round the tummy was not too unbecoming. They were reasonably athletic, I have to say, shoulders broader than the bum, and muscles developed from normal activity such as carpentry, wood cutting and hand wrestling. The small accumulation in front would soon fall away, they maintained.

They started planning already during the finishing stages of this year's Birkebeiner. They sat in comfy chairs, in front of the telly, with a few pints. There and then they started planning ahead. The big shots had just crossed the finish line, receiving well-earned tributes from onlookers; the also-rans were still dribbling in, forming a diagonal line of humanity from refreshment stands to refreshment stand, accepting scattered hurrahs, Ribena and a pat on sweaty shoulders en-route to honour and a diploma. The sun was shining, the mood was high; the TV screen oozed well-being, public rejoicing and a healthy lifestyle. Roald and Jens drank to each other, they were in our house, I remember; I had offered them freshly made coffee which they politely refused.

Our husbands started enthusiastically and made vigorous inroads into the savings accounts. They needed air permeable tracksuits, energy absorbing running shoes, a watch to monitor the pulse, up-to-date indoor clothing, new skis with all the paraphernalia, plus the very latest super-light cross-country boots. This was about 8 to 10 years ago, thank God; today the savings account raid would have been considerably higher. This was before cera powder, carbon ski sticks at 2,999 crowns a snip, underwear with infrared radiation to combat lactic acid, and preparatory camps at Gol instructing correct transfer of weight and double poling. But it was bad enough. Skis and running gear, Swix wax in every conceivable colour, klister, cork, rucksack, hat, gloves, all new.

The salary was just not adequate. Hard-earned savings, in case of unforeseen expenses, such as car repairs or water leakages, were broken into. We ladies grumbled but were told this was a sensible investment. After all, this was all about life. Investments made now would be repaid, with interest, in the shape of increased energy and 'joie de vivre'. Never mind the last one I thought to myself. I worked in a nursing home and had witnessed that increased joie de vivre was not something I aspired to. Although capacity to work was not to be sniffed at, but in which areas would this manifest itself? Would it include the home front?

Neither Rita nor I made too much fuss about all the spending. Noticed it of course but refrained from saying too much. Our men folk were, after a short period, transformed from mildly disagreeable couch potatoes to jovial athletes with decreasing paunches. They were inspired and motivated and everything was aimed at creating a positive atmosphere at home.

Roald and Jens ran and ran. Now, in early spring, there was snow only in the mountains, so skiing was limited to weekends. Their drive had never been stronger since the time when they were both confirmed, and when both, separately, had dreamt of joining Manchester United or Liverpool as professionals. They started with 30 minutes on the treadmill, had read somewhere that this was a sensible start. After two months they were walking two hours with pulses of 130 and 145. According to experts, a very commendable half-way goal. A lot of this was very enjoyable. Inspiration literally shone out of my greying, soon middle aged, husband. Body fat had been reduced from 20 to 16 % and a new light shone out of his eyes, and he was, I must admit, quite attractive. Had he missed one or other of the week-end cross-country training camps there would definitely have been a treat – at home. Although, I have to say, it did not appear that he missed these treats.

The two training mates ran every day and rushed off to the mountains every weekend, for as long as the snow lasted. They dropped News Night, Sports Night, Match of the Day and Grand Prix. The children were teenagers in those days and did not seem to mind being out of reach of their father's, from time to time, critical remarks. The sofa was mine after supper and I didn't mind that either.

In any free moment, in as far as there were any free moments, he served up animated talks about the Birkebeiner Race and he held forth with great gusto. The Birkebeiner Race (or Birken as he now called it), was started in 1932 and had run every year, bar the war years and a few others owing to bad weather. Otherwise, the annual race had grown every year. Many thousands now took part. For some, finishing the race was the most important, but not for him, nor for Jens, my one-time husband made me understand. Which I only half-heartedly believed. The race covered a distance of 54 kilometres and ran mostly over high mountain terrain, windswept and harsh. Total vertical ascend was 950 metres. Not sure why he told me all this, maybe he was frightened that I might join him. However, he lay out with a lot of charming enthusiasm and I had not the heart to tell him I already knew all this.

After all, I was there when it all began, on the sofa, when we watched that year's Birken on telly. I saw both start and finish and heard the commentary. But I was pleasant and supportive and made remarks like: "What fun it will be"; "I imagine it will be wonderful to finish"; "you're bound to make the diploma as hard as you have trained." Nice things. I noticed they helped build enthusiasm. Sometimes he marched straight into the kitchen and did the washing up.

I noticed the day he started limping. There was now no snow in the mountains, and it was all about running. Plus, various activities in the gym, mostly weightlifting, bench press and other types of weight training. They kept a diary. Jens' bench press had reached 70 kilos. Roald, who had been a smidgen ahead all the time, registered 75 kilos. Take it easy, I said. Your foot. "Shit, it's nothing", he said. "No", I said.

In the end he had to give up. Not for me but for the pain in the left ankle – the Achilles tendon. As far as Roald was concerned, running and lifting had to take a back seat. Jens was a loyal friend and accompanied him to the swimming pool. This must have been deadly boring compared to exercising in God's great outdoors. For many years this stuff about the outdoors had been underrated, it could now cure anything. Fresh air and silence, whispering wind and sunshine, gurgling streams and birdsong. Those were things they had never really noticed. The meaning of it, the benefit to the soul's tranquillity and harmony. We never contradicted them, we who fed them and looked after our teenagers. We were not against whispering wind, but we clearly lacked some of their motivation regarding outdoor life. Or at least their variety.

The heel got better with Voltarol and bathing in lukewarm water. The running continued. Autumn arrived and with it entry deadlines. Birken rules stipulate that if you have good results from previous races you can start in the so-called seeded group. They are the athletes who are on the front line and get most of the attention. If you have no results with which to show off you have to start right in the middle of the huge horde at the back. Our guys were OK with that – the first year.

Entry dues were paid, nearly 1,000 crowns, if I remember correctly. Life went on. Work, food, training. Food started to play an important role. Just after the New Year it all kicked in. No longer were fish fingers, or similar types of fast food, adequate for supper. Now it was all about proteins.

Starting in the middle of January our Birken debutants increased their training dose. With a short workout in the morning in a gym (at 50 kroner a snip); it was too dark and chilly outside. Roald left home at the crack of dawn, came home around midday for some nourishment and a quick crash recharge in the easy chair.

It is funny how what we get in small doses becomes attractive. I actually missed Roald. Missed his presence, missed him in the sitting room, our sitting room, the one we had furnished together. It was quite a nice feeling. I think I can actually admit that this period, exercise period number one, as Rita called it, really was the best time Roald and I had together. My slightly morose life partner had seen the light. That happened about 6 months into the training period, in the bathroom. The six-pack. Where the not too embarrassing sausage roll had been, right on the front of his stomach, there was now a very obvious six-pack. Body fat was by now down to 14%. It was a great moment. Roald beamed like a sun, elated. It did not matter that more domestic duties had fallen to me – I was praised. He praised the food, which he said I had taken endless trouble with, praised the system I managed to maintain in drawers and cupboards which had enabled him to find what he wanted. Things like that. He said things about me too – something I was wearing, my hair, different things.

Birken was approaching. He could no longer keep it a secret that the diploma was his goal. He bubbled over with joy, betrayed himself. Jens had by now reached 75 kilos bench press, Roald was stuck on 80. It seemed he had reached his maximum, but that was OK – he was strong enough. They had been to some institute or other to have their oxygen intake measured. Both passed with flying colours, considering their age, plus or minus 45. They were ready.

March approached. They had spent the last months on the flood-lit trails, three-hour trips with an average of 10 kilometres an hour. The technique was mastered, most things were mastered. They booked ski tuning and hotel. They deserved one night in Lillehammer. Long way to drive home having passed the finish line, tired and hungry. And thirsty. Monday was time enough; they had arranged time off in lieu. They could both do slightly better concerning oxygen intake, so they ratcheted up one more gear, got up 30 minutes early for a morning run. New measurements on March 10th and Roald had increased his intake by 2%, now up to 50, and was overjoyed.

From the beginning of January shopping took 30 minutes more. Everything had to be scrutinised, all the small writing read. Percentage content of this and that. Figures for carbohydrates must not be too high, protein content however could never be high enough. Then fat content. This needed a steady hand, not to have the misfortune of buying ordinary sausage meat with 14% fat for the evening taco. No, good minced beef, 6%. Friday evenings and favourite telly programmes were resurrected. Even a few cans of beer were justified, once a week of course.

Everything was hunky dory. Then came the bang. Rita was off on a course. She was a shop steward and of course had to keep abreast concerning her employees' welfare. She was clever like that. She was a brainy girl and spoke well. She wasn't going far but would be away from Friday to Sunday. This was the week before Birken so Jens was home. He wanted to scale down the training and concentrate on recharging. Thus, he could keep an eye on the very independent children and keep the house in order. He cooked, hoovered, washed the kitchen floor and shook the carpets in the hall, they were full of sand as there was now no snow around. Jens bravely set to work, he was in great shape. But the last duty, carpet shaking, was one exercise his body, in spite of all the training, was not ready for. That was a discipline that had not been taken into consideration. On the door step, in the hall of his and Rita's home, he suddenly and brutally seized up. It was his back. He sank to the ground and remained lying, like a wet rag, on the carpets. Later he told us that he had heard a crack.

There and then Birken ended for Jens.

Roald took it hard. They had as good as reached the end together and were supposed to have finished together too. For Jens this was 360 days poured down the can. And all because of Rita and her hysterical cleanliness. Fancy going off to a seminar at this point.

Roald wanted to take it easy the few days before the race, but now he had to let off a bit of steam. He went for a run.

The next day my husband threw in the trowel. The Achilles, right and left leg this time. Both were severely inflamed. Under normal circumstances he would have rushed off to A&E for a cortisone injection, anti-inflammatory pills, referral to a physiotherapist, laser treatment and anything else conceivable that might be useful to cure impediment and pain. But he didn't. He sat down, resigned, I suppose. The Birken day dawned. The sun was shining at Rena, there was sun and perfect conditions over Døl Mountain, Nysætra and Kvarstaddammen. Sunshine and sparkling conditions over Raufjellet, Midtfjellet, Sjusjøen, all the way to Lillehammer.

We were watching telly at home. Rita was there too. Not that she is awfully interested, but she must have learnt at the seminar that it is important, for everyone, at certain times of their life, to have support.

Rita and I ate cake and freshly brewed coffee. Jens and Roald drank ice-cold beer. Not any old beer. I had served up their favourite brew.

CHAPTER 15
THE SAMI

INTRODUCTION by Ingrid Christophersen

Modern ski equipment is now available to young Laplanders, and the romantic notion of Sami skiing on home-made local type of skis has now gone forever. They no longer wear the traditional *skaller* – reindeer-skin footwear, with upturned toe which made it easy to hook, or unhook, the boot under a simple strap. Stockings and socks were replaced by beaten *sennegrass*, a widely distributed sedge with grass-like leaves that is used by Arctic and Antarctic explorers as insulating material. When dirty and smelly, the grass is thrown away and replaced by fresh grass. *Skaller* were the height of fashion when I was young, and we all wore them in the winter. Not cheap. Today I imagine such behaviour would be called *cultural appropriation*.

Reindeer herdsmen today use snowmobiles, and snort at the idea that all cars in Norway must be carbon neutral by 2025. Where on the vast inland plateau will you find electric car charging services? They laugh at the politicians! In minus 40° Centigrade, what is the range of an electric car?

This piece from 'A New Tale of Finmark' talks about 'snowshoes' when in fact it should read 'skis'. The book was printed in 1888, the year Nansen crossed Greenland and the concept of skis and skiing had not yet been formulated.

Jens Andreas Friis (1821-1896) was a Norwegian philologist, lexicographer and author. He was a university Professor and a prominent linguist in the languages spoken by the Sami people. His is widely recognised as the founder of the studies of the Sami languages. Today he is also commonly associated with his novel 'Lajla – A New Tale of Finmark' which became the basis for a 1929 silent film.

JAAMPA ON SNOWSHOES AFTER THE WOLF by Jens Andreas Friis

Many years ago, Aslak Laagje was the richest mountain Lapp in Finmark. He owned a herd from three thousand to four thousand reindeer, and to tend these he kept serving men and maidens, not to speak of a whole troop of dogs.

Two of his hired men were named respectively 'Jaampa' and 'Jouno'. Jaampa was of pure Lapp blood and in exterior a true type of his race. His mouth was large, his nose small and somewhat flattened, his eyes small and blinking, his cheek bones high, his hair black and tangled, and his whole face furrowed and wrinkled like a piece of birch bark. Besides, he was tanned entirely brown from heat and cold, smoke and rain, hail, wind, and snow. He was not handsome, not even in a Lapp maiden's eyes. Indeed, he had fared so poorly at the hands of the female sex, that at the age of nearly forty years, he still found himself unable to procure a wife. He was not a meek man, nor could he even be called pious in a Christian sense. I am afraid, on the contrary, he must be said to have been a heathen.

He had been, sure enough, both baptised and confirmed; but his religious education had been conducted during that period of the past century when Lapp children were obliged, by law, to study the teachings of the church in Norwegian. Jaampa had thus, no doubt, learned just barely enough of the Norwegian Catechism to be admitted for confirmation by the minister; but he had, probably, according to the phrase of the time, 'nothing understood of what he had heard, read or sung'. Later in life, he had discarded the book and thereby cast his religion overboard.

Mother Laagje, who was a pious woman, and who knew a number of prayers both in Lappish, Finnish, and Norwegian, had often said to him:

"Jaampa, Jaampa, what will become of you on judgment day. You, who never pray, morning or evening?"

"I don't know Daro" (Norwegian), he would answer; "how, then, can I pray to the Norwegian God, when He doesn't understand Same" (Lappish).

To this mother Laagje never knew how to reply; for she also had heard that the Bishop, impossible as it may seem, had declared that 'our Lord would not hear Lappish, but only Norwegian prayers'.

The Bishop thought, no doubt, thereby to induce them, with so much greater eagerness, to lay hold of Norwegian. But Jaampa would not learn Norwegian, nor could he even if he wished it ever so much; for who would teach him?

What, then, did he do? He had again recourse, in secret, to the Lappish gods, who still were not quite forgotten, and whose images yet stood here and there on hill and strand. These, he thought, must at least, be just as skilled in languages as himself, or understand both Lappish and Finnish, which he spoke equally well. He prayed then, his own way; but when he prayed, where he prayed, and what his prayers were, the Lord alone knows!

Jaampa had an unruly, passionate temper. Yet he was not really a bad man. He was fondly attached to little children, and often, when he had an opportunity, showed kindness to people who were poorer than himself. But, if he became vexed or provoked, he was no better than a wild beast. For he shunned nothing, feared nothing and had no respect for things either divine or human.

Why, then, did Laagje have this man in his service?

Well, Jaampa had also his virtues and good qualities. He was uncommonly large for a Lapp, but still as nimble as a cat, and of great endurance in walking and running; especially did he excel in sliding on snowshoes. Few were as clever as he in taking care of the deer herd, in breaking them for driving, in slaughtering them, in training dogs, and above all, in chasing the wolves on snowshoes. Many a one had laid down his life because of Jaampa's knife. Half a wolf himself, he was their sworn and mortal enemy. He was therefore well-liked and prospered well at the hands of his gentle master Laagje, and had good wages. Every fall he was given three breeding deer, and of course also the calves they might have. In this manner he had, like many a one serving a mountain Lapp, procured for himself a small herd of about a hundred deer.

These were, of course, marked in the ears with his own self-chosen sign, different from his master's and all others. Jaampa drank when and where he could lay hold of liquor, and so long and in such quantities, that he would be left lying wherever he happened to be, in a house or out on the ground, in snow and cold. It sometimes happened that when he woke up after a drunken sleep, his long-tangled hair would be frozen fast in the snow and ice, so that he would have to use his knife to free himself.

Jouno differed entirely from Jaampa in being an agreeable and good-natured fellow. He talked, jested and chattered incessantly. Like many a Lapp, he was a child in mind and thought. Still he also had his virtues. He was clever in handicraft, making sledges and snowshoes, carving spoons and divers implements out of deer horns, and was skilled in fishing and capturing grouse, and handy about helping the women milk the deer, and kindred employments. Taken altogether, Jouno was a Jacob and Jaampa was an Esau. These two men shared the same tent, according to the custom and practice of the country, while, on the other hand, the serving girls slept in the family tent.

The winter when these incidents happened, Laagje had pitched his tents on Akkanas Mountain, a few miles from Karasjok, his numerous herd roaming round about.

The wolves had been already very troublesome in the early part of winter, and the servants, two and two at a time, had been out constantly both day and night, to keep watch. Still the wolves had succeeded in killing a number of deer. Several packs had been seen, and it was feared that later in the winter they would be still worse.

It had also been noticed that among the wolves there was one of unusual size, and of a slightly different colour from the common Norwegian sort. It was supposed to be a Russian wolf, come over from Siberia.

Jaampa was in constant bad temper, because this monster had killed one of his excellent sledge deer, although there had been hundreds of others to select from. He spent one day hunting this one on snowshoes, but had been obliged to give up the chase as the snow was not deep enough, and the wolf therefore, could easily get away.

Jaampa sighed and prayed, but likely not to our Lord, that there might soon come a heavy snowfall, so that he could try a race under favourable circumstances with this robber wolf.

Finally, one day the clouds began to gather and in proportion as they thickened, Jaampa's face began to clear. He put a new charge in his short Lapp rifle, selected the longest and widest snowshoes and greased them with deer fat.

Then came the snow. Silently and softly, in larger and larger flakes. It fell down from the dark vault of heaven and lay deep down in the valleys and on the heights where usually it is wont to drift away. For this reason, the wolf, when he is pursued, usually takes to the hills as he can there the more easily escape.

Jaampa's face beamed and he set extra night watches in expectation of the wolves. But several nights went by without sight or sound of them, so that it was almost believed they had gone away altogether.

Jaampa was both pleased and displeased at this. It was, of course, well that they kept away. Still, he would willingly have first tried a race, in good earnest, with that big wolf. In the meantime, he must again take up his wonted duties. One forenoon he was busy breaking a deer down on the ice of a lake right in front of the tents. The young buck had, sometime before, gone through his first lesson according to

Jaampa's educational method. This consisted of tying him with a long line or deer skin strap to the top of a tolerably tall, slim and elastic birch tree, and then letting him stand there pulling and jerking at it. The birch tree would bend every time the deer made a leap in his furious struggles to get loose. But, like the salmon on the line of a well-trained angler, it had, at last, to give in and be quiet, and submit to fate in the shape of a rein and halter. Then Jaampa, as before mentioned, took it with him down on the ice, and fastened a sledge to the end of the tug. At first, the wild animal is very suspicious of the sledge or object which it sees coming after it. It thinks perhaps that it is a wolf or some other enemy pursuing it, but gradually, as it begins to lose fear of the sledge, the tug is made shorter.

Jaampa and the deer tossed and tumbled about on the ice. Sometimes the deer being master pulled Jaampa down and dragged him along for a while. But there was no danger of jolts or bruises on the even surface of the ice and Jaampa held his own until, by and by, the deer had to submit, move slowly, and pull the empty sledge after it. Later, it would be harnessed to one partly loaded, between tamed deer, and obliged without more ado to move along with the rest.

Laagje was in his tent looking after the meat pot, which was boiling for dinner. In a mountain Lapp's household, it is the husband who cooks or minds the pot, while the wife's work consists chiefly in making clothes, shoes, dressing skins, tending the children and so on.

Jouno was engaged in working at a 'pulkka', or deér sledge. Everything breathed peace and quiet when, suddenly, someone was seen dashing down the steep hillside on the opposite shore of the lake, shouting something which was not instantly understood. It was none other than one of the serving girls who that day kept watch. Jaampa suspended his reindeer drill and listened. Then he heard distinctly the cry: "Gumpe læ botsuin!" (The wolf is after the reindeer!)

Now if there is any cry which can rouse a Lapp out of a doze, a dream, a sleep or even a drunken stupor, it is this. Yea, I am afraid that a mountain Lapp, even if he were on his knees before the altar receiving the Sacrament from the minister's hand, would spring to his feet and set off if anyone should enter the church and suddenly cry in his ear, "Gumpe læ botsuin!"

Jaampa instantly let go the deer and set off on a run up towards the tents. He also called, "Jouno, Laagje, gumpe læ botsuin!" No sooner was Jaampa's cry heard, than Jouno flung the knife and Laagje the ladle. And together, with the women and all the dogs from their lurking places, came rushing out. Everything was in an uproar, and, while the men hurried to put on their snowshoes, the panting girl related how a pack of wolves had come suddenly dashing towards them, and that, when attempting to face them, the large wolf, at the head of the others, had come close up to them and showed his teeth, so that they had drawn back in terror and defended themselves with their staffs. Then she had hurried off to the tents to give the alarm, while the other girl, as well as she could, followed the herd.

Jaampa flung his rifle over his shoulder and thrust a few deer tongues in his bosom; for he knew not how long the hunt might last. At any rate, he was not going to give it up for the first two or three days. That he promised himself. Off they started, all three, in the direction in which the reindeer had taken their flight according to the girl's report. Nor was it long before they caught sight of the large herd which again had collected itself into a close body. When they came up however, they found that the wolves had succeeded in forcing about one hundred deer out of the main troop. These had started in a north easterly direction pursued by the wolves, which, in the usual way, sought to force them apart in order afterwards, two and two to pursue single deer.

Laagje stayed behind to help the girl drive the herd back to the tents. Jaampa and Jouno kept on after the wolves. They soon found the tracks so there was no difficulty in following them. After traversing the distance of about seven miles they discovered drops of blood on the snow, causing them to suspect that the large wolf had had his teeth in a deer. Some distance farther on they found a deer torn in pieces and half-devoured by the wolves which had already taken flight again.

Jaampa examined the mark in the ears and discovered that it again was one of his own deer that the wolves had caught. If he was not enraged before he certainly became so now.

"Would that Satan or Jaampa had hold of you, damned, bloody tyrant that you are!" cried he, and then started on, following the wolf tracks. Some three miles farther on he caught sight of the large wolf with a small one following him. They were out on the ice of a lake which they were about to cross in order to reach the heights on the opposite side. Jaampa now began the chase in earnest. With lightning speed he flew down a declivity and commenced a run across the ice.

Jouno could no longer keep up with him and began to fall behind. But Jaampa's speed was not to be checked on that account.

The wolves seeing that they were pursued and finding it difficult to run in the deep snow, commenced vomiting in order to relieve themselves, as they are wont to do when closely pressed after gorging themselves with food. Jaampa, who saw this, flung away his rifle, which burdened him somewhat, and so in another way followed their example. He knew that Jouno, who came behind, would find and take it with him.

Jaampa was not far from the wolves when they reached the land, but going up the heights on the other side they got the start of him. When he again caught sight of them, the smaller wolf had parted from the large one. Perhaps he had a foreboding that it might be dangerous to keep company with him. Jaampa, of course, kept on after the large one.

The course was once more downhill, and faster and faster flew the snowshoes. The wolf was again about to cross a lake, but in the descent towards it Jaampa's speed was ten times as great as the wolf's, and he gained more and more upon him. At length he came rushing close behind him, and as he sped past he struck at him with his staff, aiming the blow across the loins, the animal's weakest point. But the wolf was an old, experienced fellow. He made a sudden turn at the instant, and parried the blow, catching the stick with his teeth. It never avails to strike at a wolf's head. Besides, as ill luck would have it, Jaampa's left snowshoe cut in under an osier twig as he struck at the wolf, causing him to fall headlong, with his face buried in the snow.

Quick as lightning the wolf was upon him, seizing his shoulder with his sharp teeth, while he tore and pulled at his deer skin coat. Fortunately, however, the coat was thick, and inside of it Jaampa had, besides, a sheepskin jacket. Although he felt the teeth, and a long time afterwards bore blue spots in the skin, he did not mind this much. He wisely remained quiet, half buried in the snow, until he got hold of his knife.

He then twisted himself suddenly about and stabbed the wolf in the shoulder, whereupon he again ran off.

Jaampa was not long in getting upon his feet to start after him. The road now lay for three miles across a long expanse of ice and the race commenced anew. The moon came up, the stars were lighted, the northern lights glimmered and glittered and glistened in millions of snow crystals. The night was clear, but no living thing was heard or seen. All was silent and still on the wide, snow-covered mountain plains.

Only these two, Jaampa and the wolf, panted and ran, without witnesses or auditors, without pause or rest, not a race for a prize, but a race for life and death.

When the wolf again reached land, he had, obviously, begun to tire somewhat. Perhaps also the wound and the loss of blood had weakened him, for he no longer attempted to ascend the heights but ran along the shore of the lake. Jaampa triumphed at the sight of the blood in his tracks and exerted himself to the utmost to overtake the brute; but the sweat dropped from him more freely than the blood from the wolf, and so heated was he that he fairly steamed. Then he tore off his heavy deerskin coat and flinging it on the snow, set forward in his short, light, sheepskin jacket. It was freezing now, so that a light crust of ice was formed on the snow. This made the snowshoes glide as smoothly as though they had been made of glass, while, on the other hand, it cut the wolf's feet. At length Jaampa tossed off his cap, as even that had become too heavy for him. Bareheaded and with streaming hair, he hurried on, to reach the end of the lake at the same time with the wolf. Here the descent was down a narrow defile, and when the wolf entered this, the act proved his destruction. Jaampa was above the wolf, and suddenly turned his course downward, so that when the beast, with grinning jaws, flew by him in the narrow gorge, he received such a well-aimed blow across his back, from Jaampa's knotty stick, that he sank down in the snow, with the hind part of the body paralyzed, unable to rise or leave the spot.

Jaampa was conqueror. He drew his breath heavily a few times as he leaned on his staff and looked at his helpless enemy. Pity was out of the question. On the contrary, in disdainful triumph at having broken the back of his mortal enemy, he exhausted his anger in all manner of abuse. "There now, I have caught you at last," he cried exultingly, "you wicked demon! You who have sneaked about in the night, but have been cowardly in the daytime, except towards little children. There you sit now with broken back and gaping jaw, you ugly brute! Do you think that I pity you? You bit my shoulder, did you? But now you shall bite no more, nor lick any more reindeer blood with your damned tongue! My knife instead shall taste your heart's blood! It was you, you thievish knave, that a month ago stole from me my best sledge deer. Yes, it was you, there is no use in your hiding and denying it; it was you, I say, or your father or your mother, or your sister, or your brother, or someone or other of your cursed kindred! Now you shall die, you shall die, do you hear, flayer, scoundrel, Satan's blood-hound! There! Here is the knife for you!"

And like a flash of lightning the blade entered the wolf's side and he rolled over on his back – dead. Jaampa flayed him, threw the skin over his shoulders and about his neck like a fur collar, and proceeded on his way homeward. After three or four miles' travel, he met Jouno, who came with his rifle, coat, and cap.

They took a short cut home, and late in the afternoon reached the tents. Jaampa did not enlarge much upon the hunt but his jaws worked all the harder on the contents of a pot of meat which had lately been taken off the fire. When one of the girls however, took his coat and sat down to repair it, he had to relate that the wolf had torn it. But Jouno, on the contrary, ate and talked as for a wager, and from him, then, they learned the exact particulars of the hunt.

QUOTE FROM AN OLD NORSE SAGA REGARDING LAPS AND SKIS

'They are so cunning that they can follow tracks like dogs, both in thawing snow and on hard crust, and they are so good on skis that nothing can escape them, whether man or beast.'

CHAPTER 16
MAGIC AND MYSTERY

THE PERFECT TURN by Dick Dorworth

A noted ski racer, coach and world-record holder, Dick Dorworth (1938) is one of skiing's most passionate journalists. He has inspired generations of skiers worldwide through his example as a leader and his ability to translate his passion for skiing into words. He is the author of Night Driving, The Perfect Turn, The Straight Course, *and* Climbing to Freedom.

Years of sun had purified his skin into a permanent crust tan with strong creases of long life in a face around peculiar blue/green/grey Pacific Ocean eyes. Bill Clarkson's hair was white, befitting an old man, but his hair had lost color at an early age. He looked the same for so many years that friends and colleagues in the ski school tended to think of Clarkson as without age, but of course he wasn't. He was an enthusiastic old man with a reverence on his mind he seldom chose to talk about.

Skiing provided much of his livelihood. His mind and spirit had been largely moulded by it, and he was on a private quest for the perfect turn on a pair of skis. He had been conscious of it for 20 years, but age had revealed to him that his path was the same from boyhood; the perfect turn. It existed in that place where snow and ski meet to sculpt man, the connector.

Clarkson had come close many times, but he never quite made it around the perfect turn. The prospect excited him. His manner, reputation and appearance, with fathomless peaceful eyes encouraged others to attribute lofty aims and levels to Bill Clarkson. Few imagined his inner expedition. He was no longer allowed the athleticism of the good young skiers on the mountain, but he was respected for the style that comes only from a lifetime's work. Serious students of skiing sought his advice, demonstration and that form of energy called encouragement, but few persisted. He spoke only of essentials. The truly determined would figure it out and Clarkson knew he could not shorten their process of discovery. The dilettante, too, always figured it out.

His students often wound up talking about two of his interests, science fiction and submarines. Sometimes lessons continued beyond skiing to several glasses of red wine in 'The Avalanche', a dining/drinking spa across from the lodge at the base of the mountain.

Clarkson loved conversation, but he rarely spoke of his privately perfect turn. He liked to talk about the ideas of 'Heinlein', 'Herbert', 'Dick', 'Bradbury', 'Clarke and Wells', and he made impassioned verbal solo runs on the importance of the submarine to man's evolution – though he had never seen a real submarine. True students don't mind eccentricity, and the coquettes were content to be in the presence of Clarkson's reputation and personality.

From November to April his days were regular and similar. He rose early and breakfasted with Eileen, his religiously-minded wife of more than 30 years and his closest friend. Their marriage had ridden the storms and endured the slack times of that institution to reach the safe harbour of familiarity, self-acceptance and habit. Their two grown children had married and moved to the city. Their favourite ongoing intimate jokes were built around the theme that while Bill hadn't quite worked out the perfect turn, he was doing as well as Eileen's God was with His world. The joke had innumerable variations.

After eating and morning talk, Clarkson kissed his wife and walked the mile from their cabin to the mountain. He enjoyed the walk. The last few years he needed it to loosen up for the day's skiing. He knew he had a fine instinctive feel for skis, snow and terrain, polished with solid technique and many years. Still, he felt his age. Certain runs – 'Elevator', 'No Deposit Chute' and 'Larry's Bowl' (named for a man killed there in an avalanche) – Clarkson wouldn't ski anymore. He could ski them if he had to, but he neither enjoyed fear nor saw merit in imposing it on himself without interest or necessity.

At the lodge he drank coffee with others in the ski school, talked about the weather (always a prime topic) the world news, the latest ski, local gossip and how the snow was likely to be that day. He relished this part of the morning, especially if Hal Sanders was pleasant. Bill and Hal were friends and skiing companions of nearly 40 years. Sanders felt like a comfortable old coat to Clarkson, warmth against the chill of unfamiliarity Clarkson felt around some of the young skiers. Most of the younger instructors were too abrasive, abrupt and insensitive, both on and off skis, in Clarkson's educated opinion, but he remembered being stupid from fighting identity battles that were no longer his concern. He was comfortable with people and things known, and his living enemies had abdicated or aged with as much élan as his own in the face of the falling inevitable. Morning coffee with Sanders was like a favorite and old piece of music to the mind and spirit of Bill Clarkson.

Then he went to the crowded ski instructors' room. People changing into uniforms. Many voices at once. Heavy ski boots stomping on a concrete floor. A ritual preparation for the day's skiing encompassing several meanings; sport, business, craft, meditation, and goal. It was a bit of each to Clarkson and the path toward a balanced mystery he thought of as the perfect turn. He believed in the grace and worth of the self-indulgence of guiding a pair of skis upon a field of snow with precision and intelligence. He bet a part of his life that the turn existed. It presented itself to his mind, over and over and over, as if it had happened before and would of necessity again. The perfect turn was wonderful to contemplate. Deja vu.

Ski lifts started an hour before classes gathered in clusters before ski school signs of ability – A*B*C*D*E*F – stuck in the snow before the lodge. More than many instructors Clarkson used that hour for his own skiing. Often he skied alone, sometimes with colleagues who had no idea of his deepest mind. It wasn't their fault they didn't know. Nor was it his. It was just that way.

Eileen knew. Sanders had an abstract comprehension. Sometimes at Instructors' gatherings when talk turned upon the theory or purpose or some such armchair concept of their profession, Sanders pontificated in the manner of the righteous that Bill Clarkson embodied the substance of skiing and knew something no one else did. Sanders was unable to determine what that something was.

During the savoured morning chair lift ride, a portion of his mind took in the matutinal mountain-light on the ridges and the white/ blue snow and the green frosty trees and the clunk-whirrrr of the cable passing over the lift support towers and the motors of the snowcats working ski runs into a smooch, soft blanket and the easy breeze rustling trees and gently swirling across the snow and the stark cold air that hit the face like a slap encountered nowhere else but in the high mountains. At such times Clarkson felt extraordinarily lucky.

At the top came the best part. The first run of the day. He felt titillation as if he had never stood upon a pair of skis, and surging doubt quickened anticipation as he debarked the lift. He knew he could ski but it was a special sensation to incinerate faint anxiety in the purifying flame of action. The act of skiing transmitted a familiar pressure to the skilled soles of his feet and up his old bones to his brain. Skiing was in that moment the entire reason for his existence. He guided his skis down the mountain along the smoothest line of least resistance, for that time master of his destiny. Excessive exertion was a waste, a sloppy turn, a mental and moral lapse in Bill Clarkson's soul. Skiing is composed of pressure and angles in constant flux. Like leaves, rivets, snowflakes and people, no two turns are the same and once made can never be retracted or redone. Each turn in life is a complete statement and Clarkson was sure the integrity of a turn persisted. It was important to make correct turns and to never give up the work of refinement – the process reaching toward the perfect turn. Two runs of several hundred turns each could be fitted in before classes.

A popular and good teacher, the consummate 'old pro', Clarkson lived off his knowledge that there's more to skiing than recreation. When business was brisk he often worked the entire day until lifts stopped, skiers left the mountain and the afternoon light began its fade. If Clarkson missed lunch, evening surely found him in The Avalanche, eating, drinking red wine and talking. He preferred to be with Sanders, another friend or an old client, but a festive mood infectiously followed him, and many a late night grew out of a sandwich and a glass of wine with Clarkson after skiing. He had a celebratory quality, but he opened only to those he chose according to the private standards of a private man. Kitty Reese was one, a 20 year old girl whose passion was photography, whose love was skiing and whose friend was Bill Clarkson. They were a sight. A pretty girl with long, light blonde hair and deep brown eyes and a quick, easy smile, and an old white-maned man with a weathered face and unfathomable, strange eyes. Easy talkers had the two as lovers, but it was not so. If he were younger or alone perhaps it could have been, but that is no more sure than the vagaries of all relationships and statements beginning with 'if'. Their friendship grew from Kitty's eagerness to photograph his skiing. She was a nuisance at first but he was kind and by consenting to ski for the camera he learned appreciation for the photographer. She took up reading science-fiction.

He critiqued her work with the unbiased eye of the non-photographer. Kitty once told Bill she would 'give anything' to ski like him. He looked at her and said nothing, his Pacific Ocean eyes flooding her with embarrassment and Kitty never said anything like that again. She settled for being pleased when he granted her skiing or photography a word of approval. Conversation between them revolved around such topics as the possibility of intelligent life in other parts of the universe, what lived in the depths of the sea, astral projection, the ethics and significance of transplanting parts of the human body, due concept of good and evil, and of the necessity to strive for the perfection which includes both the seemingly unattainable and the presently possible. Like good friends do, they spoke of the contradictions and difficulties of life.

When the skiing/photographing day ended, Kitty usually retired to the darkroom in the basement of the lodge. As a photographer Kitty was a throwback to an earlier time. She saw and searched for an essential clarity and beauty in using monochrome film to make silver halide black and white photos that, to her eye, were not available in digital photography. That search set her apart from other photographers and was part of her connection with Bill Clarkson. After she was finished with negatives, proof sheets, prints and enlargements, she studied and evaluated accomplishment and failure for that day. Then she often joined Clarkson, and usually Sanders, in The Avalanche. They joined a larger mass of skiers discussing the latest ski or ski boot or exploit of the hero of the hour, as necessary to any endeavor as bread to the Sacrament. In the altar of The Avalanche they drank red wine and enjoyed each other's company and conversation.

One clear day near season's end Clarkson volunteered to ski for Kitty and her camera. It was the first time Kitty hadn't suggested the filming and she was happy for the unforeseen chance. He was relaxed and talkative and joked that she would never see him ski so well as he would that day, green/grey eyes reflecting his private laughter at her pretty surprise.

While they rode the lift he talked about his favourite ski runs and he pointed out for her once again the beauty he perceived – the texture of snow, the vibrancy of living trees, the contour of a ridge, the honorable struggle of skiers battling their own fears and limitations, blue sky streaked with wispy cirrus clouds presaging a storm two days hence.

Shadows. Peaks. Valleys. Sharp clear air caressing lungs. Bill Clarkson told Kitty Reese that she was very pretty, as pretty as the mountain with a new mantle of snow on a cold sunny day with colour spectrum snowflake diamonds dancing in the air. And he laughed at her blush and at his own sentence.

Bill Clarkson was in a very good mood, the best Kitty had known of him. She watched his skiing through the camera viewfinder, and the elusive thought slithered through that the skier and the skiing had danced together so long that the two had become the same one. The idea passed.

Clarkson chose the spots to ski and Kitty noted the light was excellent. She shot several rolls of film. At one point she stopped photographing to simply watch him manoeuvre through an old burn of scattered dead pine trees standing nakedly branchless. Free of the camera eye, she saw him with her own. Her admiration and attention was tinged with an electric feeling of ephemerality, a sense that Bill Clarkson's skiing existed on its own, while the man himself had stepped out for lunch or a date with his love. A chill passed through her body and mind like a cloud from nowhere crossing before the sun on a warm day. The moment passed.

Clarkson skied up to her and stopped. Warmth returned.

"That's beautiful," she said. "Bill, that's lovely skiing."

"Yes," he said, smiling wide with his whole wrinkled and weathered face. "I've got it today. But I told you. I've really got it today."

They parted when the late afternoon mountain sun bathed the passes and peaks in golden contrast to the dark blue valley shadows of imminent night. He kissed her on the forehead like he sometimes did and looked into her eyes and then he skied away.

Kitty went to her darkroom, excitement and nagging anxiety floating like corks on the quiet, strong currents in the rivers of her innermost mind. For a couple of hours she was completely involved in the celluloid/chemical/time/light world of the film development process.

By the time the negatives were ready to inspect, Kitty was filled with charged anticipation. Using a magnifying glass, she began peering first at the individual frames of the strips of film she had taken that day of Bill Clarkson.

Nothing in her young life could have prepared her for what she saw. Frame after frame showed the mountains, snow, trees, the great open sky and the exact scene she had photographed in the perfect reverse focus of the negative – except that Bill Clarkson and his skiing were not there. No skier was visible in any of the film.

Kitty looked with mounting perplexity through half the negatives before the tears burst from her brown eyes and flowed down the face that Clarkson said was as pretty as the mountain with a new mantle of snow on a cold sunny day with color spectrum snowflake diamonds dancing in the air. She dropped the magnifying glass. It made a dull thud landing on the work bench. She ran, leaving the darkroom door open behind her. A growling, short-breathed sob escaped into the night air as she emerged from the lodge and sprinted across crunchy frozen snow.

With blurred, sorrowed vision she saw through the tall, plate glass windows of The Avalanche a scene from a world that would never be the same: a brightly lit, smoke-tainted room; the long table in the alcove covered with beer and wine glasses and ash trays and empty pizza trays and surrounded by ski instructors; the animated movements of conversing people, as if seen upon the silent screen of an old movie house.

And in the corner of the alcove furthest from the window, unnoticed by the others, sat Hal Sanders on a bench holding in his arms the slumped form of Bill Clarkson. Sanders looked straight ahead, his eyes wide and red, and tears streamed from them and down his old face like spring run-off from the mountains.

THE TIME OLE HAGEN SHOWED US WHAT DOWNHILL ALL IS ABOUT by Ragnar Hovland

Ragnar Hovland (1952) is a Norwegian writer, children's author, translator and musician. Striking for his narrative style is the ambiguous combination of seriousness and humour.

Translation by Ingrid Christophersen.

It happens more and more as time passes that I find myself thinking that there are really only two types of sport: ski jumping and downhill skiing. Everything else that struts around in the guise of that name is really not worthy of unloosing the shoe latchets of the two aforementioned.

Ski jumping and downhill skiing and one Norwegian, Birger Ruud, the only man to have won Olympic gold medals in both disciplines, in Garmisch Partenkirchen in 1936.

That feat has never been repeated and it is most unusual that a sportsman takes part in two such very different and demanding disciplines.

Ski jumping is a very Norwegian event, historically and anthropomorphically, and I will not elaborate here. Suffice it to say that downhill skiing is the only sport worth mentioning in my neck of the woods.

Downhill skiing is related to driving off the road in a car. In both disciplines one experiences a so-called dizzy feeling before one lands. (I am in no way blind to the differences between the two. After all, on skis you are more or less in touch with the slope most of the time, it is easier to survive without much material damage, and easier to reap honours. I cannot think of any honourable instances of driving off the road and anyhow this is not an Olympic discipline).

Downhill skiing is a clean sport. The whole point is to get to the bottom, as quickly as possible, without having to bother about those stupid gates which spoil so much in other alpine disciplines. Nor is it dependent on artificial aids, like a ski jump.

Downhill skiing is fascinating, again to a certain extent like ski jumping. There is always the off-chance that the athlete doesn't survive. However, I do not think you need to have a death wish to be a downhill skier; you just need to know that He is down there by one of the turns, looking at you.

Something else fascinating about downhill is that within a few seconds, which admittedly seem like a lifetime, the job is done. You ski down the hill, and it was either good or bad, and you can just wander off and have a beer. While those who participate in other types of sport, like cross-country skiing, have not even left the start area. It seems unfair, but we downhill addicts love the fact that that is how it is; Ski down and have done.

I think this is all that needs to be said of downhill. But I want to ask the question which probably some of the readers have been wanting to ask. Is it necessarily the best downhill skiers who emerge into the light and harvest most of the glory? The answer, as far as I can see, is no. And why I can say that is because I know one of them who would have been the greatest and why he never was will become clear.

As everyone who has visited Indre Sogn will know, the local inhabitants' character and the terrain invite sports that involve speed. The faster the better, if I can express myself clearly. Short distance sprint in the summer, downhill in the winter and motoring all the year, nothing else really matters. I have myself excelled in running and downhill skiing so I know what I am talking about, although no one entertained the idea that I would be a second Toni Sailer or a new Jean-Claude Killy. That was said about one person only... 'Ole Hagen'. (Those who knew him will know that this was not his name, and anyhow it does not concern anyone else; I have changed his name in respect to his family who are still suffering unhealed wounds). Ole Hagen possessed most of the characteristics attributed to legendary downhillers. He was tall and slim, his face bore the expression of other-worldliness and melancholy and he never made a fuss about how good he was. He always made us feel that we could be just as good. He kept to himself, without appearing to be a loner, he said little, but everyone listened to what he had to say.

He ran the 100 metres in the summer and skied downhill in the winter and drove his car all the year round, ever since he passed his driving licence. Apart from that, he stayed at home and read and listened to strange records no one had heard of.

He insisted that downhill skiing was no snob sport. The best downhillers were usually farmers' sons from the Alps.

Thinking about it now, there was maybe quite a lot missing from Ole Hagen's style. (Not to mention our style). What really characterised him was his total contempt of death and an amazing ability to stay upright. But do not forget that downhill equipment belonged to another world. It all took place on common Åsnes touring skis. And the slopes would hardly have conformed to international standards. Nevertheless, Ole Hagen won all the local races and we realised he was up to much bigger challenges. Especially after he took part in a race on the other side of the mountain and skied against the well-known Norwegian alpine skier Håkon Mjøen and beat the shit out of him.

Of course, he never trained – that goes without saying.

"If you have to train you're not a natural", he said. And he was true to his words. His equipment consisted of the following: Black boots inside rolled up jeans, a black leather jacket (which he had inherited from his uncle) and leather gloves. Nothing on his head.

Let me try and give you an impression of the state of downhill runs in Indre Sogn in those days. It must be stressed that they were strictly 'au natural'. They might start somewhere up a mountain side and terminate in the fjord. En-route they passed several more or less fatal obstacles; crags, sheep sheds, river gullies, pine clusters, clifftops and hot-tempered farmers who liked to lay traps on the course. And the speed was always extreme. It was virtually impossible to think before one was down – if one made it that far of course.

The fastest of all the runs, as many of us still remember, was 'Dead Man's Slide', and very few ever dared set foot on it. (I went down it once, survived, emerged with a glistening face and decided enough was enough. I must add that I virtually promised the heavenly powers that, if I survived, my life from here on would be one of renunciation and filled with good deeds and self-discipline).

It is not necessary to inform you that Dead Man's Slide was Ole Hagen's run. It started high up on the mountainside, ran parallel to the Teige waterfall for a bit, wound itself round some steep and sharp rocky outcrops before becoming, what one could call, a normal hill. Somewhere in the middle it was necessary to throw oneself sharply to the left in order to avoid plunging over a steep pitch which was near enough a vertical drop. Several had heard Ole Hagen say that it must surely be possible to ski straight down this drop rather than ski round it and thus lose valuable seconds. He was on the case.

One February evening Ole Hagen and I were drinking in the only bar in Indre Sogn which never closed. I had sort of got closer to him and I felt he said things I had never heard him say before and which I never thought I would hear him say. He talked about the future, his own and that of skiing in general.

"Hovland," he said (We always used our surnames, that was the custom). "The time has come to ditch Åsnes touring skis and downhill skiing such as we know it."

"It has, Hagen," I said.

"There will come a time which I do not think will do much good when downhill will be thought of differently, and it won't have much to do with downhill."

"What do you mean by that Hagen," I asked and emptied my glass.

He never answered, just looked out into the moonlit night.

"Someone must show them what downhill is," he said.

"That's right, I said. Someone must take that on."

We emptied our glasses, paid and left. We were, if not drunk, anyhow somewhat tiddly and probably staggered a bit. The moon appeared incredibly large and white and reminded me of girls I had never met. There was one called Isabella and lived in Caracas. I said things I would otherwise have been ashamed of and, for heaven's sake, even tried a few sea shanties.

"I'll show them what downhill is," said Ole Hagen and, the way he said it, I knew he meant it.

We went home and picked up our Åsnes skis and made straight for Dead Man's Slide. The going was not easy and luckily for us the moon shone brightly.

"This evening I'm going down the pitch," said Ole Hagen, and I knew what he meant. "You don't need to come all the way up," he added. "Stand by the pitch. I need an eyewitness."

I nodded. I had no burning desire to ski down Dead Man's Slide that evening.

So I remained standing at the 'top of the pitch', which, in the normal use of the term, was virtually a sheer drop of a couple of hundred metres, lent on my poles while Ole Hagen wandered up the mountain. Even at the top I could see him clearly in the moonlight.

"Come on Hagen!" I shouted. "Show us what you are good for."

He came. His skis literally emitted sparks and I have never seen him more fired up. He was at the pitch before I could even think that the moon is round; he was a black and devilish figure which rushed madly past me faster than anyone had before and then he took off and floated out over the abyss.

As most people will know, this was the last time anyone saw Ole Hagen. So, I was the last person to see him and I can only stand by what I saw. Ole Hagen took off over Dead Man's Slide and disappeared.

I never saw him land. I never saw him at the bottom of the hill, he never came home that evening or the next day or the next.

Of course, it might be easy to conclude that he killed himself but nobody has been found and there was no sign of tracks at the bottom of the hill. The closest I can come to the truth is that he disappeared – into thin air if you like.

And of course, there are plenty, as there always will be, of those who say they have seen him. But they are the types who like to emphasise their own importance, even if it means lying and spreading untruths just to appear interesting. Oh yes, Ole Hagen has been seen both here and there, cycling along the road, on the bus to Bergen, on the streets in many Norwegian and foreign cities. There was one who with great sincerity insisted that he had met Ole Hagen in a bar in Chicago, he was just the same, talked freely and asked for news from home. And even I was convinced that I saw him once coming through the doors of the Grand Hotel in the capital, but he disappeared in the crowd before I managed to reach him.

Be that as it may. Some went as far as to insist that Our Lord Himself had sent angels to grab him and anyhow many include him in their prayers. But whatever happened to Ole Hagen, and wherever he may be, he would have wanted it like that. As he predicted, downhill changed and no one uses Åsnes touring skis anymore and the legendary downhillers are few and far between.

But as far as I am concerned Ole Hagen was that person who best personified the soul of downhill skiing. One late February evening many years ago, under a white full moon he proved to anyone who wanted to know what downhill is. I don't think anyone has done that since.

THE WORLD WAS REBORN by Odd Selmer

Odd Selmer (1930) is a Norwegian journalist, novelist, crime fiction writer and playwright. His audio plays have been translated into fifteen languages. He was awarded the Ibsen Prize in 1988 for the audio play series På egne ben.

This piece translated by Ingrid Christophersen.

On Sunday November 15th, 1896 John Arntzen experienced something that would change his life for ever.

He had set off from Kirkestuen while it was still dark, groped his way over the frozen river, and climbed up the steep hill carrying the skis on his shoulder. The schoolteacher had lent him the skis, they were long and heavy but the only ones he could find anywhere. Having struggled up the hill for nearly two hours the terrain levelled off and the forest thinned out and he was able to buckle on his skis. The willow bindings were stiff and worn but he had brought along spare leather straps with which to tighten them.

John breathed heavily following the hard ascent, nevertheless he poled on energetically. The crust, topped with a thin layer of new snow, carried him sufficiently. Just below the ridge he paused for a moment and cast a glance back from where he had come. The forest below lay in semi darkness. He could no longer see the valley and the river, but smoke from the farms drifted like thin, blue streaks in the frozen air. He ran the last metres up to the ridge.

Huge mountain ridges lay ahead. They sparkled white in the sunshine; dark shadows obscured the gorges. This was the first time he had seen the mountain snow-covered. He immediately sensed the vastness of the mountain world, and yet it was different to what he had imagined. It was majestic but nevertheless appeared friendly, helpful, as though it had just opened its arms to him.

The plain was hemmed in by two long mountain ridges. Black scree appeared like warning stripes amongst all the white. Between the ridges a summit with two round peaks towered. According to the description he had been given at Kirkestuen the previous evening this was Prestkampen. He started skiing towards it. There were no signs of humans anywhere, there were not even any birds around, but only him and the mountain. The skis slid well over the granular snow and he advanced in long, undulating movements across the plain. He felt strong and fit, Prestkampen would be his in one single mouthful. But it was as though the distance continually moved away and the sun was already high in the sky before he reached the girdle of sparse birch surrounding the summit. He realised that he needed to overcome several smallish knolls before he could start the ascent of Prestkampen itself. But he started to tackle it without a rest. He criss-crossed up the hill, starting with long traverses, then shorter and shorter until he reached a steep pitch to the west of the mountain where he unbuckled his skis and carried them on his shoulder. It was necessary to kick the toe of his boot hard into the snow crust in order to get a grip on the steep wall. When the slope took on a gentler gradient, he thrust his boots into the willow bindings but had not the strength to tighten the straps before he continued to criss-cross up the hill. He panted and gasped and the sweat-soaked vest itched uncomfortably against his upper body. But he was determined not to rest before he reached the top.

But when exhausted and suddenly shivering with hunger and drooped over his poles, the sun cast long, blue shadows and he was still a long way off the top.

That is when he saw it. What made him turn his face upwards with a sudden perception of danger, was only a whisper, or a faint scratching noise. But fear suddenly took hold of him and paralysed him for he had no possibility of escaping the monster which was now unstoppably rushing towards him. Against the light backdrop all he saw was a dark shape surrounded by a halo of drifting snow, storming down the mountain side straight at him. He closed his eyes and screamed silently.

Only when the dark shape had passed him by did he realise that it was a skier. Although, he did not actually believe what he saw. No human could move at such a speed. It was not possible.

The skier held a long pole in his hand. He turned to the left, bent his knee so far it nearly touched the skis, thrust his other ski ahead, bent the other knee and swung to the right. But now he was aiming for the precipitous precipice; if he did not turn away, he would rush straight over the abyss. John wanted to scream out a warning, but there was no air left in his lungs.

The skier made no attempt at turning away. Like a tight-rope walker, pole lifted above his head, his body bent over his skis, he plunged over the gorge.

"No," whispered John, "it cannot be true."

So, the man with the pole held high was swallowed up by the dark void and John felt it was a release because it was obviously only something he had imagined. But nevertheless, he shuffled a few metres forwards over the mountainside to get a better overview.

The skier shot like an arrow out of the shadow down below. His skis clattered over the snowdrifts; sparkling snowflakes whirled around him with abandon. He continued downwards in large, serene turns, he floated effortlessly over sastrugi and bumps. When he reached the gentle slope at the foot of the mountain, he stood up and allowed his pole to drag behind. It was is if he trusted his skis to do the steering, he did not even bother to flex his legs, they were stiff and bounced him from snowdrift to snowdrift.

Suddenly he disappeared behind a small hillock. John remained standing, peering down at the dark birch thicket. He was immobilised. A raging storm of thoughts and feelings rushed around his head; But had he actually seen what he saw? Had he not read that at extreme heights climbers could from time to time experience hallucinations owing to lack of oxygen?

But he had seen it. The tracks in the snow all the way down the mountainside were frozen proof. But had a human made them? What had he actually seen? He closed his eyes in an effort to recreate the vision. But they were so fleeting; there was no face, just a hat with fluttering earflaps, a worn-out rucksack hanging floppily over a back, a grey pair of trousers with a big, black patch. And it was the black patch which ultimately convinced him that this was a mortal. No troll or fairy would wear anything so beggarly.

Exactly, beggarly. And yet this skier was the most fantastic thing John had ever seen. Nothing he had ever experienced could in any way equal this run down the mountain.

But why had no one told him that one could ski in this way? Why had Captain Dahl never as much as even insinuated something like this? The Captain had always spoken about courage, daring and patriotism. But what he had been teaching during those grey winter afternoons on Iversløkken were snowplough turns, herring-bone climbing and turning on the flat – while at the same time stressing that discipline and self-control are the skier's foremost virtues, that only bad skiers set off downhill at unknown places and that only fools allow themselves to be allured by speed.

But at the same time as John was directing embittered thoughts at Captain Dahl, he knew that not only was he being unfair, but also self-righteous. Captain Dahl and Iversløkken belonged to his boyhood. He was an independent, well-travelled and educated man of 24. Why had it never occurred to him that skis could be used for such fantastic runs?

Yes, why?

He was thought of as an accomplished skier, and he had won prizes at both Iversløkken and at St. Hanshaugen. And he knew even before he set off on this wintry mountain tour that part of the reward would be the admiration and tribute from the other wedding guests at Lawyer Kinck's. He would be received as a bold adventurer and a great sport.

And he really was only an amateur.

What he had been doing up until now was just child's play, an artistic minuet on skis. Dejected he pulled the sandwiches out of his pocket. They were wrapped in a piece of cloth; thick slices of bread and pork. He gobbled up the food in big mouthfuls. Afterwards he remained slumped over his poles while his eyes continually searched the tracks down the mountainside.

So that is how one could ski. Straight down, without braking. Go for it, without pulling back, without allowing fear to take over. It was possible. He had seen it with his own eyes. And suddenly, in a flash, it was as though the world opened up to him in a new way and he was filled with happy expectation. Up until now the difficulties, the limits, had occupied his thoughts and that was not strange, because what he had learnt during his childhood was what he could not do. But limits were not essential, the essential was what he could do. He nodded enthusiastically to himself several times.

The light over the mountain ridge had turned pale blue. The summit was no longer a possibility. He glanced again at the ski track. He could try and follow it. Not down the steep pitch of course, but just a short way.

But when he lined up with his skis in a snowplough and the poles planted solidly in front it was as though his new-found insight and enthusiasm just evaporated in the thin air. The hill below him appeared uncomfortably steep and the track was without turns to check his speed. The possibilities lying ahead of him appeared frightening. Still, he had to try.

He lifted his poles up and started to slide. Before he could gather his thoughts, before he had found a comfortable position his speed had increased to such an extent that he knew this would never work. The wind pressed against his face, his eyes filled with water and the track ahead appeared blurry and unclear. He tried feverishly to swerve to the right, he wanted to get away from the gorge, but his skis fluttered beneath him without direction. A small snowdrift brought him out of balance, and he plunged downwards, head over heels; he scraped his face against the snow crust three times.

He remained lying there, carefully moving his arms and legs. They appeared to be whole. His face was bleeding, dripping red into the snow, but so what. He got up slowly, brushed the snow off and started the tedious downhill, long traverses back and forth.

CHAPTER 17

FROM FINLAND TO MONGOLIA

LEMMINIKAINEN'S SECOND WOOING by Elias Lönnrot

'The Kalevala', a folk-tale compiled by Elias Lönnrot in the 19th century, is based on spoken Finnish mythology. It is considered the Finnish national epic and is one of the most important literary works in the Finnish language. The Kalevala contributed significantly to the development of Finnish national consciousness and has also made an impact beyond Finland. The first version of the work was published in 1835. The title is derived from Kaleva, the name of the godfather of the sung hero, and means something like 'the land of Kalevas'. The Kalevala standard text consists of 22,795 verses, which are presented in fifty songs.

Snowshoes here are skis. The concept or word 'ski' was not yet in use.

> SPAKE the ancient Lemminkainen
> To the hostess of Pohyola:
> "Give to me thy lovely daughter,
> Bring me now thy winsome maiden,
> Bring the best of Lapland virgins,
> Fairest virgin of the Northland."
>
> Louhi, hostess of Pohyola,
> Answered thus the wild magician:
> "I shall never give my daughter,
> Never give my fairest maiden,
> Not the best one, nor the worst one,
> Not the largest, nor the smallest;
> Thou hast now one wife-companion,
> Thou has taken hence one hostess,
> Carried off the fair Kyllikki."
>
> This is Lemminkainen's answer:
> To my home I took Kyllikki,
> To my cottage on the island,

To my entry-gates and kindred;
Now I wish a better hostess,
Straightway bring thy fairest daughter,
Worthiest of all thy virgins,
Fairest maid with sable tresses."

Spake the hostess of Pohyola:
"Never will I give my daughter
To a hero false and worthless,
To a minstrel vain and evil;
Therefore, pray thou for my maiden,
Therefore, woo the sweet-faced flower,
When thou bringest me the wild moose
From the Hisi fields and forests."

Then the artful Lemminkainen
Deftly whittled out his javelins,
Quickly made his leathern bow-string,
And prepared his bow and arrows,
And soliloquized as follows:
"Now my javelins are made ready,
All my arrows too are ready,
And my oaken cross-bow bended,
But my snow-shoes are not builded,

Who will make me worthy snowshoes?"
Lemminkainen, grave and thoughtful,
Long reflected, well considered,
Where the snowshoes could be fashioned,
Who the artist that could make them;
Hastened to the Kauppi smithy,
To the smithy of Lylikki,
Thus addressed the snowshoe artist:
"O thou skilful Woyalander,
Kauppi, ablest smith of Lapland,
Make me quick two worthy snowshoes,
Smooth them well and make them hardy,

That in Tapio the wild-moose,
Roaming through the Hisi forests,
I may catch and bring to Louhi,
As a dowry for her daughter."

Then Lylikki thus made answer,
Kauppi gave this prompt decision:
"Lemminkainen, reckless minstrel,
Thou wilt hunt in vain the wild moose,
Thou wilt catch but pain and torture,
In the Hisi fens and forests."

Little heeding, Lemminkainen
Spake these measures to Lylikki
"Make for me the worthy snowshoes,
Quickly work and make them ready;
Go I will and catch the blue moose
Where in Tapio it browses,
In the Hisi woods and snow fields."

Then Lylikki, snowshoe maker,
Ancient Kauppi, master artist,
Whittled in the fall his show-shoes,
Smoothed them in the winter evenings,
One day working on the runners,
All the next day making stick-rings,
Till at last the shoes were finished,
And the workmanship was perfect.
Then he fastened well the shoe straps,
Smooth as adder's skin the woodwork,
Soft as fox-fur were the stick rings;
Oiled he well his wondrous snowshoes
With the tallow of the reindeer;
When he thus soliloquizes,
These the accents of Lylikki:
"Is there any youth in Lapland,
Any in this generation,

That can travel in these snowshoes,
That can move the lower sections?"

Spake the reckless Lemminkainen,
Full of hope, and life, and vigor:
Surely there is one in Lapland.
In this rising generation,
That can travel in these snowshoes,
That the right and left can manage."

To his back he tied the quiver,
Placed the bow upon his shoulder,
With both hands he grasped his snow cane,
Speaking meanwhile words as follow:
"There is nothing in the woodlands,
Nothing in the world of Ukko,
Nothing underneath the heavens,
In the uplands, in the lowlands,
Nothing in the snow fields running,
Not a fleet deer of the forest,
That could not be overtaken
With the snow-shoes of Lylikki,
With the strides of Lemminkainen."

Wicked Hisi heard these measures,
Juntas listened to their echoes;
Straightway Hisi called the wild moose,
Juutas fashioned soon a reindeer,
And the head was made of punk wood,
Horns of naked willow branches,
Feet were furnished by the rushes,
And the legs, by reeds aquatic,
Veins were made of withered grasses,
Eyes, from daisies of the meadows,
Ears were formed of water flowers,
And the skin of tawny fir-bark,
Out of sappy wood, the muscles,

Fair and fleet, the magic reindeer.
Juutas thus instructs the wild-moose,
These the words of wicked Hisi:
Flee away, thou moose of Juutas,
Flee away, thou Hisi reindeer,
Like the winds, thou rapid courser,
To the snow-homes of the ranger,
To the ridges of the mountains,
To the snow-capped hills of Lapland,
That thy hunter may be worn out,
Thy pursuer be tormented,
Lemminkainen be exhausted."

Thereupon the Hisi reindeer,
Juutas-moose with branching antlers,
Fleetly ran through fen and forest,
Over Lapland's hills and valleys,
Through the open fields and courtyards,
Through the penthouse doors and gateways,
Turning over tubs of water,
Threw the kettles from the fire pole,
And upset the dishes cooking.
Then arose a fearful uproar,
In the court-yards of Pohyola,
Lapland-dogs began their barking,
Lapland-children cried in terror,
Lapland-women roared with laughter,
And the Lapland heroes shouted.

Fleetly followed Lemminkainen,
Followed fast, and followed faster,
Hastened on behind the wild moose,
Over swamps and through the woodlands,
Over snow-fields vast and pathless,
Over high uprising mountains,
Fire out-shooting from his runners,
Smoke arising from his snow cane:

Could not hear the wild-moose bounding,
Could not sight the flying fleet foot;
Glided on through field and forest,
Glided over lakes and rivers,
Over lands beyond the smooth sea,
Through the desert plains of Hisi,
Glided o'er the plains of Kalma,
Through the kingdom of Tuoni,
To the end of Kalma's empire,
Where the jaws of Death stand open,
Where the head of Kalma lowers,
Ready to devour the stranger,
To devour wild Lemminkainen;
But Tuoni cannot reach him,
Kalma cannot overtake him.

Distant woods are yet untraveled,
Far away a woodland corner
Stands unsearched by Kaukomieli,
In the North's extensive, borders,
In the realm of dreary Lapland.
Now the hero, on his snowshoes,
Hastens to the distant woodlands,
There to hunt the moose of Piru.
As he nears the woodland corner,
There he bears a frightful uproar,
From the Northland's distant borders,
From the dreary fields of Lapland,
Hears the dogs as they are barking,
Hears the children loudly screaming,
Hears the laughter or the women,
Hears the shouting of the heroes.
Thereupon wild Lemminkainen
Hastens forward on his snowshoes,
To the place where dogs are barking,
To the distant woods of Lapland.

When the reckless Kaukomieli
Had approached this Hisi corner,
Straightway he began to question:
"Why this laughter or the women,
Why the screaming of the children,
Why the shouting of the heroes,
Why this barking of the watch-dogs?
This reply was promptly given:
"This the reason for this uproar,
Women laughing, children screaming,
Heroes shouting, watch-dogs barking
Hisi's moose came running hither,
Hither came the Piru Reindeer,
Hither came with hoofs of silver,
Through the open fields and courtyards,
Through the penthouse doors and gateways,
Turning over tubs or water,
Threw the kettles from the firepole,
And upset the dishes cooking."

Then the hero, Lemminkainen,
Straightway summoned all his courage,
Pushed ahead his mighty snowshoes,
Swift as adders in the stubble,
Levelled bushes in the marshes,
Like the swift and fiery serpents,
Spake these words of magic import,
Keeping balance with his snow staff:
Come thou might of Lapland heroes,
Bring to me the moose of Juutas;
Come thou strength of Lapland women,
And prepare the boiling caldron;
Come, thou might of Lapland children,
Bring together fire and fuel;
Come, thou strength of Lapland kettles,
Help to boil the Hisi wild moose."

Then with mighty force and courage,
Lemminkainen hastened onward,
Striking backward, shooting forward;
With a long sweep of his snowshoe,
Disappeared from view the hero;
With the second, shooting further,
Was the hunter out of hearing,
With the third the hero glided
On the shoulders of the wild moose;
Took a pole of stoutest oak-wood,
Took some bark-strings from the willow,
Wherewithal to bind the moose-deer,
Bind him to his oaken hurdle.
To the moose he spake as follows:
"Here remain, thou moose of Juutas
Skip about, my bounding courser,
In my hurdle jump and frolic,
Captive from the fields of Piru,
From the Hisi glens and mountains."

Then he stroked the captured wild moose,
Patted him upon his forehead,
Spake again in measured accents:
"I would like awhile to linger,
I would love to rest a moment
In the cottage of my maiden,
With my virgin, young and lovely."

Then the Hisi-moose grew angry,
Stamped his feet and shook his antlers,
Spake these words to Lemminkainen:
"Surely Lempo soon will get thee,
Shouldst thou sit beside the maiden,
Shouldst thou linger by the virgin."

Now the wild-moose stamps and rushes,
Tears in two the bands of willow,

Breaks the oak-wood pole in pieces,
And upturns the hunter's hurdle,
Quickly leaping from his captor,
Bounds away with strength of freedom,
Over hills and over lowlands,
Over swamps and over snow fields,
Over mountains clothed in heather,
That the eye may not behold him,
Nor the hero's ear detect him.

Thereupon the mighty hunter
Angry grows, and much disheartened,
Starts again the moose to capture,
Gliding off behind the courser.
With his might he plunges forward;
At the instep breaks his snowshoe,
Breaks the runners into fragments,
On the mountings breaks his javelins,
In the centre breaks his snow staff,
And the moose bounds on before him,
Through the Hisi-woods and snow fields,
Out of reach of Lemminkainen.

Then the reckless Kaukomieli
Looked with bended head, ill-humored,
One by one upon the fragments,
Speaking words of ancient wisdom:
"Northland hunters, never, never,
Go defiant to thy forests,
In the Hisi vales and mountains,
There to hunt the moose of Juutas,
Like this senseless, reckless hero;
I have wrecked my magic snow-shoes,
Ruined too my useful snow staff,
And my javelins I have broken,
While the wild-moose runs in safety
Through the Hisi fields and forests."

SKIERS AND HUNTERS DITTY FROM ALTAI

A traditional song from Mongolia, a so-called Urtiin Duu or Long Song.

Within the mighty and high mountains,
With bow and arrow made of willow trees carried on his back,
Inclined ski stick is pushed with both hands,
Skis made of the red pine tree and tied to the feet,
Gliding among the pine forest rapidly,
The one who pulls the sheepskin sled on the back,
He is the brave, skilful and wise hunter.
Look at the hunter!
He can run as fast as the antelope in the grand and mighty mountains,
Travelling to and fro among the pine forest,
It's not possible to catch him,
That hunter is an excellent archer,
Shooting prey one after another,
And the preys are deer and elk,
Inclined ski stick is pushed,
Snow rolls into small balls,
And the balls, rolling and rolling,
Become a much bigger one,
It seems to be racing with the hunter,
Rolling and chasing the hunter,
While the hunter strides on fur covered skis
The snowballs fall behind such a great distance.

CHAPTER 18
THREE SHORT STORIES FROM HEMINGWAY

Ernest Hemingway (1899–1961) needs no introduction! 'A Farewell to Arms', 'The Old Man and the Sea', 'Death in the Afternoon' (about bullfighting) and, 'For Whom the Bells Toll', about the Spanish Civil War. Did the earth move for you? He was awarded the Nobel Prize for Literature in 1954. He was passionately involved in bullfighting, big game hunting, and deep-sea fishing, a macho man if ever there was one.

Until I started collecting material for this anthology, I never realised what a passionate skier he was.

CHRISTMAS ON THE ROOF OF THE WORLD by Ernest Hemingway

FROM *THE TORONTO STAR WEEKLY*: 22 DECEMBER 1923
This vignette is from 'By-Line'. Selected articles and dispatches of four decades.

While it was still dark, Ida, the little German maid, came in and lit the fire in the big porcelain stove, and the burning pine wood roared up the chimney. Out the window the lake lay steel grey far down below, with the snow-covered mountains bulking jagged beyond it, and far away beyond it the massive tooth of the Dent du Midi beginning to lighten with the first touch of morning.

It was so cold outside. The air felt like something alive as I drew a deep breath. You could swallow the air like a drink of cold water. I reached up with a boot and banged on the ceiling.

"Hey, Chink. It's Christmas!"

"Hooray!" came Chink's voice down from the little room under the roof of the chalet.

Herself was up in a warm, woollen dressing robe, with the heavy goat's wool skiing socks. Chink knocked at the door. "Merry Christmas, mes enfants," he grinned. He wore the early morning garb of big, woolly dressing robe and thick socks that made us all look like some monastic order.

In the breakfast room we could hear the stove roaring and crackling. Herself opened the door. Against the tall, white porcelain stove hung the three long skiing stockings, bulging and swollen with strange lumps and bulges. Around the foot of the stove were piled boxes.

Two new shiny pairs of ash skis lay alongside the stove, too tall to stand in the low-ceilinged chalet room. For a week we had each been making mysterious trips to the Swiss town below on the lake. Hadley and I, Chink and I, and Hadley and Chink, returning after dark with strange boxes and bundles that were concealed in various parts of the chalet. Finally we each had to make a trip alone. That was yesterday. Then last night we had taken turns on the stockings, each pledged not to sleuth.

Chink had spent every Christmas since 1914 in the army. He was our best friend. For the first time in years it seemed like Christmas to all of us.

We ate breakfast in the old, untasting, gulping, early morning Christmas way, unpacked the stockings, down to the candy mouse in the toe, each made a pile of our things for future gloating. From breakfast we rushed into our clothes and tore down the icy road in the glory of the blue-white glistening alpine morning. The train was just pulling out. Chink and I shot the skis into the baggage car, and we all three swung aboard.

All Switzerland was on the move. Ski-ing parties, men, women, boys and girls, taking the train up the mountain, wearing their tight-fitting blue caps, the girls all in riding breeches and puttees, and shouting and calling out to one another. Platforms jammed.

Everybody travels third class in Switzerland, and on a big day like Christmas the third class overflows and the overflow is crowded into the sacred red plush first class compartments.

Shouting and cheering the train crawled alongside the mountain, climbing up towards the top of the world.

There was no big Christmas dinner at noon in Switzerland. Everybody was out in the mountain air with a lunch in the rucksack and the prospect of the dinner at night. When the train reached the highest point it made in the mountains, everybody piled out, the stacks of skis were unsorted from the baggage car and transferred to an open flat car hooked on to a jerky little train that ran straight up the side of the mountain on cog wheels.

At the top we could look over the whole world, white, glistening in the powder snow, and ranges of mountains stretching off in every direction. It was the top of a bob sled run that looped and turned in icy windings far below. A bob shot past, all the crew moving in time, and as it rushed at express train speed for the first turn, the crew all cried, "Ga-a-a-r!" and the bob roared in an icy smother around the curve and dropped off down the glassy run below.

No matter how high you are in the mountains there is always a slope going up. There were long strips of seal skin harnessed on our skis, running back from the tip to the base in a straight strip with the grain of the hair pointing back, so that you pushed right ahead through the snow going uphill. If your skis had a tendency to slide back the slipping movement would be checked by the seal skin hairs. They would slide smoothly forward, but hold fast at the end of each thrusting stride. Soon the three of us were high above the shoulder of the mountain that had seemed the top of the world. We kept going up in single file, sliding smoothly up through the snow in a long, upward zig-zag.

We passed through the last of the pines and came out on a shelving plateau. Here came the first run down – a half-mile sweep ahead. At the brow the skis seemed to drop out from under and in a hissing rush we all three swooped down the slope like birds.

On the other side it was thrusting, uphill, steady climbing again. The sun was hot and the sweat poured off us in the steady up hill drive. There is no place you get so tanned as in the mountains in winter. Nor so hungry. Nor so thirsty.

Finally we hit the lunching place, a snowed-under old log cattle barn where the peasant's cattle would shelter in the summer when this mountain was green with pasture. Everything seemed to drop off sheer below us. The air at that height, about 6,200 feet, is like wine. We put on our sweaters that had been in our rucksacks coming up, unpacked the lunch and the bottle of white wine, and lay back on our rucksacks and soaked in the sun. Coming up we had been wearing sunglasses against the glare of the snowfields, and now we took off the amber shaded goggles and looked out on a bright, new world.

"I'm really too hot," Herself said. Her face had burned coming up, even through the last crop of freckles and tan.

"You ought to use lampblack on your face," Chink suggested. But there is no record of any woman that has ever yet been willing to use that famous mountaineer's specific against snow-blindness and sunburn.

It was no time after lunch and Herself's daily nap, while Chink and I practised turns and stops on the slope, before the heat was gone out of the sun and it was time to start down. We took off the seal skins and waxed our skis. Then in one long, dropping, swooping, heart-plucking rush we were off. A seven-mile run down and no sensation in the world that can compare with it. You do not make the seven miles in one run. You go as fast as you believe possible, then you go a good deal faster, then you give up all hope, then you don't know what happened, but the earth came up and over and over and you sat up and untangled yourself from your skis and looked around. Usually all three had spilled together. Sometimes there was no one in sight. But there is no place to go except down. Down in a rushing, swooping, flying, plunging rush of fast ash blades through the powder snow.

Finally, in a rush we came out on to the road on the shoulder of the mountain where the cog-wheel railway had stopped coming up. Now we were all a shooting stream of skiers. All the Swiss were coming down, too. Shooting along the road in a seemingly endless stream. It was too steep and slippery to stop. There was nothing to do but plunge along down the road as helpless as though you were in a mill race. So we went down. Herself was way ahead somewhere. We could see her blue beret occasionally before it got too dark. Down, down, down the road we went in the dusk, past chalets that were a burst of lights and Christmas merriment in the dark.

Then the long line of skiers shot into the black woods, swung to one side to avoid a team and sledge coming up the road, passed more chalets, their windows alight with the candles from the Christmas trees. As we dropped past a chalet, watching nothing but the icy road and the man ahead, we heard a shout from the lighted doorway.

"Captain! Captain! stop here!" It was the German-Swiss landlord of our chalet. We were running past it in the dark.

Ahead of us, spilled at the turn, we found Herself and we stopped in a sliding slither, knocked loose our skis, and the three of us hiked up the hill towards the lights of the chalet.

The lights looked very cheerful against the dark pines of the hill, and inside was a big Christmas tree and a real Christmas turkey dinner, the table shiny with silver, the glasses tall and thin-stemmed, the bottles narrow-necked, the turkey large and brown and beautiful, the side dishes all present, and Ida serving in a new crisp apron.

It was the kind of a Christmas you can only get on top of the world.

FROM *IN OUR TIME*

CROSS-COUNTRY SNOW by Ernest Hemingway

The Funicular car bucked once more and then stopped. It could not go farther, the snow drifted solidly across the track. The gale scouring the exposed surface of the mountain had swept the snow surface into a wind-board crust. Nick, waxing his skis in the baggage car, pushed his boots into the toe irons and shut the clamp tight. He jumped from the car sideways onto the hard wind-board, made a jump turn and crouching and trailing his sticks slipped in a rush down the slope.

On the white below George dipped and rose and dipped out of sight. The rush and the sudden swoop as he dropped down a steep undulation in the mountain side plucked Nick's mind out and left him only the wonderful flying, dropping sensation in his body. He rose to a slight up-run and then the snow seemed to drop out from under him as he went down, down, faster and faster in a rush down the last, long steep slope. Crouching so he was almost sitting back on his skis, trying to keep the centre of gravity low, the snow driving like a sandstorm, he knew the pace was too much. But he held it. He would not let go and spill. Then a patch of soft snow, left in a hollow by the wind, spilled him and he went over and over in a clashing of skis, feeling like a shot rabbit, then stuck, his legs crossed, his skis sticking straight up and his nose and ears jammed full of snow.

George stood a little farther down the slope, knocking the snow from his wind jacket with big slaps.

"You took a beauty, Mike," he called to Nick. "That's lousy soft snow. It bagged me the same way."

"What's it like over the khud?" Nick kicked his skis around as he lay on his back and stood up.

"You've got to keep to your left. It's a good fast drop with a Christy at the bottom on account of a fence."

"Wait a sec and we'll take it together."

"No, you come on and go first. I like to see you take the khuds."

Nick Adams came up past George, big back and blond head still faintly snowy, then his skis started slipping at the edge and he swooped down, hissing in the crystalline powder snow and seeming to float up and drop down as he went up and down the billowing khuds. He held to his left and at the end, as he rushed toward the fence, keeping his knees locked tight together and turning his body like tightening a screw brought his skis sharply around to the right in a smother of snow and slowed into a loss of speed parallel to the hillside and the wire fence.

He looked up the hill. George was coming down in telemark position, kneeling; one leg forward and bent, the other trailing; his sticks hanging like some insect's thin legs, kicking up puffs of snow as they touched the surface and finally the whole kneeling, trailing figure coming around in a beautiful right curve, crouching, the legs shot forward and back, the body leaning out against the swing, the sticks accenting the curve like points of light, all in a wild cloud of snow.

"I was afraid to Christy," George said, "the snow was too deep. You made a beauty."

"I can't telemark with my leg," Nick said.

Nick held down the top strand of the wire fence with his ski and George slid over. Nick followed him down to the road. They thrust bent-kneed along the road into a pine forest. The road became polished ice, stained orange and a tobacco yellow from the teams hauling logs. The skiers kept to the stretch of snow along the side. The road dipped sharply to a stream and then ran straight up-hill. Through the woods they could see a long, low-eaved, weather-beaten building. Through the trees it was a faded yellow. Closer the window frames were painted green. The paint was peeling. Nick knocked his clamps loose with one of his ski sticks and kicked off the skis.

"We might as well carry them up here," he said.

He climbed the steep road with the skis on his shoulder, kicking his heel nails into the icy footing. He heard George breathing and kicking in his heels just behind him. They stacked the skis against the side of the inn and slapped the snow off each other's trousers, stamped their boots clean, and went in.

Inside it was quite dark. A big porcelain stove shone in the corner of the room. There was a low ceiling. Smooth benches back of dark, wine-stained tables were along each side of the room. Two Swiss sat over their pipes and two decies of cloudy new wine next to the stove. The boys took off their jackets and sat against the wall on the other side of the stove. A voice in the next room stopped singing and a girl in a blue apron came in through the door to see what they wanted to drink.

"A bottle of Sion," Nick said. "Is that all right, Gidge?"

Sure," said George. "You know more about wine than I do. I like any of it."

The girl went out.

"There's nothing really can touch skiing, is there?" Nick said. "The way it feels when you first drop off on a long run."

"Huh," said George. "It's too swell to talk about."

The girl brought the wine in and they had trouble with the cork. Nick finally opened it. The girl went out and they heard her singing in German in the next room.

"Those specks of cork in it don't matter," said Nick.

"I wonder if she's got any cake."

"Let's find out." "

The girl came in and Nick noticed that her apron covered swellingly her pregnancy. I wonder why I didn't see that when she first came in, he thought.

"What were you singing?" he asked her.

"Opera, German opera." She did not care to discuss the subject. "We have some apple strudel if you want it."

"She isn't so cordial, is she?" said George.

"Oh, well. She doesn't know us and she thought we were going to kid her about her singing, maybe. She's from up where they speak German probably and she's touchy about being here and then she's got that baby coming without being married and she's touchy."

"How do you know she isn't married?"

"No ring. Hell, no girls get married around here till they're knocked up."

The door came open and a gang of woodcutters from up the road came in, stamping their boots and steaming in the room. The waitress brought in three litres of new wine for the gang and they sat at the two tables, smoking and quiet, with their hats off, leaning back against the wall or forward on the table. Outside the horses on the wood sledges made an occasional sharp jangle of bells as they tossed their heads.

George and Nick were happy. They were fond of each other. They knew they had the run back home ahead of them.

"When have you got to go back to school?" Nick asked.

"Tonight," George answered. "I've got to get the ten-forty from Montreux."

"I wish you could stick over and we could do the Dent du Lys tomorrow."

"I got to get educated," George said. "Gee, Mike, don't you wish we could just bum together? Take our skis and go on the train to where there was good running and then go on and put up at pubs and go right across the Oberland and up the Valais and all through the Engadine and just take repair kit and extra sweaters and pyjamas in our rucksacks and not give a damn about school or anything."

"Yes, and go through the Schwarzwald that way. Gee, the swell places."

"That's where you went fishing last summer, isn't it?"

"Yes."

George leaned back against the wall and shut his eyes.

"Wine always makes me feel this way," he said.

"Feel bad?" Nick asked.

"No. I feel good, but funny."

"I know," Nick said.

"Sure," said George.

"Should we have another bottle?" Nick asked.

"Not for me," George said.

They sat there, Nick leaning his elbows on the table, George slumped back against the wall.

"Is Helen going to have a baby?" George said, coming down to the table from the wall.

"Yes."

"When?"

"Late next summer."

"Are you glad?"

"Yes. Now."

"Will you go back to the States?"

'I guess so."

"Do you want to?"

"Does Helen?"

"No."

George sat silent. He looked at the empty bottle and the empty glasses.

"It's hell, isn't it?" he said.

"No. Not exactly," Nick said.

"Why not?"

"I don't know," Nick said.

"Will you ever go skiing together in the States?" George said.

"I don't know," said Nick.

"The mountains aren't much," George said.

"No," said Nick. "They're too rocky. There's too much timber and they're too far away."

"Yes," said George, "that's the way it is in California."

"Yes," Nick said, "that's the way it is everywhere I've ever been."

"Yes," said George, "that's the way it is."

The Swiss got up and paid and went out.

"I wish we were Swiss," George said.

"They've all got goiter," said Nick.

"I don't believe it," George said.

"Neither do I," said Nick.

They laughed.

"Maybe we'll never go skiing again, Nick," George said.

"We've got to," said Nick. "It isn't worthwhile if you can't."

"We'll go, all right," George said.

"We've got to," Nick agreed.

"I wish we could make a promise about it," George said.

Nick stood up. He buckled his wind jacket tight. He leaned over George and picked up the two ski poles from against the wall. He stuck one of the ski poles into the floor.

"There isn't any good in promising," he said.

They opened the door and went out. It was very cold. The snow had crusted hard. The road ran up the hill into the pine trees. They took down their skis from where they leaned against the wall in the inn. Nick put on his gloves. George was already started up the road, his skis on his shoulder. Now they would have the run home together.

FROM THE SNOWS OF KILIMANJARO by Ernest Hemingway

Now in his mind he saw a railway station at Karagatch and he was standing with his pack and that was the headlight of the Simplon-Orient cutting the dark now and he was leaving Thrace then after the retreat. That was one of the things he had saved to write, with, in the morning at breakfast, looking out the window and seeing snow on the mountains in Bulgaria and Nansen's Secretary asking the old man if it were snow and the old man looking at it and saying, "No, that's not snow. It's too early for snow." And the Secretary repeating to the other girls, "No, you see. It's not snow" and them all saying, "It's not snow we were mistaken." But it was the snow all right and he sent them on into it when he evolved exchange of populations. And it was snow they tramped along in until they died that winter.

It was snow too that fell all Christmas week that year up in the Gauertal, that year they lived in the woodcutter's house with the big square porcelain stove that filled half the room, and they slept on mattresses filled with beech leaves, the time the deserter came with his feet bloody in the snow. He said the police were right behind him and they gave him woollen socks and held the gendarmes talking until the tracks had drifted over.

In Schrunz, on Christmas day, the snow was so bright it hurt your eyes when you looked out from the Weinstube and saw everyone coming home from church. That was where they walked up the sleigh-smoothed urine-yellowed road along the river with the steep pine hills, skis heavy on the shoulder, and where they ran that great run down the glacier above the Madlener-Haus, the snow as smooth to see as cake frosting and as light as powder and he remembered the noiseless rush the speed made as you dropped down like a bird.

They were snow-bound a week in the Madlener-Haus that time in the blizzard playing cards in the smoke by the lantern light and the stakes were higher all the time as Herr Lent lost more. Finally he lost it all. Everything, the Skischule money and all the season's profit and then his capital. He could see him with his long nose, picking up the cards and then opening, "Sans Voir." There was always gambling then. When there was no snow you gambled and when there was too much you gambled. He thought of all the time in his life he had spent gambling.

But he had never written a line of that, nor of that cold, bright Christmas day with the mountains showing across the plain that Barker had flown across the lines to bomb the Austrian officers' leave train, machine-gunning them as they scattered and ran. He remembered Barker afterwards coming into the mess and starting to tell about it. And how quiet it got and then somebody saying, "You bloody murderous bastard."

Those were the same Austrians they killed then that he skied with later. No not the same. Hans, that he skied with all that year, had been in the Kaiser-Jägers and when they went hunting hares together up the little valley above the saw mill they had talked of the fighting on Pasubio and of the attack on Pertica and Asalone and he had never written a word of that. Nor of Monte Corona, nor the Siete Commun, nor of Arsiedo.

How many winters had he lived in the Vorarlberg and the Arlberg? It was four and then he remembered the man who had the fox to sell when they had walked into Bludenz, that time to buy presents, and the cherry-pit taste of good kirsch, the fast-slipping rush of running powder-snow on crust, singing "Hi! Ho! said Rolly!" as you ran down the last stretch to the steep drop, taking it straight, then running the orchard in three turns and out across the ditch and onto the icy road behind the inn. Knocking your bindings loose, kicking the skis free and leaning them up against the wooden wall of the inn, the lamplight coming from the window, where inside, in the smoky, new-wine smelling warmth, they were playing the accordion.

CHAPTER 19

MYTHS: REAL AND IMAGINED

THE STORY OF SNOWSHOE THOMPSON – VIKING OF THE SIERRA by Ron Watters

Ron Watters is the author of eight books on the outdoors. Working to recognise good outdoor writing by others, he is one of the founders and current chairman of the National Outdoor Book Awards, the largest book award programme in the outdoor world.

It is early winter, 1855. In Placerville on the west slope of California's Sierras, the prospects for any kind of reliable mail service over the mountains are bleak.

The prospects are even bleaker for the settlers living on the east slope of the Sierras in Carson Valley (south of present-day Carson City, Nevada). At least, Placerville can get news from Sacramento, only 50 miles to the west, and San Francisco beyond that. Carson Valley, however, is without any means of communication over the Sierras and is virtually cut-off from the world. The residents of Carson Valley might as well be living on an island in the middle of the ocean.

It is all because of the Sierras' snow. It grows to extraordinary depths, far beyond the experience and imagination of anyone who had to come to California since gold was discovered in 1848. Cabins – parts of towns even – drift over and disappear under the great layers of snow. The snow builds to such depths that not even stove pipes are left.

The smart ones have boarded up their cabins, braced ceiling rafters, and have gotten out before winter. They knew that snow would bring travel to a virtual standstill. Those who wait too long to get out will end up wallowing in snow, and if they manage to make it back to the valley alive (and with all their toes and fingers intact) they'll have plenty of harrowing tales of survival to tell.

About the only ones who travel in the Sierras on purpose in the winter are the mail contractors. That's their job. In the summer, it's challenging work, but, in the winter, it's downright backbreaking. To get through, they've attempted different routes through the mountains and experimented with various traveling methods. One mail contractor even resorted to using wooden mauls, beating and packing the snow, so his pack animals would have something firm to walk on. This they did mile after mile. When they got to Carson Valley they were spent. More recent attempts had been made on webs or Canadian snowshoes, with the mail carried on men's backs. But even those were not reliable. Just that December, a man by the name of Bishop took 8 days to get across the Sierras and was 'badly frozen' in the process.

That's the way things stood in 1855. Mail service over the Sierras in the winter was simply uncertain. Things, indeed, looked bleak.

Then, a strapping young Norwegian immigrant appeared on the scene.

Within a short time, this young, blond Norseman would be celebrated throughout the Sierras and become one of the most famous cross-country skiers of all time. His reputation and legend would grow by leaps, and, in time, the facts and fiction of his life would become so intermixed that it would become difficult, if not impossible, by modern historians to separate the two.

This much we do know: his name was 'John A. Thompson'. To the admiring residents of the Sierras, however, he was known simply as Snowshoe Thompson.

John Thompson immigrated with his family from Norway when he was 10 years old. In 1851, at the age of 24, Thompson arrived in California. It was just 3 years after gold had been discovered, and the mountains were crawling with recent arrivals. Prospectors had spread out all over the Sierras and more strikes were being made, particularly in a lovely region of the Sierras to the west of Lake Tahoe. It was here in a swath of mountainous country between Sacramento and Reno (60 miles to the north and south of present-day Interstate 80) that Thompson would make his mark.

This area of high peaks and preternaturally abundant snow is sometimes referred to as the Lost Sierra for its long-gone boom towns. But it abounds with much more than mining history. This is also a place where skiing history was made. Indeed, it is hallowed ground, for the Lost Sierra is the cradle of skiing in North America.

Here skis first made their appearance in great enough numbers to establish a toe hold in the New World. According to ski historian William Berry, it began with a few isolated individuals in the early 1850s. While who and when skis were first used remains murky, it is clear that by the tail end of 1850s, they were beginning to proliferate throughout the area. And by the 1860s in the Lost Sierra, they had become de rigueur.

Thompson played an important role in the popularization of skiing in the Sierras. While he probably wasn't the first, he was certainly among the earliest skiers and quickly became the most well-known. His deeds and exploits were so widely reported that, in essence, he became the sport's poster child. Television producers, had there been television in those days, would have loved him.

He would have also caught the eyes of the ladies – what few of them were around. He was, to use a more contemporary term, something of a 'hottie'. That, according to Dan DeQuille of the Territorial Enterprise who interviewed Thompson. (DeQuille, incidentally, gave a young Samuel Clemens – Mark Twain – his first newspaper job, and certainly must have had a talent for sizing up one's character.) 'John Thompson,' DeQuille wrote, was a 'man of splendid physique. His features were large, but regular and handsome. He had the blond hair and beard, and fair skin and blue eyes of his Scandinavian ancestors.'

The striking, blue-eyed Thompson had dabbled at mining in Placerville and farming near Sacramento, but, like many in those days, he was always on the look-out for other employment opportunities. Too, he had the constitution and inclinations of his Viking heritage, and a job with an adventurous slant would undoubtedly pique his interest. According to some writers, it was an ad in the Sacramento Union in 1855 that led him to the profession which would open to the door to fame: 'People Lost to the World; Uncle Sam Needs a Mail Carrier.'

The mail route referred to in the Union's ad was between Placerville, 50 miles to the east of Sacramento, to Mormon Station, 25 miles southwest to Carson City, Nevada. (Mormon Station located in the Carson River valley would eventually be renamed Genoa, Nevada.) The total distance of the route: 90 miles, all the way, from one side of the Sierras to the other.

Thompson got the job. His first run would be in early January, and for it, he planned to use skis, a method of winter travel he had learned as a boy in Norway. The term 'skis,' however, had not come into usage yet. They were called 'Norwegian Skates' by the Sacramento Union. Two other common names used by newspapers of that era included 'Long Snowshoes' and 'Norwegian Snowshoes'. What we now know as snowshoes were called 'webs,' 'Indian Snowshoes' or 'Canadian Snowshoes'.

Relying on his boyhood memory, Thompson constructed his first set of Norwegian skates out of a freshly cut (and very green) oak plank. As you can imagine, they were monstrosities. According to De Quille, Thompson weighed them when he got to Placeville and they tipped the scales at 25 pounds. He eventually got the weight down on subsequent pairs, but, even so, the skis of the 1800s were still formidable in size.

In a newspaper article some years later, Thompson described the dimensions of his skis: 9 feet long, 4 inches wide at the tip and narrowing to 3½ inches. Thickness: 1½ inches.

Since Norwegian skates were still relatively unknown, and still unproven, there were lots of doubters in Placerville. Bishop's recent ill-fated, 8-day trip across the Sierras was a case in point. Even Thompson's friends in Placerville, De Quille tells us, urged him not to do it. They were afraid that the unwieldy long boards strapped to his feet would be unmanageable and that he would 'dash his brains out against a tree' or fly off a cliff.

Thompson, however, had hedged his bets and had practiced with his skis in the high country above Placerville prior to his first trip. By the time his first trip came around, he was ready and confident enough of his skills. On January 3, 1855, he left the settlement behind and disappeared into the mountains.

Then there was silence.

A short while later, he was back. Jaws dropped open. Friends shouted hurrahs. He had done it! And far faster than anyone imagined. When he later arrived at Sacramento, his total return time from Carson Valley was an amazing three and half days. He had cut almost five days off Bishop's time and wasn't any worse for the wear. The naysayers were silenced. 'Snowshoe Thompson,' a moniker that he would pick up over the next few years, had proven that skis were an efficient and suitable mode of winter transportation in the mountains.

The Sacramento Union announced that first famous trip: 'Mr. John A. Thompson left Carson Valley on Tuesday morning and reached this city at noon yesterday. He was three days and a half in coming through from Carson Valley and used on the snow the Norwegian skates, which are manufactured of wood.'

The following month, the Union was warming up to this man Thompson, calling him an 'adventurous and hardy mountain expressman.' He regularly made the journey twice a month through the rest of the winter. His reliability, kindness and physical prowess quickly earned the admiration and respect of the Sierra residents. The seeds had been planted. The roots firmly established. A legend was about to spring forth from the Sierra soil.

His pack, weighing from 60 to 80 pounds, included mail, newspapers, periodicals, ore samples, and medicines. UPS and FedEx can't claim any originality when it comes to express service plans. Thompson long beat them to it, instituting a 2 day and 3 day service. He could run the 90-mile Placerville to Carson Valley leg in 3 days and reverse journey in 2 days.

Not all of the distance was done on skis. The snow line varied depending on the month and severity of the winter. Skis, however, were needed in 1856 and were what got him swiftly across the high, snowbound portion of the route.

He was back at it the following winter. The Sacramento Union reported that during the winter of 1856-1857, most of his 31 crossings of the Sierras were on skis. That second winter appears to be the high water mark in Thompson's trans-Sierra ski express. In 1858, he was again carrying the mail, but with improved wagon roads, he was now using horse-drawn sleighs. He continued, however, to use skis when the roads could not be broken. For the next two decades of his life, he used Norwegian skates on and off for other shorter mail routes and for privately contracted express service.

Amazingly, Snowshoe Thompson carried little in the way of bedding and clothing with him. His weighty skis and pack – and moderate Sierra winter temperatures – might have had something to do with it. Still, it's remarkable that his only indulgence to comfort was a wide- rimmed hat and Mackinaw. He kept warm during the day by the exercise of skiing. At nights, he built a large fire, lay on a bed of pine boughs and used his mail sack for a pillow. He would stretch 'himself upon this fragrant couch,' wrote Hubert Howe Bancroft, a west coast historian, 'and with his feet to the blaze and his face to the stars slept soundly and safely.'

Meals on the trail consisted of dried beef and sausage, crackers and biscuits. He didn't know about waxing. And when freshly fallen snow would warm, it would stick to his skis in great clumps. When that happened, he'd stop and wait for evening when the snowpack would glaze over and he could glide once again without the encumbrance of wet, sticky snow.

To propel himself forward on the flat and to climb hills, he used one long pole. Two poles came much later. The pole, sometimes called a 'balancing pole', was also used to assist him on downhill runs. Apparently, Thompson was a master in its use. 'He flew down the mountainside,' Dan DeQuille wrote, describing his graceful manner. 'He did not ride astride his pole or drag it to one side as was the practice of other snowshoers, but held it horizontally before him after the manner of a tightrope walker. His appearance was graceful, swaying his balance pole to one side and the other in the manner that a soaring eagle dips its wings.' Snowshoe Thompson – the man who could ski like a soaring eagle – was also known for his generosity and for his willingness to come to the aid of others. An incident early in his second year of carrying mail over the Sierras helped establish that reputation. On December 23, 1856, Thompson stopped by a cabin along his route, and found James Sisson lying on the floor, barely alive. Several days prior, Sisson had been caught in a storm and had frozen his feet. He eventually reached the cabin where Thompson found him. Thompson made the man as comfortable as possible and skied out the next day to Carson Valley. He convinced five others to go back with him, outfitting each of the rescuers in skis. Once back at the cabin, they fashioned a sled and eventually got the ailing man back to the valley by the 28th.

The story doesn't end there. In order to save the man's life, Sisson's gangrenous legs would have to be amputated, but the doctor treating him was unwilling to undertake the operation without an anaesthetic. Thompson, who must have been thoroughly knackered after the rescue, volunteered to make another trip. He again put on his skis and made the 90 mile trek to Placerville. Then travelled 50 more miles to Sacramento. There he obtained the anaesthetic, turned back around and did it all over again, retracing his path back to Carson Valley. Sisson, reportedly, recovered and eventually moved back to the east.

"Most remarkable man I ever knew, that Snowshoe Thompson," said Postmaster S. A. Kinsey. "He must be made of iron. Besides, he never thinks of himself, but he'd give his last breath for anyone else – even a total stranger."

He might have been a bit too generous. Despite the incredible physical effort he put into providing a reliable mail service, he was never ever fully compensated for his work. With the support of friends, he petitioned the Nevada legislature and the U.S. Congress, but, in the end, he never received the remuneration which he was owed. There were other life disappointments, of course. His son, and only child, died when the boy was only 11. It must have been a terrible blow to the strong Norwegian.

Life went on. DeQuille describes Thompson at the age of 49 appearing in the prime of his life. 'His eyes were bright as that of a hawk, his cheeks were ruddy, his frame muscular. His face had the look of repose, and he had that calmness of manner, which are the result of perfect self-reliance.' 'He was still skiing,' De Quille wrote. 'He would load a quarter beef on his back and ski up a steep canyon to supply miners working at the Pittsburg Mine, 20 miles south of Thompson's ranch.'

It seemed that even in middle age, the robust Snowshoe Thompson had many more years of skiing the mountains, but it was not to be. Shortly after the DeQuille interview Thompson suddenly fell ill with a liver ailment. It was springtime, and the barley on his ranch needed to be planted. Thompson struggled out to his field. Bending over to sow the seeds was too painful, so he mounted a horse and spread the seed from a bucket held out in front of him. Afterwards, unable to raise his 6 foot frame, the ever-moving Norwegian was confined to his bed. Two days later he died.

He was buried beside his son in Genoa, in Carson Valley for whose residents he had first carried the mail by snowshoes over the Sierras. Some time after his death, his wife had a tombstone placed over his grave. Carved on top of the tombstone are two crossed skis.

'To ordinary men there is something terrible in the wild winter storms that often sweep through the Sierras,' wrote De Quille. But not to Snowshoe Thompson. The mountains were his sanctuary, and storms were just another part of its raw beauty. On his skis, he could freely move across the snow-covered landscape.

The feeling of freedom must have been never more real to Thompson than when gliding downhill, holding his balance pole out in front of him, dipping it one direction and then the other, his wide-brimmed hat flapping in the wind and the Sierras spread out in front of him. At times like that, he must have felt like a soaring eagle.

AND HERE THE IMAGINED MYTH

An imagined myth takes the shape of an epic ski poem, written in 1863 in Norway by Bernt Lund, an army officer and poet. The real-life Trysil of the mid-19th century was an ideal setting for a ski epic, as the world's first official ski meet was held there in 1855, and the first ski and biathlon club was founded there in 1861. Knud was not any one person, but rather a synthesis of the young men of the town and its surrounding farms, known afar for their skiing skills. The epic was published several times and then in 1897 gained national recognition with its publication in Christiania (as Oslo then was named) in an edition illustrated with colour lithographs by artist Andreas Bloch.

The Trysil Knud epic consists of 32 stanzas of rhyming couplets, many extolling Knud's prowess in ski jumping and downhill skiing. As was then the custom, Knud is said to have jumped in military dress uniform, firing a musket while in flight, and to have skied so skillfully downhill in untracked snow that he could speed hazardously close to a tree and snatch a jacket hanging on it.

There most likely are no complete translations of the poem into English, as the best sources of translations of Norwegian literature (the National Library in Oslo and the library of St. Olaf College in Northfield, Minnesota) have none. With poetic license, the first two stanzas might in English be:

> *The Eastern Valley skiers were agreed,*
> *that they had heard of no mightier deed*
> *than Trysil-Knud descending on skis*
> *down Bratberg and Glomme with ease.*
>
> *Knud was ahead whenever it counted,*
> *steadying himself when others floundered.*
> *And in the dash down it was no surprise*
> *that he was the one to claim first prize.*

CHAPTER 20

POEMS

FOR AN EARTH LANDING by Erica Jong

Erica Jong (1942) is an American novelist, satirist, and poet, known particularly for her novel 'Fear of Flying'.
She has won numerous literary awards.

The sky sinks its blue teeth
into the mountains.
Rising on pure will

(the lurch & lift-off,
the sudden swing
into wide, white snow),
I encourage the cable.

Past the wind & crossed tips of my skis
& the mauve shadows of pines
& the spoor of bears & deer,

I speak to my fear,
rising, riding, finding myself the only thing
between snow & sky, the link
that holds it all together.

Halfway up the wire,
we stop, slide back a little
(a whirr of pulleys).

Astronauts circle above us today
in the television blue of space.

But the thin withers of alps are waiting to take us too,
& this might be the moon!

We move!
Friends, this is a toy merely for reaching mountains merely for skiing down.

& now we're dangling
like charms on the same bracelet

or upsidedown tightrope people
(a colossal circus!)
or absurd winged walkers,
angels in animal fur,

with mittened hands waving
& fear turning
& the mountain
like a fisherman, reeling us all in.

So we land
on the windy peak,
touch skis to snow,
are married to our purple shadows,
& ski back down to the unimaginable valley leaving no footprints.

TWO PAIR OF SKIS by Yevgeny Yevtushenko

Yevgeny Yevtushenko (1932–2017) was an internationally acclaimed poet with the charisma of an actor and the instincts of a politician whose defiant verse inspired a generation of young Russians in their fight against Stalinism during the Cold War.

Two pair of skis nestled tenderly against a house, silent, almost without life.
But in the house, you and I are alive.
I'm not asleep.
You are.
Our sole guardians are two pair of skis,
offended that we didn't let them lean inside the house.
On each ski is a shallow white groove, like the Milky Way.

Danger roams crunchingly across the frost.

Everything is fragile – from icicles even to us,

and, as if the skis feel the threat, they focus on the stars.

You remember – the snowy woods full of the sun and in the snow

the inscription written with the ski pole:

"G. Savel'iev."

Inside the letters a white spruce had shed its needles,

and, as if wolves had eaten him, Savel'iev himself disappeared.

And something made me fear for the life of Savel'iev,

for a son with a birthmark on his fragile fontanelle.

And you and I, and the skis, and the universe – on a tiny thread.

I am so afraid for the crystal silence, for the moonlight on the slopes of sleeping roofs ...

And did the two pair of skis leave for long a ski track from us?

Coziness,

Health – the pitiful little grabs at so-called life…

Only if they press the button and even a splinter of you will remain...

two pair of skis.

Beneath every roof… is also mankind.

Absolutely no less valued than Paris is our home

Where on a porch lit by the moon

are two pair of skis

And listening with keen attention to the endless,

Where you move your lips in sleep,

two pair of skis support eternity on their tips.

CHAPTER 21
MISCELLANEOUS

GETTING READY FOR THE NEW SEASON

PRE SKI SEASON TRAINING

Ski season is almost here! Hence, the following list of exercises to get you prepared:

1. Visit your local butcher and pay £30 to sit in the walk-in freezer for a half an hour. Afterwards, burn two £50 bills to warm up.

2. Soak your gloves and store them in the freezer after every use.

3. Fasten a small, wide rubber band around the top half of your head before you go to bed each night.

4. If you wear glasses, begin wearing them with glue smeared on the lenses.

5. Throw away a fify-pound bill now.

6. Find the nearest ice rink and walk across the ice 20 times in your ski boots carrying two pairs of skis, accessory bag and poles. Pretend you are looking for your car. Sporadically drop things.

7. Place a small but angular pebble in your shoes, line them with crushed ice, and then tighten a C-clamp around your toes.

8. Buy a new pair of gloves and immediately throw one away.

9. Secure one of your ankles to a bed post and ask a friend to run into you at high speed.

10. Go to McDonald's and insist on paying £8.50 for a hamburger. Be sure you are in the longest line.

11. Clip a lift ticket to the zipper of your jacket and ride a motorcycle fast enough to make the ticket lacerate your face.

12. Drive slowly for five hours – anywhere – as long as it's in a snowstorm and you're following an 18-wheeler.

13. Fill a blender with ice, hit the pulse button and let the spray blast your face. Leave the ice on your face until it melts. Let it drip into your clothes.

14. Dress up in as many clothes as you can and then proceed to take them off because you have to go to the bathroom.

15. Slam your thumb in a car door. Don't go see a doctor.

16. Repeat all of the above every Saturday and Sunday until it's time for the real thing!

STRAUSS INTERMEZZO

SYNOPSIS

Setting: Vienna and Grundlsee during a 1920s winter

The composer Storch is leaving for a conducting tour, and his wife Christine helps him pack, arguing and nagging along the way. Seeking relief from loneliness she goes tobogganing and collides with a skier, a young Baron who befriends her. They dance together at a ball and she arranges for him to lodge in the house of her notary. The friendship is soured when the Baron asks Christine for financial assistance. She opens a letter, supposedly for her husband, from a lady arranging an assignation. She immediately telegrams Storch demanding they part for ever. In tears, she seeks solace in her son's bedroom but he defends his father.

Storch is playing skat with friends in Vienna when the telegram arrives, and is bewildered by the accusations. Stroh, a conductor friend, admits that he knows the lady and surmises that his and Storch's surnames must have been confused. Christine visits the notary to demand a divorce, but he is unwilling to pursue the matter. She sends the Baron to Vienna to gather evidence of infidelity. Packing to leave, she receives a telegram from her husband saying that Stroh will explain the misunderstanding. Even after Stroh's visit she is reluctant to accept the truth. Storch returns home, and an argument ensues. The Baron arrives with evidence that Stroh rather than Storch had indeed known the lady and Christine dismisses him, assured that her husband is blameless. Storch forgives her anger and teases her about her dalliance with the Baron. Husband and wife declare a renewed love.

Surely, the only Opera that mentions, however briefly, skiing.

SOME STATISTICS

World Speed skiing records, set in 2016 in Vars, France
Men: 254.958 km/h (158.424 mph) set by Ivan Origone, Italy
Women 247.083 km/h (153.530 mph) set by Valentina Greggio, Italy.

World Longest Ski Jump, set in 2017 at Vikersundbakken in Norway
253.5 m (832 ft), Stefan Kraft, Austria

The Birkebeiner Race has been held since 1932, and commemorates a trip made by the Birkebeiner loyalists Torstein Skevla and Skjervald Skrukka to save the infant heir to the Norwegian throne, Håkon Håkonsson, in 1206. All participants carry a backpack weighing at least 3.5 kg, symbolizing the weight of the then one-year-old king. The race starts at Rena and ends at Lillehammer, a distance of 54 km. Present record held by Petter Eliassen, Norway in 2.19.28 set in 2015, faster than his 2019 time.

50-kilometre cross country, on a prepared track

It is difficult to make comparisons as the courses vary from country to country, but the fastest Holmenkollen Ski Festival 50-kilometre, skied on the same course each year, was set by Sjur Røthe Norway in 2015 in a time of 1:54.44.

Amundsen to the South Pole

Amundsen and his crew returned to their base camp on 25 January 1912, 99 days and roughly 1400 nautical miles after their departure.

World speed record on a snowboard

In 2015 Frenchman Edmond Plawczyk broke the world record for fastest speed recorded on a snowboard, with a speed of 203kph (126mph).

Mürren Inferno

Start Kleines Schilthorn 2970 m to Lauterbrunnen 800 m, 14.9 km. Fastest man Kuno Michel 13.20 min. Fastest lady Marianne Rubi 14.32 min.

TO SWANK OR NOT TO SWANK by A H D'Egville

A H D'Egville was one of the early pioneers of British skiing. This vignette is from his book 'Modern Skiing' published in 1927

I must say at once that I do not like the word, but then I do not like what it implies, and am therefore quite prepared to dub a bad quality with a bad name. Skiing, like cricket, skating, and ball-room dancing, is a game which gives the most magnificent opportunities for swank, and because people are herded together for long periods in hotels during the winter season, this habit is more irritating than anything else I know of. Let me say at once that I do not imagine that you personally are going to swank! But it is such an easy fault to fall into that I wanted to warn you of it at once and put you on your guard against those who indulge in it. You will suffer from it quite enough at the hands of others sooner or later. To have to listen to interminable stories as to exactly how such and such a run was performed, how such and such a turn was made on such and such a steep slope is perfectly maddening.

Mr. Arnold Lunn once wrote a very clever article for the Bystander, which I took much pleasure in illustrating, in which, with great delicacy and wit, he dealt with this subject. He pointed out various methods of swanking, among which was the case of the woman who tells you how angry her husband was with her for going down Lone Tree Slope straight. With infinite guile she pretends to harp upon the anger. What she is really doing is finding an excuse for letting you know about Lone Tree Slope. Another method is to lead a party of honest skiers to a point from which an excellent view is obtained of a single track running down the steep side of the Schiltgrat. With a careless manner, the adept swanker asks whose tracks they can be and then remembers, with studied confusion, and loud voice that they are his own. Dear, dear!

Still another well-known method is to advise someone not to go straight down a certain steep place. 'I took it straight yesterday. I didn't fall, but it was most unpleasant.'

Those, of course, are subtle methods, and subtlety deserves some praise. What deserves no praise at all is the habit of blatantly showing off in public. It is really never worth doing because it is so easy. Most of us can do something, some little trick that the others can't do. But this does not justify our believing that others couldn't do it if they tried as hard as we have. A favourite method of swank in public is to wait till all the competitors are gathered at the top of a Slalom course, when some three hundred spectators are gathered near the finishing post, and then to take the hill straight, thus :

Securing a free field.

Receiving the admiration of those who have only just arrived in Switzerland.

Driving the time-keeper mad, and

Keeping all the other competitors waiting.

Then there is the "practice sloper." You can see him standing at the top of the slope waiting until the right people are looking. If they are not, he may be perceived pretending to adjust his binding and dithering with his stick.

Then, assured that Miss Thingummy is at last looking his way he darts off downhill in a series of well-prepared turns on a well-prepared line, and perhaps Miss Thingummy is duly impressed and gives him Nos. 6 and 7 at the dance that evening, and during the interval between 6 and 7 you may bet your boots that the conversation will be skiing.

Another nuisance is the man who says he wishes he could do a Christiania like Snoggitt, knowing full well he can do it better, or that he has a better method, and immediately goes and does it, to the discomfiture of Snoggitt, if he is very serious, and to his great amusement, if he has any sense of humour at all.

Worst of all is the 'Never-turn' pest, or the 'non stick' person. The first is forever telling us how aggravating it is that he is not able to turn, so that everything, however steep, has to be taken straight. Great Heavens! Not only is the 'non-turner' a pest and great nuisance verbally, but a great danger practically, and quite useless as a ski-runner.

The 'non-sticker' is rarer, but no less a nuisance. His particular form of swank is to run without sticks, which, if he only guessed it , we know to be slow, tiring and completely.

The "non-sticker " is rarer, but no less a nuisance. His particular form of swank is to run without sticks, which, if he only guessed it , we know to be slow, tiring and completely futile and pointless.

Of the man who repeatedly tells us that such and such a slope terrifies him, that he is frightened before he starts and that he knows he is going to fall-and doesn't, we will say nothing.

Skiing should allow of no swank for the reason that –

The beginner, because a beginner, has nothing to show off.

The expert never needs to because he is expert.

What one does want to do is to ski with more confidence than one's skill warrants in order to push up one's standard. One wants to' attempt much, always rather more than one expects to be able to do.

But this is swanking inwardly and not outwardly – to others.

Modesty on the snow is an essential to progress in every way. Above all things avoid telling people about your falls.

We all fall. We have seen hundreds of others fall hundreds of times. We are completely versed in all forms of falling. It is useless to tell us you have had an amazing fall, in the firm belief that it is something delightfully novel. You got your ski-point down the back of your neck? We know. We knew it years ago. But this one was in a deep gully ? We know ! They all are. You couldn't get up ? No one ever can. Don't be ashamed of falling. Be ashamed of retailing it.

CHAPTER 22
QUOTES

JACQUES DE LA TOCNAYE

In 1799 French traveller Jacques de la Tocnaye visited Norway and wrote in his travel diary:

"In winter, the mail is transported through the Filefjell mountain pass by a man on a kind of snow skates moving very quickly without being obstructed by snow drifts that would engulf both people and horses. People in this region move around like this. I've seen it repeatedly. It requires no more effort than what is needed to keep warm. The day will surely come when even those of other European nations are learning to take advantage of this convenient and cheap mode of transport."

VARIOUS QUOTES

The sensation of downhill skiing is easy to appreciate (and become addicted to) but sometimes hard to put into words. Here's a list of some pretty good attempts.

"Gotta use your brain, it's the most important part of your equipment."
Kevin Andrews and Warren Miller, Extreme Skiing

"There is nothing in the world like going out onto an untouched, open, virgin mountain slope drenched under a thick blanket of new powder snow. It gives a supreme feeling of freedom, mobility. A great sense of flying, moving anywhere in a great white paradise."
Hans Gmoser

"Skiing combines outdoor fun with knocking trees down with your face."
Dave Barry

"Powder skiing is not fun. It's life, fully lived, life lived in a blaze of reality."
Dolores LaChapelle

"You won't get hurt skiing if you don't fall."
Warren Miller

"Backcountry skiing is full of surprises."
David Goodman

"It is better to go skiing and think of God, than go to church and think of sport."
Fridtjof Nansen

"Obviously, you always want to win, but you want to win by skiing a race that you're proud of and you feel like you really challenged yourself and left it all out there."
Bode Miller

"Cooking is like snow skiing: If you don't fall at least 10 times, then you're not skiing hard enough."
Guy Fieri

"For me, skiing is a physical necessity. I have a need for risk."
Jean-Marie Messier

"Skiing is a dance, and the mountain always leads."
Author Unknown

"The quality of life is so much higher any place you can ski in the morning and surf in the evening, there's something to be said for that."
Ian Somerhalder

"I don't put anything in front of taking ski racing and sports seriously."
Bode Miller

"Traverse: One of two ways to stop while skiing. Tree: The other method."
Author Unknown

"There's no waiting for friends on a powder day."
Author Unknown

"There is no such thing as too much snow."
Doug Coombs

"Skiing can be thought of as a control and guidance activity, sliding down on a varying surface."
David W. Murrie

"Here in the deep powder snow you don't hear yourself ski. You don't hear your long turns or your short turns. You just float. The faster you go, the better. The less you struggle, the better. You move through the deep light snow, through the deep snow with some crust on it, through the deep snow with some wind in it."
Jacques Labrie

"You are one with your skis and nature. This is something that develops not only the body but the soul as well, and it has a deeper meaning for a people than most of us perceive."
Fridtjof Nansen

"Skiing is the best way in the world to waste time."
Glen Plake

"How could I live without powder?"
Dolores LaChapelle

"The sensual caress of waist deep cold smoke... glory in skiing virgin snow, in being the first to mark the powder with the signature of their run."
Tim Cahill

"Ski fast and and leave narrow tracks."
Warren Witherall

"For me, personally, skiing holds everything. I used to race cars, but skiing is a step beyond that. It removes the machinery and puts you one step closer to the elements. And it's a complete physical expression of freedom."
Robert Redford

"I'm never tired of winning, and I'm never tired of skiing."
Lindsey Vonn

"It is unbecoming for a cardinal to ski badly."
John Paul II

"I loved Kirk so much I would have skied down Mount Everest in the nude with a carnation up my nose."
Joyce McKinney, former US beauty queen

"Skiing is better than sex actually, because for me a good round of sex might be seven minutes. Skiing you can do for seven hours."
Spalding Gray

"Sometimes it's all about the win, sometimes it's about the skiing."
Bode Miller

"I do uphill skiing; I don't do downhill skiing. I think that's for herd amateurs."
Judah Friendlander

1911: The 1,600 Mile Ski Race "A century ago, the ski had its ultimate triumph when Roald Amundsen and four other Norwegians won the fight for the South Pole. They skied up to the coveted spot on December 14 1911, well ahead of their British rivals under Robert Falcon Scott. The last great terrestrial discovery had simply turned out to be the longest ski race in history. In figures, the round trip was 2,714 kilometres (1,686 miles), taking 99 days, with a daily average of 27 km at a speed of roughly 4 km per hour."
Roland Huntford (Der Schneehase, Edition 38, Swiss Academic Ski Club)

1916: Lenin Recommends Skiing
"Do you ski? Do it without fail! Learn how and set off for the mountains – you must. In the mountains winter is wonderful! It's sheer delight."

Advice from Vladimir Lenin to his mistress, French socialist and feminist Inessa Armand, less than a year before the Bolsheviks seized power in Petrograd in 1917.
William D. Frank, Everyone to Skis! Northern Illinois University Press, 2013

1938: As if there weren't enough reasons to hate Hitler. Hitler was dismissive of the supposed joys of winter Alpine life, and in particular the attraction of skiing – "What pleasure can there be in prolonging the horrible winter artificially by staying in the mountains. If I had my way I'd forbid these sports, with all the accidents people have doing them."
David Faber, p.252, 'Munich, 1938' published 2008 by Simon & Schuster

"The English have loudly and openly told the world that ski and dogs are unusable in these regions and that fur clothes are rubbish. We will see, we will see."
Roald Amundsen (1872–1928)

CHAPTER 23

JUST SKIING

TENDER AND VIOLENT ELIZABETH by Henri Troyat

Henri Troyat (1911-2007) was a Russian-born French author, biographer, historian and novelist. He was greatly loved in France and won major literary prizes. The chapter below, from his novel 'Tender and Violent Elizabeth', is the fourth in the series of Troyat's warm and brilliant novels of French life.

As the cable car passed the first tower, it jolted suddenly and a few feminine squeals rang out.

"It's coming apart. It's going to fall!"

"Don't worry. There's an emergency cable."

"Besides, if we fall down, I'll get there ahead of you and catch you!"

The car progressed slowly toward the heights with its tightly packed contingent of skiers talking loudly and laughing at the slightest provocation. Pushed into the centre, Monsieur and Madame Grevy were clinging to the vertical post which held up the roof. They were both wearing Basque berets. Their noses, coated with a protective white cream, stuck out of their faces like cardboard appendages. Elizabeth was struck by their old and sensible air in this group of young, bronzed faces. Of the eight women in the cabin, there were two, pretty and elegantly dressed, who were certainly going up Rochebrune not to ski but to get suntanned.

Three dashing young athletes were standing near them. The tallest wore a black ski suit with a red silk scarf at his neck. His eyes were set deep under a prominent ridge. A mocking smile exposed his teeth and the almost canine set of his mouth. He was staring insolently at Elizabeth. She remembered having seen him on the Megève streets and on the ski slopes the year before, but he had never looked at her like that. Afraid of showing her embarrassment, she turned to Madame Grevy and said suddenly,

"What a change from last year. Remember how hard it was and how long it took to climb up here on sealskins?"

"Yes," said Madame Grevy. "But, all in all, I rather liked it. At least you could enjoy nature. Now you only want to make time."

"When you learn how to ski better, you'll understand us," said Monsieur Grevy.

Jacques leaned over to admire the scenery, and Elizabeth found herself flattened against the window. The man with the red scarf disappeared from her view. Below, a white abyss dotted by the dark cones of the pine trees opened up. The valley slipped away as if in a dream. Megève was already merely a heap of tiny boxes with frosted roofs and chocolate foundations surrounding the bulbous steeple.

"Can you see the hotel from here?" Jacques asked.

"Yes. There, on the left, away from the village, on that road that trails off."

"There it is," said Jacques, in a strangely moved voice.

Then, taking advantage of a new shake of the cabin, he plucked up enough courage to put his hand on Elizabeth's shoulder. Suddenly a wild, strident laugh jarred the girl's nerves: the man with the red scarf was laughing at a friend's remark.

"Here we are," said Jacques.

The cable car operator, a peasant with a bashed-in forehead and a defiant look, planted himself firmly in front of the door. His clothes reeked of the stable. "Stop shoving," he growled. "Won't get there any faster by pushing, y' know. Everybody gets his chance."

The vibrating car settled awkwardly on a level with the landing. The mass of passengers disgorged violently onto the platform. Those who were most excited rushed to the ski rack attached to the car. Impatient hands searched for their treasures in the cluster of skis. The operator tried to re-establish order by telling the riders not to help themselves.

"I can't manage any faster, y' know… Only mess me up for nothing… I'm telling you… Some people are taking advantage…"

No one listened to him. Jacques, his parents and Elizabeth, having retrieved their skis, left the station and headed toward the starting point of the trails. The brisk air filled their lungs. The sun beat down on the snow as if on a shield. From afar, the summits of the Mont Blanc range were encrusted with ice under the blue sky.

"Your mother was right," said Madame Grevy. "The weather has cleared up. What a superb view! Is that really Mont Joly which we are facing?"

Elizabeth had already recited the list of mountains to many guests. She extended her arm toward the horizon: "Mont Joly; behind it, Mont Blanc; beside it, Mont Blanc du Tacul, l'Aiguille du Gouter…"

"Well, are we going?" asked Jacques.

"Wait a second!" said Madame Grevy. "It's so beautiful that I can't stop looking."

Actually, she was in no hurry to risk the slope. All around her, the speed demons were kneeling to adjust their bindings with hands numbed by the cold. The man with the red scarf passed Elizabeth. They stared at each other again. His eyelids narrowed as he smiled. His bony chin glistened in the sun. She put on her sunglasses and tried to avoid thinking about him. Meanwhile, he put on his mittens and slipped his hands into the loops of his ski poles.

Then he leaped and dived behind a powdery bank. Instinctively she craned her neck. On the snow, the red scarf was whipping along, dancing like a flame. Disdaining the ordinary slopes, the stranger was plunging toward Mouillebiau. His companions were trailing behind, having difficulty following him. Elizabeth admired him but was relieved when she lost sight of him.

The more prudent skiers rushed forward on the right, toward the path of Trail A, open between two rows of pines. They crisscrossed paths at varying speeds, diminished in size and finally disappeared.

Jacques was sliding his skis back and forth on the tightly packed snow while leaning on his ski poles. "Hurry up, Mama," he said.

"I haven't decided yet," said Madame Grevy in a feeble voice. She looked at the start of the trail and bent her knees slightly, throwing her chest back in order to resist the pull of the void.

"Really, Madame, it's very easy, once you're on it," said Elizabeth.

"Yes, Estelle," said Monsieur Grevy. "We aren't going to do championship skiing, you know. You see that little mountain? Aim across the slope at that. When you reach it, make a quick turn. You'll manage that very well. Then…"

"Let me get used to it, Marc," said Madame Grevy, sighing. "For the moment I'm concentrating, studying the terrain."

"In a few minutes a new load of skiers is going to arrive and we'll be caught in the crowd," Jacques said.

"Then go along with your father and Elizabeth," his mother said mournfully. "If necessary, I'll go down in the cable car."

"Oh, no!" Monsieur Grevy exclaimed. "If you give up, you'll never learn. Trust me. We'll take all the time you need. Jacques and Elizabeth can go on ahead." Elizabeth vainly protested that she could very well stay with Madame Grevy and encourage her in the difficult moments. Monsieur Grevy refused to share his responsibility with anyone. Jacques hastened to approve his father. "Yes, Mama will manage best with you."

Madame Grevy lowered her head in confusion. Elizabeth pulled off her mittens and fiddled with one binding.

"I'm going first," said Jacques.

She watched him go, legs stiff, shoulders hunched, elbows close to his body in a tense, defiant attitude which instructors had never been able to correct. He tried to make a turn and fell, picked himself up and continued his run more slowly. Elizabeth was a better skier than he. In two seasons of winter sports, she had acquired enough ease (thanks to a daily workout) to be able to enjoy the difficulties of the slope. Jacques had stopped at the top of a steep drop off and was catching his breath while leaning on his ski poles.

Elizabeth started off down the trail which had been packed and polished by hundreds of runs. Skis parallel, one ski tip in front of the other, she felt that speed did not depend on the steepness of the slope but rather on her desire to go even faster. The wind was blowing heavily on her cheeks. The irregularities of the terrain were reflected in the staccato movements of her legs. When she came to a bump, she would launch herself off the ground with a mixed feeling of fright and elation. Her skis would hit the snow again with a dull, prolonged thud that unbalanced her for a second and then helped her to increase her speed even more. Faster, faster, she flew. The snow was blue-green through the coloured lenses of her glasses. As she caught up with Jacques, she braked sharply, going into a Christy which raised a white powder spray all around her.

"It's wonderful," said Jacques. "You're even better than last year. I'm just terrible. Did you see the flop I took? My edges again. I can't get used to steel edges. When I start a turn they bite too much into the snow and I fall."

"Yes," said Elizabeth, "but edges are marvellous for fast turns. You're more assured and you can direct yourself better."

The expression of tenderness and gravity in Jacques' face alarmed Elizabeth.

"Shall we continue?" she asked.

Instead of answering, he said with feeling, "I'd like to be able to stay in Megève all through the winter."

"When are you leaving?"

"In the middle of January."

"Definitely?"

"Almost. Now that I've finally passed my exams the second time around, my father wants to take me into the business. And he has to be in Paris on the fifteenth, so…"

"He'll give you some extra vacation days at the last minute. He seems so kind!"

"A few days won't be enough!" Jacques sighed. He gazed at her with dramatic intensity, not daring to say more, begging her to understand his hint.

Elizabeth was sorry he wasn't older or more attractive. Throwing her head back, she said gaily, "Let's go through there and we can get back on the trail at the entrance to the forest. All right?"

He stammered, "If you like."

She dashed off, making a curve in the untouched, deep snow. Jacques followed in her tracks. She turned around. "See how easy it is with the edges!"

She had just stopped speaking when a crashing meteor blocked her path, almost knocking her down. She caught a glimpse of Maxime Poitou, a law student from the annex. He skied badly but with such scorn of danger that no spill, it seemed, could discourage him. A few feet down, he side-slipped, bent his knee in an attempt at a telemark, rolled over head first and almost exploded onto the slope, skis crossed, ski poles lost. She thought he had hurt himself and sped to his aid. He was laughing, however, lying on his back like a beetle, skis twisted, face wet with snow, white flakes in his hair.

"I noticed you from up there," he said breathlessly. "I wanted to catch up with you. But I put on too much speed! Besides, I've never been able to try a telemark without breaking my neck. What an eggbeater of a fall. You were afraid, weren't you, Mademoiselle?"

"Of course. It's idiotic to do that. You haven't hurt yourself?"

"No," he said. "I even feel like trying again."

"Do you enjoy falling?"

"In front of you, yes," he said, and winked.

"You're being silly!"

She helped him straighten his skis and start up. He couldn't stop laughing. He was shorter than

Jacques but more substantially built. Square-jawed and with an open face. Snowflakes were melting in his collar.

"Brrr!" he said. "It's going all the way down. It feels good."

Jacques caught up with them. He was out of breath and furious.

"May I join you?" Maxime Poitou asked.

There was no way to refuse. Elizabeth took flight. Under her narrow, rapidly moving skis, the compact snow of the trail was soon succeeded by the unpacked snow of the fields. Maxime Poitou skied along in the girl's wake, shouting comically from time to time,

"Not so fast, Mademoiselle. I'm going to fall again!"

Far behind them, Jacques was following in a snowplough position. They entered a stretch of denuded forest. Lining the trail were black fir trees as erect and grave as monks. Elizabeth stopped to wait for her companions at a curve in the trail. Unfamiliar skiers went past her. Some were as fleet as birds, others seemed to cling to the ground, their rear ends sticking out, ski poles dragging on the snow, with anxious looks on their faces.

Maxime Poitou slowed down as best he could and swerved slightly against Elizabeth. "Excuse me," he said. "I think it's still the best way to stop."

"Have you been skiing long?" she asked.

"Three years, but never more than two weeks at a time. It's not enough. I see your skis are made of ash?"

"Yes," said Elizabeth.

"You don't prefer hickory?"

"I don't know… Ash is lighter."

Jacques' arrival interrupted their conversation. He eyed both of them suspiciously. Obviously Maxime Poitou's presence was spoiling his outing. Is he jealous? Elizabeth wondered. The thought amused her. She felt very beautiful and important. The sun and the snow were her domain. The entire mountain was conspiring with her to bewitch two young men. She pushed off with her ski poles, and they darted after her. She sensed that they were competing in skill and daring to catch up to her. After having gained distance on them, she stopped at the edge of a drop-off. Again, it was Maxime Poitou who caught up with her first.

He was exhausted and happy. The perspiration poured down his suntanned face. How old could he be? Twenty? Twenty-one?

"Bravo!" she cried. "You really have determination."

"I don't ski as well when I'm alone," he said.

"Why?"

"Because I have no goal."

"And now you have one?"

"Yes."

"What?"

"To catch up with you as fast as possible."

She had heard what she wanted to hear. Maxime Poitou should definitely not add to it. By persisting he would spoil the charm of the flirtatious but meaningless jokes which enabled Elizabeth to measure her power over young men without offering them anything in exchange.

"You ought to take your glasses off," he murmured.

"What an idea! Don't be silly."

"I don't see your eyes."

She waved her hand to greet Jacques Grevy, who, having corrected his stance somewhat, was sideslipping toward her, erect on his skis, following the Swiss technique. He had tied his jacket around his waist and unbuttoned the collar of his shirt.

"Antoine must have waxed my skis with glue," he grumbled as he stopped. "What a mess!"

"Do you want to go ahead?" she asked.

"And hold you back even more? No, thanks! No, do go on. Don't bother about me. I'll get there when I get there."

This uncompetitive attitude annoyed Elizabeth. She shrugged her shoulders. "As you like."

At least Maxime Poitou was ready to break his neck to follow her. They went off together, leaving the faltering phantom of reproach far behind them. Down below, an eager crowd was surrounding the cable car station. The wooden staircase trembled beneath the heavy boots climbing to the ticket window. One car, packed with the lucky ones, was on its way to the summit. Another was coming down, revealing the shameful silhouette of a passenger who could not ski. Winter athletes, springing out of nowhere onto the icy slopes, were heading down the trail, exerting themselves to execute their most beautiful Christies of the afternoon for an audience of connoisseurs. Elsewhere, on the gentle slopes, instructors were encouraging the beginnings of a regiment of large-pawed and awkward bears. Maxime Poitou suggested going right back up Rochebrune, but Jacques was tired; he preferred waiting for his parents.

Friendship and propriety required that the girl stay with him, but the temptation of another run was stronger. Elizabeth joined Maxime Poitou in the crowd of skiers lined up in front of the gate.

They made two more runs. The setting sun was blazing in the sky when they finally decided to go back. A sharp cold enveloped them. At the foot of the trail the cable car was luring only a few aficionados. Jacques had disappeared. At the spot where the ski school students had been sliding about not long ago, the snow was now deserted. All was calm. The mountains were almost completely dark. A bell clanged. The village was calling its own back before nightfall. Some giggling women, looking chilled, were piling on a blue wood sleigh. The driver spread a goatskin over their legs. A bearded old horse was snorting clouds of vapor from his nostrils.

"That was wonderful!" said Maxime Poitou. "Now what do we do?"

"We go back to the hotel," said Elizabeth.

'How about having a cup of tea with me at the Mauvais Pas? We can dance…"

Elizabeth smiled, pleased and shy. "I'd love to, but it's impossible. My parents expect me. I'm already very late."

"Another time, then?"

"Maybe."

They skied down to the hotel. In front of the door, Elizabeth unbuckled her straps, slapped her two skis together to get rid of the snow and placed them against the wall. Maxime Poitou, however, who was in a hurry to change, continued gliding toward the annex, which was located about seventy yards farther down, on the Glaise road.

The girl felt the welcoming warmth of the house on her chilled face as she entered the lobby. Friquette, her backside quivering, jumped on her. Several guests were having tea and toast at round tables. The whole Grevy clan was there.

"Well!" Madame Grevy exclaimed. "There's our little champion. Are you happy with your afternoon?"

"The snow was marvellous!" said Elizabeth. "And did it go well for you, Madame?"

"She did extremely well!" said Monsieur Grevy, glowing with conjugal pride.

"Except on the big drop, after the forest, where I did a stretch sitting down!" said Madame Grevy.

"Oh, that doesn't count," said Elizabeth.

She was annoyed. Jacques was gazing at her reproachfully. She reflected that he looked like a sheep. Suddenly he knitted his brows and lowered his eyes into his cup. Was he going to cry into it?

"I'm going to straighten up a bit. I'll come back," Elizabeth said casually. She was heading for the staircase when her mother, coming out of the pantry, intercepted her.

"Did you just get back?"

"Yes, Mama," said Elizabeth.

"Where were you?"

"Rochebrune."

"The Grevys came back an hour ago!"

"I wanted to make another run."

"Alone?"

"No."

"With whom?"

"With Maxime Poitou."

"Maxime Poitou!" Amelie cried. "Congratulations! What sort of impression could you have made on that trail with a young man you hardly know?"

"Oh, Mama, he's a guest of the hotel!"

"A student!" Amelie said with restrained anger. They were alone in the corridor, but the servants could surprise them.

"What difference does it make if he's a student?" Elizabeth asked.

"I know what I'm saying," said Amelie.

"If you look at it that way, Jacques is also a student."

"Jacques is a boy from a good family. As for Maxime Poitou, I don't even know where he comes from. I don't like his manners. From now on you will do me the favour of avoiding private outings with strangers. You can just as well ski alone or with a group. It's more respectable and certainly as much fun."

"All right, Mama," Elizabeth said with resignation. Her arms drooped lifelessly down to her hips. Her mother really came from another era. She refused to acknowledge that relations between boys and girls had changed since her youth. And yet the gay life of Megève should have cured her of these old-fashioned ideas.

As Elizabeth stared at her mother in silent judgment, Amelie straightened up slightly and said, "Now go get ready. You look like a wild woman with your hair that way." Elizabeth dashed up the staircase, and her iron-tipped boots clattered on the steps. Friquette trotted behind her.

"Don't run, Elizabeth," Amelie shouted once more. The girl continued her climb more quietly. When she reached the third floor, she pushed a door marked 23. The year before, she had still been obliged to change her room according to the fluctuation in the clientele. There were even several occasions when her parents had made her sleep in their room on a folding bed, in order not to refuse anyone. But since the beginning of the season, she finally had, in Amelie's words, 'her own little domain all to herself'. Each time she came back to it a feeling of independence surged through her. Everything in this slope-ceilinged room had been chosen and arranged with care: the sofa bed, the cretonne curtains, the bedside lamp shaped like a flat candlestick, the bookcase with a few odd volumes, the writing table where some letters and photographs were buried. Facing the window was an old black fir whose top leaned slightly toward the house, the better to see what went on in the room.

Elizabeth undressed to her waist and splashed the top of her body over the basin. The warm water flowed gently over her body and on her breasts. She caressed the plump curves with the wash mitt, and the tips stood out, pink and impertinent. Her skin was smooth and taut. A mole marked her left shoulder. She could touch it with her lips by turning her head. After she finished washing, she combed her short brown hair, trying to give the silky mass a tousled look.

She had decided that it suited her best to look wind-blown. No powder. A slight suntan coloured her face evenly. Just a touch of red to outline her mouth. Friquette, seated on her cushion, gazed at her mistress with adoration. Elizabeth grabbed her, kissed her passionately behind the ears, and thought of Maxime Poitou's invitation. Had she been right to refuse? The Mauvais Pas held a magic attraction for her. The orchestra was excellent, the crowd young, the atmosphere 'divine'. She adored dancing so much that she would have gladly spent all her evenings in the place. But, all things considered, Maxime Poitou did not please her enough to risk another scolding. If it had only been Andre Lebreuil, last year's love, she would have undoubtedly been less good. She accorded him a nostalgic thought, replaced Friquette on her cushion and lifted up the mattress to take out her beautiful dark blue slacks, which were lying full length, the seam knife-sharp, on the grey and white striped box spring. There were steps creaking and voices raised in the corridor. Some of the guests were going back to their rooms.

The pensive old fir was balancing its head in the wind. Elizabeth dressed again, smiled at her reflection in the mirror and decided that she would be very friendly toward Jacques this evening.

TOP OF THE HILL by Irwin Shaw

Irwin Shaw (1913-1984) was a prolific American playwright, screenwriter, and author of critically acclaimed short stories and best-selling novels. Shaw's experiences in the U.S. Army in Europe during World War II led to his writing 'The Young Lions' (1948; filmed 1958), a novel about three young soldiers (one German and two Americans) in wartime; it became a best-seller, and thereafter Shaw devoted most of the rest of his career to writing novels. Among the best known of his 12 novels are 'Two Weeks in Another Town' (1960), 'Evening in Byzantium' (1973), and 'Beggarman, Thief' (1977).

He was having a nightmare. He was going down a steep, icy slope on skis, with mean little rocks showing in the bare spots and sparks flying up from his skis as the steel edges hit the rocks and threw him off balance. He was going faster and faster and below him there was a deep, dark gully. The wind was screaming past his ears and his speed became greater and greater as he neared the gully. He tried to stop, but he knew it was impossible on that ice. He screamed, but the wind took the sound out of his mouth. He knew he was going to crash and he knew it was going to be bad and he resigned himself to how bad it was going to be.

Then the telephone rang and he awoke, sweating. He didn't know how long it had been ringing. His hand shook as he reached out for the receiver.

It was Dave Cully. He sounded happy. "Mike," he said, "it's really coming down. There should be over a foot of new powder by morning. I'm opening the lifts at nine. How about making the first run of the season with me?"

"Great," Michael said, trying to keep his voice steady. "I'll be there. What time is it now?"

"Quarter to eleven," Cully said. "Did I wake you?"

"No," Michael said, his voice stronger. "I was doing some research on monsoons."

"What?" Cully asked, puzzled.

"Indian storms," Michael said. "No matter."

"See you at nine," Cully said and hung up.

Another husband who finds me attractive, Michael thought, grateful for the ringing of the telephone that had awakened him. For other reasons, no doubt.

He looked at his watch to see if Cully had had the time right. Twelve minutes before eleven. It had been a full day. He got out of bed and went to the window and looked out. The snow was coming down heavily, beautifully, evenly glittering in the light of the driveway lampposts in the windless night. Then he saw Eva Heggener walking in the snow in high after-ski boots that came up to the bottom of her thick fur coat, the dog gambolling and rolling deliciously in the new snow. After what happened in the cottage, he thought resentfully, where does she get the energy?

He left the drapes pulled open so he could watch the snow falling and got into bed and tried to sleep again, but the phone rang again. It was Susan Hartley, calling from New York.

"Hey," Susan said. "It's falling like Siberia in New York. How is it up there?"

"There'll be at least a foot of powder in the morning."

"Will the lifts be open?"

"Nine a.m."

"Oh, bliss. I'll take a week off and then there's the Thanksgiving weekend, that'll give me ten days. Antoine's with me now, can you find a room for him, too?"

"How is he?"

"Suicidal."

"Don't tell me," Michael said. "I'm having a good time."

"He says skiing will take his mind off disaster. How's the hotel you're staying in?"

"Bliss," he said, imitating her.

"Get me a room adjoining yours," she said playfully.

"This is Vermont," Michael said sternly. "They frown on such things here. And stop teasing Antoine. And tell him I will make sure that you will get a room in the attic, three floors up from mine and on the other side of the building."

"Ski heil," she said airily. "We'll arrive late Friday night. Stay up for us."

He hung up. He stared at the phone. He didn't know whether he was pleased or not pleased that his friends were coming. Well, he thought, at least Susan would be good for some laughs. Thanksgiving. He had forgotten about Thanksgiving. Did he have anything to be thankful for? He would look into the pros and cons before the holiday and act accordingly.

He sank back into bed, pulling the blankets around him, half-hypnotized by the steady, straight, silent fall of snow outside the window and fell asleep quickly and did not dream.

Cully was waiting for him at the chair lift exactly at nine. The word had not yet gone out that the lifts were working and they were alone. The slopes above them shone untracked in the sunlight. Cully had an expression of faraway, almost sensual pleasure on his weathered, tough face as he looked up, but all he said as Michael greeted him was, "It's about time we had it."

As they were putting on their skis, a grey-haired, black man of about fifty, his skin almost copper-coloured, came out of the shed. He was wearing an old tufted down-lined parka and a peaked corduroy woodman's cap with earflaps. He had a battered old pipe stuck in his mouth and was puffing contentedly.

"Everything ready, Harold?" Cully asked.

"Ready for the thundering herd," the man said. "Enjoy yourself, Dave, this is the last moment of peace you'll have for a long time."

"Harold," Cully said, "this is Mike Storrs. He's working for me this winter. Mike, Harold Jones."

Michael shook the man's hand. It felt like a steel clamp. Jones looked at him closely.

"Didn't I see you someplace before, young fella?" His accent was exactly the same as Cully's.

"Maybe. I was here a long time ago for a winter."

Jones nodded. "I thought so. You did all those crazy tricks, like once I saw you somersaulting over a six-foot-high pile of stacked cordwood."

Cully laughed. "The same."

"How many bones you broke since then, Mr. Storrs?" Jones asked.

"None," Michael said. He told himself that the man was referring to skiing and that ribs cracked in bar-room brawls didn't count.

"God takes care of fools and drunkards," said Jones. He held the chair that was swinging around on the overhead cable for them and they slipped onto it and started up.

"Who is that old guy?" Michael asked.

"Our chief engineer. Fix anything from a cotter pin to a fractured skull."

"He sounds as if he's from around here."

"He was born here. His great grandfather's got a picture of himself in the town library. He came up from the South on the underground railroad before the Civil War and liked it and stayed, farming a little, doing odd jobs, and some painter who came through town painted his picture. This was a lumbering and farming town until the 1920s. No ski bunnies up from New York and Boston then and no drinking on Sundays, either. The town was dying on the limb during the Depression but the family stayed and then the skiing craze caught on and it turns out Jones owns about a thousand acres he'd been buying up for peanuts all around town. One smart fella. He could retire if he wanted to but you'd have to call an armed guard to get him away from his machinery. His kid works at the Alpina, the waitress. Smart kid, finished high school at the age of fifteen, but she refuses to go to college. Her old man doesn't care one way or the other, he's told me – he's seen the college kids come up here and he says he wouldn't give a broken ski pole for the lot of them."

They rose steadily upward through the swath cut in the forest for the chair lift, the branches of the pines still laden with snow in the below zero sunshine. A deer looked up at them inquiringly but without fear from a spot under a spreading tree where there was still some dried grass showing. There was a slight whirr from the cable but otherwise the silence was absolute and both men understood that to break it would mar that particular moment of the morning of their first ascent of the year to the mountain. Here and there below them, too, there were rabbit tracks and a track that Michael thought was that of a fox. New York, he thought, was continents, ages away.

At the top, they skied down the little slope off the lift and Cully waved to the man who was on duty in the shed in which the great round wheel returned the chairs downhill again.

Without saying anything, Cully skied off on a traverse on the bald top of the mountain. Michael followed him. He had never skied this side of the hill before, because the lift had been installed after his time and new trails cut through the woods. Finally, Cully stopped and they both looked down. A hill as steep as any Michael had skied anywhere before, in America or in Europe, dropped, almost sheer, below them, for a straight hundred yards, then veered sharply to the left, out of sight, into the forest.

"I see," Michael said. "We do the easy ones first and gradually work our way up to the beginners' slopes."

Cully grinned. "They call this run the Black Knight. All the kids do it," he said.

"I'm sure," said Michael. "With parachutes."

"Remember what the man said – fools and drunkards."

"Follow me, you son of a bitch," Michael said and skated off and down, the powder fountaining like foam from the prow of a ship behind him. He whistled tunelessly as he sped straight downhill, to remember to breathe. He had wanted to schuss the whole thing to the turn, but he knew he was out of control halfway down and it wouldn't do to wind up smeared against a tree on the first run of the winter with Cully. As he made his turn to brake his speed, he saw Cully glide past him, his skis together, pointed straight downhill. "Showboat," Michael called and Cully waved a pole debonairly at him. Michael was relieved to see that at least Cully didn't schuss the whole face, but made four turns before stopping and waiting at the place where the run curved into the forest.

"Pretty good for an old fart," Michael said when he stopped beside Cully. Somehow, he could talk to Cully on the hill in a way that he never could on the flat.

Cully grinned again. "After this it becomes more technical."

"I am with you, friend."

"What I mean by that," Cully said jovially, "is that it narrows and becomes a little steeper and there's a boulder about two hundred yards down in the middle of the trail that you don't see until you're right on it, because it's in a little clearing right after you make a sharp turn out of the woods."

"It sounds like fun," Michael said. "Allez, allez."

From then on, Cully was merciless. Comradely, smiling, but merciless. It was impossible to believe that he spent most of his days at a desk. Huge, overweight, paunchy, balding, he never stopped, never looked back, jumped bumps twenty feet in the air, landed lightly as a bird, a bird made out of steel springs that would not reveal any signs of metal fatigue even under x-ray examination after ten thousand flights.

Michael hung on doggedly, sweating through his parka, his city muscles screaming within his legs, fell twice, wanted to just lie there in the cooling snow, abandoning himself to shameless defeat, but made himself scramble up and pound down after the inexorable broad back below him.

It was nearly noon, and they had done every run on the two hills of the ski area, with only the blessed respite of the trips up on the lifts to allow him time to regain his breath, when Cully finally stopped. From two hundred yards above him, Michael saw Cully bend to take off his skis near the lodge which abutted the parking space. He put on one last, groaning burst of speed and stopped flashily, throwing a great spray of snow over Cully.

Cully looked up. "Showboat," he said, smiling. "Have a good morning?"

"Never had a better," Michael gasped, leaning bent forward on his ski poles. "Thanks."

"It was nothing," Cully said. "But I didn't notice you doing any somersaults."

"I like to do things like that when there are girls around."

"There's one." Cully pointed up the hill. "Maybe she'd like a sample."

Michael turned with difficulty, too tired to take off his skis. High up the slope a slender figure in red was making swift, perfect short turns through the powder. "I think I'll leave tricks to later in the season," Michael said.

Cully laughed. "Maybe you ought to get more sleep at night." He patted Michael's shoulder. "You'll do," he said. "I thought I could shake you and I couldn't." Michael knew that he had been put to some private, simple-minded test of Cully's and he had passed it. It was silly, but he was happy. He knew he had done nothing that should make him feel guilty in Cully's presence, but he had still felt uneasy until now. Cully, he saw now, was doing everything he could, in his taciturn, heavy-handed and merciless way, to show him that he liked him and that they could be friends.

Michael wiped the sweat off his face and forehead with a handkerchief and watched the girl in red come swooping down the hill. When she got near enough, he saw that it was Rita, the waitress from the hotel, Harold Jones's daughter. "Holy man," Michael said, "she really can ski."

"She ought to," Cully said. "She's been on skis since the age of three. Hi, Rita," he said, as she came to a neat, modest stop in front of the two men. "Nice morning?"

"Splendiferous," she said, beaming, looking more like ten years old than sixteen. "It makes you sad, too."

"Why?" Michael asked.

"Tomorrow it will be crawling with people. Today I owned the mountain. Except for you two. I saw your tracks wherever I went," she said, stepping out of the bindings of her skis. "Hey, Mr. Storrs," she said, "those were pretty fancy tracks you made."

"They were Dave's," Michael said. "Mine looked as though they were made by a drunken webbed animal."

She laughed. "I can recognize Dave's. He's been signing his name on these hills since before I was born."

"Listen, you two," Michael said, finally recovered enough to bend and get out of his skis, "I'm dying of thirst. Let's go into the lodge and I'll treat you to something cold."

"I'm not thirsty," Cully said.

"You dog," Michael said.

"Anyway, I have to go back to the office. I've played hooky long enough. Mike, come in if you have time later. You might as well sign the contract. It will make you a rich man for three or four hours, if you don't do anything extravagant, like buying a sandwich."

"I'll be there," Michael said. "How about you, Rita? You got time for a drink?"

"Fifteen minutes. Then I have to get back to the hotel. I'm on for lunch today."

"I'll drive you," Michael said. "That'll give you more time." He picked up her skis and with his own on the other shoulder started toward the lodge, while Cully went to where his battered station wagon was parked.

"You shouldn't carry my skis, Mr. Storrs," Rita said in a low voice as she walked by his side toward the steps leading up to the lodge.

"Why not?"

"Not everybody in this town is like you," Rita said flatly. "And if they told Mrs. Heggener you were seen carrying my skis, she would say it wasn't seemly."

"Nonsense, Rita," he said, sharply. Then, more lightly, "I make a point of always being seemly."

"I don't want you to get any wrong ideas," Rita said hastily. "Mr. Cully is not one of those people. Not in a million years."

"I know," Michael said, still keeping his tone light. "He's most seemly, too – in his own rough way, of course."

He leaned the two pairs of skis against a wall and poked the poles into the snow beside them. "I've been dreaming about a cold beer since nine thirty this morning," he said. "Following good old Dave Cully down the hill is warm work."

"Isn't that man something?" Rita shook her head admiringly. She had been skiing without a cap and her cropped black hair trembled as she moved and there were still little flakes of snow in it that made gleaming highlights over her forehead. Her skin, Michael noticed, was considerably darker than her father's, and was glistening with youthful health. "Imagine being that old and fat and still skiing like that," she said.

"He's not much older than I am," Michael said with dignity as they mounted the steps.

"Oh, I'm sorry." Rita put up her hand to her mouth, abashed. "I didn't mean to offend you. Anyway, you're not fat." She giggled.

"I will be," Michael said, "if you keep giving me those huge portions at the hotel every meal."

"If you're going to ski with Dave Cully, you better keep your strength up."

At the self-service counter inside, he picked up a cold beer and she took a Coke. They sat at a corner table, after Michael had taken off his parka. His shirt, he saw, embarrassed, was dark with sweat, but Rita didn't say anything about it. She drank slowly, through a straw, while he finished the beer in three voracious gulps, then went back for a second. "Nectar," he said with a sigh, after he had taken the first swallow of the second bottle. "One day I would like to own a brewery and swim in the vats."

"Mr. Heggener likes beer, too. He always has a bottle before dinner."

Michael was tempted to ask about Mr. Heggener, but refrained. Whatever the girl might say, however innocent, she might regret later.

"I want to thank you," Michael said, "for remembering to leave a bottle of wine for me each night." He had gotten into the guilty habit of rinsing out the second glass and drying it and returning it to exactly the same position it had arrived on the tray so that in the morning whoever came in to clean up would suppose that he had drunk the whole bottle himself. Better the reputation of a drunkard than of a lecher.

"With Madam Heggener around, we make sure we don't forget anything."

Michael got off the subject of Mrs. Heggener quickly. "You ski awfully well, you know."

Rita shrugged. "I was born here. I ski like all the kids."

"I know. I met your father this morning."

"He was whistling when he left the house at dawn," Rita said. "At last his lifts were working."

"He remembered me. Not too fondly. He said God protects fools and drunkards."

"That's daddy." She laughed. "He's an outspoken man." She had unzipped the top of her ski suit and dropped it around her waist. She was wearing a boy's cotton shirt and he noticed that there was no sign of perspiration coming through the thin cloth. She was flat and thin and angular and he saw that he could have put his fingers easily, with something to spare, around her fine-boned wrists. "Rita," he said, "have you ever been hurt? Skiing, I mean?"

She looked surprised. "No. Should I have?"

"I mean, you're so slender and your bones..."

"Skinny, you mean." She looked wistful. "My mama swears I'm going to develop. I'm stronger than I look. I have to be. I've been rassling with my brother all my life."

"Have you ever raced?"

Rita laughed, something surprisingly condescending in the sound, as you might laugh at a child who had amused you with a silly question. In a moment she was an adult. "Have you ever heard of a black downhill racer?"

"Not really," Michael said, sensitive to what was behind the question. "Still, before Jackie Robinson, there never was a black second baseman in the National League, either."

"I've talked about it with my daddy," she said seriously. "Give it another fifty years, my daddy says. In fifty years I'll be sixty six. How many sixty six year-old girls, black or white, do you know of in the Olympics? And I'm not even the good one in the family. You ought to see my brother..."

"How old is he?"

"Eighteen."

"What does he do?"

"He works with my father."

"Maybe we can all three of us ski together one day," Michael said.

"He gets Thursdays off." She looked pleased with the invitation. She changed from moment to moment, child to adult, adult to child.

"And you?"

"Mornings, mostly. I usually start work at lunch and go on till ten p.m."

"Maybe we can arrange it for next Thursday," Michael said. "One day a month with Dave Cully does it for me, thank you. And I don't like to ski alone."

"That would be very nice. If you're not busy with Madam."

"Oh," he said, "you know about my being assigned to her?"

"News gets around. A little town..."

"How does she ski?"

"Very well," Rita said. Again, she sounded condescending, but this time not because of her colour. "Considering her age."

Michael laughed. "You know," he said, "I'm older than she is."

Rita giggled, suddenly very childish. "I did it again. I'm sorry."

"That's all right," Michael said, thinking that he had to get used to people Rita's age regarding everyone over thirty as decrepit and on the brink of extinction.

They finished their drinks and went out to where the Porsche was parked, with Michael carrying the two pairs of skis and Rita not objecting now. He put the skis in the rack and the poles in the back of the car and Rita sank luxuriously into the passenger seat. "Mr. Storrs," she said, "do me a favour, please."

"Of course."

"Drive slowly through town. I want everybody to see me in this car."

Michael drove sedately along the main street of the town. There were two people on the street whom she knew and she waved, grandly, all the time babbling excitedly. Skiing didn't interest her all that much, she said, what she really wanted to be was a singer. She sang in the church choir and was one of its soloists, but that wasn't what she meant. "What I want," she said, "is to go out dressed in a crazy costume, all feathers and spangles and long stockings, red is my favourite colour, maybe after purple, and see twenty thousand people out there screaming 'Rita, Rita!' at me and pick up a microphone and belt out one song after another and have them go crazy and rip out the chairs and travel with my own band – New York, San Francisco, London, Paris... with the money coming in so fast I'd have to hire three college graduates just to count it."

Michael laughed at the girl's dreadful vision of the good life and hoped, for her sake, that her ambition would never be fulfilled. But he didn't have the heart to remind her of the many popular singers whose admirers had staged riots in their honour and who had wound up suicides or dead from drugs before the age of thirty. Instead he said, "There's a friend of mine, a Frenchman, who plays the piano and sings in bars and who's very good indeed. He's coming up here in a few days and he's very nice and I'm sure I can arrange to let him listen to you and give you some useful pointers."

"You're kidding..." She gasped at the grandeur of what he was offering as she said it.

"No. Honestly."

"Mr. Storrs," she said emotionally, "you're just the nicest man I ever met."

"I hope," he said, embarrassed by her intensity, "I hope later you'll find someone, lots of someones, a good deal nicer, Rita."

She leaned her head back against the leather bucket seat and closed her eyes, a dreamy smile on her face as he drove the last few hundred yards to the hotel. When he took her skis off the rack, she said, "Better take yours off, too. They steal skis around here if they're left unlocked. Up to now it looks like heaven in Green Hollow, but when there's snow on the ground we get some real uglies up here."

Obediently, as Rita hurried in to begin her working day, Michael took his skis off the rack and put them and his poles in the hotel ski room. Then he went to the front desk and asked if there were any messages for him from Mrs. Heggener. There was a message. Mrs. Heggener wished to ski at two thirty this afternoon. He hoped she wouldn't be as active on the slopes as she was in bed.

CHECKERS by John Marsden

John Marsden (1950) is an Australian writer, teacher and school principal. Marsden's books have been translated into eleven languages, including Norwegian, French, German, Swedish, Dutch, Danish, Italian, Polish, and Spanish.

One night Dad announced we were going skiing. He took me by surprise. He hadn't done anything spontaneous for months, apart from punching out the reporter.

There was still a week of school to go but that didn't bother him: there'd been a good dump, the best of the year, and he wanted to go tomorrow, tonight, this instant.

We went the next day. The worst thing was putting Checkers into kennels. I felt like I'd abandoned him when I saw his sad face peering through the wire netting of his pen and heard his yelping begin as I walked away. Poor thing, he'd never been left before. The lady who owned the kennels made it worse by laughing at Checkers when she saw him.

"Goodness, he's an unusual one," she said. "Where'd you get him?"

I'd never actually asked Dad where he got Checkers.

He'd said something about a friend who'd been looking for a home for a dog, that was all. In the car on the way back from the kennels I asked him some more. I was always kind of nervous when I was alone with Dad, so it was good to have a topic to talk about for once; a safe topic.

"Oh, I got him from a business friend," he said vaguely, as he tried to sneak through a gap in the traffic at a roundabout. "No one you've met."

"How many puppies were in the litter?"

"Just the two. The mother wasn't meant to breed with the father. She's a pedigree cocker spaniel, he's a crossbreed Border collie from down the road. Your dog's lucky he wasn't drowned at birth."

"What happened to the other one?"

"They kept him, I think. His wife, I think she wanted to have him. She was the one who stopped them being drowned in the first place."

"Does Checkers look like his brother?"

"Yes, very, as I recall. I didn't take a lot of notice. It all happened kind of quickly, on the spur of the moment. I was so excited about... there was so much happening that day... well, my mind was on other things, put it that way."

The next morning we left for Mt Whiteman. That's always been my favourite, that and Tremblant, when we've been to Canada a few times. Whiteman's a long drive, and I get carsick going up the last bit, but it's a small price to pay. We stopped at Bronson for lunch and to hire some chains (Dad hadn't got around to buying new ones since we changed cars) and I bought some very cool, very expensive Ray Bans. Everyone seemed more relaxed, happier, even Mum. She doesn't like skiing, and we'd had to work hard to persuade her to come, but I was glad we had when I saw her going through the clothes racks in the ski shop, just like old times.

The weather was pretty foul, but we got to the carpark without using the chains and caught a Toyota up to the hotel. We were staying in The Max, a new place, very big, a bit over the top with all the white marble and chandeliers, but at least the rooms weren't pokey like they are in a lot of ski lodges. Mark and I had to share a room because the place was so heavily booked, but even though he dropped his stuff all over the floor as per usual, I could still get from the bed to the door and back without breaking a leg.

I saw Susy Thieu the moment I arrived. I assumed she'd given school the flick for a few days, same as me, but it turned out she was with the PLC ski team, training for the inter-schools. Within three minutes she introduced me to six guys, so I was set. I knew I wouldn't be seeing much of Mummy and Daddy, let alone little brother, for the next week.

I've got a theory about skiing, and that is that you improve over the summer without having to do anything. In other words, whatever standard you're at when one season ends, you start the next season at a higher standard. It's not very logical, but I honestly believe it works that way. So, I felt good the next morning. I'd had the skis tuned and waxed and whatever else they do to them, the snow was good, I'd been on 195s for half of last season and was confident, so I just went for it. The weather was lousy: windy and cold, with bad visibility, little ice particles blowing straight into our faces. Hardly anyone was around. Mark came with me but Mum and Dad were still in bed.

For three hours we skied our asses off. Mark's better than me, technically, but I'm more aggressive, and that morning he really had to struggle to keep up. "Suck on it, little brother," I thought, skiing straight onto yet another lift without him.

"What's the hurry?" he asked me at one point. "It'll still be here tomorrow, you know."

I didn't know what the hurry was. I still don't. I wasn't thinking about it. I just wanted to go as far and as fast as I could. I flashed past people at Concorde speed, not caring if I ran them off the slopes or into trees. I made my knees work like they were on springs. I skied every slope on the mountain and invented a few runs of my own. "You're crazy," Mark said as he caught up with me in the lift queue, still huffing and puffing from a great route I'd just found, down the side of McCaskills Shoulder.

He was right, of course, and my being in here proves it. Except I more or less know why I'm in here. I don't know why I was crazy that day. But suddenly it was over.

Suddenly I felt the numb coldness of my face, the burning red skin, the sandblasted cheeks. I felt the ache of my knees. I felt the rumbles of ravenous hunger in my stomach. I turned to Mark.

"I'm going back," I said.

"I thought you'd never ask," he grumbled.

I wasn't actually asking, just telling, but I think he was too wrecked to know the difference.

The rest of the six days was totally different to that first morning. I hung round with Susy and the PLC squad, stole their guys off them (well, tried to) gave my fake ID a huge workout, partied, skied, and partied some more. You don't have time to get tired because everything just keeps happening around you and all you've gotta do is hang on to the roller coaster and not think about how tired you are and how long it is since you last had a sleep.

Somewhere in the world right now, I guess, people are skiing and drinking and partying and cracking on to each other but in here our one pathetic attempt has ended with Cindy stabbing her wrist till she's got bloody gashes all over it and then being taken off in an ambulance to a closed ward.

THE ADVENTURES OF A SKIER by Italo Calvino
(Translated, from the Italian, by Ann Goldstein)

Italo Calvino was born in Cuba and grew up in Italy. He was a journalist and writer of short stories and novels. His best-known works include the 'Our Ancestors' trilogy (1952-1959), the 'Cosmicomics' collection of short stories (1965), and the novels 'Invisible Cities' (1972) and 'If On a Winter's Night a Traveller' (1979).

There was a line at the ski lift. The group of boys who had come on the bus had joined it, one next to the other, skis parallel, and every time it advanced it was long and, instead of going straight, as in fact it could have, zigzagged randomly, sometimes upward, sometimes down. They stepped up or slid down sideways, depending on where they were, and immediately propped themselves on their poles again, often resting their weight on the neighbour below, or trying to free their poles from under the skis of the neighbour above, stumbling on skis that had got twisted, leaning over to adjust their bindings and bringing the whole line to a halt, pulling off windbreakers or sweaters or putting them back on as the sun appeared or disappeared, tucking strands of hair under their woollen headbands, or the billowing tails of their checked shirts into their belts, digging in their pockets for handkerchiefs and blowing their red, frozen noses, and for all these operations taking off and then putting back on their big gloves, which sometimes fell in the snow and had to be picked up with the tip of a pole. That flurry of small disjointed gestures coursed through the line and became frenzied at the front, when the skier had to unzip every pocket to find where he'd stuck his ticket money or his badge, and hand it to the lift operator to punch, and then he had to put it back in his pocket, and readjust his gloves, and join his two poles together, the tip of one stuck in the basket of the other so that they could be held with one hand – all this while climbing the small slope in the open space where he had to be ready to position the T-bar under his bottom and let it tug him jerkily upward.

The boy in the green goggles was at the midway point of the line, numb with cold, and next to him was a fat boy who kept pushing. As they stood there, a girl in a sky-blue hood passed. She didn't get in line; she kept going, up, on the path. And she moved uphill on her skis as lightly as if she were walking.

"What's that girl doing? She's going to walk?" the fat boy who was pushing asked.

"She's got climbing skins," the boy in the green goggles said.

"Well, I'd like to see her up where it gets steep," the fat boy said.

"She's not as smart as she thinks she is – you can bet on that."

The girl moved easily, her high knees (she had very long legs, in close-fitting pants, snug at the ankles) moving rhythmically, in time with the raising and lowering of her shiny poles. In that frozen white air the sun looked like a precise yellow drawing, with all its rays: on the expanses of snow where there was no shadow, only the glint of sunlight indicated humps and crevices and the trampled course of the trails. Framed by the hood of the sky-blue windbreaker, the blonde girl's face was a shade of pink that turned red on her cheeks against the white plush lining of the hood. She laughed at the sun, squinting slightly. She moved nimbly on her climbing skins. The boys in the group from the bus, with their frozen ears, chapped lips, sniffling noses, couldn't take their eyes off her and began shoving one another in the line, until she climbed over a ledge and disappeared.

Gradually, as their turn came, the boys in the group, after many initial stumbles and false starts, began to ascend, two by two, pulled along the almost vertical track. The boy in the green goggles ended up on the same T-bar as the fat boy who kept pushing. And there, halfway up, they saw her again.

"How did that girl get up here?"

At that point the lift skirted a sort of hollow, where a packed-down trail advanced between high dunes of snow and occasional fir trees fringed with embroideries of ice. The sky-blue girl was proceeding effortlessly, with that precise stride of hers and that push forward of her gloved hands, gripping the handles of her poles.

"Oooh!" the boys on the lift shouted, holding their legs stiff as they ascended. "She might even beat the rest of us!" She had a delicate smile on her lips, and the boy in the green goggles was confused. He didn't dare to keep up the banter, because when she lowered her eyelids he felt as if he'd been erased.

As soon as he reached the top, he started down the slope, behind the fat boy, both of them as heavy as sacks of potatoes. But what he was looking for, as he made his way along the trail, was a glimpse of the sky-blue windbreaker, and he hurtled straight down, so that he'd appear bold and at the same time hide his clumsiness on the turns. "Look out! Look out!" he called, in vain, because the fat boy, too, and all the boys in the group were descending at breakneck speed, shouting, "Look out! Look out!" And one by one they fell, backward or forward, and he alone was cutting through the air, bent double over his skis, until he saw her. The girl was still going up, off the trail, in the fresh snow. The boy in the green goggles grazed her, shooting by like an arrow, rammed the fresh snow, and disappeared into it, face forward.

But at the bottom of the slope, breathless, dusted in snow from head to foot, c'mon, there he was again with all the others in line for the lift, and then up, up again to the top. This time when he met her, she, too, was going down. How did she go? For the boys, a champion was someone who sped straight down like a lunatic. "Well, she's no champion, the blonde," the fat boy said quickly, relieved. The sky-blue girl was coming down unhurriedly, making her turns with precision, or, rather, in such a way that until the last moment they couldn't tell if she'd turn or what she'd do, and then suddenly they'd see her descending in the opposite direction. She was taking her time, you might have said, stopping every so often to study the trail, upright on her long legs, but still the boys from the bus couldn't keep up. Until even the fat boy admitted, "No kidding! She's incredible!"

They wouldn't have been able to explain why, but this was what held them spellbound: all her movements were as simple as possible and perfectly suited to her person; she never exaggerated by a centimetre, never showed a hint of agitation or effort or determination to do a thing at all costs, but did it naturally; and, depending on the state of the trail, she even made a few uncertain moves, like someone walking on tiptoe, which was her way of overcoming the difficulties without revealing whether she was taking them seriously or not – in other words, not with the confident air of one who does things as they should be done but with a trace of reluctance, as if she were trying to imitate a good skier but always ended up skiing better. This was the way the sky-blue girl moved on her skis.

Then, one after the other, awkward, heavy, snapping the christies, forcing snowplow turns into a slalom, the boys from the bus plunged down after her, trying to follow her, to pass her, shouting, making fun of one another. But everything they did was a messy downhill tumble, with disjointed shoulder movements, arms holding poles out straight, skis that crossed, bindings that broke off boots, and wherever they went the snow was gouged by crashing bottoms, hips, head-over-heels dives.

After every fall, they raised their heads and immediately looked for her. Passing through the avalanche of boys, the sky-blue girl went along lightly; the straight creases of her close-fitting pants scarcely angled as her knees bent, and you couldn't tell if her smile was in sympathy with the exploits and mishaps of her downhill companions or was instead a sign that she didn't even notice them.

Meanwhile, the sun, instead of getting stronger as midday approached, froze, and disappeared, as if soaked up by blotting paper. The air was full of light, colourless crystals flying slantwise. It was sleet: you couldn't see from here to there. The boys skied blindly, shouting and calling to one another, and they were continually going off the trail and, c'mon, falling. Air and snow were now the same colour, opaque white, but by peering intently into that whiteness, so that it almost became less dense, the boys could make out the sky-blue shadow, suspended in the midst of it, flying this way and that as if on a violin string.

The sleet had scattered the crowd at the lift. The boy in the green goggles found himself, without realising it, near the hut at the lift station. There was no sign of his companions. The girl in the sky-blue hood was already there. She was waiting for the T-bar, which was now making its turn. "Quick!" the lift man shouted to him, grabbing the T-bar and holding it so that the girl wouldn't set off alone. With limping herringbones, the boy in the green goggles managed to position himself next to the girl just in time to depart with her, but he nearly caused her to fall as he grabbed hold of the bar. She kept them both balanced until he righted himself, muttering self-reproaches, to which she responded with a low laugh like the 'glu-glu' of a guinea hen, muffled by the windbreaker drawn up over her mouth. Now the sky-blue hood, like the helmet of a suit of armour, left uncovered only her nose, her eyes, a few curls on her forehead, and her cheekbones. So he saw her, in profile, the boy in the green goggles, and didn't know whether to be happy to find himself on the same T-bar or to be ashamed of being there, all covered with snow, the hair pasted to his temples, his shirt puffing out between sweater and belt – he didn't dare tuck it in, in case he lost his balance by moving his arms; and he was partly glancing sideways at her, partly keeping an eye on the position of his skis, so that they wouldn't go off the track at moments of traction too slow or too taut, and it was always she who kept them balanced, laughing her guinea hen glu-glu, while he didn't know what to say.

The snow had stopped. Now there was a break in the fog, and in the break the sky appeared, blue at last, and the shining sun and, one by one, the clear, frozen mountains, their peaks feathered here and there by soft shreds of the snow cloud. The mouth and chin of the hooded girl reappeared.

"It's nice again," she said. "I said it would be."

"Yes," the boy in the green goggles said, "nice. Then the snow will be good."

"A little soft."

"Oh, yes."

"But I like it," she said, "and going down in the fog isn't bad."

"As long as you know the trail," he said.

"No," she said, "guessing."

"I've already done it three times," the boy said.

"Good for you. I've only done it once, but I went up without the lift."

"I saw you. You'd put on climbing skins."

"Yes. Now that the sun's out I'll go up to the pass."

"To the pass where?"

"Farther up, above where the lift goes. Up to the top."

"What's up there?"

"The glacier seems so close it's as if you could touch it. And the white hares."

"The what?"

"The hares. At this altitude mountain hares put on a white coat. Also the partridges."

"Up there?"

"White partridges. Their feathers are all white. In summer their feathers are pale brown. Where are you from?"

"Italy."

"I'm Swiss."

They had arrived. They pulled away from the lift, he clumsily, she holding the bar with her hand through the whole turn. She took off her skis, stood them upright, removed the climbing skins from the bag she wore at her waist, and fastened them to the bottoms of the skis. He watched, rubbing his cold fingers in his gloves. Then, when she began to climb, he followed.

The ascent from the lift to the summit of the pass was difficult.

The boy in the green goggles worked hard, sometimes herring-boning, sometimes stepping, sometimes trudging up and sliding back, holding on to his poles like a lame man his crutches. And already she was up where he couldn't see her.

He reached the pass in a sweat, tongue out, half blinded by the glittering radiance all around. There the world of ice began. The blonde girl had taken off her sky-blue windbreaker and tied it around her waist. She, too, had put on a pair of goggles. "There! Did you see? Did you see?"

"What is it?" he said, dazed. Had a white hare leaped out? A partridge?

"It's not there anymore," she said.

Below, over the valley, cawing blackbirds fluttered as usual at two thousand metres. Midday had turned perfectly clear, and from up there you could see the trails, the open slopes thronged with skiers, children sledding, the lift station and the line, which had re-formed, the hotel, the parked buses, the road that wove in and out of the black forest of fir trees.

The girl had set off on the descent, going back and forth in her tranquil zigzags, and had already reached the point where the trails were more trafficked by skiers, yet her figure, faintly sketched, like an oscillating parenthesis, didn't get lost in the confusion of darting interchangeable profiles: it remained the only one that could be picked out and followed, removed from chance and disorder. The air was so clear that the boy in the green goggles could divine in the snow the dense network of ski tracks, straight and oblique, of abrasions, mounds, holes, and pole marks, and it seemed to him that there, in the shapeless jumble of life, was hidden a secret line, a harmony, traceable only to the sky-blue girl, and this was the miracle of her: that at every instant in the chaos of innumerable possible movements she chose the only one that was right and clear and light and necessary, the only gesture that, among an infinity of wasted gestures, counted.

MAN AND DAUGHTER IN THE COLD by John Updike

John Hoyer Updike (1932–2009) was an American writer. Updike published more than 20 novels and collections of short stories, as well as several collections of essays and poetry collections. He was known for his careful craftsmanship and realistic but subtle depiction of American middle-class life.

"Look at that girl ski!" The exclamation arose at Ethan's side as if, in the disconnecting cold, a rib of his had cried out; but it was his friend, friend and fellow teacher, an inferior teacher but superior skier, Matt Langley, admiring Becky, Ethan's own daughter. It took an effort, in this air like slices of transparent metal interposed everywhere, to make these connections and to relate the young girl, her round face red with windburn as she skimmed down the run-out slope, to himself. She was his daughter, age thirteen. Ethan had twin sons, two years younger, and his attention had always been focused on their skiing, on the irksome comedy of their double needs – the four boots to lace, the four mittens to find – and then their cute yet grim competition as now one and now the other gained the edge in the expertise of geländesprungs and slalom form. On their trips north into the White Mountains, Becky had come along for the ride. "Look how solid she is," Matt went on. "She doesn't cheat on it like your boys – those feet are absolutely together." The girl, grinning as if she could hear herself praised, wiggle-waggled to a flashy stop that sprayed snow over the men's ski tips.

"Where's Mommy?" she asked.

Ethan answered, "She went with the boys into the lodge. They couldn't take it." Their sinewy little male bodies had no insulation; weeping and shivering, they had begged to go in after a single T-bar run.

"What sissies," Becky said.

Matt said, "This wind is wicked. And it's picking up. You should have been here at nine; Lord, it was lovely. All that fresh powder, and not a stir of wind."

Becky told him, "Dumb Tommy couldn't find his mittens, we spent an hour looking, and then Daddy got the Jeep stuck." Ethan, alerted now for signs of the wonderful in his daughter, was struck by the strange fact that she was making conversation. Unafraid, she was talking to Matt without her father's intercession.

"Mr. Langley was saying how nicely you were skiing."

"You're Olympic material, Becky."

The girl perhaps blushed; but her cheeks could get no redder. Her eyes, which, were she a child, she would have instantly averted, remained a second on Matt's face, as if to estimate how much he meant it. "It's easy down here," Becky said. "It's babyish."

Ethan asked, "Do you want to go up to the top?" He was freezing standing still, and the gondola would give shelter from the wind.

Her eyes shifted to his, with another unconsciously thoughtful hesitation.

"Sure. If you want to."

"Come along, Matt?"

"Thanks, no. It's too rough for me; I've had enough runs. This is the trouble with January – once it stops snowing, the wind comes up. I'll keep Elaine company in the lodge." Matt himself had no wife, no children. At thirty eight, he was as free as his students, as light on his skis and as full of brave know-how. "In case of frostbite," he shouted after them, "rub snow on it."

Becky effortlessly skated ahead to the lift shed. The encumbered motion of walking on skis, not natural to Ethan, made him feel asthmatic: a fish out of water. He touched his parka pocket, to check that the inhalator was there. As a child he had imagined death as something attacking from outside, but now he knew that it was carried within; we nurse it for years, and it grows. The clock on the lodge wall said a quarter to noon. The giant thermometer read two degrees above zero. The racks outside were dense as hedges with idle skis. Crowds, any sensation of crowding or delay, quickened his asthma; as therapy he imagined the emptiness, the blue freedom, at the top of the mountain. The clatter of machinery inside the shed was comforting, and enough teenage boys were boarding gondolas to make the ascent seem normal and safe. Ethan's breathing eased. Becky proficiently handed her poles to the loader with their points up; her father was always caught by surprise, and often as not fumbled the little manoeuvre of letting his skis be taken from him. Until, seven years ago, he had become an assistant professor at a New Hampshire college, he had never skied; he had lived in those Middle Atlantic cities where snow, its moment of virgin beauty by, is only an encumbering nuisance, a threat of suffocation. In those seven years, his children had grown up on skis.

Alone with his daughter in the rumbling isolation of the gondola, he wanted to explore her, and found her strange – strange in her uninquisitive child's silence, her accustomed poise in this ascending egg of metal. A dark figure with spreading legs veered out of control beneath them, fell forward, and vanished. Ethan cried out, astonished; he imagined that the man had buried himself alive. Becky was barely amused and looked away before the dark spots struggling in the drift were lost from sight. As if she might know, Ethan asked, "Who was that?"

"Some kid." Kids, her tone suggested, were in plentiful supply; one could be spared. He offered to dramatize the adventure ahead of them:

"Are we going to freeze at the top?"

"Not exactly."

"What do you think it'll be like?"

"Miserable."

"Why are we doing this?"

"Because we paid the money for the all-day lift ticket."

"Becky, you think you're pretty smart, don't you?"

"Not really."

The gondola rumbled and lurched into the shed at the top; an attendant opened the door, and there was a howling mixed of wind and of boys whooping to keep warm. He was roughly handed two pairs of skis, and the handler, muffled to the eyes with a scarf, stared as if amazed that Ethan was so old. All the others struggling into skis in the lee of the shed were adolescent boys. Students: after fifteen years of teaching, Ethan tended to flinch from youth – its harsh noises, its cheerful rapacity, its cruel onward flow as one class replaced another, taking with it another year of his life.

Away from the shelter of the shed, the wind was a high monotonous pitch of pain. His cheeks instantly ached. His septum tingled and burned. He inhaled through his nose, and pushed off. Drifts ribbed the trail, obscuring Becky's ski tracks seconds after she made them; at each push through the heaped snow, his scope of breathing narrowed. By the time he reached the first steep section, the left half of his back hurt as it did only in the panic of a full asthmatic attack, and his skis, ignored, too heavy to manage, spread and swept him toward a snowbank at the side of the trail. He was bent far forward but kept his balance; the snow kissed his face lightly, instantly, all over; he straightened up, refreshed by the shock, thankful not to have lost a ski.

Down the slope, Becky had halted and was staring upward at him, worried. A huge blowing feather, a partition of snow, came between them. The cold, unprecedented in his experience, shone through his clothes like furious light, and as he rummaged through his parka for the inhalator he seemed to be searching glass shelves backed by a black wall. He found it, its icy plastic the touch of life, a clumsy key to his insides. Gasping, he exhaled, put it into his mouth, and inhaled; the isoproterenol spray, chilled into drops, opened his lungs enough for him to call to his daughter, "Keep moving! I'll catch up!"

Solid on her skis, as Matt had said, she swung down among the moguls and wind-bared ice, and became small, and again waited. The moderate slope seemed a cliff; if he fell and sprained anything, he would freeze. His entire body would become locked tight against air and light and thought. His legs trembled; his breath moved in and out of a narrow slot beneath the pain in his back. The cold and blowing snow all around him constituted an immense crowding, but there was no way out of this white cave except to slide downward toward the dark spot that was his daughter. He had forgotten all his skiing lessons. Leaning backward in an infant's tense snowplow, he floundered through alternating powder and ice.

"You O.K., Daddy?" Her stare was wide, its fright underlined by a pale patch on her cheek.

He used the inhalator again and gave himself breath to tell her, "I'm fine. Let's get down."

In this way, in steps of her leading and waiting, they worked down the mountain, out of the worst wind, into the lower trail that ran between birches and hemlocks. The cold had the quality not of absence but of force: an inverted burning. The last time Becky stopped and waited, the colourless crescent on her scarlet cheek disturbed him, reminded him of some injunction, but he could find in his brain, whittled to a dim determination to persist, only the advice to keep going, toward shelter and warmth. She told him, at a division of trails, "This is the easier way."

"Let's go the quicker way," he said, and in this last descent he recovered the rhythm – knees together, shoulders facing the valley, weight forward as if in the moment of release from a diving board – not a resistance but a joyous acceptance of falling. They reached the base lodge, and with unfeeling hands removed their skis. Pushing into the cafeteria, Ethan saw in the momentary mirror of the door window that his face was a spectre's; chin, nose, and eyebrows had retained the snow from that near-fall near the top. "Becky, look," he said, turning in the crowded warmth and clatter inside the door. "I'm a monster."

"I know, your face was absolutely white, I didn't know whether to tell you or not. I thought it might scare you."

He touched the pale patch on her cheek. "Feel anything?"

"No."

"Damn. I should have rubbed snow on it."

Matt and Elaine and the twins, flushed and stripped of their parkas, had eaten lunch; shouting and laughing with a strange guilty shrillness, they said that there had been repeated loudspeaker announcements not to go up to the top without face masks, because of frostbite. They had expected Ethan and Becky to come back down on the gondola, as others had, after tasting the top.

"It never occurred to us," Ethan said. He took the blame upon himself by adding, "I wanted to see the girl ski."

Their common adventure, and the guilt of his having given her frostbite, bound Becky and Ethan together in loose complicity for the rest of the day. They arrived home as sun was leaving even the tips of the hills; Elaine had invited Matt to supper, and while the windows of the house burned golden Ethan shovelled out the Jeep. The house was a typical New Hampshire farmhouse, less than two miles from the college, on the side of a hill, overlooking what had been a pasture, with the usual capacious porch running around three sides, cluttered with cordwood and last summer's lawn furniture. The woodsy, sheltered scent of these porches never failed to please Ethan, who had been raised in a Jersey City semi-detached, then a West Side apartment besieged by other people's cooking smells and noises. The wind had been left behind in the mountains. The air was as still as the stars. Shovelling the light dry snow became a lazy dance. But when he bent suddenly, his knees creaked, and his breathing shortened so that he had to pause.

A sudden rectangle of light was flung from the shadows of the porch. Becky came out into the cold with him. She was carrying a lawn rake.

He asked her, "Should you be out again? How's your frostbite?" Though she was a distance away, there was no need, in the immaculate air, to raise his voice.

"It's O.K. It kind of tingles. And under my chin. Mommy made me put on a scarf."

"What's the lawn rake for?"

"It's a way you can make a path. It really works."

"O.K., you make a path to the garage, and after I get my breath I'll see if I can get the Jeep back in."

"Are you having asthma?"

"A little."

"We were reading about it in biology. Dad, see, it's kind of a tree inside you, and every branch has a little ring of muscle around it, and they tighten." From her gestures in the dark she was demonstrating, with mittens on.

What she described, of course, was classic unalloyed asthma, whereas his was shading into emphysema, which could only worsen. But he liked being lectured to – preferred it, indeed, to lecturing – and as the minutes of companionable silence with his daughter passed he took inward notes on the bright, quick impressions flowing over him like a continuous voice. The silent cold. The stars. Orion behind an elm. Minute scintillae in the snow at his feet. His daughter's strange black bulk against the white; the solid grace that had stolen upon her over time. He remembered his father shovelling their car free from a sudden unwelcome storm in the mid-Atlantic region. The undercurrent of desperation, his father a salesman and must get to Camden. Got to get to Camden, boy, get to Camden or bust. Dead of a heart attack at forty-seven.

Ethan tossed a shovelful into the air so the scintillae flashed in the steady golden chord from the house windows. He saw again Elaine and Matt sitting flushed at the lodge table, parkas off, in déshabillé, as if sitting up in bed. Matt's enviable way of turning a half-circle on the top of a mogul, light as a diver, compared with the cancerous unwieldiness of Ethan's own skis. The callousness of students. The flawless cruelty of the stars, Orion intertwined with the silhouetted elm. A black tree inside him. His daughter, busily sweeping with the rake, childish yet lithe, so curiously demonstrating this preference for his company. It was female of her, he supposed, to forgive him her frostbite. A plow a half mile away painstakingly scraped. He was missing the point of this silent lecture. The point was unstated: an absence. He was looking upon his daughter as a woman, but without lust. There was no need to possess her; she was already his. The music around him was being produced, in the zero air, like a finger on a glass rim, by this hollowness, this biological negation. Sans lust, sans jealousy. Space seemed love, bestowed to be free in, and coldness the price. He felt joined to the great dead whose words it was his duty to teach.

The Jeep came up unprotestingly from the fluffy snow. It looked happy to be penned in the garage with Elaine's station wagon, and the skis, and the oiled chain saw, and the power mower dreamlessly waiting for spring. Ethan was so full of happiness that, rather than his soul shatter, he uttered a sound: "Becky?"

"Yeah?"

"You want to know what else Mr. Langley said?"

"What?" They trudged toward the porch, up the path the gentle rake had cleared.

"He said you ski better than the boys."

"I bet," she said, and raced to the porch, and in the precipitate way, evasive and pleased, that she flung herself to the top step he glimpsed something generic and joyous, a pageant that would leave him behind.